Essays in Literary Criticism
of George Santayana

ESSAYS IN LITERARY CRITICISM

OF
George Santayana

SELECTED AND EDITED, WITH AN INTRODUCTION,

by Irving Singer

CHARLES SCRIBNER'S SONS NEW YORK

Selections from: *Reason in Art* and *Reason in Religion,* copyright 1905 by Charles
Scribner's Sons, 1933 by George Santayana; *The Last Puritan,* copyright 1935 by
Charles Scribner's Sons.

Grateful acknowledgement is made for the use of the following copyrighted
material:
  To Harvard University Press for the selections from *Three Philosophical
     Poets* by George Santayana, copyright 1910, 1938 by Harvard University
     Press.
  To The Marchesa Iris Origo and Oxford University Press for George Santa-
     yana's Preface to *Leopardi* by Iris Origo.
  To University Press, Inc. for "Hamlet" by George Santayana, copyright 1908
     by University Press, Inc., 1936 by William Dana Orcutt.

A Note about This Edition

I<small>N</small> making this edition, I found that the essays fell naturally into three Parts. Part I is entirely composed of *Three Philosophical Poets*, which stands by itself as a unit. Part II is made up of scattered essays on particular authors and works of literature. Part III comprises writings about the nature of poetry and prose in general. The essays are not arranged in the order of their composition, but roughly in accordance with the historical and philosophical continuity of their subject-matter. I have generally left Santayana's material as I found it, though in several instances slight adjustments had to be made. For example, the first sentence of the essay "Hints of Egotism in Goethe" originally appeared as the last lines of the previous chapter in the book *Egotism in German Philosophy*. It is included in order to give the reader some idea of how Santayana uses the word "transcendentalism." In the selections from *The Last Puritan* the sub-title "Critical Excerpts" is mine, the excerpts themselves having been included to show how Santayana uses literary criticism as a way of demonstrating the character of Peter Alden, Caleb Wetherbee, and Oliver Alden respectively. The titles "Literary Form" and "Expression in Literature" are also mine, the selections having originally appeared in *The Sense of Beauty*. Finally, the reader may be interested in knowing that "Speech and Signification" and "Poetry and Prose" are chapters from *Reason in Art*, "Literary Psychology" is a chapter from *Scepticism and Animal Faith*, and "Mythology" is a chapter from *Reason in Religion*.

I.S.

Contents

vii

PART III

Introduction: SANTAYANA AS
A LITERARY CRITIC

BY IRVING SINGER

PHILOSOPHERS are not generally noted for their literary criticism,
just as literary critics have rarely distinguished themselves as philosophers. For all its integrity, the philosophic mind always runs
the danger of becoming tendentious: it knows too much, and cannot become as a little child. On the other hand, the literary mind
all too often resembles the ghost of Hamlet's father: 'tis here, 'tis
there, a perturbed and insubstantial spirit that flits about in mysterious darkness. It is a rare genius who can combine good philosophy with good literary criticism. George Santayana was a
genius of this sort. One is even tempted to say that his genius was
pre-eminently of this sort, and that in the special province of
philosophical literary criticism his contribution was more unique
and more permanently outstanding than in any other field. In the
last two hundred years there have been better philosophers and
better essayists, and certainly better poets and novelists, but hardly
any critics who have blended philosophical and literary insights
with as free and authentic a hand as Santayana. Even among the
greatest literary critics there have been few who could do Santayana's "job of work."

Just what kind of work was it? The practice is almost lost among
American writers. In the last fifty years our philosophers and
critics alike have become technical, minute, and pedagogical in
a way that Santayana never was. Ours is an age of instruments:
we are devoted to examining the telescope, as Santayana would
say, instead of looking through it. Santayana wanted to look. He
was an intellectual astronomer with good eyesight and a refined
sense of distance. Unlike recent critics, he was not particularly
interested in the principles of rhetoric. For better or for worse, his
criticism generally avoids both exegesis and linguistic analysis.

He shows how the Homeric Hymns, for instance, exemplify the imaginative function of religion, but he largely ignores the poetic devices they employ. He defines religion in terms of myth and metaphor, but he never attempts a thorough analysis of either myth or metaphor. Except for a few remarks about euphony and euphuism, he has little to say about the rudiments of poetry. What excites the muse in him, and what makes his criticism so exciting, is rather an awareness of the human significance of literature— the way in which it can be used to communicate a sense of what is real and important. Santayana wished to treat literary works of art as expressions of an attitude towards the world which could be examined and criticized, not merely accepted or rejected. In this attempt he tried to make his astronomical reports as comprehensive as possible. He filled them with philosophical commentary reinforced by psychological insights, historical and biographical observations, and the expressions of his own moral and aesthetic taste. All of this contributes to a ricochet of ideas, a cross-fire that is brilliant, even dazzling—so much so that the prose occasionally explodes in a burst of elegance and one has difficulty separating the literary criticism from partisan manœuvering, on the one hand, and stylistic fire-works on the other.

Comparison with Hegel is inevitable, and in the Preface to *The Life of Reason* Santayana reports that the first suggestion for that work came to him after reading the *Phaenomenologie des Geistes*. At the same time, however, Santayana claims that Hegel approached their common subject, the history of human ideas, with sophistry and romantic madness. A similar complaint could not be made against Santayana, whatever his critical or philosophical faults may have been. He never thought that his astronomy disclosed a universe governed by Germanic (or other) orderliness, and he never allowed his own perspective to cripple and cramp everything else in the name of Universal Will. There were marches *in* history, but no march *of* history. If anything, history was a series of aimless dances. One had to catch their individual rhythms, one had to use what Keats called "negative capability" instead of forcing everything into the Hegelian three-step. All the same, there is one respect in which Santayana resembled Hegel: he had a definite point of view. Like Hegel, Santayana wrote within the framework of a personal philosophy that made up his telescope more than he may sometimes have admitted. In giving his "excuse" for writing about the three philosophical poets, Santayana says that "they have revealed to me certain aspects of nature and of philosophy which I am prompted by mere sincerity to express." But as we read on, we find that these "aspects of nature and of philosophy" turn out to be aspects within Santayana's own nature and philosophy. The philosophical poets have not been chosen at random; they serve a definite philosophical purpose, however little they may be forced to *sub*serve it. Santayana's intention, clearly, was to choose in accordance with his personal and doctrinal needs, but then, having chosen, to report accurately and honestly what he saw. His criticism would then be a projection of himself without being a distortion of his subject-matter.

In reading Santayana's criticism as a projection of his own philosophy, we must always remember that the climate of his opinions altered as he grew older. In some ways it became warmer, more tolerant and less demanding; in other ways, colder, more remote and detached from ordinary human interests. For instance, compare "The Poetry of Barbarism" (1900) with "Penitent Art" (1922). In both essays Santayana is describing what he considers to be significant but inferior art, the work of strangely misguided genius. But where the earlier essay almost sounds like a charge of the light brigade against the dark and irrational forces of Whitman's sensualism and Browning's activism, the later essay is a melancholy sigh, a gentle shaking of the deploring head, as if Santayana had come to see that it was only fitting for the tragic twentieth century to express itself in an abstract, incomplete, and self-caricaturing manner. Similarly, in "The Absence of Religion in Shakespeare" (1896) Santayana is shocked to find that Shakespeare has little of the "cosmic consciousness," whereas in "Tragic Philosophy" (1936) he is more tolerant of a poet who spoke to an age that "needed no mastering living religion." It is not clear whether the later Santayana finds Shakespeare's secularism adequate for the needs of great poetry; but as against the criticism of T. S. Eliot, he defends Shakespeare for having "stuck fast in the facts of life" and he pits him against Dante in a way that one could hardly have anticipated from the early essay.

Throughout this changing climate, there perseveres a way of looking at things, an attitude or general perspective, that might be called the desire to harmonize. In book after book, Santayana defined the life of reason as the harmonization between opposing interests. In his aesthetics and literary criticism he works out patterns of harmonization between a great many divergent principles, most of which can be approached in terms of the following themes: Platonism vs. naturalism, classicism vs. romanticism, "idealisation" vs. realism, and poetry vs. prose. Each conflict poses separate problems, but the problems overlap and much of what we say about one will also apply to the others.

I

The struggle between naturalism and Platonism is the most striking of the four themes. Throughout all of Santayana's work there is an ambivalence of sentiment, a yearning towards the extremes of naturalism with its emphasis upon the brute materiality of existent things and Platonism with its reliance upon the value of formal characteristics. Santayana wanted to harness both, the black horse of the body and the white horse of the soul, and he wanted them to run in neatly parallel lines. In order to effect this harmonization, he used each extreme to chasten the other. They were the two masks of his drama, and his prose bristles with their dialogue. Speaking in the person of naturalism, he finds Platonism superstitious and absurdly optimistic. Because there are human values in the world, Platonism assumes that ideal entities, or purposive divinities as Christianity made them into, must provide the ultimate explanation for the existence of everything. Nothing could be farther from the materialistic truth. But speaking in the person of Platonism, Santayana finds traditional naturalism barren of hope and ignorant of spiritual goods. Devoted as it is to facts, naturalism ignores the fact of human aspiration and the quest for purified ideals. In *The Last Puritan*, where the spirituality of Oliver Alden is pitted against the naturalism of Mario Van de Weyer, the contrast between the two sides of Santayana's nature shows through time and again, sometimes with astonishing stridency. In one scene Oliver is completing an essay on Plato's *Symposium*. As his hand writes the word "philosophy" he is interrupted by Mario, who describes an unhappy carnal encounter from which he has just come and then boards a train on his way to see his dying mother. Oliver returns to his room and finds that he had not finished writing the word "philosophy." The last five letters had yet to be put down. Thus, as "philosophy" is split into its two halves, of love and wisdom, and Mario pursues the former while Oliver is characteristically arrested in his attempt to reach the latter, so too is man composed of two disparate, warring elements—matter and spirit. Santayana's thinking always has its feet on the ground and its head in the clouds. Whether there is, or ought to be, anything in-between remains a matter of controversy.

The character of Santayana's naturalism is best reflected in the essays on Lucretius and Dickens. In explaining the sense in which Lucretius is a "poet of matter," Santayana distinguishes between five different kinds of "naturalists" in poetry. Lucretius is a philosophical or cosmological naturalist—for him nature means "the principle of birth or genesis, the universal mother, the great cause, or system of causes." As a philosophical naturalist, Lucretius is contrasted with: the descriptive poet who paints a word picture of the scenery of nature, the symbolist poet who breaks up nature into elements that he re-shuffles by means of random association, the idealist poet who uses these elements of nature to construct a utopian dream-world, and the humanistic poet who depicts the moral effects that can be derived from living "in" nature. These are all naturalists, but of an inferior sort. The descriptive poet ignores Lessing's scruples about representing spatial objects in a temporal medium; the Symbolists "play with things luxuriously, making them symbols for their thoughts, instead of mending their thoughts intelligently, to render them symbols for things"; the idealistic poet is blind to the dynamism in things; the humanistic poet, such as Wordsworth, limits himself to a tiny part of the cosmic process—"adventitious human matters." Only a poet like Lucretius has his finger on the pulse of nature—its character as a force, a power, a generating and destroying agency. Only Lucretius, we may add, concerns himself with what Santayana later called "The Realm of Matter." It is interesting to note that Santayana praises Lucretius for writing "the poetry of things themselves" and in his "Apologia Pro Mente Sua" (1940) he calls himself a "true poet" inasmuch as his own poetry is "not a poetry of words or concepts, but a poetry of things." And yet, is this sufficient basis for elevating Lucretius above Wordsworth and the Symbolists? That a kinship of interest should make Lucretius dearer to Santayana is not at all surprising; but Santayana does not *seem* to be expressing a mere preference. He seems to be evaluating poetry on the basis of objective standards of criticism. This kind of problem recurs continually.

Since philosophical naturalism investigates the principles of genesis and decay, it is fitting that the essay on Lucretius hovers about the dualism of life and death, creation and destruction, love and strife, peace and warfare—as symbolized in *De Rerum Natura* by Venus and Mars. This awareness of the "double colouring" of things characterizes all of Santayana's writing. In his essay "A Long Way Round to Nirvana," Santayana defends the Freudian notion that a universal death instinct counterbalances the drive for self-preservation. Like all philosophy, the concept of a death instinct had to be taken as a metaphoric suggestion, and not as scientific truth, but if one did take it as such one discovered something that Santayana considered a fair report of "the general movement and the pertinent issue of material facts." In emphasizing death as one of the facts of life, Santayana's philosophy wears the same tragic cast as existentialism. He wished to construct his system on the basis of a radical disillusionment. Once man *realized* that he was dust, that there was no other world, and that someday he would be dead 100%, he could freely and honestly search for the good. Santayana felt that it would be cheating for man to be bribed into virtue by hopes of a future life or by optimistic assurances that the good would win out eventually. There was no prearranged harmony, no ultimate dialectic, no *élan vital* that guaranteed anything. Death and evil were as indigenous to nature as life and goodness. They were to be observed and analyzed, not wished out of existence.

This naturalistic analysis takes up much of the essay on Lucretius and reappears in the succeeding ones on Dante and Goethe. The Paolo-Francesca scene, for instance, is treated as a continuation of Lucretius' theme about Venus and Mars. Paolo and Francesca are in hell because their union is unnatural, as intimacy must always be when it makes separateness and individuality impossible. An eternity of possession in a void, of inescapable love and no exit into anything or anyone else, causes the destruction of Mars in a way that prevents Venus from savoring her conquest. "Only an inspired poet could be so subtle a moralist," Santayana concludes. "Only a sound moralist could be so tragic a poet." Similarly, Mephistopheles is compared to the Mars of Lucretius, and Santayana delights in Goethe's ability to express the nothingness of things by means of him. Santayana denies that Mephistopheles can be fitted into a Hegelian dialectic, as the nay-saying that makes a higher yea-saying possible and thus unintentionally contributes to the good. On the one hand, Santayana sees the sense in which Mephistopheles is consciously, not unintentionally, benevolent: for Mephistopheles destruction is better than creation and it is destruction that he knowingly and gladly chooses. On the other hand, Santayana refuses to bleach the blackness of Mephistopheles. Creation is one thing; destruction is another. Sentimentality or barbaric romanticism results from confusing the two, from making the colors run so that neither has a determinate quality of its own.

It is a comparable desire to keep the black and the white distinct that Santayana admires most in Dickens. He finds in Dickens the same love of common people that Walt Whitman had, except that Dickens is free of all impressionistic wishy-washiness. Whereas Whitman interpreted everything else in terms of himself, Dickens saw the differences in things. Unlike Whitman, Dickens saw life as "a concourse of very distinct, individual bodies, natural and social, each with its definite interests and story." This naturalistic clarity enabled him to sympathize with the aspirations of others, to "love the love in everything" as Santayana says in "Ultimate Religion," without forgetting that vice is really vice and must be annihilated for the greater good of mankind.

In seeing Dickens as an outstanding example of uncontaminated naturalism, Santayana also takes him as the prototype of all comedy. Comedy sees things externally, as brute occurrences in nature which have no necessary reason for being. The existence of anything is, as the existentialists would say, "absurd"—we can never prove deductively that anything must or must not be. Comedy cuts beneath convention in order to show the absurdity of everything, in order to reduce every existent to its fundamental materiality. Comedy requires courage, and is usually cruel. Dickens had the courage, but not the cruelty. Santayana praises him for combining naturalistic insight with a universal kindness which tempers his savage strokes and allows the reader to enjoy the comic spectacle in which he is himself a participant.

If Santayana's naturalistic mask is comic, his Platonic one is tragic. As a naturalist, Santayana joins with Sancho Panza in laughing at misadventures that result from neglecting the facts of daily life; as a Platonist, he feels the compelling pathos of a Don Quixote whose madness flows directly from his "sense of what is good." In the Preface to *The Last Puritan* Santayana complains that the critics have misunderstood the tragedy of his hero. That Oliver died young or was killed in an accident did not make him tragic, but rather "that he stopped himself, not trusting his inspiration." And in "Tragic Philosophy" he says that tragedy is the "conflict between inspiration and truth." Tragedy shows us human beings from their own inward point of view—as they are motivated by desires and aspirations that are serious to them, not at all absurd, though doomed to more or less failure. The life of man is tragic because it is always striving towards the accomplishment of ideals which, in the nature of the case, can never be attained. For the Platonist the actual world is inevitably the scene of tragedy.

Santayana's Platonism is most fully expressed in the essays on "Platonic Love in Some Italian Poets," "Dante," and "Shelley." Each deals with Platonism in a different setting; and each displays the critic in a slightly different posture. In the first essay, Santayana recites the story of Beatrice and Dante, and then shrewdly reminds us that despite his life-long devotion Dante took a wife just as Beatrice had taken a husband. Did Dante's marriage fulfill his naturalistic needs and thereby release him for the more essential love of an ideal? Or did it force him into a "species of infidelity" towards Beatrice as well as his wife? Santayana never gives us a straight reply. He documents the achievement of the Platonizing Italian poets, and he praises their intense contemplation, which "disentangles the idea from the idol of sense." At the same time, he also realizes that Platonic love is based upon pervasive frustration: for the Platonist "all beauties attract by suggesting the ideal and then fail to satisfy by not fulfilling it." Platonism fascinates him by the purity of its transcendence, but he is too this-worldly to drop his naturalism completely.

xvi

In the essay on "Dante" as the second of the philosophical poets, Santayana is both sharper in his criticism and more enthusiastic in his praise. Like Christianity itself, Dante offends by having turned Platonism into a historical drama, thus making it the kind of *super*naturalism that Santayana could not accept. Dante evinces all the imperfections of Christian superstition and anthropocentrism, such as the belief in original sin and retributive justice. Finally, Santayana suggests that Dante was dedicated to a kind of love that is neither normal nor healthy nor natural nor manly; and he adds that "the poet who wishes to pass convincingly from love to philosophy (and that seems a natural progress for a poet) should accordingly be a hearty and complete lover—a lover like Goethe and his Faust—rather than like Plato and Dante." Still, these naturalistic complaints are only one side of the coin; the reverse is pure eulogy. The merits of Dante's world-view redeem all his defects, for they are the merits of the Platonizing imagination writ large, of the sense of good and evil operating on a cosmic scale. The essay ends with Santayana putting Dante forth as "a successful example of the *highest species* of poetry."

The essay on Shelley is more serene than the other two: one feels that Santayana's philosophical position had developed to the point where he was more confident of reconciling the best of Platonism with the best of naturalism. And it is clear that in Shelley he sees the best of Platonism. He speaks of Shelley as a pure, winged spirit whose love of the ideal was sincere and spontaneous. Shelley was not limited by Christian beliefs and his Platonism emanated from sympathy with the misery of everything in nature, rather than personal disappointment. Although he was ignorant of the dynamic workings of matter, Shelley knew what was good and bad in things. If his poetry destroyed the everyday world, it was only to reconstruct it in a playful, selfless way "nearer to the heart's desire." Shelley's idealism is the same as the idealistic naturalism that Santayana had previously compared to Lucretius' philosophical naturalism. As a kind of naturalism, he there considered it inferior to what Lucretius gave us. But as a type of idealism, he now finds it supreme poetry. Dickens and Shelley, between them, seem to make up Santayana's vision, just as Lucretius and Dante do. Dickens rollicks through the natural world, above which the skylark Shelley soars in search of universal freedom; Lucretius hears the voice of things themselves, while Dante documents the uses to which the spirit can put them.

II

In moving to our second theme, we are confronted by questions of interpretation that did not arise in the first. Although it is obvious that Santayana wishes to stereoscope the partial views of naturalism and Platonism, it is not immediately evident that he wants to do the same with classicism and romanticism. Santayana is known as the defender of the one and the critic of the other; and much could be cited in favor of this interpretation. Nevertheless, it is, I think, a superficial interpretation which has to be much subtilized before it can be accepted. For one thing, we ought not to confuse "barbarism," as Santayana uses that term, with romanticism as a whole. Barbarism is only one kind of romanticism: it is romanticism which refuses to be harmonized. The barbarian is "the man who does not know his derivations nor perceive his tendencies, but who merely feels and acts, valuing in his life its force and its filling, but being careless of its purpose and its form." The romanticist values the experiential flow of his life; he becomes a barbarian when he values nothing else, when he *merely* feels and acts. Thus, it is barbarism, and not necessarily romanticism, which is incompatible with the classical sense of purpose and form that Santayana wants to advocate.

Santayana's attack upon nineteenth century barbarism is guided by the same kind of historical or sociological analysis that T. S. Eliot took as a premise of his own literary criticism. Examining barbaric poetry "in relation to the general moral crisis and imaginative disintegration of which it gives a verbal echo," Santayana finds that the imagination of western man bears a duality of inspiration. It derives in part from classic literature, in part from Christianity. The confusion of barbaric poetry reflects the modern inability to serve both masters, or either one, or any other. Whitman and Browning are "poets of barbarism" because they reject both traditions without fully understanding them and without having anything to put in their place. They express sensations and emotions without fitting them into a rational system

xviii

of any sort. To Santayana's ear and eye they are like the players Hamlet describes as created by nature's journeymen: "neither having the accent of Christians nor the gait of Christian, pagan, nor man." Even when it studies the past, as historicism did, barbarism examines a corpse instead of communicating with a vital tradition. If history preoccupies modern poets, Santayana reminds his readers at the turn of the century, it is because they are so greatly conscious of a separation from the past.

That Santayana's caustic remarks about barbarism are not intended to cover all romantic poetry is apparent from his treatment of Goethe, whom he ranks with Dante and Lucretius rather than with Whitman and Browning. The saving grace of Goethe, as Santayana sees him, is his real and honest attempt to fit romanticism into a framework of classicism. *Faust* is a return to Lucretius, though with a difference. The difference is the emphasis on life itself, on "experience in its immediacy, variety, and apparent groundlessness." This is what all romanticism emphasizes, but in Goethe it is accompanied by moments of sad and classic wisdom. One of these occurs when Faust calls forth the Earth-Spirit, the symbol of unlimited and indiscriminate experience. The ugly spectacle of unformed and unorganized life in all its infinite variations horrifies Faust. He learns, as Eliot was to say, that "human kind cannot bear very much reality," that the life of *mere* experience is not worth living. To be happy one must recognize the limits of one's nature, one must temper the fervor of youth with the discipline of age, one must make oneself by means of calculated choice. This is the classical point of view, and it is the morality Santayana expounded throughout his life.

If this classical side of Goethe redeems him in the eyes of Santayana, it is nevertheless too meager to raise him as high as Lucretius and Dante. In drawing his conclusions, Santayana arranges the three philosophical poets hierarchically: at the top, Dante, the poet of salvation; next, Lucretius, the poet of nature; and at the bottom, Goethe, the poet of life. The basis of this arrangement is not entirely clear. On the one hand, Santayana specifically denies that he is trying to indicate which of the poets is best. "Each is the best in his own way, and none is the best in every way. To express a preference is not so much a criticism as a personal confession." Just two pages later, however, Santayana sounds as if his hierarchy was based on something more objective than personal taste. ". . . taken formally, and in respect to their type of philosophy and imagination, Dante is on a higher plane than Lucretius, and Lucretius on a higher plane than Goethe." Without pausing to examine the difficulties in Santayana's statement, we should here notice that his hierarchy places the representative of Platonism first, and the representative of romanticism last. Santayana wishes to harmonize Platonism with naturalism and classicism with romanticism; but he insists upon a specific *kind* of harmonization: one in which naturalism is subordinated to Platonism, and romanticism to classicism. It is this implicit standard which leads Santayana, in the early essays at least, to place Shakespeare below the level of Homer, Virgil, and Dante. Like Goethe, Shakespeare is a romantic poet without being a poet of barbarism. Although he was "not unacquainted with speculation," Shakespeare generally restricts himself to the poetry of ordinary experience: he chooses positivism rather than religion, and society rather than the cosmos. Even in the case of *Hamlet*— "here is no necessary human tragedy, no universal destiny or divine law." And yet, Santayana has also noted that Hamlet "lays bare the heart of a whole race, or, perhaps we should rather say, expresses a conflict to which every soul is more or less liable." But if this is so, why not admit the supremely philosophical achievement of Shakespeare? Granted that Shakespeare is not philosophical in the same sense in which Lucretius and Dante are, why not recognize and admit his equally profound understanding of everything there is to understand?

The answer to these questions turns on Santayana's imperfect appreciation of romanticism. In subordinating romanticism to classicism, he dissolves, or at least ignores, the problems that troubled the romantics. In lamenting the absence of religion in Shakespeare, he overlooks the fact that Shakespeare's philosophic interest was of a different sort. Shakespeare, like Goethe, like Whitman and Browning, and like a great many other modern writers, saw the world in terms of moral problems. Religion did not concern him since it was unable to settle the ethical doubts that structured his world-outlook. Hamlet, like all of Shakespeare's major characters, is tormented by problems of action that Shakespeare analyzes to a remarkable degree of precision. Likewise, one could interpret the trial of Faust in terms of the need to *do* something: Mephistopheles is to win his wager if he can debase Faust's libido to the point where he will do virtually anything; Faust drops dead when he passively acquiesces in the passing moment; his soul is saved because, until the moment of his death, he was unflagging in his active aspiration. The root dilemma of all romanticism was formulated by Schopenhauer when he defined the human lot as the miserable alternation between boredom and dissatisfaction. The bored man has nothing for which to act; the unsatisfied man is forced to act in any way that will relieve his discomfiture. How then can man be free? How can he act with intelligence and spontaneous good-will? Santayana ignores these problems. They did not trouble him in the way that religious problems did. It may be fortunate that he pursued his own interests. But the fact remains that these interests prevented him from penetrating to the deepest stratum of the romantic soul.

III

The next theme takes us into the critical theory that underlies most of Santayana's practice. His preference for classicism over romanticism, as well as his preference for Platonism over naturalism, derives from his conception of "idealisation," an aesthetic principle that runs through all his criticism but receives full treatment only in *The Sense of Beauty*.

To explain what Santayana means by idealisation, we must first put it in the context of his general aesthetics. At the very outset Santayana defines aesthetic experience in terms of "objectified pleasure," i.e. pleasure that is taken to be an attribute of an object more or less in the way that its color is. According to Santayana, the difference between "this painting pleases me" and "this painting is beautiful" consists in the fact that the first statement describes an effect that the painting has upon the speaker whereas the second statement speaks of the painting as *itself* embodying the pleasure it causes. To the literal, scientific mind it makes no sense to speak of an object embodying pleasures; but the aesthetic experience is neither literal nor scientific. Santayana takes it to be a hangover from the primitive, animistic tendency to read into objects all of the effects that they have upon human observers. The sense of beauty causes us to project our feelings without realizing what we are doing; and this, I think, is the sense in which Santayana would say that all art is "illusion."

There is, however, a further sense of illusion which is more relevant to the underlying notion of idealisation. For after defining beauty as objectified pleasure, Santayana goes on to discuss three different kinds of beauty: the beauty of materials, of form, and of expression. Of these three the greatest is form, and in the aesthetics of form the most significant factor is the creation of types—the class concepts or general ideas by reference to which we identify particular objects. Types are especially important to the artist because they enable him to remain true to experience without *copying,* without duplicating something that has existed and therefore possesses an indefinite number of properties which are aesthetically irrelevant. In discussing the origin of types, Santayana rejects the Platonic theory which considers them independent of ordinary sense-experience. Santayana insists that a type —the general idea of man, tree, whale, or what not—is merely a lowest common denominator, a residue of particular sense-experiences on particular occasions. When Santayana later developed the doctrine of essences, he moved closer to Platonism inasmuch as he denied that the naturalistic origin of types prevented them from being independent of experience in other, and more important, respects. What remained constant in both the earlier and the later theories was the belief that typical form is the most important kind of aesthetic form.

Now we are in a position to see how Santayana conceives of idealisation, and how he reconciles it with aesthetic truth. Having defined beauty in terms of pleasure, and typical form in terms of observable recurrences, Santayana then says that typical form can have its greatest effect only if it is modified "in the direction of the observer's pleasure" and thereby turned into an "idealisation." This means that the artist must not content himself with a merely realistic portrayal of a type, any more than a realistic representation of a particular object. The former would be an unaesthetic copy as much as the latter, although a copy of "the average of things" rather than specific characteristics of particular things. Since the sense of beauty is the experience of pleasure in the object, the sense of formal beauty must be the experience of a type which has been modified for the sake of giving greater pleasure. "The mind is thus peopled by general ideas in which beauty is the chief quality; and these ideas are at the same time the types of things."

In this manner, Santayana hopes to combine the sense of reality with the sense of beauty. A mere sense of reality would disclose typical forms that might very well be harsh, shocking, brutal. A mere sense of beauty would provide indiscriminate pleasure. But when the forms themselves have been modified in the direction of pleasure, they embody human ideals as well as depicting human realities. Santayana insists that these ideals would be "true to" reality since they would be refinements of actual forms rather than fanciful ones invented by a raving artist. At the same time, they would be much more significant than the photographs of nature that so-called "realists" provide.

Thus, despite his emphasis on idealisation, Santayana does not wish to ignore the aesthetic relevance of truth. When he discusses the nature of expression in literature, he reminds us that great works often employ accurate and honest representation. But having said this, he quickly adds that "such instruction does not of itself constitute an aesthetic pleasure: the other conditions of beauty remain to be fulfilled." These other conditions are fulfilled only when the vehicle, the art object itself, provides pleasure in its direct effect, which is to say that the expression of truth cannot be aesthetic except in its subordination to the beauty of form and materials. And since the beauty of form is at its highest when it employs idealisation, the supreme aesthetic production will have to subordinate realistic representation to the creation of ideal types. In a similar vein, Santayana denies that the expression of evil can itself be aesthetic. He goes to great lengths to show that tragedies are aesthetic only in spite of the evil they represent, never because of it. Since the expression of evil is unpleasant and therefore unaesthetic, the tragedian must always cushion it by means of pleasing idealisations. With this theory in mind, it is not surprising that Santayana should prefer Platonism and classicism to naturalism and romanticism.

In applying the conception of ideal types to the specific problems of characterization, Santayana enriches it by saying that the great characters of literature are always individuals as well as idealisations. Universal characters, such as Hamlet, Don Quixote, and Achilles, are not just particular men candidly observed. Nor are they averages or realistic types. They are idealised types which have been given uniqueness or individuality. Goethe's Gretchen had no original, but is herself "the original to which we may occasionally think we see some likeness in real maidens. It is the fiction here that is the standard of naturalness." And Santayana concludes that "on this, as on so many occasions, we may repeat the saying that poetry is truer than history."

Santayana's conception of idealisation also underlies his celebrated identification of religion with poetry. As he sees it, religion is primarily poetic idealisation extended to the cosmic scene. "Poetry is called religion when it intervenes in life, and religion, when it merely supervenes upon life, is seen to be nothing but poetry." Santayana realizes that religious people have not usually *thought* that their religion was a kind of elevated poetry. They have generally taken it to be a superior science. This side of religion Santayana considers sheer superstition. In identifying religion with poetry, he is trying to release those imaginative values which can remain to the enlightened and sensitive intellect after all pseudo-scientific claims have been discounted. This residue he relates to idealisation because he thinks that a religion can fulfil its function only by symbolizing desired perfections. The religion of Apollo, for example, he considers a true religion because "the mythology which created the god rested on a deep, observant sense for moral values, and drew a vivid, if partial, picture of the ideal, attaching it significantly to its natural ground." He points out that the Christ men have loved is "an ideal of their own hearts"; and he asserts that "no poet has ever equalled the perfection or significance of these religious creations."

The trouble with Santayana's theory of idealisation is that it seems to minimize the importance of truth. Idealisations do not tell us how things are, but how they ought to be, or how the "heart's desire" would like them to be. If aesthetic excellence is primarily determined by idealisation, art is treated as wish fulfillment more than anything else. As long as we concern ourselves with the artist's idealisation, we are not especially interested in what he tells us about the world: what matters most is his dream of perfection, his prophetic blueprint. If realism ignores ideals, it will have to be subordinated; if tragedy expresses sad and bitter truths, it will have to do so in a way that is ultimately pleasurable and uplifting. Dante idealises to the fullest. He is therefore considered "the type of a supreme poet." Lucretius, Goethe, and Shakespeare idealise proportionately less, and they are fitted into the hierarchy of value accordingly. Santayana never faces up to the possibility that *a priori* there is no reason to favor idealisation over realism; and he fails to see how this preferred kind of harmonization distorts much of what is generally considered to be essential in both poetry and religion.

IV

Related difficulties attend Santayana's way of reconciling poetry with prose. Santayana begins with the assumption that poetry and prose are two distinct modes of discourse: the former devoted to the sound and texture of words, and to the immediate experiences they can evoke or symbolize; the latter designed for practical adaptation to the material environment. Poetry *gives* us the world; prose tells us about it discursively. Poetry portrays life in its full immediacy; prose, as in science or philosophy, does the very opposite: it theorizes and tries to understand. How then are the two to be joined? Santayana is convinced that neither poetry nor prose can achieve its aesthetic mission without the other. He criticizes the shallow aestheticism which decrees that art and reason are incompatible and that poetry must ignore the problems of the real world. "Clarification of ideas and disentanglement of values are as essential to aesthetic activity as to intelligence. A failure of reason is a failure of art and taste." The "rational poet" whom Santayana deifies throughout his early writing unites intelligence with imagination: "A rational poet's vision would have the same moral functions which myth was asked to fulfil, and fulfilled so treacherously. . . . His poetry, without ceasing to be a fiction in its method and ideality, would be an ultimate truth in its practical scope. It would present in graphic images the total efficacy of real things." Such poetry succeeds by digesting prose, by putting it to aesthetic employment rather than spewing it forth.

But just how is the harmonization between poetry and prose to be effected? Santayana returns to the problem in the Introduction to *Three Philosophical Poets*. He wonders whether poetry is capable of supporting the analytical reasoning of philosophy. He replies that it cannot and that it should not, and yet that philosophical poetry is poetry at its best. He concludes that philosophy itself is poetic to the extent that it terminates in "a steady contemplation of all things in their order and worth." It was to the study of contemplation in this sense that Santayana dedicated much of his later philosophy. By "contemplation" he means the intuition of essences. By "essence" he means, as he says in the note on Proust, "the recognizable character of any object or feeling, all of it that can actually be possessed in sensation or recovered in memory, or transcribed in art, or conveyed to another mind." To discover essences one had to limit oneself to experience as it came, experience devoid of interpretation and the discursive processes of reason. In conveying a complex essence of things in their order and worth, philosophical poetry remained non-discursive, and therefore distinctively poetical, at the same time as it incorporated the over-arching visions of philosophy. Poetry was the language of intuition; in being harmonized with prose, it became the language of significant, and possibly truthful, intuitions.

Although the doctrine of essences was not fully developed until late in Santayana's life, it enters into most of his early writing. I have recently tried to show that it is basic to all his theories of art and aesthetics.* I also believe that it renders most of them philosophically unacceptable. Here I can only suggest that Santayana's reliance upon intuition subordinates the ordinary processes of thought to a kind of quasi-mystical trance which no one has ever succeeded in describing with any clarity. And even if it made sense to speak of contemplation in the way that Santayana does, one still wonders how any of this is relevant to art or the definition of great poetry. That philosophical poetry depends upon general insights about the world one may well admit; but that these insights are intuitions of a special and inherently non-discursive sort one cannot believe without a considerable amount of faith.

The nature of Santayana's faith is indicated by the extent to

* Cf. my forthcoming book, *Santayana's Aesthetics: A Critical Introduction*, Harvard University Press.

which the doctrine of essences led him to revise his earlier aesthetics. At some points, the revisions were minor; at others, extensive. In changing his definition of beauty, he said that he still adhered to its major import and was mainly altering the language. He no longer felt the necessity of talking about the objectification of pleasure, since on the doctrine of essences pleasure "does not need to be objectified in order to be fused into an image felt to be beautiful: if felt at all, pleasure is already an object of intuition." The idea of a special aesthetic attitude, at once intuitive and pleasurable, had always been present in Santayana's thinking; the doctrine of essences merely gave him a new, and more original, way of formulating his conception.

On the question of aesthetic excellence and the importance of philosophical poetry, however, Santayana's later views differed sharply from his earlier ones. His change of heart sounds almost like a recantation. It runs as follows:

> So anxious was I, when younger, to find some rational justification for poetry and religion, and to show that their magic was significant of true facts, that I insisted too much, as I now think, on the need of relevance to fact even in poetry. Not only did I distinguish good religion from bad by its expression of practical wisdom and of the moral discipline that makes for happiness in this world, but I maintained that the noblest poetry also must express the moral burden of life and must be rich in wisdom. Age has made me less exacting, and I can now find quite sufficient perfection in poetry, like that of the Chinese and Arabians, without much philosophic scope, in mere grace and feeling and music and cloud-castles and frolic. . . . When living substance is restored beneath the surface of experience, there is no longer any reason for assuming that the first song of a bird may not be infinitely rich and as deep as heaven, if it utters the vital impulses of that moment with enough completeness. The analogies of this utterance with other events, or its outlying suggestions, whilst they may render it more intelligible to a third person, would not add much to its inward force and intrinsic beauty. Its lyric adequacy, though of course not independent of nature, would be independent of wisdom. If besides being an adequate expression of the soul, the song expressed the lessons of a broad experience, which that soul had gathered and digested, this fact certainly would lend a great tragic sublimity to that song; but to be poetical or religious intrinsically, the mystic cry is enough.

This statement appeared in 1922, eleven years after *Three Philosophical Poets*. Since almost all of Santayana's literary criticism was written before the 'twenties, the later standard had virtually no effect upon it. Although essays such as "Penitent Art," "Tragic Philosophy," and "Literary Psychology" reflect the change of doctrine, Santayana never attempted to reconstruct his earlier criticism. It is, therefore, extremely difficult to say just how much of his great writings on literature the older Santayana would readily have acknowledged. And what would his essays have been like if he had employed the later rather than the earlier standard? The question is intriguing, as such questions always are, but perhaps we do best to leave it as a question, since all speculation in this matter is sure to be utterly fruitless.

PART I

Three Philosophical Poets
(*selections*)

THREE PHILOSOPHICAL
POETS

I. INTRODUCTION

THE SOLE advantage in possessing great works of literature lies in
what they can help us to become. In themselves, as feats performed
by their authors, they would have forfeited none of their truth or
greatness if they had perished before our day. We can neither take
away nor add to their past value or inherent dignity. It is only they,
in so far as they are appropriate food and not poison for us, that
can add to the present value and dignity of our minds. Foreign
classics have to be retranslated and reinterpreted for each generation, to render their old naturalness in a natural way, and keep
their perennial humanity living and capable of assimilation. Even
native classics have to be reapprehended by every reader. It is this
continual digestion of the substance supplied by the past that alone
renders the insights of the past still potent in the present and for
the future. Living criticism, genuine appreciation, is the interest
we draw from year to year on the unrecoverable capital of human
genius.

Regarded from this point of view, as substances to be digested,
the poetic remains of Lucretius, Dante, and Goethe (though it is
his *Faust* only that I shall speak of) afford rather a varied feast. In
their doctrine and genius they may seem to be too much opposed
to be at all convergent or combinable in their wisdom. Some, who
know and care for one, perhaps, of these poets, may be disposed to
doubt whether they have anything vital to learn from the other
two. Yet it is as a pupil—I hope a discriminating pupil—of each
in turn that I mean to speak; and I venture to maintain that in
what makes them great they are compatible; that without any
vagueness or doubleness in one's criterion of taste one may admire

3

enthusiastically the poetry of each in turn; and that one may accept the essential philosophy, the positive intuition, of each, without lack of definition or system in one's own thinking.

Indeed, the diversity of these three poets passes, if I may use the Hegelian dialect, into a unity of a higher kind. Each is typical of an age. Taken together they sum up all European philosophy. Lucretius adopts the most radical and the most correct of those cosmological systems which the genius of early Greece had devised. He sees the world to be one great edifice, one great machine, all its parts reacting upon one another, and growing out of one another in obedience to a general pervasive process or life. His poem describes the nature, that is, the birth and composition, of all things. It shows how they are compounded out of elements, and how these elements, which he thinks are atoms in perpetual motion, are being constantly redistributed, so that old things perish and new things arise. Into this view of the world he fits a view of human life as it ought to be led under such conditions. His materialism is completed by an aspiration towards freedom and quietness of spirit. Allowed to look once upon the wonderful spectacle, which is to repeat itself in the world for ever, we should look and admire, for to-morrow we die; we should eat, drink, and be merry, but moderately and with much art, lest we die miserably, and die to-day.

This is one complete system of philosophy,—materialism in natural science, humanism in ethics. Such was the gist of all Greek philosophy before Socrates, of that philosophy which was truly Hellenic and corresponded with the movement which produced Greek manners, Greek government, and Greek art—a movement towards simplicity, autonomy, and reasonableness in everything, from dress to religion. Such is the gist also of what may be called the philosophy of the Renaissance, the reassertion of science and liberty in the modern world, by Bacon, by Spinoza, by the whole contemporary school that looks to science for its view of the facts, and to the happiness of men on earth for its ideal. This system is called naturalism; and of this Lucretius is the unrivalled poet.

Skip a thousand years and more, and a contrasting spectacle is before us. All minds, all institutions, are dominated by a religion that represents the soul as a pilgrim upon earth; the world is fallen and subject to the devil; pain and poverty are considered normal,

4

happiness impossible here and to be hoped for only in a future life, provided the snares and pleasures of the present life have not entrapped us. Meantime a sort of Jacob's ladder stretches from the stone on which the wayfarer lays his head into the heaven he hopes for; and the angels he sees ascending and descending upon it are beautiful stories, wonderful theories, and comforting rites. Through these he partakes, even on earth, of what will be his heavenly existence. He partly understands his destiny; his own history and that of the world are transfigured before him and, without ceasing to be sad, become beautiful. The raptures of a perfect conformity with the will of God, and of union with Him, overtake him in his prayers. This is supernaturalism, a system represented in Christendom chiefly by the Catholic Church, but adopted also by the later pagans, and widespread in Asia from remote antiquity down to the present time. Little as the momentary temper of Europe and America may now incline to such a view, it is always possible for the individual, or for the race, to return to it. Its sources are in the solitude of the spirit and in the disparity, or the opposition, between what the spirit feels it is fitted to do, and what, in this world, it is condemned to waste itself upon. The unmatched poet of this supernaturalism is Dante.

Skip again some five hundred years, and there is another change of scene. The Teutonic races that had previously conquered Europe have begun to dominate and understand themselves. They have become Protestants, or protesters against the Roman world. An infinite fountain of life seems to be unlocked within their bosom. They turn successively to the Bible, to learning, to patriotism, to industry, for new objects to love and fresh worlds to conquer; but they have too much vitality, or too little maturity, to rest in any of these things. A demon drives them on; and this demon, divine and immortal in its apparent waywardness, is their inmost self. It is their insatiable will, their radical courage. Nay, though this be a hard saying to the uninitiated, their will is the creator of all those objects by which it is sometimes amused, and sometimes baffled, but never tamed. Their will summons all opportunities and dangers out of nothing to feed its appetite for action; and in that ideal function lies their sole reality. Once attained, things are transcended. Like the episodes of a spent dream, they are to be smiled at and forgotten; the spirit that feigned and

5

discarded them remains always strong and undefiled; it aches for new conquests over new fictions. This is romanticism. It is an attitude often found in English poetry, and characteristic of German philosophy. It was adopted by Emerson and ought to be sympathetic to Americans; for it expresses the self-trust of world-building youth, and mystical faith in will and action. The greatest monument to this romanticism is Goethe's *Faust*.

Can it be an accident that the most adequate and probably the most lasting exposition of these three schools of philosophy should have been made by poets? Are poets, at heart, in search of a philosophy? Or is philosophy, in the end, nothing but poetry? Let us consider the situation.

If we think of philosophy as an investigation into truth, or as reasoning upon truths supposed to be discovered, there is nothing in philosophy akin to poetry. There is nothing poetic about the works of Epicurus, or St. Thomas Aquinas, or Kant; they are leafless forests. In Lucretius and in Dante themselves we find passages where nothing is poetical except the metre, or some incidental ornament. In such passages the form of poetry is thrown over the substance of prose, as Lucretius himself confesses where he says: "As when physicians would contrive to administer loathsome wormwood to little boys they first moisten the rim of the cup round about with sweet and golden honey, that the children's unsuspecting youth may be beguiled—to the lips, but no further— while they drink down the bitter potion, by deception not betrayed, but rather by that stratagem made whole and restored; . . . so I have willed to set forth our doctrine before thee in sweetsounding Pierian song, and to smear it, as it were, with the Muses' honey."[1]

But poetry cannot be spread upon things like butter; it must play upon them like light, and be the medium through which we

[1]Lucretius, I. 936–47:
> Veluti pueris absinthia tetra medentes
> Cum dare conantur, prius oras pocula circum
> Contingunt mellis dulci flavoque liquore,
> Ut puerorum aetas improvida ludificetur
> Labrorum tenus, interea perpotet amarum
> Absinthi laticem, deceptaque non capiatur,
> Sed potius tali pacto recreata valescat:
> Sic ego nunc . . . volui tibi suaviloquenti
> Carmine Pierio rationem exponere nostram,
> Et quasi musaeo dulci contingere melle.

see them. Lucretius does himself an injustice. If his philosophy had been wormwood to him, he could not have said, as he does just before this passage: "Like a sharp blow of the thyrsus, a great hope of praise vibrates through my heart and fills my breast with tender love of the Muses, whereby now, instinct with flowering fancy, I traverse pathless haunts of the Pierides, by no man's foot trodden before. It is joy to reach undefiled fountains and quaff; it is joy to gather fresh flowers and weave a matchless crown for my head of those bays with which never yet the Muses veiled the brow of any man; first, in that I teach sublime truths and come to free the soul from the strangling knots of superstition; then, in that on so dark a theme I pour forth so clear a song, suffusing all with poetic beauty, . . . if haply by such means I might keep thy mind intent upon my verses, until thine eye fathoms the whole structure of nature, and the fixed form that makes it beautiful."[2]

Here, I think, we have the solution to our doubt. The reasonings and investigations of philosophy are arduous, and if poetry is to be linked with them, it can be artificially only, and with a bad grace. But the vision of philosophy is sublime. The order it reveals in the world is something beautiful, tragic, sympathetic to the mind, and just what every poet, on a small or on a large scale, is always trying to catch.

In philosophy itself investigation and reasoning are only preparatory and servile parts, means to an end. They terminate in insight, or what in the noblest sense of the word may be called *theory*, θεωρία,—a steady contemplation of all things in their order and worth. Such contemplation is imaginative. No one can reach

---

[2]Lucretius, I. 922-34, 948-50:

Acri
Percussit thyrso laudis spes magna meum cor
Et simul incussit suavem mi in pectus amorem
Musarum, quo nunc instinctus mente vigenti
Avia Pieridum peragro loca nullius ante
Trita solo: iuvat integros accedere fontes,
Atque haurire; iuvatque novos decerpere flores,
Insignemque meo capiti petere inde coronam,
Unde prius nulli velarint tempora musae.
Primum, quod magnis doceo de rebus, et artis
Religionum animum nodis exsolvere pergo:
Deinde, quod obscura de re tam lucida pango
Carmina, musaeo contingens cuncta lepore. . . .
Si tibi forte animum tali ratione tenere
Versibus in nostris possem, dum perspicis omnem
Naturam rerum, qua constet compta figura.

it who has not enlarged his mind and tamed his heart. A philosopher who attains it is, for the moment, a poet; and a poet who turns his practised and passionate imagination on the order of all things, or on anything in the light of the whole, is for that moment a philosopher.

Nevertheless, even if we grant that the philosopher, in his best moments, is a poet, we may suspect that the poet has his worst moments when he tries to be a philosopher, or rather, when he succeeds in being one. Philosophy is something reasoned and heavy; poetry something winged, flashing, inspired. Take almost any longish poem, and the parts of it are better than the whole. A poet is able to put together a few words, a cadence or two, a single interesting image. He renders in that way some moment of comparatively high tension, of comparatively keen sentiment. But at the next moment the tension is relaxed, the sentiment has faded, and what succeeds is usually incongruous with what went before, or at least inferior. The thought drifts away from what it had started to be. It is lost in the sands of versification. As man is now constituted, to be brief is almost a condition of being inspired.

Shall we say, then,—and I now broach an idea by which I set some store,—that poetry is essentially short-winded, that what is poetic is necessarily intermittent in the writings of poets, that only the fleeting moment, the mood, the episode, can be rapturously felt, or rapturously rendered, while life as a whole, history, character, and destiny are objects unfit for imagination to dwell on, and repellent to poetic art? I cannot think so. If it be a fact, as it often is, that we find little things pleasing and great things arid and formless, and if we are better poets in a line than in an epic, that is simply due to lack of faculty on our part, lack of imagination and memory, and above all to lack of discipline.

This might be shown, I think, by psychological analysis, if we cared to rely on something so abstract and so debatable. For in what does the short-winded poet himself excel the common unimaginative person who talks or who stares? Is it that he thinks even less? Rather, I suppose, in that he feels more; in that his moment of intuition, though fleeting, has a vision, a scope, a symbolic something about it that renders it deep and expressive. Intensity, even momentary intensity, if it can be expressed at all, comports fullness and suggestion compressed into that intense moment. Yes,

8

everything that comes to us at all must come to us at some time or other. It is always the fleeting moment in which we live. To this fleeting moment the philosopher, as well as the poet, is actually confined. Each must enrich it with his endless vistas, vistas necessarily focused, if they are to be disclosed at all, in the eye of the observer, here and now. What makes the difference between a moment of poetic insight and a vulgar moment is that the passions of the poetic moment have more perspective. Even the short-winded poet selects his words so that they have a magic momentum in them which carries us, we know not how, to mountaintops of intuition. Is not the poetic quality of phrases and images due to their concentrating and liberating the confused promptings left in us by a long experience? When we feel the poetic thrill, is it not that we find sweep in the concise and depth in the clear, as we might find all the lights of the sea in the water of a jewel? And what is a philosophic thought but such an epitome?

If a short passage is poetical because it is pregnant with suggestion of a few things, which stretches our attention and makes us rapt and serious, how much more poetical ought a vision to be which was pregnant with all we care for? Focus a little experience, give some scope and depth to your feeling, and it grows imaginative; give it more scope and more depth, focus all experience within it, make it a philosopher's vision of the world, and it will grow imaginative in a superlative degree, and be supremely poetical. The difficulty, after having the experience to symbolize, lies only in having enough imagination to hold and suspend it in a thought; and further to give this thought such verbal expression that others may be able to decipher it, and to be stirred by it as by a wind of suggestion sweeping the whole forest of their memories.

Poetry, then, is not poetical for being short-winded or incidental, but, on the contrary, for being comprehensive and having range. If too much matter renders it heavy, that is the fault of the poet's weak intellect, not of the outstretched world. A quicker eye, a more synthetic imagination, might grasp a larger subject with the same ease. The picture that would render this larger subject would not be flatter and feebler for its extent, but, on the contrary, deeper and stronger, since it would possess as much unity as the little one with greater volume. As in a supreme dramatic crisis all our life seems to be focused in the present, and used in colouring our consciousness and shaping our decisions, so for each philosophic poet the whole world of man is gathered together; and he is never so much a poet as when, in a single cry, he summons all that has affinity to him in the universe, and salutes his ultimate destiny. It is the acme of life to understand life. The height of poetry is to speak the language of the gods. . . .

II. LUCRETIUS

. . . We are told of the old Xenophanes that he looked up into the round heaven and cried, "The All is One." What is logically a truism may often be, imaginatively, a great discovery, because no one before may have thought of the obvious analogy which the truism registers. So, in this case, the unity of all things is logically an evident, if barren, truth; for the most disparate and unrelated worlds would still be a multitude, and so an aggregate, and so, in some sense, a unity. Yet it was a great imaginative feat to cast the eye deliberately round the entire horizon, and to draw mentally the sum of all reality, discovering that reality makes such a sum, and may be called one; as any stone or animal, though composed of many parts, is yet called one in common parlance. It was doubtless some prehistoric man of genius, long before Xenophanes, who first applied in this way to all things together that notion of unity and wholeness which everybody had gained by observation of things singly, and who first ventured to speak of "the world." To do so is to set the problem for all natural philosophy, and in a certain measure to anticipate the solution of that problem; for it is to ask how things hang together, and to assume that they do hang together in one way or another.

To cry "The All is One," and to perceive that all things are in one landscape and form a system by their juxtaposition, is the rude beginning of wisdom in natural philosophy. But it is easy to go farther, and to see that things form a unity in a far deeper and more mysterious way. One of the first things, for instance, that impresses the poet, the man of feeling and reflection, is that these objects that people the world all pass away, and that the place thereof knows them no more. Yet, when they vanish, nothingness does not succeed; other things arise in their stead. Nature remains always young and whole in spite of death at work everywhere; and what takes the place of what continually disappears is often remarkably like it in character. Universal instability is not incompatible with a great monotony in things; so that while Heraclitus lamented that everything was in flux, Ecclesiastes, who was also entirely convinced of that truth, could lament that there was nothing new under the sun.

This double experience of mutation and recurrence, an experience at once sentimental and scientific, soon brought with it a very great thought, perhaps the greatest thought that mankind has ever hit upon, and which was the chief inspiration of Lucretius. It is that all we observe about us, and ourselves also, may be so many passing forms of a permanent substance. This substance, while remaining the same in quantity and in inward quality, is constantly redistributed; in its redistribution it forms those aggregates which we call things, and which we find constantly disappearing and reappearing. All things are dust, and to dust they return; a dust, however, eternally fertile, and destined to fall perpetually into new, and doubtless beautiful, forms. This notion of substance lends a much greater unity to the outspread world; it persuades us that all things pass into one another, and have a common ground from which they spring successively, and to which they return.

The spectacle of inexorable change, the triumph of time, or whatever we may call it, has always been a favourite theme for lyric and tragic poetry, and for religious meditation. To perceive universal mutation, to feel the vanity of life, has always been the beginning of seriousness. It is the condition for any beautiful, measured, or tender philosophy. Prior to that, everything is barbarous, both in morals and in poetry; for until then mankind has not learned to renounce anything, has not outgrown the instinctive egotism and optimism of the young animal, and has not removed the centre of its being, or of its faith, from the will to the imagination.

To discover substance, then, is a great step in the life of reason, even if substance be conceived quite negatively as a term that serves merely to mark, by contrast, the unsubstantiality, the vanity, of all particular moments and things. That is the way in which Indian poetry and philosophy conceived substance. But the step taken by Greek physics, and by the poetry of Lucretius, passes beyond. Lucretius and the Greeks, in observing universal mutation and the vanity of life, conceived behind appearance a great intelligible process, an evolution in nature. The reality became interesting, as well as the illusion. Physics became scientific, which had previously been merely spectacular.

Here was a much richer theme for the poet and philosopher, who was launched upon the discovery of the ground and secret causes of this gay or melancholy flux. The understanding that enabled him to discover these causes did for the European what no Indian mystic, what no despiser of understanding anywhere, suffers himself to do; namely, to dominate, foretell, and transform this changing show with a virile, practical intelligence. The man who discovers the secret springs of appearances opens to contemplation a second positive world, the workshop and busy depths of nature, where a prodigious mechanism is continually supporting our life, and making ready for it from afar by the most exquisite adjustments. The march of this mechanism, while it produces life and often fosters it, yet as often makes it difficult and condemns it to extinction. This truth, which the conception of natural substance first makes intelligible, justifies the elegies which the poets of illusion and disillusion have always written upon human things. It is a truth with a melancholy side; but being a truth, it satisfies and exalts the rational mind, that craves truth as truth, whether it be sad or comforting, and wishes to pursue a possible, not an impossible, happiness.

So far, Greek science had made out that the world was one, that there was a substance, that this was a physical substance, distributed and moving in space. It was matter. The question remained, What is the precise nature of matter, and how does it produce the appearances we observe? The only answer that concerns us here is that given by Lucretius; an answer he accepted from Epicurus, his master in everything, who in turn had accepted it from Democritus. Now Democritus had made a notable advance over the systems that selected one obvious substance, like water, or collected all the obvious substances, as Anaxagoras had done, and tried to make the world out of them. Democritus thought that the substance of everything ought not to have any of the qualities present in some things and absent in others; it ought to have only the qualities present in all things. It should be *merely* matter. Materiality, according to him, consisted of extension, figure, and solidity; in the thinnest ether, if we looked sharp enough, we should find nothing but particles possessing these properties. All other qualities of things were apparent only, and imputed to them by a convention of the mind. The mind was a born mythologist, and projected its feelings into their causes. Light, colour, taste, warmth, beauty, excellence, were such imputed and conventional qualities; only space and matter were real. But empty space was no less real than matter. Consequently, although the atoms of matter never changed their form, real changes could take place in nature, because their position might change in a real space.

Unlike the useless substance of the Indians, the substance of Democritus could offer a calculable ground for the flux of appearances; for this substance was distributed unequally in the void, and was constantly moving. Every appearance, however fleeting, corresponded to a precise configuration of substance; it arose with that configuration and perished with it. This substance, accordingly, was physical, not metaphysical. It was no dialectical term, but a scientific anticipation, a prophecy as to what an observer who should be properly equipped would discover in the interior of bodies. Materialism is not a system of metaphysics; it is a speculation in chemistry and physiology, to the effect that, if analysis could go deep enough, it would find that all substance was homogeneous, and that all motion was regular.

Though matter was homogeneous, the forms of the ultimate particles, according to Democritus, were various; and sundry combinations of them constituted the sundry objects in nature. Motion was not, as the vulgar (and Aristotle) supposed, unnatural, and produced magically by some moral cause; it had been eternal and was native to the atoms. On striking, they rebounded; and the mechanical currents or vortices which these contacts occasioned formed a multitude of stellar systems, called worlds, with which infinite space was studded.

Mechanism as to motion, atomism as to structure, materialism as to substance, that is the whole system of Democritus. It is as wonderful in its insight, in its sense for the ideal demands of method and understanding, as it is strange and audacious in its simplicity. Only the most convinced rationalist, the boldest prophet, could embrace it dogmatically; yet time has largely given it the proof. If Democritus could look down upon the present state of science, he would laugh, as he was in the habit of doing, partly at the confirmation we can furnish to portions of his philosophy, and partly at our stupidity that cannot guess the rest.

There are two maxims in Lucretius that suffice, even to this day, to distinguish a thinker who is a naturalist from one who is not. "Nothing," he says, "arises in the body in order that we may use it, but what arises brings forth its use."[1] This is that discarding of final causes on which all progress in science depends. The other maxim runs: "One thing will grow plain when compared with another: and blind night shall not obliterate the path for thee, before thou hast thoroughly scanned the ultimate things of nature; so much will things throw light on things."[2] Nature is her own standard; and if she seems to us unnatural, there is no hope for our minds.

The ethics of Democritus, in so far as we may judge from scanty evidence, were merely descriptive or satirical. He was an aristocratic observer, a scorner of fools. Nature was laughing at us all; the wise man considered his fate and, by knowing it, raised himself in a measure above it. All living things pursued the greatest happiness they could see their way to; but they were marvellously short-sighted; and the business of the philosopher was to foresee and pursue the greatest happiness that was really possible. This, in so rough a world, was to be found chiefly in abstention and retrenchment. If you asked for little, it was more probable that the event would not disappoint you. It was important not to be a fool, but it was very hard.

The system of Democritus was adopted by Epicurus, but not because Epicurus had any keenness of scientific vision. On the contrary, Epicurus, the Herbert Spencer of antiquity, was in his natural philosophy an encyclopaedia of second-hand knowledge. Prolix and minute, vague and inconsistent, he gathered his scientific miscellany with an eye fixed not on nature, but on the exigencies of an inward faith,—a faith accepted on moral grounds, deemed necessary to salvation, and defended at all costs, with any available

[1]Lucretius, IV. 834, 835:
        Nil . . . natumst in corpore, ut uti
        Possemus, sed quod natumst id procreat usum.
[2]Ibid., I. 1115–18:
            Alid ex alio clarescet, nec tibi caeca
            Nox iter eripiet, quin ultima naturai
            Pervideas: ita res accendent lumina rebus.

weapon. It is instructive that materialism should have been adopted at that juncture on the same irrelevant moral grounds on which it has usually been rejected.

Epicurus, strange as it may sound to those who have heard, with horror or envy, of wallowing in his sty, Epicurus was a saint. The ways of the world filled him with dismay. The Athens of his time, which some of us would give our eyes to see, retained all its splendour amid its political decay; but nothing there interested or pleased Epicurus. Theatres, porches, gymnasiums, and above all the agora, reeked, to his sense, with vanity and folly. Retired in his private garden, with a few friends and disciples, he sought the ways of peace; he lived abstemiously; he spoke gently; he gave alms to the poor; he preached against wealth, against ambition, against passion. He defended free-will because he wished to exercise it in withdrawing from the world, and in not swimming with the current. He denied the supernatural, since belief in it would have a disquieting influence on the mind, and render too many things compulsory and momentous. There was no future life: the art of living wisely must not be distorted by such wild imaginings.

All things happened in due course of nature; the gods were too remote and too happy, secluded like good Epicureans, to meddle with earthly things. Nothing ruffled what Wordsworth calls their "voluptuous unconcern." Nevertheless, it was pleasant to frequent their temples. There, as in the spaces where they dwelt between the worlds, the gods were silent and beautiful, and wore the human form. Their statues, when an unhappy man gazed at them, reminded him of happiness; he was refreshed and weaned for a moment from the senseless tumult of human affairs. From those groves and hallowed sanctuaries the philosopher returned to his garden strengthened in his wisdom, happier in his isolation, more friendly and more indifferent to all the world. Thus the life of Epicurus, as St. Jerome bears witness, was "full of herbs, fruits, and abstinences." There was a hush in it, as of bereavement. His was a philosophy of the decadence, a philosophy of negation, and of flight from the world.

Although science for its own sake could not interest so monkish a nature, yet science might be useful in buttressing the faith, or in removing objections to it. Epicurus therefore departed from the reserve of Socrates, and looked for a natural philosophy that might support his ethics. Of all the systems extant—and they were legion —he found that of Democritus the most helpful and edifying. Better than any other it would persuade men to renounce the madness that must be renounced and to enjoy the pleasures that may be enjoyed. But, since it was adopted on these external and pragmatic grounds, the system of Democritus did not need to be adopted entire. In fact, one change at least was imperative. The motion of the atoms must not be wholly regular and mechanical. Chance must be admitted, that Fate might be removed. Fate was a terrifying notion. It was spoken of by the people with superstitious unction. Chance was something humbler, more congenial to the man in the street. If only the atoms were allowed to deflect a little now and then from their courses, the future might remain unpredictable, and free-will might be saved. Therefore, Epicurus decreed that the atoms deflected, and fantastic arguments were added to show that this intrusion of chance would aid in the organization of nature; for the declension of the atoms, as it is called, would explain how the original parallel downpour of them might have yielded to vortices, and so to organized bodies. Let us pass on.

Materialism, like any system of natural philosophy, carries with it no commandments and no advice. It merely describes the world, including the aspirations and consciences of mortals, and refers all to a material ground. The materialist, being a man, will not fail to have preferences, and even a conscience, of his own; but his precepts and policy will express, not the logical implications of his science, but his human instincts, as inheritance and experience may have shaped them. Any system of ethics might accordingly coexist with materialism; for if materialism declares certain things (like immortality) to be impossible, it cannot declare them to be undesirable. Nevertheless, it is not likely that a man so constituted as to embrace materialism will be so constituted as to pursue things which he considers unattainable. There is therefore a psychological, though no logical, bond between materialism and a homely morality.

The materialist is primarily an observer; and he will probably be such in ethics also; that is, he will have no ethics, except the emotion produced upon him by the march of the world. If he is an *esprit fort* and really disinterested, he will love life; as we all love perfect vitality, or what strikes us as such, in gulls and porpoises. This, I think, is the ethical sentiment psychologically consonant with a vigorous materialism: sympathy with the movement of things, interest in the rising wave, delight at the foam it bursts into, before it sinks again. Nature does not distinguish the better from the worse, but the lover of nature does. He calls better what, being analogous to his own life, enhances his vitality and probably possesses some vitality of its own. This is the ethical feeling of Spinoza, the greatest of modern naturalists in philosophy; and we shall see how Lucretius, in spite of his fidelity to the ascetic Epicurus, is carried by his poetic ecstasy in the same direction.

But mark the crux of this union: the materialist will love the life of nature when he loves his own life; but if he should hate his own life, how should the life of nature please him? Now Epicurus, for the most part, hated life. His moral system, called hedonism, recommends that sort of pleasure which has no excitement and no risk about it. This ideal is modest, and even chaste, but it is not vital. Epicurus was remarkable for his mercy, his friendliness, his utter horror of war, of sacrifice, of suffering. These are not sentiments that a genuine naturalist would be apt to share. Pity and repentance, Spinoza said, were vain and evil; what increased a man's power and his joy increased his goodness also. The naturalist will believe in a certain hardness, as Nietzsche did; he will incline to a certain scorn, as the laughter of Democritus was scornful. He will not count too scrupulously the cost of what he achieves; he will be an imperialist, rapt in the joy of achieving something. In a word, the moral hue of materialism in a formative age, or in an aggressive mind, would be aristocratic and imaginative; but in a decadent age, or in a soul that is renouncing everything, it would be, as in Epicurus, humanitarian and timidly sensual.

We have now before us the antecedents and components of Lucretius' poem on nature. There remains the genius of the poet himself. The greatest thing about this genius is its power of losing itself in its object, its impersonality. We seem to be reading not the poetry of a poet about things, but the poetry of things themselves. That things have their poetry, not because of what we make them symbols of, but because of their own movement and life, is what Lucretius proves once for all to mankind.

Of course, the poetry we see in nature is due to the emotion the spectacle produces in us; the life of nature might be as romantic and sublime as it chose, it would be dust and ashes to us if there were nothing sublime and romantic in ourselves to be stirred by it to sympathy. But our emotion may be ingenuous; it may be concerned with what nature really is and does, has been and will do for ever. It need not arise from a selfish preoccupation with what these immense realities involve for our own persons or may be used to suggest to our self-indulgent fancy. No, the poetry of nature may be discerned merely by the power of intuition which it awakens and the understanding which it employs. These faculties, more, I should say, than our moodiness or stuffy dreams, draw taut the strings of the soul, and bring out her full vitality and music. Naturalism is a philosophy of observation, and of an imagination that extends the observable; all the sights and sounds of nature enter into it, and lend it their directness, pungency, and coercive stress. At the same time, naturalism is an intellectual philosophy; it divines substance behind appearance, continuity behind change, law behind fortune. It therefore attaches all those sights and sounds to a hidden background that connects and explains them. So understood, nature has depth as well as surface, force and necessity as well as sensuous variety. Before the sublimity of this insight, all forms of the pathetic fallacy seem cheap and artificial. Mythology, that to a childish mind is the only possible poetry, sounds like bad rhetoric in comparison. The naturalistic poet abandons fairy land, because he has discovered nature, history, the actual passions of man. His imagination has reached maturity; its pleasure is to dominate, not to play.

Poetic dominion over things as they are is seen best in Shakespeare for the ways of men, and in Lucretius for the ways of nature. Unapproachably vivid, relentless, direct in detail, he is unflinchingly grand and serious in his grouping of the facts. It is the truth that absorbs him and carries him along. He wishes us to be convinced and sobered by the fact, by the overwhelming evidence of thing after thing, raining down upon us, all bearing witness with one voice to the nature of the world.

Suppose, however,—and it is a tenable supposition,—that Lucretius is quite wrong in his science, and that there is no space, no substance, and no nature. His poem would then lose its pertinence to our lives and personal convictions; it would not lose its imaginative grandeur. We could still conceive a world composed as he describes. Fancy what emotions those who lived in such a world would have felt on the day when a Democritus or a Lucretius revealed to them their actual situation. How great the blindness or the madness dissipated, and how wonderful the vision gained! How clear the future, how intelligible the past, how marvellous the swarming atoms, in their unintentional, perpetual fertility! What the sky is to our eyes on a starry night, that every nook and cranny of nature would resemble, with here and there the tentative smile of life playing about those constellations. Surely that universe, for those who lived in it, would have had its poetry. It would have been the poetry of naturalism. Lucretius, thinking he lived in such a world, heard the music of it, and wrote it down.

And yet, when he set himself to make his poem out of the system of Epicurus, the greatness of that task seems to have overwhelmed him. He was to unfold for the first time, in sonorous but unwieldy Latin, the birth and nature of all things, as Greek subtlety had discerned them. He was to dispel superstition, to refute antagonists, to lay the sure foundations of science and of wisdom, to summon mankind compellingly from its cruel passions and follies to a life of simplicity and peace. He was himself combative and distracted enough—as it is often our troubles, more than our attainments, that determine our ideals. Yet in heralding the advent of human happiness, and in painting that of the gods, he was to attain his own, soaring upon the strong wings of his hexameters into an ecstasy of contemplation and enthusiasm. When it is so great an emotion to read these verses, what must it have been to compose them? Yet could he succeed? Could such great things fall to his lot? Yes, they might, if only the creative forces of nature, always infinite and always at hand, could pass into his brain and into his spirit; if only the seeds of corruption and madness, which were always coursing through the air, could be blown back for a moment; and if the din of civil conflicts could be suspended while he thought and wrote. To a fortunate conjunction of atoms, a child owes his first being. To a propitious season and atmosphere, a poet owes his inspiration and his success. Conscious that his undertaking hangs upon these chance conjunctions, Lucretius begins by invoking the powers he is about to describe, that they may give him breath and genius enough to describe them. And at once these powers send him a happy inspiration, perhaps a happy reminiscence of Empedocles. There are two great perspectives which the moralist may distinguish in the universal drift of atoms,—a creative movement, producing what the moralist values, and a destructive movement, abolishing the same. Lucretius knows very well that this distinction is moral only, or as people now say, subjective. No one else has pointed out so often and so clearly as he that nothing arises in this world not helped to life by the death of some other thing;[3] so that the destructive movement creates and the creative movement destroys. Yet from the point of view of any particular life or interest, the distinction between a creative force and a destructive force is real and all-important. To make it is not to deny the mechanical structure of nature, but only to show how this mechanical structure is fruitful morally, how the outlying parts of it are friendly or hostile to me or to you, its local and living products.

This double colouring of things is supremely interesting to the philosopher; so much so that before his physical science has reached the mechanical stage, he will doubtless regard the double aspect which things present to him as a dual principle in these things themselves. So Empedocles had spoken of Love and Strife as two forces which respectively gathered and disrupted the elements, so as to carry on between them the Penelope's labour of the world, the one perpetually weaving fresh forms of life, and the other perpetually undoing them.[4]

It needed but a slight concession to traditional rhetoric in order to exchange these names, Love and Strife, which designated divine powers in Empedocles, into the names of Venus and Mars, which designated the same influences in Roman mythology. The Mars and Venus of Lucretius are not moral forces, incompatible with the mechanism of atoms; they are this mechanism itself, in so far as it now produces and now destroys life, or any precious enterprise, like this of Lucretius in composing his saving poem. Mars and Venus, linked in each other's arms, rule the universe together; nothing arises save by the death of some other thing. Yet when what arises is happier in itself, or more congenial to us, than what

[3]Lucretius, I. 264, 265:
> Alid ex alio reficit natura, nec ullam
> Rem gigni patitur, nisi morte adiuta aliena.

[4]An excellent expression of this view is put by Plato into the mouth of the physician Eryximachus in the *Symposium*, pp. 186–88.

is destroyed, the poet says that Venus prevails, that she woos her captive lover to suspend his unprofitable raging. At such times it is spring on earth; the storms recede (I paraphrase the opening passage),[5] the fields are covered with flowers, the sunshine floods the serene sky, and all the tribes of animals feel the mighty impulse of Venus in their hearts. . . .

In treating of the soul and of immortality Lucretius is an imperfect psychologist and an arbitrary moralist. His zeal to prove that the soul is mortal is inspired by the wish to dispel all fear of future punishments, and so to liberate the mind for the calm and tepid enjoyment of this world. There is something to be gained in this direction, undoubtedly, especially if tales about divine vengeance to come are used to sanction irrational practices, and to prevent poor people from improving their lot. At the same time, it is hardly fair to assume that hell is the only prospect which immortality could possibly open to any of us; and it is also unfair not to observe that the punishments which religious fables threaten the dead with are, for the most part, symbols for the actual degradation which evil-doing brings upon the living; so that the fear of hell is not more deterrent or repressive than experience of life would be if it were clearly brought before the mind.

There is another element in this polemic against immortality which, while highly interesting and characteristic of a decadent age, betrays a very one-sided and, at bottom, untenable ideal. This element is the fear of life. Epicurus had been a pure and tender moralist, but pusillanimous. He was so afraid of hurting and of being hurt, so afraid of running risks or tempting fortune, that he wished to prove that human life was a brief business, not subject to any great transformations, nor capable of any great achieve-

[5]Lucretius, I. 1–13:
Æneadum genetrix, hominum divomque voluptas,
Alma Venus, caeli subter labentia signa
Quae mare navigerum, quae terras frugiferentis
Concelebras; per te quoniam genus omne animantum
Concipitur, visitque exortum lumina solis:
Te, dea, te fugiunt venti, te nubila caeli,
Adventumque tuum: tibi suaves daedala tellus
Submittit flores; tibi rident aequora ponti,
Placatumque nitet diffuso lumine caelum.
Nam simul ac species patefactast verna diei,
Et reserata viget genitabilis aura favoni;
Aëriae primum volucres te, diva, tuumque
Significant initum, perculsae corda tua vi.

ments. He taught accordingly that the atoms had produced already all the animals they could produce, for though infinite in number the atoms were of few kinds. Consequently the possible sorts of being were finite and soon exhausted; this world, though on the eve of destruction, was of recent date. The worlds around it, or to be produced in future, could not afford anything essentially different. All the suns were much alike, and there was nothing new under them. We need not, then, fear the world; it is an explored and domestic scene,—a home, a little garden, six feet of earth for a man to stretch in. If people rage and make a great noise, it is not because there is much to win, or much to fear, but because people are mad. Let me not be mad, thought Epicurus; let me be reasonable, cultivating sentiments appropriate to a mortal who inhabits a world morally comfortable and small, and physically poor in its infinite monotony. The well-known lines of Fitzgerald echo this sentiment perfectly:

> A Book of Verses underneath the Bough,
> A Jug of Wine, a Loaf of Bread—and Thou
>   Beside me singing in the Wilderness—
> Oh, Wilderness were Paradise enow!

But what if the shadow of incalculable possibilities should fall across this sunny retreat? What if after death we should awake in a world to which the atomic philosophy might not in the least apply? Observe that this suggestion is not in the least opposed to any of the arguments by which science might prove the atomic theory to be correct. All that Epicurus taught about the universe now before us might be perfectly true of it; but what if to-morrow a new universe should have taken its place? The suggestion is doubtless gratuitous, and no busy man will be much troubled by it; yet when the heart is empty it fills itself with such attenuated dreams. The muffled pleasures of the wise man, as Epicurus conceived him, were really a provocation to supernaturalism. They left a great void; and before long supernaturalism—we shall see it in Dante—actually rushed in to quicken the pulses of life with fresh hopes and illusions, or at least (what may seem better than nothing) with terrors and fanatical zeal. With such tendencies already afoot as the myths and dogmas of Plato had betrayed, it was imperative for Epicurus to banish anxiously all thought of what might follow death. To this end are all his arguments about the material nature of the soul and her incapacity to survive the body.

To say that the soul is material has a strange and barbarous sound to modern ears. We live after Descartes, who taught the world that the essence of the soul was consciousness; and to call consciousness material would be to talk of the blackness of white. But ancient usage gave the word soul a rather different meaning. The essence of the soul was not so much to be conscious as to govern the formation of the body, to warm, move, and guide it. And if we think of the soul exclusively in this light, it will not seem a paradox, it may even seem a truism, to say that the soul must be material. For how are we to conceive that preëxisting consciousness should govern the formation of the body, move, warm, or guide it? A spirit capable of such a miracle would in any case not be human, but altogether divine. The soul that Lucretius calls material should not, then, be identified with consciousness, but with the ground of consciousness, which is at the same time the cause of life in the body. This he conceives to be a swarm of very small and volatile atoms, a sort of ether, resident in all living seeds, breathed in abundantly during life and breathed out at death.

Even if this theory were accepted, however, it would not prove the point which Lucretius has chiefly at heart, namely, that an after-life is impossible. The atoms of the soul are indestructible, like all atoms; and if consciousness were attached to the fortunes of a small group of them, or of one only (as Leibniz afterwards taught), consciousness would continue to exist after these atoms had escaped from the body and were shooting through new fields of space. Indeed, they might be the more aroused by that adventure, as a bee might find the sky or the garden more exciting than the hive. All that Lucretius urges about the divisibility of the soul, its diffused bodily seat, and the perils it would meet outside fails to remove the ominous possibility that troubles him.

To convince us that we perish at death he has to rely on vulgar experience and inherent probability: what changes is not indestructible; what begins, ends; mental growth, health, sanity, accompany the fortunes of the body as a whole (not demonstrably those of the soul-atoms); the passions are relevant to bodily life and to an earthly situation; we should not be ourselves under a different

23

mask or in a new setting; we remember no previous existence if we had one, and so, in a future existence, we should not remember this. These reflections are impressive, and they are enforced by Lucretius with his usual vividness and smack of reality. Nothing is proved scientifically by such a deliverance, yet it is good philosophy and good poetry, it brings much experience together and passes a lofty judgement upon it. The artist has his eye on the model; he is painting death to the life.

If these considerations succeed in banishing the dread of an after-life, there remains the distress which many feel at the idea of extinction; and if we have ceased to fear death, like Hamlet, for the dreams that may come after it, we may still fear death instinctively, like a stuck pig. Against this instinctive horror of dying Lucretius has many brave arguments. Fools, he says to us, why do you fear what never can touch you? While you still live, death is absent; and when you are dead, you are so dead that you cannot know you are dead, nor regret it. You will be as much at ease as before you were born. Or is what troubles you the childish fear of being cold in the earth, or feeling its weight stifling you? But you will not be there; the atoms of your soul—themselves unconscious—will be dancing in some sunbeam far away, and you yourself will be nowhere; you will absolutely not exist. Death is by definition a state that excludes experience. If you fear it, you fear a word.

To all this, perhaps, Memmius, or some other recalcitrant reader, might retort that what he shrank from was not the metaphysical state of being dead, but the very real agony of dying. Dying is something ghastly, as being born is something ridiculous; and, even if no pain were involved in quitting or entering this world, we might still say what Dante's Francesca says of it: *Il modo ancor m' offende,* —"I shudder at the way of it." Lucretius, for his part, makes no attempt to show that everything is as it should be; and if our way of coming into this life is ignoble, and our way of leaving it pitiful, that is no fault of his nor of his philosophy. If the fear of death were merely the fear of dying, it would be better dealt with by medicine than by argument. There is, or there might be, an art of dying well, of dying painlessly, willingly, and in season,—as in those noble partings which Attic gravestones depict,—especially if we were allowed, as Lucretius would allow us, to choose our own time.

But the radical fear of death, I venture to think, is something quite different. It is the love of life. Epicurus, who feared life, seems to have missed here the primordial and colossal force he was fighting against. Had he perceived that force, he would have been obliged to meet it in a more radical way, by an enveloping movement, as it were, and an attack from the rear. The love of life is not something rational, or founded on experience of life. It is something antecedent and spontaneous. It is that Venus Genetrix which covers the earth with its flora and fauna. It teaches every animal to seek its food and its mate, and to protect its offspring; as also to resist or fly from all injury to the body, and most of all from threatened death. It is the original impulse by which good is discriminated from evil, and hope from fear.

Nothing could be more futile, therefore, than to marshal arguments against that fear of death which is merely another name for the energy of life, or the tendency to self-preservation. Arguments involve premises, and these premises, in the given case, express some particular form of the love of life; whence it is impossible to conclude that death is in no degree evil and not at all to be feared. For what is most dreaded is not the agony of dying, nor yet the strange impossibility that when we do not exist we should suffer for not existing. What is dreaded is the defeat of a present will directed upon life and its various undertakings. Such a present will cannot be argued away, but it may be weakened by contradictions arising within it, by the irony of experience, or by ascetic discipline. To introduce ascetic discipline, to bring out the irony of experience, to expose the self-contradictions of the will, would be the true means of mitigating the love of life; and if the love of life were extinguished, the fear of death, like smoke rising from that fire, would have vanished also.

Indeed, the force of the great passage against the fear of death, at the end of the third book of Lucretius, comes chiefly from the picture it draws of the madness of life. His philosophy deprecates covetousness, ambition, love, and religion; it takes a long step towards the surrender of life, by surrendering all in life that is ardent, on the ground that it is painful in the end and ignominious. To escape from it all is a great deliverance. And since genius must be ardent about something, Lucretius pours out his enthusiasm on Epicurus, who brought this deliverance and was the saviour of mankind. Yet this was only a beginning of salvation, and the same principles carried further would have delivered us from the Epicurean life and what it retained that was Greek and naturalistic: science, friendship, and the healthy pleasures of the body. Had it renounced these things also, Epicureanism would have become altogether ascetic, a thorough system of mortification, or the pursuit of death. To those who sincerely pursue death, death is no evil, but the highest good. No need in that case of elaborate arguments to prove that death should not be feared, because it is nothing; for in spite of being nothing—or rather because it is nothing—death can be loved by a fatigued and disillusioned spirit, just as in spite of being nothing—or rather because it is nothing—it must be hated and feared by every vigorous animal.

One more point, and I have done with this subject. Ancient culture was rhetorical. It abounded in ideas that are verbally plausible, and pass muster in a public speech, but that, if we stop to criticize them, prove at once to be inexcusably false. One of these rhetorical fallacies is the maxim that men cannot live for what they cannot witness. What does it matter to you, we may say in debate, what happened before you were born, or what may go on after you are buried? And the orator who puts such a challenge may carry the audience with him, and raise a laugh at the expense of human sincerity. Yet the very men who applaud are proud of their ancestors, care for the future of their children, and are very much interested in securing legally the execution of their last will and testament. What may go on after their death concerns them deeply, not because they expect to watch the event from hell or heaven, but because they are interested ideally in what that event shall be, although they are never to witness it. Lucretius himself, in his sympathy with nature, in his zeal for human enlightenment, in his tears for Iphigenia, long since dead, is not moved by the hope of observing, or the memory of having observed, what excites his emotion. He forgets himself. He sees the whole universe spread out in its true movement and proportions; he sees mankind freed from the incubus of superstition, and from the havoc of passion. The vision kindles his enthusiasm, exalts his imagination, and swells his verse into unmistakable earnestness.

If we follow Lucretius, therefore, in narrowing the sum of our personal fortunes to one brief and partial glimpse of earth, we must not suppose that we need narrow at all the sphere of our moral interests. On the contrary, just in proportion as we despise superstitious terrors and sentimental hopes, and as our imagination becomes self-forgetful, we shall strengthen the direct and primitive concern which we feel in the world and in what may go on there, before us, after us, or beyond our ken. If, like Lucretius and every philosophical poet, we range over all time and all existence, we shall forget our own persons, as he did, and even wish them to be forgotten, if only the things we care for may subsist or arise. He who truly loves God, says Spinoza, cannot wish that God should love him in return. One who lives the life of the universe cannot be much concerned for his own. After all, the life of the universe is but the locus and extension of ours. The atoms that have once served to produce life remain fit to reproduce it; and although the body they might animate later would be a new one, and would have a somewhat different career, it would not, according to Lucretius, be of a totally new species; perhaps not more unlike ourselves than we are unlike one another, or than each of us is unlike himself at the various stages of his life.

The soul of nature, in the elements of it, is then, according to Lucretius, actually immortal; only the human individuality, the chance composition of those elements, is transitory; so that, if a man could care for what happens to other men, for what befell him when young or what may overtake him when old, he might perfectly well care, on the same imaginative principle, for what may go on in the world for ever. The finitude and injustice of his personal life would be broken down; the illusion of selfishness would be dissipated; and he might say to himself, I have imagination, and nothing that is real is alien to me.

The word nature has many senses; but if we preserve the one which etymology justifies, and which is the most philosophical as well, nature should mean the principle of birth or genesis, the universal mother, the great cause, or system of causes, that brings phenomena to light. If we take the word nature in this sense, it may be said that Lucretius, more than any other man, is the poet of nature. Of course, being an ancient, he is not particularly a poet of landscape. He runs deeper than that; he is a poet of the source of landscape, a poet of matter. A poet of landscape might try to suggest, by well-chosen words, the sensations of light, movement, and form which nature arouses in us; but in this attempt he would encounter the insuperable difficulty which Lessing long ago pointed out, and warned poets of: I mean the unfitness of language to render what is spatial and material; its fitness to render only what, like language itself, is bodiless and flowing,—action, feeling, and thought.

It is noticeable, accordingly, that poets who are fascinated by pure sense and seek to write poems about it are called not impressionists, but symbolists; for in trying to render some absolute sensation they render rather the field of association in which that sensation lies, or the emotions and half-thoughts that shoot and play about it in their fancy. They become—against their will, perhaps —psychological poets, ringers of mental chimes, and listeners for the chance overtones of consciousness. Hence we call them symbolists, mixing perhaps some shade of disparagement in the term, as if they were symbolists of an empty, super-subtle, or fatuous sort. For they play with things luxuriously, making them symbols for their thoughts, instead of mending their thoughts intelligently, to render them symbols for things.

A poet might be a symbolist in another sense,—if he broke up nature, the object suggested by landscape to the mind, and reverted to the elements of landscape, not in order to associate these sensations lazily together, but in order to build out of them in fancy a different nature, a better world, than that which they reveal to reason. The elements of landscape, chosen, emphasized, and recombined for this purpose, would then be symbols for the ideal world they were made to suggest, and for the ideal life that might be led in that paradise. Shelley is a symbolic landscape poet in this sense. To Shelley, as Francis Thompson has said, nature was a toyshop; his fancy took the materials of the landscape and wove them into a gossamer world, a bright ethereal habitation for new-born irresponsible spirits. Shelley was the musician of landscape; he traced out its unrealized suggestions; transformed the things he saw into the things he would fain have seen. In this idealization it was spirit that guided him, the bent of his wild and exquisite imagination, and he fancied sometimes that the grosser landscapes of earth were likewise the work of some half-spiritual stress, of some restlessly dreaming power. In this sense, earthly landscape seemed to him the symbol of the earth spirit, as the starlit crystal landscapes of his verse, with their pensive flowers, were symbols in which his own fevered spirit was expressed, images in which his passion rested.

Another sort of landscape poetry is to be found in Wordsworth, for whom the title of poet of nature might perhaps be claimed. To him the landscape is an influence. What he renders, beyond such pictorial touches as language is capable of, is the moral inspiration which the scene brings to him. This moral inspiration is not drawn at all from the real processes of nature which every landscape manifests in some aspect and for one moment. Such would have been the method of Lucretius; he would have passed imaginatively from the landscape to the sources of the landscape; he would have disclosed the poetry of matter, not of spirit. Wordsworth, on the contrary, dwells on adventitious human matters. He is no poet of genesis, evolution, and natural force in its myriad manifestations. Only a part of the cosmic process engages his interest, or touches his soul—the strengthening or chastening of human purposes by the influences of landscape. These influences are very real; for as food or wine keeps the animal heart beating, or quickens it, so large spaces of calm sky, or mountains, or dells, or solitary stretches of water, expand the breast, disperse the obsessions that cramp a man's daily existence, and even if he be less contemplative and less virtuous than Wordsworth, make him, for the moment, a friend to all things, and a friend to himself.

Yet these influences are vague and for the most part fleeting. Wordsworth would hardly have felt them so distinctly and so constantly had he not found a further link to bind landscape to moral sentiment. Such a link exists. The landscape is the scene of human life. Every spot, every season, is associated with the sort of existence which falls to men in that environment. Landscape for Wordsworth's age and in his country was seldom without figures. At least, some visible trace of man guided the poet and set the key for his moral meditation. Country life was no less dear to Wordsworth than landscape was; it fitted into every picture; and while the march of things, as Lucretius conceived it, was not present to Wordsworth's imagination, the revolutions of society—the French Revolution, for instance—were constantly in his thoughts. In so far as he was a poet of human life, Wordsworth was truly a poet of nature. In so far, however, as he was a poet of landscape, he was still fundamentally a poet of human life, or merely of his personal experience. When he talked of nature he was generally moralizing, and altogether subject to the pathetic fallacy; but when he talked of man, or of himself, he was unfolding a part of nature, the upright human heart, and studying it in its truth.

Lucretius, a poet of universal nature, studied everything in its truth. Even moral life, though he felt it much more narrowly and coldly than Wordsworth did, was better understood and better sung by him for being seen in its natural setting. It is a fault of idealists to misrepresent idealism, because they do not view it as a part of the world. Idealism *is* a part of the world, a small and dependent part of it. It is a small and dependent part even in the life of men. This fact is nothing against idealism taken as a moral energy, as a faculty of idealization and a habit of living in the familiar presence of an image of what would, in everything, be best. But it is the ruin of idealism taken as a view of the central and universal power in the world. For this reason Lucretius, who sees human life and human idealism in their natural setting, has a saner and maturer view of both than has Wordsworth, for all his greater refinement. Nature, for the Latin poet, is really nature. He loves and fears her, as she deserves to be loved and feared by her creatures. Whether it be a wind blowing, a torrent rushing, a lamb bleating, the magic of love, genius achieving its purpose, or a war, or a pestilence, Lucretius sees everything in its causes, and in its total career. One breath of lavish creation, one iron law of change, runs through the whole, making all things kin in their inmost elements and in their last end. Here is the touch of nature indeed, her largeness and eternity. Here is the true echo of the life of matter. . . .

III. DANTE

In the *Phaedo* of Plato there is an incidental passage of supreme interest to the historian. It foreshadows, and accurately defines, the whole transition from antiquity to the middle age, from naturalism to supernaturalism, from Lucretius to Dante. Socrates, in his prison, is addressing his disciples for the last time. The general subject is immortality; but in a pause in the argument Socrates says: "In my youth . . . I heard some one reading, as he said, from a book of Anaxagoras, that Reason was the disposer and cause of all, and I was delighted at this notion, which appeared quite admirable, and I said to myself: 'If Reason is the disposer, Reason will dispose all for the best, and put each particular in the best place;' and I argued that if any desired to find out the cause of the generation or destruction or existence of anything, he must find out what . . . was best for that thing. . . . And I rejoiced to think that I had found in Anaxagoras a teacher of the causes of existence such as I desired, and I imagined that he would tell me first whether the earth is flat or round; and whichever was true, he would proceed . . . to show the nature of the best, and show that this was best; and if he said that the earth was in the centre [of the universe], he would further explain that this position was the best, and I should be satisfied with the explanation given, and not want any other sort of cause. . . . For I could not imagine that when he spoke of Reason as the disposer of things, he would give any other account of their being, except that this was best. . . . These hopes I would not have sold for a large sum of money, and I seized the books and read them as fast as I could, in my eagerness to know the better and the worse.

"What expectations I had formed and how grievously was I disappointed! As I proceeded, I found my philosopher altogether forsaking Reason or any other principle of order, but having recourse to air, and ether, and water, and other eccentricities. . . . Thus one man makes a vortex all round, and steadies the earth by the heaven; another gives the air as a support to the earth, which is a sort of bread trough. Any power which in arranging them as they are arranges them for the best never enters into their minds; and instead of finding any superior strength in it, they rather expect to discover another Atlas of the world who is stronger and more everlasting and more containing than the good; of the obligatory and containing power of the good they think nothing; and yet this is the principle which I would fain learn if anyone would teach me."[1]

Here we have the programme of a new philosophy. Things are to be understood by their uses or purposes, not by their elements or antecedents; as the fact that Socrates sits in his prison, when he

[1] Plato, *Phaedo*, 97B–99C, Jowett's translation. I have changed the rendering of νοῦς from "mind" to "reason."

might have escaped to Euboea, is to be understood by his allegiance to his notion of what is best, of his duty to himself and to his country, and not by the composition of his bones and muscles. Such reasons as we give for our actions, such grounds as might move the public assembly to decree this or that, are to be given in explanation of the order of nature. The world is a work of reason. It must be interpreted, as we interpret the actions of a man, by its motives. And these motives we must guess, not by a fanciful dramatic mythology, such as the poets of old had invented, but by a conscientious study of the better and the worse in the conduct of our own lives. For instance, the highest occupation, according to Plato, is the study of philosophy; but this would not be possible for man if he had to be continually feeding, like a grazing animal, with its nose to the ground. Now, to obviate the necessity of eating all the time, long intestines are useful; therefore the cause of long intestines is the study of philosophy. Again, the eyes, nose, and mouth are in the front of the head, because (says Plato) the front is the nobler side,—as if the back would not have been the nobler side (and the front side) had the eyes, nose, and mouth been there! This method is what Molière ridicules in *Le Malade Imaginaire*, when the chorus sings that opium puts people to sleep because it has a dormitive virtue, the nature of which is to make the senses slumber.

All this is ridiculous physics enough; but Plato knew—though he forgot sometimes—that his physics were playful. What it is important for us now to remember is rather that, under this childish or metaphorical physics, there is a serious morality. After all, the *use* of opium is that it is a narcotic; no matter why, physically, it is one. The *use* of the body *is* the mind, whatever the origin of the body may be. And it seems to dignify and vindicate these uses to say that they are the "causes" of the organs that make them possible. What is true of particular organs or substances is true of the whole frame of nature. Its *use* is to serve the good—to make life, happiness, and virtue possible. Therefore, speaking in parables, Plato says with his whole school: Discover the right principle of action, and you will have discovered the ruling force in the universe. Evoke in your rapt aspiration the essence of a supreme good, and you will have understood why the spheres revolve, why the earth is fertile, and why mankind suffers and exists. Observation must yield to dialectic; political art must yield to aspiration.

It took many hundred years for the revolution to work itself out; Plato had a prophetic genius, and looked away from what he was (for he was a Greek) to what mankind was to become in the next cycle of civilization. In Dante the revolution is complete, not merely intellectually (for it had been completed intellectually long before, in the Neoplatonists and the Fathers of the Church), but complete morally and poetically, in that all the habits of the mind and all the sanctions of public life had been assimilated to it. There had been time to reinterpret everything, obliterating the natural lines of cleavage in the world, and substituting moral lines of cleavage for them. Nature was a compound of ideal purposes and inert matter. Life was a conflict between sin and grace. The environment was a battle-ground between a host of angels and a legion of demons. The better and the worse had actually become, as Socrates desired, the sole principles of understanding.

Having become Socratic, the thinking part of mankind devoted all its energies henceforward to defining good and evil in all their grades, and in their ultimate essence; a task which Dante brings to a perfect conclusion. So earnestly and exclusively did they speculate about moral distinctions that they saw them in almost visible shapes, as Plato had seen his ideas. They materialized the terms of their moral philosophy into existing objects and powers. The highest good—in Plato still chiefly a political ideal, the aim of policy and art—became God, the creator of the world. The various stages or elements of perfection became persons in the Godhead, or angelic intelligences, or aerial demons, or lower types of the animal soul. Evil was identified with matter. The various stages of imperfection were ascribed to the grossness of various bodies, which weighted and smothered the spark of divinity that animated them. This spark, however, might be released; then it would fly up again to its parent fire and a soul would be saved.

This philosophy was not a serious description of nature or evolution; but it was a serious judgment upon them. The good, the better, the best, had been discerned; and a mythical bevy of powers, symbolizing these degrees of excellence, had been first talked of and then believed in. Myth, when another man has invented it, can pass for history; and when this man is a Plato, and has lived long ago, it can pass for revelation. In this way moral values came to be regarded as forces working in nature. But if they worked in nature, which was a compound of evil matter and perfect form, they must exist outside: for the ideal of excellence beckons from afar; it is what we pine for and are not. The forces that worked in nature were accordingly supernatural virtues, dominations, and powers; each natural thing had its supernatural incubus, a guardian angel, or a devil that possessed it. The supernatural—that is, something moral or ideal regarded as a power and an existence—was all about us. Everything in the world was an effect of something beyond the world; everything in life was a step to something beyond life.

Into this system Christianity fitted easily. It enriched it by adding miraculous history to symbolic cosmology. The Platonists had conceived a cosmos in which there were higher and lower beings, marshalled in concentric circles, around this vile but pivotal lump of earth. The Christians supplied a dramatic action for which the stage seemed admirably fitted, a story in which the whole human race, or the single soul, passed successively through these higher and lower stages. There had been a fall, and there might be a salvation. In a sense, even this conception of descent from the good, and ascent towards it again, was Platonic. According to the Platonists, the good eternally shed its vital influence, like light, and received (though unawares and without increase of excellence to itself) reflected rays that, in the form of love and thought, reverted to it from the ends of the universe. But according to the Platonist this radiation of life and focusing of aspiration were both perpetual. The double movement was eternal. The history of the world was monotonous; or rather the world had no significant history, but only a movement like that of a fountain playing for ever, or like the circulation of water that is always falling from the clouds in rain and always rising again in vapour. This fall, or emanation of the world from the deity, was the origin of evil for the Platonists; evil consisted merely in finitude, materiality, or otherness from God. If anything besides God was to exist, it had to be imperfect; instability and conflict were essential to finitude and to existence. Salvation, on the other hand, was the return current of aspiration on the part of the creature to revert to its source; an aspiration which was expressed in various types of being, fixed in the eternal, —types which led up, like the steps of a temple, to the ineffable good at the top.

In the Christian system this cosmic circulation became only a figure or symbol expressing the true creation, the true fall, and the true salvation; all three being really episodes in an historical drama, occurring only once. The material world was only a scene, a stage-setting, designed expressly to be appropriate for the play; and this play was the history of mankind, especially of Israel and of the Church. The persons and events of this history had a philosophic import; each played some part in a providential plan. Each illustrated creation, sin, and salvation in some degree, and on some particular level.

The Jews had never felt uncomfortable at being material; even in the other world they hoped to remain so, and their immortality was a resurrection of the flesh. It did not seem plausible to them that this excellent frame of things should be nothing but a faint, troubled, and unintended echo of the good. On the contrary, they thought this world so good, intrinsically, that they were sure God must have made it expressly, and not by an unconscious effluence of his virtue, as the Platonists had believed. Their wonder at the power and ingenuity of the deity reached its maximum when they thought of him as the cunning contriver of nature, and of themselves. Nevertheless the work seemed to show some imperfections; indeed, its moral excellence was potential rather than actual, a suggestion of what might be, rather than an accomplished fact. And so, to explain the unexpected flaws in a creation which they thought essentially good, they put back at the beginning of things an experience they had daily in the present, namely, that trouble springs from bad conduct.

The Jews were intent watchers of fortune and of its vicissitudes. The careers of men were their meditation by day and by night; and it takes little attention to perceive that frivolity, indifference, knavery, and debauchery do not make for well-being in this world. And like other hard-pressed peoples, the ancient Jews had a pathetic admiration for safety and plenty. How little they must have known these things, to think of them so rapturously and so poetically! Not merely their personal prudence, but their corporate and religious zeal made them abhor that bad conduct which defeated prosperity. It was not mere folly, but wickedness and the abomination of desolation. With the lessons of conduct continually in mind, they framed the theory that all suffering, and even death, were the wages of sin. Finally they went so far as to attribute evil in all creation to the casual sin of a first man, and to the taint of it transmitted to his descendants; thus passing over the suffering and death of all creatures that are not human with an indifference that would have astonished the Hindoos.

The imperfection of things, in the Hebraic view, was due to accidents in their operation; not, as in the Platonic view, to their essential separation from their source and their end. It is in harmony with this that salvation too should come by virtue of some special act, like the incarnation or death of Christ. Just so, the Jews had conceived salvation as a revival of their national existence and greatness, to be brought about by the patience and fidelity of the elect, with tremendous miracles supervening to reward these virtues.

Thus their conception of the fall and of the redemption was historical. And this was a great advantage to a man of imagination inheriting their system; for the personages and the miracles that figured in their sacred histories afforded a rich subject for fancy to work upon, and for the arts to depict. The patriarchs from Adam down, the kings and prophets, the creation, Eden, the deluge, the deliverance out of Egypt, the thunders and the law of Sinai, the temple, the exile—all this and much more that fills the Bible was a rich fund, a familiar tradition living in the Church, on which Dante could draw, as he drew at the same time from the parallel classic tradition which he also inherited. To lend all these Biblical persons and incidents a philosophical dignity he had only to fit them, as the Fathers of the Church had done, into the Neoplatonic cosmology, or, as the doctors of his own time were doing, into the Aristotelian ethics.

So interpreted, sacred history acquired for the philosopher a new importance besides that which it had seemed to have to Israel in exile, or to the Christian soul conscious of sin. Every episode became the symbol for some moral state or some moral principle. Every preacher in Christendom, as he repeated his homily on the gospel of the day, was invited to rear a structure of spiritual interpretations upon the literal sense of the narrative, which nevertheless he was always to hold and preserve as a foundation for the others.[2] In a world made by God for the illustration of his glory,

[2]"Est pro fundamento tenenda veritas historiae et desuper spirituales expositiones fabricandae." Thomas Aquinas, *Summa Theologiae*, I. quaest. 102, conclusio.

things and events, though real, must be also symbolical; for there is intention and propriety behind them. The creation, the deluge, the incarnation, crucifixion, and resurrection of Christ, the coming of the Holy Ghost with flames of fire and the gift of tongues, were all historical facts. The Church was heir to the chosen people; it was an historic and political institution, with a destiny in this world, in which all her children should share, and for which they should fight. At the same time all those facts were mysteries and sacraments for the private soul; they were channels for the same moral graces that were embodied in the order of the heavenly spheres, and in the types of moral life on earth. Thus the Hebrew tradition brought to Dante's mind the consciousness of a providential history, a great earthly task,—to be transmitted from generation to generation,—and a great hope. The Greek tradition brought him natural and moral philosophy. These contributions, joined together, had made Christian theology.

Although this theology was the guide to Dante's imagination, and his general theme, yet it was not his only interest; or rather he put into the framework of orthodox theology theories and visions of his own, fusing all into one moral unity and one poetical enthusiasm. The fusion was perfect between the personal and the traditional elements. . . .

Thus, throughout the *Divine Comedy*, meaning and meaning lurk beneath the luminous pictures; and the poem, besides being a description of the other world, and of the rewards and punishment meted out to souls, is a dramatic view of human passions in this life; a history of Italy and of the world; a theory of Church and State; the autobiography of an exile; and the confessions of a Christian, and of a lover, conscious of his sins and of the miracle of divine grace that intervenes to save him.

The subject-matter of the *Divine Comedy* is accordingly the moral universe in all its levels,—romantic, political, religious. To present these moral facts in a graphic way, the poet performed a double work of imagination. First he chose some historical personage that might plausibly illustrate each condition of the soul. Then he pictured this person in some characteristic and symbolic attitude of mind and of body, and in an appropriate, symbolic environment. To give material embodiment to moral ideas by such a method would nowadays be very artificial, and perhaps impossible; but in Dante's time everything was favourable to the attempt. We are accustomed to think of goods and evils as functions of a natural life, sparks struck out in the chance shock of men with things or with one another. For Dante, it was a matter of course that moral distinctions might be discerned, not merely as they arise incidentally in human experience, but also, and more genuinely, as they are displayed in the order of creation. The Creator himself was a poet producing allegories. The material world was a parable which he had built out in space, and ordered to be enacted. History was a great charade. The symbols of earthly poets are words or images; the symbols of the divine poet were natural things and the fortunes of men. They had been devised for a purpose; and this purpose, as the Koran, too, declares, had been precisely to show forth the great difference there is in God's sight between good and evil.

In Platonic cosmology, the concentric spheres were bodies formed and animated by intelligences of various orders. The nobler an intelligence, the more swift and outward, or higher, was the sphere it moved; whence the identification of "higher" with better, which survives, absurdly, to this day. And while Dante could not attribute literal truth to his fancies about hell, purgatory, and heaven, he believed that an actual heaven, purgatory, and hell had been fashioned by God on purpose to receive souls of varying deserts and complexion; so that while the poet's imagination, unless it reëchoed divine revelation, was only human and not prophetic, yet it was a genuine and plausible imagination, moving on the lines of nature, and anticipating such things as experience might very well realize. Dante's objectification of morality, his art of giving visible forms and local habitations to ideal virtues and vices, was for him a thoroughly serious and philosophical exercise. God had created nature and life on that very principle. The poet's method repeated the magic of Genesis. His symbolical imagination mirrored this symbolical world; it was a sincere anticipation of fact, no mere laboured and wilful allegory.

This situation has a curious consequence. Probably for the first and last time in the history of the world a classification worked out by a systematic moralist guided the vision of a great poet. Aristotle had distinguished, named, and classified the various virtues, with their opposites. But observe: if the other world was made on purpose—as it was—to express and render palpable those moral distinctions which were eternal, and to express and render them palpable in great detail, with all their possible tints and varieties; and if Aristotle had correctly classified moral qualities, as he had —then it follows that Aristotle (without knowing it) must have supplied the ground-plan, as it were, of hell and of heaven. Such was Dante's thought. With Aristotle's *Ethics* open before him, with a supplementary hint, here and there, drawn from the catechism, and with an ingrained preference (pious and almost philosophic) for the number three and its multiples, he needed not to voyage without a chart. The most visionary of subjects, life after death, could be treated with scientific soberness and deep sincerity. This vision was to be no wanton dream. It was to be a sober meditation, a philosophical prophecy, a probable drama,—the most poignant, terrible, and consoling of all possible truths.

The good—this was the fundamental thought of Aristotle and of all Greek ethics,—the good is the end at which nature aims. The demands of life cannot be radically perverse, since they are the judges of every excellence. No man, as Dante says, could hate his own soul; he could not at once be, and contradict, the voice of his instincts and emotions. Nor could a man hate God; for if that man knew himself, he would see that God was, by definition, his natural good, the ultimate goal of his actual aspirations.[3] Since it was impossible, according to this insight, that our faculties should be intrinsically evil, all evil had to arise from the disorder into which these faculties fall, their too great weakness or strength in relation to one another. If the animal part of man was too strong for his reason, he fell into incontinence,—that is, into lust, gluttony, avarice, wrath, or pride. Incontinence came from an excessive or ill-timed pursuit of something good, of a part of what nature aims at; for food, children, property, and character are natural goods. These sins are accordingly the most excusable and the least odious. Dante puts those who have sinned through love in the first circle of hell, nearest to the sunlight, or in the topmost round of purgatory,

---

[3] *Purgatorio*, XVII. 106–11:

> Or perchè mai non può dalla salute
> Amor del suo suggetto volger viso,
> Dall' odio proprio son le cose tute:
> E perchè intender non si può diviso,
> E per sè stante, alcuno esser dal primo,
> Da quello odiare ogni affetto è deciso.

nearest to the earthly paradise. Below the lovers, in each case, are the gluttons,—where a northern poet would have been obliged to place his drunkards. Beneath these again are the misers,—worse because less open to the excuse of a merely childish lack of self-control.

The disorder of the faculties may arise, however, in another way. The combative or spirited element, rather than the senses, may get out of hand, and lead to crimes of violence. Violence, like incontinence, is spontaneous enough in its personal origin, and would not be odious if it did not inflict, and intend to inflict, harm on others; so that besides incontinence, there is malice in it. Ill-will to others may arise from pride, because one loves to be superior to them, or from envy, because one abhors that they should seem superior to oneself; or through desire for vengeance, because one smarts under some injury. Sins of these kinds are more serious than those of foolish incontinence; they complicate the moral world more; they introduce endless opposition of interests, and perpetual, self-propagating crimes. They are hateful. Dante feels less pity for those who suffer by them: he remembers the sufferings these malefactors have themselves caused, and he feels a sort of joy in joining the divine justice, and would gladly lash them himself.

Worse still than violence, however, is guile: the sin of those who in the service of their intemperance or their malice have abused the gift of reason. *Corruptio optimi pessima;* and to turn reason, the faculty that establishes order, into a means of organizing disorder, is a perversity truly satanic: it turns evil into an art. But even this perversity has stages; and Dante distinguishes ten sorts of dishonesty or simple fraud, as well as three sorts of treachery.

Besides these positive transgressions there is a possibility of general moral sluggishness and indifference. This Dante, with his fervid nature, particularly hates. He puts the Laodiceans in the fringe of his hell; within the gate, that they may be without hope, but outside of limbo, that they may have torments to endure, and be stung by wasps and hornets into a belated activity.[4]

To these vices, known to Aristotle, the Catholic moralist was obliged to add two others: original sin, of which spontaneous dis-

4*Inferno,* III. 64–66:

> Questi sciaurati, che mai non fur vivi,
> Erano ignudi e stimolati molto
> Da mosconi e da vespe ch' erano ivi.

belief is one consequence, and heresy, or misbelief, after a revelation has been given and accepted. Original sin, and the paganism that goes with it, if they lead to nothing worse, are a mere privation of excellence and involve in eternity merely a privation of joy: they are punished in limbo. There sighs are heard, but no lamentation, and the only sorrow is to live in desire without hope. This fate is most appropriately imputed to the noble and clear-sighted in the hereafter, since it is so often their experience here. Dante was never juster than in this stroke.[5] Heresy, on the other hand, is a kind of passion when honest, or a kind of fraud when politic; and it is punished as pride in fiery tombs,[6] or as faction by perpetual gaping wounds and horrible mutilations.[7]

So far, with these slight additions, Dante is following Aristotle; but here a great divergence sets in. If a pagan poet had conceived the idea of illustrating the catalogue of vices and virtues in poetic scenes, he would have chosen suitable episodes in human life, and painted the typical characters that figured in them in their earthly environment; for pagan morality is a plant of earth. Not so with Dante. His poem describes this world merely in retrospect; the foreground is occupied by the eternal consequences of what time had brought forth. These consequences are new facts, not merely, as for the rationalist, the old facts conceived in their truth; they often reverse, in their emotional quality, the events they represent. Such a reversal is made possible by the theory that justice is partly retributive; that virtue is not its own sufficient reward, nor vice its own sufficient punishment. According to this theory, this life contains a part of our experience only, yet determines the rest. The other life is a second experience, yet it does not contain any

[5]*Ibid.*, IV. 41, 42:

> Semo perduti, e sol di tanto offesi
> Che senza speme vivemo in disio.

Cf. *Purgatorio*, III. 37–45, where Virgil says:

> "State contenti, umana gente, al *quia;*
>   Chè se potuto aveste veder tutto,
>   Mestier non era partorir Maria;
> E disiar vedeste senza frutto
>   Tai, che sarebbe lor disio quetato,
>   Ch' eternalmente è dato lor per lutto.
> Io dico d' Aristotele e di Plato,
>   E di molti altri." E qui chinò la fronte;
>   E più non disse, e rimase turbato.

[6]*Inferno*, IX. 106–33, and x.
[7]*Ibid.*, XXVIII.

41

novel adventures. It is determined altogether by what we have done on earth; as the tree falleth so it lieth, and souls after death have no further initiative.

The theory Dante adopts mediates between two earlier views; in so far as it is Greek, it conceives immortality ideally, as something timeless; but in so far as it is Hebraic, it conceives of a new existence and a second, different taste of life. Dante thinks of a second experience, but of one that is wholly retrospective and changeless. It is an epilogue which sums up the play, and is the last episode in it. The purpose of this epilogue is not to carry on the play indefinitely: such a romantic notion of immortality never entered Dante's mind. The purpose of the epilogue is merely to vindicate (in a more unmistakable fashion than the play, being ill acted, itself could do) the excellence of goodness and the misery of vice. Were this life all, he thinks the wicked might laugh. If not wholly happy, at least they might boast that their lot was no worse than that of many good men. Nothing would make an overwhelming difference. Moral distinctions would be largely impertinent and remarkably jumbled. If I am a simple lover of goodness, I may perhaps put up with this situation. I may say of the excellences I prize what Wordsworth says of his Lucy: there may be none to praise and few to love them, but they make all the difference to me.

Dante, however, was not merely a simple lover of excellence: he was also a keen hater of wickedness, one that took the moral world tragically and wished to heighten the distinctions he felt into something absolute and infinite. Now any man who is *enragé* in his preferences will probably say, with Mohammed, Tertullian, and Calvin, that good is dishonoured if those who contemn it can go scot-free, and never repent of their negligence; that the more horrible the consequences of evil-doing, the more tolerable the presence of evil-doing is in the world; and that the everlasting shrieks and contortions of the damned alone will make it possible for the saints to sit quiet, and be convinced that there is perfect harmony in the universe. On this principle, in the famous inscription which Dante places over the gate of hell, we read that primal love, as well as justice and power, established that torture-house; primal love, that is, of that good which, by the extreme punishment of those who scorn it, is honoured, vindicated, and made to shine like the sun. The damned are damned for the glory of God.

This doctrine, I cannot help thinking, is a great disgrace to human nature. It shows how desperate, at heart, is the folly of an egotistic or anthropocentric philosophy. This philosophy begins by assuring us that everything is obviously created to serve our needs; it then maintains that everything serves our ideals; and in the end, it reveals that everything serves our blind hatreds and superstitious qualms. Because my instinct taboos something, the whole universe, with insane intensity, shall taboo it for ever. This infatuation was inherited by Dante, and it was not uncongenial to his bitter and intemperate spleen. Nevertheless, he saw beyond it at times. Like many other Christian seers, he betrays here and there an esoteric view of rewards and punishments, which makes them simply symbols for the intrinsic quality of good and evil ways. The punishment, he then seems to say, is nothing added; it is what the passion itself pursues; it is a fulfilment, horrifying the soul that desired it.

For instance, spirits newly arrived in hell require no devil with his prong to drive them to their punishment. They flit towards it eagerly, of their own accord.[8] Similarly, the souls in purgatory are kept by their own will at the penance they are doing. No external force retains them, but until they are quite purged they are not able, because they are not willing, to absolve themselves.[9] The whole mountain, we are told, trembles and bursts into psalmody when any one frees himself and reaches heaven. Is it too much of a gloss to say that these souls change their prison when they change their ideal, and that an inferior state of soul is its own purgatory, and determines its own duration? In one place, at any rate, Dante proclaims the intrinsic nature of punishment in express terms. Among the blasphemers is a certain king of Thebes, who defied the thunderbolts of Jupiter. He shows himself indifferent to his punishment and says: "Such as I was alive, such I am dead." Where-

[8] *Inferno*, III. 124–26:

> E pronti sono a trapassar lo rio,
> Chè la divina giustizia gli sprona
> Sì che la tema si volge in disio.

[9] *Purgatorio*, XXI. 61–69:

> Della mondizia sol voler fa prova,
> Che, tutta libera a mutar convento,
> L' alma sorprende, e di voler le giova. . . .
> Ed io che son giaciuto a questa doglia
> Cinquecento anni e più, pur mo sentii
> Libera volontà di miglior soglia.

upon Virgil exclaims, with a force Dante had never found in his
voice before: "In that thy pride is not mortified, thou art punished
the more. No torture, other than thy own rage, would be woe
enough to match thy fury."[10] And indeed, Dante's imagination cannot outdo, it cannot even equal, the horrors which men have
brought upon themselves in this world. If we were to choose the most
fearful of the scenes in the *Inferno,* we should have to choose the
story of Ugolino, but this is only a pale recital of what Pisa had
actually witnessed.

A more subtle and interesting instance, if a less obvious one, may
be found in the punishment of Paolo and Francesca da Rimini.
What makes these lovers so wretched in the Inferno? They are
still together. Can an eternity of floating on the wind, in each
other's arms, be a punishment for lovers? That is just what their
passion, if left to speak for itself, would have chosen. It is what
passion stops at, and would gladly prolong for ever. Divine judgement has only taken it at its word. This fate is precisely what Aucassin, in the well-known tale, wishes for himself and his sweetheart
Nicolette,—not a heaven to be won by renunciation, but the possession, even if it be in hell, of what he loves and fancies. And a
great romantic poet, Alfred de Musset, actually upbraids Dante for
not seeing that such an eternal destiny as he has assigned to Paolo
and Francesca would be not the ruin of their love,[11] but the perfect fulfilment of it. This last seems to be very true; but did Dante
overlook the truth of it? If so, what instinct guided him to choose

[10]*Inferno,* XIV. 63–66:

> "O Capaneo, in ciò che non s' ammorza
> La tua superbia, se' tu più punito:
> Nullo martiro, fuor che la tua rabbia,
> Sarebbe al tuo furor dolor compito."

[11]Alfred de Musset, *Poésies Nouvelles, Souvenir:*

> Dante, pourquoi dis-tu qu'il n'est pire misère
> Qu'un souvenir heureux dans les jours de douleur?
> Quel chagrin t'a dicté cette parole amère,
> Cette offense au malheur?

> . . . Ce blasphème vanté ne vient pas de ton cœur.
> Un souvenir heureux est peut-être sur terre
> Plus vrai que le bonheur. . . .

> Et c'est à ta Françoise, à ton ange de gloire,
> Que tu pouvais donner ces mots à prononcer,
> Elle qui s'interrompt, pour conter son histoire,
> D'un éternel baiser!

just the fate for these lovers that they would have chosen for themselves?

There is a great difference between the apprentices in life, and the masters,—Aucassin and Alfred de Musset were among the apprentices; Dante was one of the masters. He could feel the fresh promptings of life as keenly as any youngster, or any romanticist; but he had lived these things through, he knew the possible and the impossible issue of them; he saw their relation to the rest of human nature, and to the ideal of an ultimate happiness and peace. He had discovered the necessity of saying continually to oneself: Thou shalt renounce. And for this reason he needed no other furniture for hell than the literal ideals and fulfilments of our absolute little passions. The soul that is possessed by any one of these passions nevertheless has other hopes in abeyance. Love itself dreams of more than mere possession; to conceive happiness, it must conceive a life to be shared in a varied world, full of events and activities, which shall be new and ideal bonds between the lovers. But unlawful love cannot pass out into this public fulfilment. It is condemned to be mere possession—possession in the dark, without an environment, without a future. It is love among the ruins. And it is precisely this that is the torment of Paolo and Francesca—love among the ruins of themselves and of all else they might have had to give to one another. Abandon yourself, Dante would say to us,—abandon yourself altogether to a love that is nothing but love, and you are in hell already. Only an inspired poet could be so subtle a moralist. Only a sound moralist could be so tragic a poet.

The same tact and fine feeling that appear in these little moral dramas appear also in the sympathetic landscape in which each episode is set. The poet actually accomplishes the feat which he attributes to the Creator; he evokes a material world to be the fit theatre for moral attitudes. Popular imagination and the precedents of Homer and Virgil had indeed carried him halfway in this symbolic labour, as tradition almost always carries a poet who is successful. Mankind, from remotest antiquity, had conceived a dark subterranean hell, inhabited by unhappy ghosts. In Christian times, these shades had become lost souls, tormented by hideous demons. But Dante, with the Aristotelian chart of the vices before

him, turned those vague windy caverns into a symmetrical labyrinth. Seven concentric terraces descended, step by step, towards
the waters of the Styx, which in turn encircled the brazen walls of
the City of Dis, or Pluto. Within these walls, two more terraces led
down to the edge of a prodigious precipice—perhaps a thousand
miles deep—which formed the pit of hell. . . .

Never before or since has a poet lived in so large a landscape as
Dante; for our infinite times and distances are of little poetic value
while we have no graphic image of what may fill them. Dante's
spaces were filled; they enlarged, to the limits of human imagination, the habitations and destinies of mankind. Although the saints
did not literally inhabit the spheres, but the empyrean beyond,
yet each spirit could be manifested in that sphere the genius of
which was most akin to his own. In Dante's vision spirits appear as
points of light, from which voices also flow sometimes, as well as
radiance. Further than reporting their words (which are usually
about the things of earth) Dante tells us little about them. He has
indeed, at the end, a vision of a celestial rose; tier upon tier of saints
are seated as in an amphitheatre, and the Deity overarches them in
the form of a triple rainbow, with a semblance of man in the midst.
But this is avowedly a mere symbol, a somewhat conventional picture to which Dante has recourse unwillingly, for want of a better
image to render his mystical intention. What may perhaps help us
to divine this intention is the fact, just mentioned, that according
to him the celestial spheres are not the real seat of any human soul;
that the pure rise through them with increasing ease and velocity,
the nearer they come to God; and that the eyes of Beatrice—the
revelation of God to man—are only mirrors, shedding merely reflected beauty and light.

These hints suggest the doctrine that the goal of life is the very
bosom of God; not any finite form of existence, however excellent,
but a complete absorption and disappearance in the Godhead. So
the Neoplatonists had thought, from whom all this heavenly landscape is borrowed; and the reservations that Christian orthodoxy
requires have not always remained present to the minds of Christian mystics and poets. Dante broaches this very point in the
memorable interview he has with the spirit of Piccarda, in the
third canto of the *Paradiso*. She is in the lowest sphere of heaven,
that of the inconstant moon, because after she had been stolen

from her convent and forcibly married, she felt no prompting to renew her earlier vows. Dante asks her if she never longs for a higher station in paradise, one nearer to God, the natural goal of all aspiration. She answers that to share the will of God, who has established many different mansions in his house, is to be truly one with him. The wish to be nearer God would actually carry the soul farther away, since it would oppose the order he has established.[12]

Even in heaven, therefore, the Christian saint was to keep his essential fidelity, separation, and lowliness. He was to feel still helpless and lost in himself, like Tobias, and happy only in that the angel of the Lord was holding him by the hand. For Piccarda to say that she accepts the will of God means not that she shares it, but that she submits to it. She would fain go higher, for her moral nature demands it, as Dante—incorrigible Platonist—perfectly perceived; but she dare not mention it, for she knows that God, whose thoughts are not her thoughts, has forbidden it. The inconstant sphere of the moon does not afford her a perfect happiness; but, chastened as she is, she says it brings her happiness enough; all that a broken and a contrite heart has the courage to hope for.

Such are the conflicting inspirations beneath the lovely harmonies of the *Paradiso*. It was not the poet's soul that was in conflict here; it was only his traditions. The conflicts of his own spirit had been left behind in other regions; on that threshing-floor of earth which, from the height of heaven, he looked back upon with wonder,[13] surprised that men should take so pas-

[12]*Paradiso,* III. 73–90:

> "Se disiassimo esser più superne,
> Foran discordi li nostri disiri
> Dal voler di colui che qui ne cerne, . . .
> E la sua volontate è nostra pace;
> Ella è quel mare al qual tutto si move
> Ciò ch' ella crea, e che natura face."
> Chiaro mi fu allor com' ogni dove
> In cielo è Paradiso, e sì la grazia
> Del sommo ben d' un modo non vi piove.

[13]*Paradiso,* XXII. 133–39:

> Col viso ritornai per tutte e quante
> Le sette spere, evidi questo globo
> Tal, ch' io sorrisi del suo vil sembiante;
> E quel consiglio per migliore approbo
> Che l' ha per meno; e chi ad altro pensa
> Chiamar si puote veramente probo.

sionately this trouble of ants, which he judges best, says Dante, who thinks least of it.

In this saying the poet is perhaps conscious of a personal fault; for Dante was far from perfect, even as a poet. He was too much a man of his own time, and often wrote with a passion not clarified into judgement. So much does the purely personal and dramatic interest dominate us as we read of a Boniface or an Ugolino that we forget that these historical figures are supposed to have been transmuted into the eternal, and to have become bits in the mosaic of Platonic essences. Dante himself almost forgets it. The modern reader, accustomed to insignificant, wayward fictions, and expecting to be entertained by images without thoughts, may not notice this lack of perspective, or may rejoice in it. But, if he is judicious, he will not rejoice in it long. The Bonifaces and the Ugolinos are not the truly deep, the truly lovely figures of the *Divine Comedy*. They are, in a relative sense, the vulgarities in it. We feel too much, in these cases, the heat of the poet's prejudice or indignation. He is not just, as he usually is; he does not stop to think, as he almost always does. He forgets that he is in the eternal world, and dips for the moment into a brawl in some Italian market-place, or into the council-chamber of some factious *condottiere*. The passages— such as those about Boniface and Ugolino—which Dante writes in this mood are powerful and vehement, but they are not beautiful. They brand the object of their invective more than they reveal it; they shock more than they move the reader.

This lower kind of success—for it is still a success in rhetoric— falls to the poet because he has abandoned the Platonic half of his inspiration and has become for the moment wholly historical, wholly Hebraic or Roman. He would have been a far inferior mind if he had always moved on this level. With the Platonic spheres and the Aristotelian ethics taken out, his *Comedy* would not have been divine. Persons and incidents, to be truly memorable, have to be rendered significant; they have to be seen in their place in the moral world; they have to be judged, and judged rightly, in their dignity and value. A casual personal sentiment towards them, however passionate, cannot take the place of the sympathetic insight that comprehends and the wide experience that judges.

Again (what is fundamental with Dante) love, as he feels and renders it, is not normal or healthy love. It was doubtless real

48

enough, but too much restrained and expressed too much in fancy; so that when it is extended Platonically and identified so easily with the grace of God and with revealed wisdom, we feel the suspicion that if the love in question had been natural and manly it would have offered more resistance to so mystical a transformation. The poet who wishes to pass convincingly from love to philosophy (and that seems a natural progress for a poet) should accordingly be a hearty and complete lover—a lover like Goethe and his Faust— rather than like Plato and Dante. Faust, too, passes from Gretchen to Helen, and partly back again; and Goethe made even more passages. Had any of them led to something which not only was loved, but deserved to be loved, which not only could inspire a whole life, but which ought to inspire it—then we should have had a genuine progress.

In the next place, Dante talks too much about himself. There is a sense in which this egotism is a merit, or at least a ground of interest for us moderns; for egotism is the distinctive attitude of modern philosophy and of romantic sentiment. In being egotistical Dante was ahead of his time. His philosophy would have lost an element of depth, and his poetry an element of pathos, had he not placed himself in the centre of the stage, and described everything as his experience, or as a revelation made to himself and made for the sake of his personal salvation. But Dante's egotism goes rather further than was requisite, so that the transcendental insight might not fail in his philosophy. It extended so far that he cast the shadow of his person not only over the terraces of purgatory (as he is careful to tell us repeatedly), but over the whole of Italy and of Europe, which he saw and judged under the evident influence of private passions and resentments.

Moreover, the personality thrust forward so obtrusively is not in every respect worthy of contemplation. Dante is very proud and very bitter; at the same time, he is curiously timid; and one may tire sometimes of his perpetual tremblings and tears, of his fainting fits and his intricate doubts. A man who knows he is under the special protection of God, and of three celestial ladies, and who has such a sage and magician as Virgil for a guide, might have looked even upon hell with a little more confidence. How far is this shivering and swooning philosopher from the laughing courage of Faust, who sees his poodle swell into a monster, then into a cloud, and finally change into Mephistopheles, and says at once: *Das also war des Pudels Kern!* Doubtless Dante was mediaeval, and contrition, humility, and fear of the devil were great virtues in those days; but the conclusion we must come to is precisely that the virtues of those days were not the best virtues, and that a poet who represents that time cannot be a fair nor an ultimate spokesman for humanity.

Perhaps we have now reviewed the chief objects that peopled Dante's imagination, the chief objects into the midst of which his poetry transports us; and if a poet's genius avails to transport us into his enchanted world, the character of that world will determine the quality and dignity of his poetry. Dante transports us, with unmistakable power, first into the atmosphere of a visionary love; then into the history of his conversion, affected by this love, or by the divine grace identified with it. The supreme ideal to which his conversion brought him back is expressed for him by universal nature, and is embodied among men in the double institution of a revealed religion and a providential empire. To trace the fortunes of these institutions, we are transported next into the panorama of history, in its great crises and its great men; and particularly into the panorama of Italy in the poet's time, where we survey the crimes, the virtues, and the sorrows of those prominent in furthering or thwarting the ideal of Christendom. These numerous persons are set before us with the sympathy and brevity of a dramatist; yet it is no mere carnival, no *danse macabre:* for throughout, above the confused strife of parties and passions, we hear the steady voice, the implacable sentence, of the prophet that judges them.

Thus Dante, gifted with the tenderest sense of colour, and the firmest art of design, has put his whole world into his canvas. Seen there, that world becomes complete, clear, beautiful, and tragic. It is vivid and truthful in detail, sublime in its march and in its harmony. This is not poetry where the parts are better than the whole. Here, as in some great symphony, everything is cumulative: the movements conspire, the tension grows, the volume redoubles, the keen melody soars higher and higher; and it all ends, not with a bang, not with some casual incident, but in sustained reflection, in the sense that it has not ended, but remains by us in its totality, a revelation and a resource for ever. It has taught us to love and to renounce, to judge and to worship. What more could a poet do?

Dante poetized all life and nature as he found them. His imagination dominated and focused the whole world. He thereby touched the ultimate goal to which a poet can aspire; he set the standard for all possible performance, and became the type of a supreme poet. This is not to say that he is the "greatest" of poets. The relative merit of poets is a barren thing to wrangle about. The question can always be opened anew, when a critic appears with a fresh temperament or a new criterion. Even less need we say that no greater poet can ever arise; we may be confident of the opposite. But Dante gives a successful example of the *highest species* of poetry. His poetry covers the whole field from which poetry may be fetched, and to which poetry may be applied, from the inmost recesses of the heart to the uttermost bounds of nature and of destiny. If to give imaginative value to something is the minimum task of a poet, to give imaginative value to all things, and to the system which things compose, is evidently his greatest task.

Dante fulfilled this task, of course under special conditions and limitations, personal and social; but he fulfilled it, and he thereby fulfilled the conditions of supreme poetry. Even Homer, as we are beginning to perceive nowadays, suffered from a certain conventionality and one-sidedness. There was much in the life and religion of his time that his art ignored. It was a flattering, a euphemistic art; it had a sort of pervasive blandness, like that which we now associate with a fashionable sermon. It was poetry addressed to the ruling caste in the state, to the conquerors; and it spread an intentional glamour over their past brutalities and present self-deceptions. No such partiality in Dante; he paints what he hates as frankly as what he loves, and in all things he is complete and sincere. If any similar adequacy is attained again by any poet, it will not be, presumably, by a poet of the supernatural. Henceforth, for any wide and honest imagination, the supernatural must figure as an idea in the human mind,—a part of the natural. To conceive it otherwise would be to fall short of the insight of this age, not to express or to complete it. Dante, however, for this very reason, may be expected to remain the supreme poet of the supernatural, the unrivalled exponent, after Plato, of that phase of thought and feeling in which the supernatural seems to be the key to nature and to happiness. This is the hypothesis on which, as yet, moral unity has been best attained in this world. Here, then, we have the most complete idealization and comprehension of things achieved by mankind hitherto. Dante is the type of a consummate poet.

IV. GOETHE'S FAUST

In approaching the third of our philosophical poets, there is a scruple that may cross the mind. Lucretius was undoubtedly a philosophical poet; his whole poem is devoted to expounding and defending a system of philosophy. In Dante the case is almost as plain. The *Divine Comedy* is a moral and personal fable; yet not only are many passages explicitly philosophical, but the whole is inspired and controlled by the most definite of religious systems and of moral codes. Dante, too, is unmistakably a philosophical poet. But was Goethe a philosopher? And is *Faust* a philosophical poem?

If we say so, it must be by giving a certain latitude to our terms. Goethe was the wisest of mankind; too wise, perhaps, to be a philosopher in the technical sense, or to try to harness this wild world in a brainspun terminology. It is true that he was all his life a follower of Spinoza, and that he may be termed, without hesitation, a naturalist in philosophy and a pantheist. His adherence to the general attitude of Spinoza, however, did not exclude a great plasticity and freedom in his own views, even on the most fundamental points. Thus Goethe did not admit the mechanical interpretation of nature advocated by Spinoza. He also assigned, at least to privileged souls, like his own, a more personal sort of immortality than Spinoza allowed. Moreover, he harboured a generous sympathy with the dramatic explanations of nature and history current in the Germany of his day. Yet such transcendental idealism, making the world the expression of a spiritual endeavour, was a total reversal of that conviction, so profound in Spinoza, that all moral energies are resident in particular creatures, themselves sparks in an absolutely infinite and purposeless world. In a word, Goethe was not a systematic philosopher. His feeling for the march of things and for the significance of great personages and great ideas was indeed philosophical, although more romantic than scientific. His thoughts upon life were fresh and miscellaneous. They voiced the genius and learning of his age. They did not express a firm personal attitude, radical and unified, and transmissible to other times and persons. For philosophers, after all, have this advantage over men of letters, that their minds, being more organic, can more easily propagate themselves. They scatter less influence, but more seeds.

If from Goethe we turn to *Faust*—and it is as the author of *Faust* only that we shall consider him—the situation is not less ambiguous. In the play, as the young Goethe first wrote it, philosophy appeared in the first line,—*Hab nun ach die Philosophey;* but it appeared there, and throughout the piece, merely as a human experience, a passion or an illusion, a fund of images or an ambitious art. Later, it is true, under the spell of fashion and of Schiller, Goethe surrounded his original scenes with others, like the prologue in heaven, or the apotheosis of Faust, in which a philosophy of life was indicated; namely, that he who strives strays, yet in that straying finds his salvation. This idea left standing all that satirical and Mephistophelian wisdom with which the whole poem abounds, the later parts no less than the earlier. Frankly, it was a moral that adorned the tale, without having been the seed of it, and without even expressing fairly the spirit which it breathes. *Faust* remained an essentially romantic poem, written to give vent to a pregnant and vivid genius, to touch the heart, to bewilder the mind with a carnival of images, to amuse, to thrill, to humanize; and, if we must speak of philosophy, there were many express maxims in the poem, and many insights, half betrayed, that exceeded in philosophic value the belated and official moral which the author affixed to it, and which he himself warned us not to take too seriously.[1]

Faust is, then, no philosophical poem, after an open or deliberate fashion; and yet it offers a solution to the moral problem of existence as truly as do the poems of Lucretius and Dante. Heard philosophies are sweet, but those unheard may be sweeter. They may be more unmixed and more profound for being adopted unconsciously, for being lived rather than taught. This is not merely to say what might be said of every work of art and of every natural object, that it could be made the starting-point for a chain of inferences that should reveal the whole universe, like the flower in the crannied wall. It is to say, rather, that the vital straining towards

[1]Eckermann, Conversation of May 6, 1827: "Das ist zwar ein wirksamer, manches erklärender, guter Gedanke, aber es ist keine Idee die dem Ganzen . . . zugrunde liege."

an ideal, definite but latent, when it dominates a whole life, may express that ideal more fully than could the best-chosen words.

Now *Faust* is the foam on the top of two great waves of human aspiration, merging and heaping themselves up together,—the wave of romanticism rising from the depths of northern traditions and genius, and the wave of a new paganism coming from Greece over Italy. These are not philosophies to be read into *Faust* by the critic; they are passions seething in the drama. It is the drama of a philosophical adventure; a rebellion against convention; a flight to nature, to tenderness, to beauty; and then a return to convention again, with a feeling that nature, tenderness, and beauty, unless found there, will not be found at all. Goethe never depicts, as Dante does, the object his hero is pursuing; he is satisfied with depicting the pursuit. Like Lessing, in his famous apologue, he prefers the pursuit of the ideal to the ideal itself; perhaps, as in the case of Lessing, because the hope of realizing the ideal, and the interest in realizing it, were beginning to forsake him.

The case is somewhat as that of Dante would have been if, instead of recognizing and loving Beatrice at first sight and rising into a vision of the eternal world, ready-made and perfectly ordered, Dante had passed from love to love, from *donna gentile* to *donna gentile,* always longing for the eyes of Beatrice without ever meeting them. The *Divine Comedy* would then have been only human, yet it might have suggested and required the very consummation that the *Divine Comedy* depicts; and without expressing this consummation, our human comedy might have furnished materials and momentum for it, such that, if ever that consummation came to be expressed, it would be more deeply felt and more adequately understood. Dante gives us a philosophical goal, and we have to recall and retrace the journey; Goethe gives us a philosophic journey, and we have to divine the goal.

Goethe is a romantic poet; he is a novelist in verse. He is a philosopher of experience as it comes to the individual; the philosopher of life, as action, memory, or soliloquy may put life before each of us in turn. Now the zest of romanticism consists in taking what you know is an independent and ancient world as if it were material for your private emotions. The savage or the animal, who should not be aware of nature or history at all, could not be romantic about them, nor about himself. He would be blandly idiotic, and take everything quite unsuspectingly for what it was in him. The romanticist, then, should be a civilized man, so that his primitiveness and egotism may have something paradoxical and conscious about them; and so that his life may contain a rich experience, and his reflection may play with all varieties of sentiment and thought. At the same time, in his inmost genius, he should be a barbarian, a child, a transcendentalist, so that his life may seem to him absolutely fresh, self-determined, unforeseen, and unforeseeable. It is part of his inspiration to believe that he creates a new heaven and a new earth with each revolution in his moods or in his purposes. He ignores, or seeks to ignore, all the conditions of life, until perhaps by living he personally discovers them.[2] Like Faust, he flouts science, and is minded to make trial of magic, which renders a man's will master of the universe in which he seems to live. He disowns all authority, save that mysteriously exercised over him by his deep faith in himself. He is always honest and brave; but he is always different, and absolves himself from his past as soon as he has outgrown or forgotten it. He is inclined to be wayward and foolhardy, justifying himself on the ground that all experience is interesting, that the springs of it are inexhaustible and always pure, and that the future of his soul is infinite. In the romantic hero the civilized man and the barbarian must be combined; he should be the heir to all civilization, and, nevertheless, he should take life arrogantly and egotistically, as if it were an absolute personal experiment. . . . The souls of Rousseau, Byron, and Shelley are pre-incarnate in this Faust, the epitome of all romantic rebellions. They coexist there with the souls of Paracelsus and Giordano Bruno. The wild aspects of nature, he thinks, will melt and renew his heart, while magic reveals the mysteries of cosmic law and helps him to exploit them.

Full of these hopes, Faust opens his book of magic at the sign of the Macrocosm: it shows him the mechanism of the world, all

---

[2]*Faust*, Part II. Act v. 375–82:

> Ich bin nur durch die Welt gerannt;
> Ein jed' Gelüst ergriff ich bei den Haaren,
> Was nicht genügte, liess ich fahren,
> Was mir entwischte, liess ich ziehn.
> Ich habe nur begehrt und nur vollbracht
> Und abermals gewünscht und so mit Macht
> Mein Leben durchgestürmt; erst gross und mächtig,
> Nun aber geht es weise, geht bedächtig.

forces and events playing into one another and forming an infinite chain. The spectacle entrances him; he seems to have attained one of his dearest ambitions. But here he comes at once upon the other half, or, as Hegel would call it, the other moment, of the romantic life. Every romantic ideal, once realized, disenchants. No matter what we attain, our dissatisfaction must be perpetual. Thus the vision of the universe, which Faust now has before him, is, he remembers, only a vision; it is a theory or conception.[3] It is not a rendering of the inner life of the world as Shakespeare, for instance, feels and renders it. Experience, as it comes to him who lives and works, is not given by that theoretical vision; in science experience is turned into so many reviewed events, the passage of so much substance through so many forms. But Faust does not want an image or description of reality; he yearns to enact and to become the reality itself.

In this new search, he fixes his eye on the sign of the Earth-Spirit, which seems more propitious to his present wish. This sign is the key to all experience. All experience tempts Faust; he shrinks from nothing that any mortal may have endured; he is ready to undertake everything that any mortal may have done. In all men he would live; and with the last man he will be content to die.[4] So mighty is his yearning for experience that the Earth-Spirit is softened and appears at his bidding. In a red flame he sees its monstrous visage, and his enthusiasm is turned to horror. Outspread before him is the furious, indiscriminate cataract of life, the merciless flux, the infinite variety, the absolute inconstancy of it. This general life is not for any individual to rehearse; it bursts all bounds of personality. Each man may assimilate that part only which falls within his understanding, only that aspect which things wear from his particular angle, and to his particular interests. *Du*

[3]*Faust*, Part I., *Studierzimmer*, I.:
> Welch Schauspiel! aber, ach! ein Schauspiel nur!
> Wo fass' ich dich, unendliche Natur?
> Euch, Brüste, wo?

[4]*Faust*, Part I., *Studierzimmer:*
> Du, Geist der Erde, bist mir näher;
> Schon fühl' ich meine Kräfte höher,
> Schon glüh' ich wie von neuem Wein;
> Ich fühle Mut, mich in die Welt zu wagen,
> Der Erde Weh, der Erde Glück zu tragen, . . .
> Mit Stürmen mich herumzuschlagen
> Und in des Schiffbruch's Knirschen nicht zu zagen.

gleichst, the Earth-Spirit cries to him,—*du gleichst dem Geist den du begreifst, nicht mir.*

This saying—that the life possible and good for man is the life of reason, not the life of nature—is a hard one to the romantic, unintellectual, insatiable Faust. He thinks, like many another philosopher of feeling, that since his is a part of the sum of experience, the whole of experience should be akin to his. But in fact the opposite is far nearer the truth. Man is constituted by his limitations, by his station contrasted with all other stations, and his purposes chosen from amongst all other purposes. Any great scope he can attain must be due to his powers of representation. His understanding may render him universal; his life never can. Faust, as he hears this sentence from the departing Earth-Spirit, collapses under it. He feels impotent to gainsay what the tumult of the world is thundering at him, but he will not accept on authority so unwelcome and chastening a truth. All his long experience to come will scarcely suffice to convince him of it.

These are the chief philosophical ideas that appear in the two earlier versions of Goethe's *Faust,*—the *Urfaust* and the *Fragment.* What Mephistopheles says to the young student is only a clever expansion of what Faust had said in his first monologue about the vanity of science and of the learned professions. . . .

In the two earlier versions of *Faust,* Mephistopheles appears without introduction; we find him amusing himself by giving ambiguous advice to an innocent scholar, and accompanying Faust in his wanderings. His mocking tone and miraculous powers mark him at once as the devil of the legend; but several passages prove that he is a deputy of the Earth-Spirit evoked by Faust in the beginning. That he should be both devil and world-demon ought not to surprise the learned.[5] The devils of popular mediaeval religion were not cut out of whole cloth: they were simply the Neoplatonic

[5]*Faust,* Part I., *Wald und Höhle:*
>Erhabner Geist, du gabst mir, gabst mir alles,
>Warum ich bat. Du hast mir nicht umsonst
>Dein Angesicht ım Feuer zugewendet. . . .
>> O, dass dem Menschen nichts Vollkommnes wird,
>Empfind' ich nun. Du gabst zu dieser Wonne,
>Die mich den Göttern nah und näher bringt,
>Mir den Gefährten, &c.

Also, ibid., *Trüber Tag:* Grosser herrlicher Geist, der du mir zu erscheinen würdig-test, der du mein Herz kennest und meine Seele, warum an den Schandgesellen mich schmieden, der sich am Schaden weidet und am Verderben sich letzt?

demons of the air, together with the gods of Olympus and the more ancient chthonic deities, blackened by sectarian zeal, and degraded by a coarse and timid imagination. Many of these pagan sprites, indeed, had been originally impish and mischievous, since not all the aspects of nature are lovely or propitious, nor all the dreams of men. But as a whole they were without malice in their irresponsible, elemental life,—winged powers darting through space between the earth and the moon. They were not dwellers in a subterranean hell; they were not tormentors nor tormented. Often they swarmed and sang blithely, as they do in *Faust* and even in the *Wonder-working Magician;* and if at other times they croaked or hooted, it was like frogs and owls, less lovely creatures than humming-birds, but not less natural.

One of these less amiable spirits of the atmosphere, especially of its ambient fire, is the Mephistopheles of Goethe. Why he delighted in evil rather than in good he himself explains in a profound and ingenious fashion. Darkness or nothingness, he says, existed alone before the birth of light. Nothingness or darkness still remains the fundamental and, to his mind, the better part of that mixture of being and privation which we call existence. Nothing that exists can be preserved, nor does it deserve to be; therefore it would have been better if nothing had ever existed.[6] To deny the value of whatever is, and to wish to destroy it, according to him, is the only rational ambition; he is the spirit that denies continually, he is the everlasting No. This spirit—which we might compare with the Mars of Lucretius—has great power in the world; every change, in one of its aspects, expresses it, since in one of its aspects, every change is the destruction of something. This spirit is always willing evil, for it wills death, with all the folly, crime, and despair

[6]*Faust*, Part I., *Studierzimmer*, II.:
> Ich bin der Geist, der stets verneint!
> Und das mit Recht; denn alles, was entsteht,
> Ist wert, dass es zu Grunde geht;
> Drum besser wär's, dass nichts entstünde. . . .
> Ich bin ein Teil des Teils, der anfangs alles war,
> Ein Teil der Finsternis, die sich das Licht gebar. . . .
> Was sich dem Nichts entgegenstellt,
> Das Etwas, diese plumpe Welt,
> So viel als ich schon unternommen,
> Ich wusste nicht ihr beizukommen. . . .
> Wie viele hab' ich schon begraben!
> Und immer cirkuliert ein neues, frisches Blut.
> So geht es fort, man möchte rasend werden!

that minister to death. But in willing evil, it is always accomplishing good; for these evils make for nothingness, and nothingness is the true good. The famous couplet—

Ein Teil von jener Kraft
Die stets das Böse will, und stets das Gute schafft—

is far from expressing the Hegelian commonplace with which it is usually identified. It does not mean that destruction serves a good purpose after all because it clears the way for "something higher." Mephistopheles is not one of those philosophers who think change and evolution a good in themselves. He does not admit that his activity, while aiming at evil, contributes unintentionally to the good. It contributes to the good intentionally, because the evil it does is, in his opinion, less than the evil it cures. He is the cruel surgeon to the disease of life.

If he admitted the other interpretation, he would be *ipso facto* converted to the view of the Lord in the *Prologue*. His naughtiness would become, in his own eyes, a needful service in the cause of life,—a condition of life being really vital and worth living. He might then continue his sly operations and biting witticisms, without one drop more of kindness, and yet be sanctioned in everything by the Absolute, and adopt the smile and halo of the optimist. He would have perceived that he was the spice of life, the yeast and red pepper of the world, necessary to the perfect savour of the providential concoction. As it is, Mephistopheles is far more modest. He says that he wills evil, because what he wills is contrary to what his victims will; he is the great contradictor, the blaster of young hopes. Yet he does good, because these young hopes, if let alone, would lead to misery and absurdity. His contradiction nips the folly of living in the bud. To be sure, as he goes on to acknowledge, the destructive power never wins a decisive victory. While everything falls successively beneath his sickle, the seeds of life are being scattered perpetually behind his back. The Lucretian Venus has her innings, as well as the Lucretian Mars. The eternal see-saw, the ancient flux, continues without end and without abatement.

Thus Mephistopheles has a philosophy, and is justified and consistent in his own eyes; yet in the course of the drama he wears various masks and has various moods. All he says and does cannot be made altogether compatible with the essence of his mind, as Goethe finally conceived it. The dramatic figure of Mephistopheles had been fixed long before in its graphic characteristics. Mephistopheles, for instance, is extremely old; he feels older than the universe. There is nothing new for him; he has no illusions. His feeling for anyone he sees is choked, as happens to old people, by his feelings for the infinite number of persons he remembers. He is heartless, because he is impersonal and universal. He is altogether inhuman; he has not the shames nor the tastes of man. He often assumes the form of a dog,—it is his favourite mask in this earthly carnival. He is not averse to the witches' kitchen, with its senseless din and obscenity. He puts up good-naturedly with the grotesque etiquette of the spirit-world, observes all the rules about signing contracts in blood, knocking thrice, and respecting pentagrams. Why should he not? Dogs and demons of the air are forms of the Earth-Spirit as much as man; man has no special dignity that Mephistopheles should respect. Man's morality is one of the moralities, his conventions are not less absurd than the conventions of other monkeys. Mephistopheles has no prejudice against the snake; he understands and he despises his cousin, the snake, also. He understands and he despises himself; he has had time to know himself thoroughly.

His understanding, however, is not impartial, because he is the advocate of death; he cannot sympathize with the other half of the Earth-Spirit, which he does not represent,—the creative, propulsive, enamoured side, the side that worships the ideal, the love that makes the world go round. What enchants an ingenuous soul can only amuse Mephistopheles; what torments it gives him a sardonic satisfaction. Thus he comes to be in fact a sour and mocking devil. At other times, when he opposes the silliness and romanticism of Faust, he seems to be the spokesman of all experience and reason; as when he warns Faust that to be at all you must be something in particular. Yet even this he says by way of checking and denying Faust's passion for the infinite. The soberest truth, when unwelcome, may seem to the sentimental as diabolical as the most cynical lie; so that in spite of the very unequal justness of his various sentiments, Mephistopheles retains his dramatic unity. We recognize his tone and, under whatever mask, we think him a villain and find him delightful.

Such is the spirit, and such are the conditions, in which Faust undertakes his adventures. He thirsts for all experience, including all experience of evil; he fears no hell; and he hopes for no happiness. He trusts in magic; that is, he believes, or is willing to make believe, that apart from any settled conditions laid down by nature or God, personal will can evoke the experience it covets by its sheer force and assurance. His bond with Mephistopheles is an expression of this romantic faith. It is no bargain to buy pleasures on earth at the cost of torments hereafter; for neither Goethe, nor Faust, nor Mephistopheles believes that such pleasures are worth having, or such torments possible. . . .

The secret of what is serious in the moral of *Faust* is to be looked for in Spinoza,—the source of what is serious in the philosophy of Goethe. Spinoza has an admirable doctrine, or rather insight, which he calls seeing things under the form of eternity. This faculty is fundamental in the human mind; ordinary perception and memory are cases of it. Therefore, when we use it to deal with ultimate issues, we are not alienated from experience, but, on the contrary, endowed with experience and with its fruits. A thing is seen under the form of eternity when all its parts or stages are conceived in their true relations, and thereby conceived together. The complete biography of Caesar is Caesar seen under the form of eternity. Now the complete biography of Faust, Faust seen under the form of eternity, shows forth his salvation. God and Faust himself, in his last moment of insight, see that to have led such a life, in such a spirit, *was* to be saved; it was to be the sort of man a man should be. The blots on that life were helpful and necessary blots; the passions of it were necessary and creative passions. To have felt such perpetual dissatisfaction is truly satisfactory; such desire for universal experience is the right experience. You are saved in that you lived well; saved not after you have stopped living well, but during the whole process. Your destiny has been to be the servant of God. That God and your own conscience should pronounce this sentence is your true salvation. Your worthiness is thereby established under the form of eternity.

The play, in its philosophic development, ends here; but Goethe added several more details and scenes, with that abundance, that love, of symbolic pictures and poetic epigrams which characterizes the whole second part. As Faust expires, or rather before he does so, Mephistopheles posts one of his little demons at each aperture of the hero's body, lest the soul should slip out without being caught. At the same time a bevy of angels descends, scattering the red roses of love and singing its praises. These roses, if they touch Mephistopheles and his demons, turn to balls of fire; and although fire is their familiar element, they are scorched and scared away. The angels are thus enabled to catch the soul of Faust at their leisure, and bear it away triumphantly.

It goes without saying that this fight of little boys over a fluttering butterfly cannot be what really determines the issue of the wager and the salvation of Faust; but Goethe, in his conversations with Eckermann, justifies this intervention of a sort of mechanical accident, by the analogy of Christian doctrine. Grace is needed, besides virtue; and the intercession of Gretchen and the Virgin Mary, like that of the Virgin Mary, Lucia, and Beatrice, in Dante's case, and the stratagem of the balls of fire, all stand for this external condition of salvation.

This intervention of grace is, at bottom, only a new symbol for the essential justification, under the form of eternity, of what is imperfect and insufficient in time. The chequered and wilful life of Faust is not righteous in any of its parts; yet righteousness is imputed to it as a whole; divine love accepts it as sufficient; speculative reason declares that to be the best possible life which, to humdrum understanding, seems a series of faults and of failures. If the foretaste of his new Holland fills, from a distance, the dying Faust with satisfaction, how much more must the wonderful career of Faust himself deserve to be accepted and envied, and proclaimed to be its own excuse for being! The faults of Faust in time are not counted against him in eternity. His crimes and follies were blessings in disguise. Did they not render his life interesting and fit to make a poem of? Was it not by falling into them, and rising out of them, that Faust was Faust at all? This insight is the higher reason, the divine love, supervening to save him. What ought to be imperfect in time is, because of its very imperfection there, perfect when viewed under the form of eternity. To live, to live just as we do, that—if we could only realize it—is the purpose and the crown of living. We must seek improvement; we must be dissatisfied with ourselves; that is the appointed attitude, the histrionic pose, that is to keep the ball rolling. But while we feel this dissatisfaction we are perfectly satisfactory, and while we play our game and constantly lose it, we are winning the game for God.

Even this scene, however, did not satisfy the prolific fancy of the poet, and he added a final one,—the apotheosis or *Himmelfahrt* of Faust. In the Campo Santo at Pisa Goethe had seen a fresco representing various anchorites dwelling on the flanks of some sacred mountain, Sinai, Carmel, or Athos,—each in his little cave or hermitage; and above them, in the large space of sky, flights of angels were seen rising towards the Madonna. Through such a landscape the poet now shows us the soul of Faust carried slowly upwards.

This scene has been regarded as inspired by Catholic ideas, whereas the *Prologue in Heaven* was Biblical and Protestant; and Goethe himself says that his "poetic intention" could best be rendered by images borrowed from the tradition of the mediaeval church. But in truth there is nothing Catholic about the scene, except the names or titles of the personages. What they say is all sentimental landscape-painting or vague mysticism, such as might go with any somewhat nebulous piety; and much is actually borrowed from Swedenborg. What is Swedenborgian, however,—such as the notion of heavenly instruction, passage from sphere to sphere, and looking through other people's eyes,—is in turn a mere form of expression. The "poetic intention" of the author is, as we have seen, altogether Spinozitic. Undoubtedly he conceives that the soul of Faust is to pass, in another world, through some new series of experiences. But that destiny is not his salvation; it is the continuance of his trial. The famous chorus at the very end repeats, with an interesting variation, the same contrast we have seen before between the point of view of time and that of eternity. Everything transitory, says the mystic chorus,[7] is only an image; here (that is, under the form of eternity) the insufficient is turned into something actual and complete; and what seemed in experi-

[7]*Faust,* Part II. Act v., *Himmel:*

> Alles Vergängliche
> Ist nur ein Gleichnis;
> Das Unzulängliche,
> Hier wird's Ereignis;
> Das Unbeschreibliche,
> Hier ist es gethan;
> Das Ewig-Weibliche
> Zieht uns hinan.

ence an endless pursuit becomes to speculation a perfect fulfilment. The ideal of something infinitely attractive and essentially inexhaustible—the eternal feminine, as Goethe calls it—draws life on from stage to stage.

Gretchen and Helen had been symbols of this ideal; Goethe's green old age had felt, to the very last, the charm of woman, the sweetness and the sorrow of loving what he could not hope to possess, and what, in its ideal perfection, necessarily eludes possession. He had reconciled himself, not without tears, to this desire without hope, and, like Piccarda in the *Paradiso,* he had blessed the hand that gave the passion and denied the happiness.[8] Thus, in dreaming of one satisfaction and renouncing it, he had found a satisfaction of another kind. *Faust* ends on the same philosophical level on which it began,—the level of romanticism. The worth of life lies in pursuit, not in attainment; therefore, everything is worth pursuing, and nothing brings satisfaction—save this endless destiny itself.

Such is the official moral of *Faust,* and what we may call its general philosophy. But, as we saw just now, this moral is only an afterthought, and is far from exhausting the philosophic ideas which the poem contains. Here is a scheme for experience; but experience, in filling it out, opens up many vistas; and some of these reveal deeper and higher things than experience itself. The path of the pilgrim and the inns he stops at are neither the whole landscape he sees as he travels, nor the true shrine he is making for. And the incidental philosophy or philosophies of Goethe's *Faust* are, to my mind, often better than its ultimate philosophy. The first scene of the second part, for instance, is better, poetically and philosophically, than the last. It shows a deeper sense for the realities of nature and of the soul, and it is more sincere. Goethe there is interpreting nature with Spinoza; he is not dreaming with Swedenborg, nor talking equivocal paradoxes with Hegel.

In fact, the great merit of the romantic attitude in poetry, and of the transcendental method in philosophy, is that they put us

[8]Cf. *Trilogie der Leidenschaft,* 1823:

> Mich treibt umher ein unbezwinglich Sehnen;
> Da bleibt kein Rat als grenzenlose Thränen. . . .
> Und so das Herz erleichtert merkt behende
> Dass es noch lebt und schlägt und möchte schlagen, . . .
> Da fühlte sich—o, dass es ewig bliebe!—
> Das Doppelglück der Töne wie der Liebe.

back at the beginning of our experience. They disintegrate convention, which is often cumbrous and confused, and restore us to ourselves, to immediate perception and primordial will. That, as it would seem, is the true and inevitable starting-point. Had we not been born, had we not peeped into this world, each out of his personal eggshell, this world might indeed have existed without us, as a thousand undiscoverable worlds may now exist; but for us it would not have existed. This obvious truth would not need to be insisted on but for two reasons: one that conventional knowledge, such as our notions of science and morality afford, is often top-heavy; asserts and imposes on us much more than our experience warrants,—our experience, which is our only approach to reality. The other reason is the reverse or counterpart of this; for conventional knowledge often ignores and seems to suppress parts of experience no less actual and important for us as those parts on which the conventional knowledge itself is reared. The public world is too narrow for the soul, as well as too mythical and fabulous. Hence the double critical labour and reawakening which romantic reflection is good for,—to cut off the dead branches and feed the starving shoots. This philosophy, as Kant said, is a cathartic: it is purgative and liberating; it is intended to make us start afresh and start right.

It follows that one who has no sympathy with such a philosophy is a comparatively conventional person. He has a second-hand mind. Faust has a first-hand mind, a truly free, sincere, courageous soul. It follows also, however, that one who has no philosophy but this has no wisdom; he can say nothing that is worth carrying away; everything in him is attitude and nothing is achievement. Faust, and especially Mephistopheles, do have other philosophies on top of their transcendentalism; for this is only a method, to be used in reaching conclusions that shall be critically safeguarded and empirically grounded. Such outlooks, such vistas into nature, are scattered liberally through the pages of *Faust*. Words of wisdom diversify this career of folly, as exquisite scenes fill this tortuous and overloaded drama. The mind has become free and sincere, but it has remained bewildered.

The literary merits of Goethe's *Faust* correspond accurately with its philosophical excellences. In the prologue in the theatre Goethe himself has described them; much scenery, much wisdom, some folly, great wealth of incident and characterization; and behind, the soul of a poet singing with all sincerity and fervour the visions of his life. Here is profundity, inwardness, honesty, waywardness; here are the most touching accents of nature, and the most varied assortment of curious lore and grotesque fancies. This work, says Goethe (in a quatrain intended as an epilogue, but not ultimately inserted in the play),—this work is like human life: it has a beginning, it has an end; but it has no totality, it is not one whole.[9] How, indeed, should we draw the sum of an infinite experience that is without conditions to determine it, and without goals in which it terminates? Evidently all a poet of pure experience can do is to represent some snatches of it, more or less prolonged; and the more prolonged the experience represented is the more it will be a collection of snatches, and the less the last part of it will have to do with the beginning. Any character which we may attribute to the whole of what we have surveyed would fail to dominate it, if that whole had been larger, and if we had had memory or foresight enough to include other parts of experience differing altogether in kind from the episodes we happen to have lived through. To be miscellaneous, to be indefinite, to be unfinished, is essential to the romantic life. May we not say that it is essential to all life, in its immediacy; and that only in reference to what is not life—to objects, ideals, and unanimities that cannot be experienced but may only be conceived—can life become rational and truly progressive? Herein we may see the radical and inalienable excellence of romanticism; its sincerity, freedom, richness, and infinity. Herein, too, we may see its limitations, in that it cannot fix or trust any of its ideals, and blindly believes the universe to be as wayward as itself, so that nature and art are always slipping through its fingers. It is obstinately empirical, and will never learn anything from experience.

V. CONCLUSION

It may be possible, after studying these three philosophical poets, to establish some comparison between them. By a compari-

---

[9] *Aus dem Nachlass, Abkündigung:*
> Des Menschen Leben ist ein ähnliches Gedicht;
> Es hat wohl einen Anfang, hat ein Ende,
> Allein ein Ganzes ist es nicht.

son is not meant a discussion as to which of our poets is the best. Each is the best in his way, and none is the best in every way. To express a preference is not so much a criticism as a personal confession. If it were a question of the relative pleasure a man might get from each poet in turn, this pleasure would differ according to the man's temperament, his period of life, the language he knew best, and the doctrine that was most familiar to him. By a comparison is meant a review of the analysis we have already made of the type of imagination and philosophy embodied in each of the poets, to see what they have in common, how they differ, or what order they will fall into from different points of view. Thus we have just seen that Goethe, in his *Faust*, presents experience in its immediacy, variety, and apparent groundlessness; and that he presents it as an episode, before and after which other episodes, differing from it more and more as you recede, may be conceived to come. There is no possible totality in this, for there is no known ground. Turn to Lucretius, and the difference is striking. Lucretius is the poet of substance. The ground is what he sees everywhere; and by seeing the ground, he sees also the possible products of it. Experience appears in Lucretius, not as each man comes upon it in his own person, but as the scientific observer views it from without. Experience for him is a natural, inevitable, monotonous round of feelings, involved in the operations of nature. The ground and the limits of experience have become evident together.

In Dante, on the other hand, we have a view of experience also in its totality, also from above and, in a sense, from outside; but the external point of reference is moral, not physical, and what interests the poet is what experience is best, what processes lead to a supreme, self-justifying, indestructible sort of existence. Goethe is the poet of life; Lucretius the poet of nature; Dante the poet of salvation. Goethe gives us what is most fundamental,—the turbid flux of sense, the cry of the heart, the first tentative notions of art and science, which magic or shrewdness might hit upon. Lucretius carries us one step farther. Our wisdom ceases to be impressionistic and casual. It rests on understanding of things, so that what happiness remains to us does not deceive us, and we can possess it in dignity and peace. Knowledge of what is possible is the beginning of happiness. Dante, however, carries us much farther than that. He, too, has knowledge of what is possible and impossible. He has collected the precepts of old philosophers and saints, and the more recent examples patent in society around him, and by their help has distinguished the ambitions that may be wisely indulged in this life from those which it is madness to foster,—the first being called virtue and piety and the second folly and sin. What makes such knowledge precious is not only that it sketches in general the scope and issue of life, but that it paints in the detail as well,—the detail of what is possible no less than that (more familiar to tragic poets) of what is impossible.

Lucretius' notion, for instance, of what is positively worth while or attainable is very meagre: freedom from superstition, with so much natural science as may secure that freedom, friendship, and a few cheap and healthful animal pleasures. No love, no patriotism, no enterprise, no religion. So, too, in what is forbidden us, Lucretius sees only generalities,—the folly of passion, the blight of superstition. Dante, on the contrary, sees the various pitfalls of life with intense distinctness; and seeing them clearly, and how fatal each is, he sees also why men fall into them, the dream that leads men astray, and the sweetness of those goods that are impossible. Feeling, even in what we must ultimately call evil, the soul of good that attracts us to it, he feels in good all its loveliness and variety. Where, except in Dante, can we find so many stars that differ from other stars in glory; so many delightful habitations for excellences; so many distinct beauties of form, accent, thought, and intention; so many delicacies and heroisms? Dante is the master of those who know by experience what is worth knowing by experience; he is the master of *distinction*.

Here, then, are our three poets and their messages: Goethe, with human life in its immediacy, treated romantically; Lucretius, with a vision of nature and of the limits of human life; Dante, with spiritual mastery of that life, and a perfect knowledge of good and evil.

You may stop at what stage you will, according to your sense of what is real and important; for what one man calls higher another man calls unreal; and what one man feels to be strength smells rank to another. In the end, we should not be satisfied with any one of our poets if we had to drop the other two. It is true that taken formally, and in respect to their type of philosophy and imagination, Dante is on a higher plane than Lucretius, and Lucretius on

68

a higher plane than Goethe. But the plane on which a poet dwells is not everything; much depends on what he brings up with him to that level. Now there is a great deal, a very great deal, in Goethe that Lucretius does not know of. Not knowing of it, Lucretius cannot carry this fund of experience up to the intellectual and naturalistic level; he cannot transmute this abundant substance of Goethe's by his higher insight and clearer faith; he has not woven so much into his poem. So that while to see nature, as Lucretius sees it, is a greater feat than merely to live hard in a romantic fashion, and produces a purer and more exalted poem than Goethe's magical medley, yet this medley is full of images, passions, memories, and introspective wisdom that Lucretius could not have dreamed of. The intellect of Lucretius rises, but rises comparatively empty; his vision sees things as a whole, and in their right places, but sees very little of them; he is quite deaf to their intricacy, to their birdlike multiform little souls. These Goethe knows admirably; with these he makes a natural concert, all the more natural for being sometimes discordant, sometimes over-loaded and dull. It is necessary to revert from Lucretius to Goethe to get at the volume of life.

So, too, if we rise from Lucretius to Dante, there is much left behind which we cannot afford to lose. Dante may seem at first sight to have a view of nature not less complete and clear than that of Lucretius; a view even more efficacious than materialism for fixing the limits of human destiny and marking the path to happiness. But there is an illusion here. Dante's idea of nature is not genuine; it is not sincerely put together out of reasoned ob-servation. It is a view of nature intercepted by myths and worked out by dialectic. Consequently, he has no true idea either of the path of happiness or of its real conditions. His notion of nature is an inverted image of the moral world, cast like a gigantic shadow upon the sky. It is a mirage.

Now, while to know evil, and especially good, in all their forms and inward implications is a far greater thing than to know the natural conditions of good and evil, or their real distribution in space and time, yet the higher philosophy is not safe if the lower philosophy is wanting or is false. Of course it is not safe practically; but it is not safe even poetically. There is an attenuated texture and imagery in the *Divine Comedy*. The voice that sings it, from beginning to end, is a thin boy-treble, all wonder and naïveté. This art does not smack of life, but of somnambulism. The reason is that the intellect has been hypnotized by a legendary and verbal philosophy. It has been unmanned, curiously enough, by an excess of humanism; by the fond delusion that man and his moral nature are at the centre of the universe. Dante is always thinking of the divine order of history and of the spheres; he believes in controlling and chastening the individual soul; so that he seems to be a cosmic poet, and to have escaped the anthropocentric conceit of romanticism. But he has not escaped it. For, as we have seen, this golden cage in which his soul sings is artificial; it is constructed on purpose to satisfy and glorify human distinctions and human preferences. The bird is not in his native wilds; man is not in the bosom of nature. He is, in a moral sense, still at the centre of the universe; his ideal is the cause of everything. He is the appointed lord of the earth, the darling of heaven; and history is a brief and prearranged drama, with Judea and Rome for its chief theatre.

Some of these illusions are already abandoned; all are undermined. Sometimes, in moments when we are unnerved and uninspired, we may regret the ease with which Dante could reconcile himself to a world, so imagined as to suit human fancy, and flatter human will. We may envy Dante his ignorance of nature, which enabled him to suppose that he dominated it, as an infinite and exuberant nature cannot be dominated by any of its parts. In the end, however, knowledge is good for the imagination. Dante himself thought so; and his work proved that he was right, by infinitely excelling that of all ignorant contemporary poets. The illusion of knowledge is better than ignorance for a poet; but the reality of knowledge would be better than the illusion; it would stretch the mind over a vaster and more stimulating scene; it would concentrate the will upon a more attainable, distinct, and congenial happiness. The growth of what is known increases the scope of what may be imagined and hoped for. Throw open to the young poet the infinity of nature; let him feel the precariousness of life, the variety of purposes, civilizations, and religions even upon this little planet; let him trace the triumphs and follies of art and philosophy, and their perpetual resurrections—like that of the downcast Faust. If, under the stimulus of such a scene, he does not some day compose a natural comedy as much surpassing Dante's divine comedy in sublimity and richness as it will surpass it in truth, the fault will not lie with the subject, which is inviting and magnificent, but with the halting genius that cannot render that subject worthily.

Undoubtedly, the universe so displayed would not be without its dark shadows and its perpetual tragedies. That is in the nature of things. Dante's cosmos, for all its mythical idealism, was not so false as not to have a hell in it. Those rolling spheres, with all their lights and music, circled for ever about hell. Perhaps in the real life of nature evil may not prove to be so central as that. It would seem to be rather a sort of inevitable but incidental friction, capable of being diminished indefinitely, as the world is better known and the will is better educated. In Dante's spheres there could be no discord whatever; but at the core of them was eternal woe. In the star-dust of our physics discords are everywhere, and harmony is only tentative and approximate, as it is in the best earthly life; but at the core there is nothing sinister, only freedom, innocence, inexhaustible possibilities of all sorts of happiness. These possibilities may tempt future poets to describe them; but meantime, if we wish to have a vision of nature not fundamentally false, we must revert from Dante to Lucretius.

Obviously, what would be desirable, what would constitute a truly philosophical or comprehensive poet, would be the union of the insights and gifts which our three poets have possessed. This union is not impossible. The insights may be superposed one on the other. Experience in all its extent, what Goethe represents, should be at the foundation. But as the extent of experience is potentially infinite, as there are all sorts of worlds possible and all sorts of senses and habits of thought, the widest survey would still leave the poet, where Goethe leaves us, with a sense of an infinity beyond. He would be at liberty to summon from the limbo of potentiality any form that interested him; poetry and art would recover their early freedom; there would be no beauties forbidden and none prescribed. For it is a very liberating and sublime thing to summon up, like Faust, the image of *all* experience. Unless that has been done, we leave the enemy in our rear; whatever interpretations we offer for experience will become impertinent and worthless if the experience we work upon is no longer at hand. Nor will any construction, however broadly based, have an *absolute* authority; the indomitable freedom of life to be more, to be new, to be what it has not entered into the heart of man as yet to conceive, must always remain standing. With that freedom goes the modesty of reason, both in physics and in morals, that can lay claim only to partial knowledge, and to the ordering of a particular soul, or city, or civilization.

Poetry and philosophy, however, are civilized arts; they are proper to some particular genius, which has succeeded in flowering at a particular time and place. A poet who merely swam out into the sea of sensibility, and tried to picture all possible things, real or unreal, human or inhuman, would bring materials only to the workshop of art; he would not be an artist. To the genius of Goethe he must add that of Lucretius and Dante.

There are two directions in which it seems fitting that rational art should proceed, on the basis which a limited experience can give it. Art may come to buttress a particular form of life, or it may come to express it. All that we call industry, science, business, morality, buttresses our life; it informs us about our conditions and adjusts us to them; it equips us for life; it lays out the ground for the game we are to play. This preliminary labour, however, need not be servile. To do it is also to exercise our faculties; and in that exercise our faculties may grow free,—as the imagination of Lucretius, in tracing the course of the atoms, dances and soars most congenially. One extension of art, then, would be in the direction of doing artistically, joyfully, sympathetically, whatever we have to do. Literature in particular (which is involved in history, politics, science, affairs) might be throughout a work of art. It would become so not by being ornate, but by being appropriate; and the sense of a great precision and justness would come over us as we read or wrote. It would delight us; it would make us see how beautiful, how satisfying, is the art of being observant, economical, and sincere. The philosophical or comprehensive poet, like Homer, like Shakespeare, would be a poet of business. He would have a taste for the world in which he lived, and a clean view of it.

There remains a second form of rational art, that of expressing the ideal towards which we would move under these improved conditions. For as we react we manifest an inward principle, expressed in that reaction. We have a nature that selects its own direction, and the direction in which practical arts shall transform the world. The outer life is for the sake of the inner; discipline is for the sake of freedom, and conquest for the sake of self-possession. This inner life is wonderfully redundant; there is, namely, very much more in it than a consciousness of those acts by which the body adjusts itself to its surroundings. *Am farbigen Abglanz haben wir das Leben;* each sense has its arbitrary quality, each language its arbitrary euphony and prosody; every game has its creative laws, every soul its own tender reverberations and secret dreams. Life has a margin of play which might grow broader, if the sustaining nucleus were more firmly established in the world. To the art of working well a civilized race would add the art of playing well. To play with nature and make it decorative, to play with the overtones of life and make them delightful, is a sort of art. It is the ultimate, the most artistic sort of art, but it will never be practised successfully so long as the other sort of art is in a backward state; for if we do not know our environment, we shall mistake our dreams for a part of it, and so spoil our science by making it fantastic, and our dreams by making them obligatory. The art and the religion of the past, as we see conspicuously in Dante, have fallen into this error. To correct it would be to establish a new religion and a new art, based on moral liberty and on moral courage.

Who shall be the poet of this double insight? He has never existed, but he is needed nevertheless. It is time some genius should appear to reconstitute the shattered picture of the world. He should live in the continual presence of all experience, and respect it; he should at the same time understand nature, the ground of that experience; and he should also have a delicate sense for the ideal echoes of his own passions, and for all the colours of his possible happiness. All that can inspire a poet is contained in this task, and nothing less than this task would exhaust a poet's inspiration. We may hail this needed genius from afar. Like the poets in Dante's limbo, when Virgil returns among them, we may salute him, saying: *Onorate l'altissimo poeta.* Honour the most high poet, honour the highest possible poet. But this supreme poet is in limbo still.

PART II

Critical Essays

THE HOMERIC
HYMNS

W<small>E OF</small> this generation look back upon a variety of religious
conceptions and forms of worship, and a certain unsatisfied hunger in our own souls attaches our attention to the spectacle. We
observe how literally fables and mysteries were once accepted
which can have for us now only a thin and symbolical meaning.
Judging other minds and other ages by our own, we are tempted
to ask if there ever was any fundamental difference between religion and poetry. Both seem to consist in what the imagination
adds to science, to history, and to morals. Men looked attentively
on the face of Nature: their close struggle with her compelled
them to do so: but before making statistics of her movements
they made dramatisations of her life. The imagination enveloped
the material world, as yet imperfectly studied, and produced the
cosmos of mythology.

Thus the religion of the Greeks was, we might say, nothing but
poetry: nothing but what imagination added to the rudiments
of science, to the first impressions of a mind that pored upon
natural phenomena and responded to them with a quick sense of
kinship and comprehension. The religion of the Hebrews might
be called poetry with as good reason. Their "sense for conduct"
and their vivid interest in their national destiny carried them past
any prosaic record of events or cautious theory of moral and social laws. They rose at once into a bold dramatic conception of
their race's covenant with Heaven: just such a conception as the
playwright would seek out in order to portray with awful ac-
celeration the ways of passion and fate. Finally, we have apparently a third kind of poetry in what has been the natural religion

of the detached philosophers of all ages. In them the imagination touches the precepts of morals and the ideals of reason, attributing to them a larger scope and more perfect fulfilment than experience can show them to have. Philosophers even tend to clothe the harmonies of their personal thought with universal validity and to assign to their ideals a latent omnipotence and an ultimate victory over the forces of unreason. This which is obviously a kind of poetry is at the same time the spontaneous religion of conscience and thought.

Yet religion in all these cases differs from a mere play of the imagination in one important respect; it reacts directly upon life; it is a factor in conduct. Our religion is the poetry in which we believe. Mere poetry is an ineffectual shadow of life; religion is, if you will, a phantom also, but a phantom guide. While it tends to its own expansion, like any growth in the imagination, it tends also to its application in practice. Such an aim is foreign to poetry. The inspirations of religion demand fidelity and courageous response on our part. Faith brings us not only peace, not only the contemplation of ideal harmonies, but labour and the sword. These two tendencies—to imaginative growth and to practical enbodiment—coexist in every living religion, but they are not always equally conspicuous. In the formatives ages of Christianity, for instance, while its legends were being gathered and its dogma fixed, the imaginative expansion absorbed men's interest; later, when the luxuriant branches of the Church began to shake off their foliage, and there came a time of year

> *When yellow leaves, or none, or few, do hang*
> *Upon those boughs which shake against the cold,*

the energy of religious thought, released from the enlargement of doctrine, spent itself upon a more rigid and watchful application of the residuum of faith.

In the Pagan religion the element of applicability might seem at first sight to be lacking, so that nothing would subsist but a poetic fable. An unbiassed study of antiquity, however, will soon dispel that idea. Besides the gods whom we may plausibly regard as impersonations of natural forces, there existed others; the spirits of ancestors, the gods of the hearth, and the ideal patrons of war and the arts. Even the gods of Nature inspired reverence and secured a cultus only as they influenced the well-being of man. The worship of them had a practical import. The conception of their nature and presence became a sanction and an inspiration in the conduct of life. When the figments of the fancy are wholly divorced from reality they can have no clearness or consistency; they can have no permanence when they are wholly devoid of utility. The vividness and persistence of the figures of many of the gods came from the fact that they were associated with institutions and practices which controlled the conception of them and kept it young. The fictions of a poet, whatever his genius, do not produce illusion because they do not attach themselves to realities in the world of action. They have character without power and names without local habitations. The gods in the beginning had both. Their image, their haunts, the reports of their apparitions and miracles, gave a nucleus of empirical reality to the accretions of legend. The poet who came to sing their praise, to enlarge upon their exploits, and to explain their cultus, gave less to the gods in honour than he received from them in inspiration. All his invention was guided by the genius of the deity, as represented by the traditions of his shrine. This poetry, then, even in its most playful mood, is not mere poetry, but religion. It is a poetry in which men believe; it is a poetry that beautifies and justifies to their minds the positive facts of their ancestral worship, their social unity, and their personal conscience.

These general reflections may help us to approach the hymns of Homer in a becoming spirit. For in them we find the extreme of fancy, the approach to a divorce between the imagination and the faith of the worshipper. Consequently there is danger that we may allow ourselves to read these lives of the gods as the composition of a profane poet. If we did so we should fail to understand not only their spirit as a whole but many of their parts, in which notes are struck now of devotion and affectionate pride, now of gratitude and entreaty. These may be addressed, it is true, to a being that has just been described as guilty of some signal vice or treachery, and the contradiction may well stagger a Puritan critic. But the lusts of life were once for all in the blood of the Pagan gods, who were the articulate voices of Nature and of passion. The half-meant exaggeration of a well-known trait in the divinity would not render the poets that indulged in it unwelcome to the god; he could feel the sure faith and affection of his worshippers even in their good-humoured laughter at his imaginary plights and naughtiness. The clown was not excluded from these rites. His wit also counted as a service.

The Homeric Hymns, if we may trust the impression they produce on a modern, are not hymns and are not Homer's. They are fragments of narrative in Ionic hexameter recited during the feasts and fairs at various Greek shrines. They are not melodies to be chanted with a common voice by the assemblage during a sacrifice; they are tales delivered by the minstrel to the listening audience of citizens and strangers. They usually have a local reference. Thus we find under the title of a hymn to Apollo a song of Delos and one of Delphi. Delos is a barren rock; its wealth was due to the temple that attracted to the place pilgrimages and embassies, not without rich offerings, from many Greek cities. Accordingly we hear how Leto or Latona, when about to become the mother of Apollo, wandered about the cities and mountains of Greece and Asia, seeking a birthplace for her son. None would receive her, but all the islands trembled at the awful honour of such a nativity, profitable as the honour might eventually prove,—

> Until at length
> The lovely goddess came to Delos' side
> And, making question, spake these wingèd words:
> "Delos, were it thy will to be the seat
> Of my young son Apollo, brightest god,
> And build him a rich fane, no other power
> Should ever touch thee or work ill upon thee.
> I tell thee not thou shalt be rich in kine
> Or in fair flocks, much fruit, or myriad flowers;
> But when Apollo of the far-felt dart
> Hath here his shrine, all men will gather here
> Bringing thee hecatombs. . . . And though thy soil
>   be poor,
> The gods shall make thee strong against thy foes."

The spirit of the island is naturally not averse to so favourable a proposition but, like some too humble maiden wooed by a great prince, has some misgivings lest this promise of unexpected good fortune should veil the approach of some worse calamity. "When the god is born into the light of day," she says, "will he not despise me, seeing how barren I am, and sink me in the sea

> *That ever will*
> *Oppress my heart with many a watery hill?*
> *And therefore let him choose some other land,*
> *Where he shall please, to build at his command*
> *Temple and grove set thick with many a tree.*
> *For wretched polypuses breed in me,*
> *Retiring chambers, and black sea-calves den*
> *In my poor soil, for penury of men.*[1]

Leto reassures the island, however, and swears to build a great temple there which her son will haunt perpetually, preferring it to all his other shrines. Delos consents, and Apollo is born amid the ministrations of all the goddesses except Hera, who sits indignant and revengeful in the solitudes of Olympus. The child is bathed in the stream and delicately swaddled; but after tasting the nectar and ambrosia which one of the nymphs is quick to offer him, he bursts his bands, calls for his bow and his lyre, and flies upward into the sky announcing that he will henceforth declare the will of Zeus to mortals. Thereupon—

> *All the immortals stood*
> *In deep amaze. . . .*
> *All Delos, looking on him, all with gold*
> *Was loaded straight, and joy'd to be extoll'd.*
> *. . . For so she flourished, as a hill that stood*
> *Crown'd with the flower of an abundant wood.*[2]

This legend, with all that accompanies it concerning the glories of Delos and its gods, and the pilgrimages and games that enlivened the island, was well-conceived to give form and justification to the cultus of the temple, and to delight the votaries whom custom or vague instincts of piety had gathered there. The sacred poet, in another part of this hymn, does the same service to the even greater sanctuary of Delphi. He tells us how Apollo wandered over many lands and waters, and he stops lovingly to recall the names of the various spots that claimed the honour of having at

[1]Chapman's version.
[2]Chapman's version.

some time been visited by the god. The minstrels, wanderers themselves, loved to celebrate in this way the shores they had seen or heard of, and to fill at the same time their listeners' minds with the spell of sonorous names, the sense of space and the thrill of mystery. In his journeys Apollo, the hymn tells us, finally came to the dell and fountain of Delphusa on the skirts of Parnassus. The nymph of the spot, fearing the encroachments of so much more powerful a deity, deceived him and persuaded him to plant his temple on another site, where Parnassus fronts the west, and the overhanging rocks form a cavern. There Apollo established his temple for the succour and enlightenment of mankind, while Trophonius and Agamedes, sons of Erginus, men dear to the immortal gods, built the approaches of stone.

Thus the divine origin of the temple is vindicated, the structure described, and the human architects honoured, whose descendants, very likely, were present to hear their ancestors' praise. But here a puzzling fact challenges the attention and stimulates the fancy of the poet: Apollo was a Dorian deity, yet his chief shrine was here upon Phocian ground. Perhaps some traditions remained to suggest an explanation of the anomaly; at any rate the poet is not at a loss for an account of the matter. The temple being established, Apollo bethought himself what race of priests he should make its ministers: at least, such is the naïve account in the poem, which expects us to forget that temples do not arise in the absence of predetermined servants and worshippers. While pondering this question, however, Apollo cast his eyes on the sea where it chanced that a swift ship, manned by many and excellent Cretans, was merrily sailing: whereupon the god, taking the form of a huge dolphin, leapt into the ship, to the infinite surprise and bewilderment of those worthy merchants, who, as innocent as the fishers of the Galilæan Lake of the religious destiny that awaited them, were thinking only of the pecuniary profits of their voyage. The presence of the god benumbed their movements, and they stood silent while the ship sailed before the wind. And the blast, veering at this place with the changed configuration of the coast, blew them irresistibly to the very foot of Parnassus, to the little haven of Crissa. There Apollo appeared to them once more, this time running down to the beach to meet them in the form of

A stout and lusty fellow,
His mighty shoulders covered with his mane;
Who sped these words upon the wings of sound:
"Strangers, who are ye? and whence sail ye hither
The watery ways? Come ye to traffic justly
Or recklessly like pirates of the deep
Rove ye, adventuring your souls, to bring
Evil on strangers? Why thus sit ye grieving,
Nor leap on land, nor strike the mast and lay it
In your black ship? For so should traders do
When, sated with the labour of the sea,
They quit their painted galley for the shore,
And presently the thought of needful food
Comes gladsomely upon them." So he spake,
Putting new courage in their breasts. To whom
The Cretan captain in his turn replied:
"Since thou art nothing like to things of earth
In form or stature, but most like the gods
That ever live, Hail, and thrice hail, O Stranger,
And may the gods pour blessings on thy head.
Now tell me truly, for I need to know,
What land is this, what people, from what race
Descended? As for us, over the deep
Broad sea, we sought another haven, Pylos,
Sailing from Crete, for thence we boast to spring;
But now our ship is cast upon this shore,
For some god steered our course against our will."
Then the far-darter spoke and answered them.
"Friends, in well-wooded Cnossus hitherto
Ye have had homes, but ye shall not again
Return to your good native town, to find
Each his fair house and well-belovèd wife,
But here shall ye possess my temple, rich
And greatly honoured by the tribes of men.
For I am son to Zeus. Apollo is
My sacred name. 'Twas I that led you hither
Over the mighty bosom of the deep,
Intending you no ill; for ye shall here

Possess a temple sacred to me, rich,
And greatly honoured of all mortal men.
The counsels of the deathless gods shall be
Revealed to you, and by their will your days
Shall pass in honour and in peace for ever.
Come then and, as I bid, make haste to do.
. . . Build by the sea an altar; kindle flame;
Sprinkle white barley grains thereon, and pray,
Standing about the altar. And as first
Ye saw me leap into your swift black bark
In likeness of a dolphin, so henceforth
Worship me by the name Delphinius,
And Delphian ever be my far-seen shrine."

Thus the establishment of the Dorian god in Phocis is explained, and the wealth and dignity of his temple are justified by prophecy and by divine intention. For Apollo is not satisfied with repeatedly describing the future temple, by an incidental epithet, as opulent; that hint would not have been enough for the simplicity of those merchant sailors, new as they were to the mysteries of priestcraft. It was necessary for Apollo to allay their fears of poverty by a more explicit assurance that it will be easy for them to live by the altar. And what is more, Hermes and all the thieves he inspires will respect the shrine; its treasures, although unprotected by walls, shall be safe for ever.

These were truly, as we see, the hymns of a levitical patriotism. With Homeric breadth and candour they dilated on the miracles, privileges, and immunities of the sacred places and their servitors, and they thus kept alive in successive generations an awe mingled with familiar interest toward divine persons and things which is characteristic of that more primitive age. Gods and men were then nearer together, and both yielded more frankly to the tendency, inherent in their nature, to resemble one another.

The same quality is found in another fragment, the most beautiful and the most familiar of all. This is the hymn to Demeter in which two stories are woven together, one telling of the rape of Persephone, and the other of the reception of Demeter, disguised in her sorrow, into the household of Celeus, where she becomes the nurse of his infant son Demophoon. Both stories belong to the religion of Eleusis, where this version of them seems intended to be sung. The place was sacred to Demeter and Persephone and its mysteries dealt particularly with the passage of souls to the nether world and with their habitation there. The pathetic beauty of the first fable—in which we can hardly abstain from seeing some symbolical meaning—expresses for us something of the mystic exaltation of the local rites; while the other tale of Celeus, his wife, his daughters, and his son, whom his nurse, the disguised goddess, almost succeeds in endowing with immortality, celebrates the ancient divine affinities of the chiefs of the Eleusinian state.

The first story is too familiar to need recounting; who has not heard of the gentle Persephone gathering flowers in the meadow and suddenly swallowed by the yawning earth and carried away to Hades, the god of the nether world, to share his sombre but sublime dominion over the shades?—a dignity of which she is not insensible, much as she grieves at the separation from her beloved mother; and how Demeter in turn is disconsolate and (in her wrath and despair at the indifference of the gods) conceals her divinity, refuses the fruits of the earth, and wanders about in the guise of an old woman, nursing her grief, until at last Zeus sends his messenger to Hades to effect a compromise; and Persephone, after eating the grain of pomegranate that obliges her to return yearly to her husband, is allowed to come back to the upper world to dwell for two-thirds of the year in her mother's company.

The underlying allegory is here very interesting. We observe how the genius of the Greek religion, while too anthropomorphic to retain any clear consciousness of the cosmic processes that were symbolised by its deities and their adventures, was anthropomorphic also in a moral way, and tended to turn the personages which it ceased to regard as symbols of natural forces into types of human experience. So the parable of the seed that must die if it is to rise again and live an immortal, if interrupted, life in successive generations, gives way in the tale of Demeter and Persephone, to a prototype of human affection. The devotee, no longer reminded by his religion of any cosmic laws, was not reduced to a mere superstition,—to a fable and a belief in the efficacy of external rites,— he was encouraged to regard the mystery as the divine counterpart of his own experience. His religion in forgetting to be natural had succeeded in becoming moral; the gods were now models of human endurance and success; their histories offered sublime consolations to mortal destiny. Fancy had turned the aspects of Nature into persons; but devotion, directed upon these imaginary persons, turned them into human ideals and into patron saints, thereby relating them again to life and saving them from insignificance.

A further illustration of the latter transformation may be found in the second story contained in our hymn. Demeter, weary of her wanderings and sick at heart, has come to sit down beside a well, near the house of Celeus. His four young daughters, dancing and laughing, come to fetch water in their golden jars,—

> *As hinds or heifers gambol in the fields*
> *When Spring is young.*

They speak kindly to the goddess, who asks them for employment. "And for me," she says,—

> *And for me, damsels, harbour pitiful*
> *And favouring thoughts, dear children, that I come*
> *To some good man's or woman's house, to ply*
> *My task in willing service of such sort*
> *As agèd women use. A tender child*
> *I could nurse well and safely in my arms,*
> *And tend the house, and spread the master's couch*
> *Recessed in the fair chamber, or could teach*
> *The maids their handicraft.*

The offer is gladly accepted, for Celeus himself has an infant son, Demophoon, the hope of his race. The aged woman enters the dwelling, making in her long-robed grief a wonderful contrast to the four sportive girls:—

> *Who lifting up their ample kirtle-folds*
> *Sped down the waggon-furrowed way, and shook*
> *Their curls about their shoulders—yellow gold*
> *Like crocuses in bloom.*

Once within the house, which she awes with her uncomprehended presence, the goddess sits absorbed in grief, until she is compelled to smile for a moment at the jests of the quick-witted maid Iambe, and consents to take in lieu of the wine that is offered her, a beverage of beaten barley, water, and herbs. These details are of course introduced to justify the ritual of Eleusis, in which the clown and the barley-water played a traditional part.

Thus Demeter becomes nurse to Demophoon, but she has ideas of her duties differing from the common, and worthy of her unusual qualifications. She neither suckles nor feeds the infant but anoints him with ambrosia and lays him at night to sleep on the embers of the hearth. This his watchful mother discovers with not unnatural alarm; when the goddess reveals herself and departs, foiled in her desire to make her nursling immortal.

The spirit that animates this fable is not that poetic frivolity which we are accustomed to associate with Paganism. Here we find an immortal in profoundest grief and mortals entertaining an angel unawares; we are told of supernatural food, and of a burning fire that might make this mortal put on immortality did not the generous but ignorant impulses of the natural man break in upon that providential purpose and prevent its consummation. Eleusis was the natural home for such a myth, and we may well believe that those initiated into the mysteries there were taught to dwell on its higher interpretation.

But there are other hymns in a lighter vein in which the play of fancy is not guided by any moral intuition. The hymn to Hermes is one perpetual ebullition of irresponsible humour.

Hermes is the child of Maia, a nymph of Cyllene whose cave Zeus has surreptitiously visited while the white-armed Juno—for, unsympathetic prude as this goddess may be, she must still be beautiful—slept soundly in Olympus. The child is hardly born when he catches a tortoise, kills it, scoops out the shell, and makes a lute of it, upon which he begins to play delicious music. Not satisfied with that feat, however, he escapes from his cradle, and drives from their pasture the kine that Apollo has left feeding there. Accused afterward of this mischief, he defends himself after the following fashion, while he lies in his crib, holding his new-made lyre lightly in his hand under the bedclothes. I quote Shelley's version:—

> "An ox-stealer should be both tall and strong
>   And I am but a little new-born thing
> Who yet, at least, can think of nothing wrong.
>   My business is to suck, and sleep, and fling

The cradle-clothes about me all day long,
  Or, half-asleep, hear my sweet mother sing
And to be washed in water clean and warm
And hushed and kissed and kept secure from harm."

  .   .   .   .   .

Sudden he changed his plan, and with strange skill
  Subdued the strong Latonian, by the might
Of winning music, to his mightier will.
  His left hand held the lyre, and in his right
The plectrum struck the chords: unconquerable
  Up from beneath his hand in circling flight
The gathering music rose—and sweet as Love
The penetrating notes did live and move

Within the heart of great Apollo. He
  Listened with all his soul, and laughed for pleasure.
Close to his side stood harping fearlessly
  The unabashèd boy, and to the measure
Of the sweet lyre there followed loud and free
  His joyous voice: for he unlocked the treasure
Of his deep song, illustrating the birth
Of the bright Gods, and the dark desert Earth;

And how to the Immortals every one
  A portion was assigned of all that is.
But chief Mnemosyne did Maia's son
  Clothe in the light of his loud melodies.
And, as each god was born or had begun,
  He in their order due and fit degrees
Sung of his birth and being—and did move
Apollo to unutterable love.

In fact, after the most enthusiastic encomiums on the young god's art, and on the power of music in general, Apollo offers the child his protection and friendship:—

Now, since thou hast, although so very small,
  Science of arts so glorious, thus I swear,—
And let this cornel javelin, keen and tall,

> *Witness between us what I promise here,—*
> *That I will lead thee to the Olympian hall,*
>   *Honoured and mighty, with thy mother dear,*
> *And many glorious gifts in joy will give thee*
> *And even at the end will ne'er deceive thee.*

Hermes is not insensible to this offer and its advantages; he accepts it with good grace and many compliments, nor does he wish to remain behind in the exchange of courtesies and benefits: he addresses Apollo thus:—

> *Thou canst seek out and compass all that wit*
>   *Can find or teach. Yet, since thou wilt, come, take*
> *The lyre—be mine the glory giving it—*
>   *Strike the sweet chords, and sing aloud, and wake*
> *The joyous pleasure out of many a fit*
>   *Of trancèd sound—and with fleet fingers make*
> *Thy liquid-voicèd comrade speak with thee,—*
> *It can talk measured music eloquently.*
>
> *Then bear it boldly to the revel loud,*
>   *Love-wakening dance, or feast of solemn state,*
> *A joy by night or day: for those endowed*
>   *With art and wisdom who interrogate*
> *It teaches, babbling in delightful mood*
>   *All things which make the spirit most elate,*
> *Soothing the mind with sweet familiar play,*
> *Chasing the heavy shadows of dismay.*
>
> *To those that are unskilled in its sweet tongue,*
>   *Though they should question most impetuously*
> *Its hidden soul, it gossips something wrong—*
>   *Some senseless and impertinent reply.*
> *But thou, who art as wise as thou art strong,*
>   *Canst compass all that thou desirest. I*
> *Present thee with this music-flowing shell,*
> *Knowing thou canst interrogate it well. . . .*

Apollo is not slow to learn the new art with which he is ever after to delight both gods and men; but he is not at first quite at ease in his mind, fearing that Hermes will not only recapture the lyre but steal his friend's bow and arrows into the bargain. Hermes, however, swears by all that is holy never to do so, and the friendship of the two artful gods is sealed for ever. The minstrel does not forget, at this point, to remind his hearers, among whom we may imagine not a few professional followers of Hermes to have been mixed, that the robber's honour is pledged by his divine patron to respect the treasures of Apollo's shrines. Let not the votary think, he adds, that Apollo's oracles are equally useful to good and to bad men; these mysteries are truly efficacious only for the pious and orthodox who follow the established traditions of the temple and honour its servants. Apollo says:—

> *He who comes consigned*
> *By voice and wings of perfect augury*
> *To my great shrine shall find avail in me:*
>
> *Him I will not deceive, but will assist.*
> *But he who comes relying on such birds*
> *As chatter vainly, who would strain and twist*
> *The purpose of the gods with idle words,*
> *And deems their knowledge light, he shall have missed*
> *His road—whilst I among my other hoards*
> *His gifts deposit. . . .*

The wildest fairy-story thus leads easily to a little drama not without its human charm and moral inspiration; while the legend is attached to the cultus, and the cultus is intertwined with the practice and sanctions of daily life. Even here, in its most playful mood, therefore, this mythological poetry retains the spirit and function of religion. Even here sacerdotal interests are not forgotten. Delphi shall be safe; the lyre is Apollo's by right although it be Hermes' by invention. A certain amiable harmony is after all drawn from the riot of foolishness. All is sweet and unmalicious and lovable enough, and the patronage of both the friendly gods, the enthusiast and the wag, may be invoked with confidence and benefit.

Not less remarkable, although for other reasons, is the hymn to Aphrodite. Here we find a more human fable and a more serious tone: while the poem, if we choose to consider it in its allegorical meaning, touches one of the deepest convictions of the Greek con-science. All the gods save three—Athena, Artemis, and Hestia,—are subject to the power of Aphrodite, Zeus at least as much as the rest. In revenge for this subjection, Zeus determines to make Aph-rodite feel the passion which she boasts to be able to inspire in others.

The fair shepherd Anchises feeds his flocks upon Mount Ida, and with him Aphrodite is made to fall in love. She presents herself to him in a human disguise, and meets his advances with a long ac-count of her birth and parentage, and begs him to take her back to her parents, and having asked for her hand and fulfilled all cus-tomary formalities, to lead her away as his lawful wife. The pas-sion which at the same time, however, she is careful to breathe into him cannot brook so long a delay: and she yields to his impatience. When about to leave him she awakes him from his sleep, turns upon him the full glance of her divinity, and reveals her name and his destiny. She will bear him a son, Æneas, who will be one of the greatest princes and heroes of Troy; but he himself will be stricken with feebleness and a premature old age, in punishment for the involuntary sacrilege which he has committed.

The description of the disguised goddess, with its Homeric pomp and elaborate propriety, is a noble and masterly one, under-lined, as it were, with a certain satirical or dramatic intention; we have the directness of a Nausicaa, with a more luxurious and pas-sionate beauty. The revelation of the goddess is wonderfully made, with that parallel movement of natural causes and divine workings which is so often to be admired in Homer. The divinity of the visitant appears only at the moment of her flight, when she be-comes a consecration and an unattainable memory. The sight of deity leaves the eyes dull, like those of the Platonic prisoners re-turning from the sunlight of truth into the den of appearance. Nay more, a communion with the divinity, closer than is consonant with human fraility, leaves the seer impotent and a burden upon the world; but this personal tragedy is not without its noble fruits to posterity. Anchises suffers, but his son Æneas, the issue of that divine though punishable union, lives to bear, not only the aged Anchises himself, but the gods of Ilium, out of the ruins of Troy.

Such analogies carry us, no doubt, far beyond the intention of the hymn or of the exoteric religion to which it ministers. The story-teller's delight in his story is the obvious motive of such compositions, even when they reflect indirectly the awe in which the divine impersonations of natural forces were held by the popular religion. All that we may fairly imagine to have been in the mind of the pious singer is the sense that something divine comes down among us in the crises of our existence, and that this visitation is fraught with immense although vague possibilities of both good and evil. The gods sometimes appear, and when they do they bring us a foretaste of that sublime victory of mind over matter which we may never gain in experience but which may constantly be gained in thought. When natural phenomena are conceived as the manifestation of divine life, human life itself, by sympathy with that ideal projection of itself, enlarges its customary bounds, until it seems capable of becoming the life of the universe. A god is a conceived victory of mind over Nature. A visible god is the consciousness of such a victory momentarily attained. The vision soon vanishes, the sense of omnipotence is soon dispelled by recurring conflicts with hostile forces; but the momentary illusion of that realised good has left us with the perennial knowledge of good as an ideal. Therein lies the essence and the function of religion.

That such a function was fulfilled by this Homeric legend, with all its love of myth and lust of visible beauty, is witnessed by another short hymn, which we may quote almost entire by way of conclusion. It is addressed to Castor and Polydeuces, patrons of sailors no less than of horsemen and boxers. It is impossible to read it without feeling that the poet, however entangled he may have been in superstition and fable, grasped that high essence of religion which makes religion rational. He felt the power of contemplation to master the contradictions of life and to overspread experience, sublime but impalpable, like a rainbow over retreating storms:—

> Ye wild-eyed Muses, sing the Twins of Jove
> . . . Mild Pollux, void of blame,
> And steed-subduing Castor, heirs of fame.
> These are the powers who earth-born mortals save
> And ships, whose flight is swift along the wave.
> When wintry tempests o'er the savage sea
> Are raging, and the sailors tremblingly

Call on the Twins of Jove with prayer and vow,
Gathered in fear upon the lofty prow,
And sacrifice with snow-white lambs—the wind
And the huge billow bursting close behind
Even then beneath the weltering waters bear
The staggering ship,—they suddenly appear,
On yellow wings rushing athwart the sky,
And lull the blasts in mute tranquillity
And strew the waves on the white ocean's bed,
Fair omen of the voyage; from toil and dread
The sailors rest, rejoicing in the sight,
And plough the quiet sea in safe delight.[3]

[3]Shelley's translation.

PLATONIC LOVE IN
SOME ITALIAN POETS

W HEN THE fruits of philosophic reflection, condensed into some phrase, pass into the common language of men, there does not and there cannot accompany them any just appreciation of their meaning or of the long experience and travail of soul from which they have arisen. Few doctrines have suffered more by popularisation than the intuitions of Plato. The public sees in Platonic sayings little more than phrases employed by unpractical minds to cloak the emptiness of their yearnings. Finding these fragments of an obsolete speech put to bad uses, we are apt to ignore and despise them, much as a modern peasant might despise the fragment of a frieze or a metope which he found built into his cottage wall. It is not only the works of plastic art that moulder and disintegrate to furnish materials for the barbarous masons of a later age: the great edifices of reason also crumble, their plan is lost, and their fragments, picked where they happen to lie, become the materials of a feebler thought. In common speech we find such bits of ancient wisdom embedded; they prove the intelligence of some ancestor of ours, but are no evidence of our own. When used in ignorance of their meaning, they become misplaced flourishes, lapses into mystery in the businesslike plainness of our thought.

Yet there is one man, the archæologist, to whom nothing is so interesting as just these stones which a practical builder would have rejected. He forgives the ignorance and barbarism that placed them where they are; he is absorbed in studying their sculptured surface and delighted if his fancy can pass from them to the idea of the majestic whole to which they once belonged. So in the presence of a much-abused philosophic phrase, we may be interested in re-

94

constructing the experience which once gave it meaning and form. Words are at least the tombs of ideas, and the most conventional formulas of poets or theologians are still good subjects for the archæologist of passion. He may find a treasure there; or at any rate he may hope to be rewarded for his labour by the ideal restoration of some one beautiful temple of Athena.

Something of this kind is what we may now attempt to do with regard to one or two Platonic ideas, ideas which under the often ironical title of Platonic love, are constantly referred to and seldom understood. These ideas may be defined as the transformation of the appreciation of beautiful things into the worship of an ideal beauty and the transformation of the love of particular persons into the love of God. These mystical phrases may acquire a new and more human meaning if we understand, at least in part, how they first came to be spoken. We shall then not think of them merely as the reported sayings of Plato or Plotinus, Porphyry or Proclus; we shall not learn them by rote, as the unhappy student learns the enigmas, which, in the histories of philosophy, represent all that survives of the doctrine of a Thales or a Pythagoras. We shall have some notion of the ideas that once prompted such speech.

And we shall be the better able to reconstruct those conceptions inasmuch as the reflection by which they are bred has recurred often in the world—has recurred, very likely, in our own experience. We are often Platonists without knowing it. In some form or other Platonic ideas occur in all poetry of passion when it is seasoned with reflection. They are particularly characteristic of some Italian poets, scattered from the thirteenth to the sixteenth centuries. These poets had souls naturally Platonic; even when they had heard something of Plato they borrowed nothing from him. They repeated his phrases, when they did so, merely to throw the authority of an ancient philosopher over the spontaneous suggestions of their own minds. Their Platonism was all their own: it was Christian, mediæval, and chivalrous, both in origin and expression. But it was all the more genuine for being a reincarnation rather than an imitation of the old wisdom.

Nothing, for example, could be a better object-lesson in Platonism than the well-known sentimental history of Dante. There is no essential importance in the question whether Dante could have read anything of Plato or come indirectly under his influence.

The Platonism of Dante is, in any case, quite his own. It is the expression of his inner experience moulded by the chivalry and theology of his time. He tells us the story himself very quaintly in the *Vita Nuova*.

At the age of nine he saw, at a wedding-feast in Florence, Beatrice, then a child of seven, who became, forthwith, the mistress of his thoughts. This precocious passion ruled his imagination for life, so that, when he brings to an end the account of the emotions she aroused in him by her life and death, he tells us that he determined to speak no more about her until he should be able to do so more worthily, and to say of her what had never been said of any woman. In the *Divine Comedy,* accordingly, where he fulfils this promise, she appears transfigured into a heavenly protectress and guide, whose gentle womanhood fades into an impersonation of theological wisdom. But this life-long devotion of Dante to Beatrice was something purely mental and poetical; he never ventured to woo; he never once descended or sought to descend from the sphere of silent and distant adoration; his tenderness remained always tearful and dreamy, like that of a supersensitive child.

Yet, while his love of Beatrice was thus constant and religious, it was by no means exclusive. Dante took a wife as Beatrice herself had taken a husband; the temptations of youth, as well as the affection of married life, seem to have existed beneath this ideal love, not unrebuked by it, indeed, but certainly not disturbing it. Should we be surprised at this species of infidelity? Should we regard it as proof of the artificiality and hollowness of that so transcendental passion, and smile, as people have done in the case of Plato himself, at the thin disguise of philosophy that covers the most vulgar frailties of human nature? Or, should we say, with others, that Beatrice is a merely allegorical figure, and the love she is said to inspire nothing but a symbol for attachment to wisdom and virtue? These are old questions, and insoluble by any positive method, since they cannot be answered by the facts but only by our interpretation of them. Our solution can have little historical value, but it will serve to test our understanding of the metaphysics of feeling.

To guide us in this delicate business we may appeal to a friend of Dante, his fellow-poet Guido Cavalcanti, who will furnish us with another example of this same sort of idealisation, and this same sort of inconstancy, expressed in a manner that will repay analysis. Guido Cavalcanti had a Beatrice of his own—something of the kind was then expected of every gentle knight and poet— and Guido's Beatrice was called Giovanna. Dante seems to acknowledge the parity of his friend's passion with his own by coupling the names of the two ladies, Monna Vanna and Monna Bice, in one or two of the sonnets he addresses to Guido. Now it came to pass that Guido, in the fervour of his devotion, at once chivalrous and religious, bethought him of making a pilgrimage to the tomb of Saint James the Apostle, at Compostela in Spain. Upon this journey—a journey beguiled, no doubt, by thoughts of the beautiful Giovanna he had left in Florence—he halted in the city of Toulouse. But at Toulouse, as chance would have it, there lived a lovely lady by the name of Mandetta, with whom it was impossible for the chivalrous pilgrim not to fall in love; for chivalry is nothing but a fine emblazoning of the original manly impulse to fight every man and love every woman. Now in an interesting sonnet Guido describes the conflict of these two affections, or perhaps we should rather say, their union.

> *There is a lady in Toulouse so fair,*
> *So young, so gentle, and so chastely gay,*
> *She doth a true and living likeness bear*
> *In her sweet eyes to Love, whom I obey.*

The word I have, to avoid confusion, here rendered by "Love" is the original "la Donna mia," "my Lady"; so that we have our poet falling in love with Mandetta on account of her striking resemblance to Giovanna. Is this inconstancy or only a more delicate and indirect homage? We shall see; for Guido goes on to represent his soul, according to his custom, as a being that dwells and moves about in the chambers of his heart; and speaking still of Mandetta, the lady of Toulouse, he continues:—

> *Within my heart my soul, when she appeared,*
> *Was filled with longing and was fain to flee*
> *Out of my heart to her, yet was afeared*
> *To tell the lady who my Love might be.*
> *She looked upon me with her quiet eyes,*
> *And under their sweet ray my bosom burned,*
> *Cheered by Love's image, that within them lies.*

So far we have still the familiar visible in the new and making its power; Mandetta is still nothing but a stimulus to reawaken the memory of Giovanna. But before the end there is trouble. The sting of the present attraction is felt in contrast to the eternal ideal. There is a necessity of sacrifice, and he cries, as the lady turns away her eyes:—

> *Alas! they shot an arrow as she turned,*
> *And with a death-wound from the piercing dart*
> *My soul came sighing back into my heart.*

Perhaps this merely means that the lady was disdainful; had she been otherwise the poet might never have written sonnets about her, and surely not sonnets in which her charms were reduced to a Platonic reminiscence of a fairer ideal. But it is this turning away of the face of love, this ephemeral quality of its embodiments, that usually stimulates the imagination to the construction of a super-sensible ideal in which all those evaporated impulses may meet again and rest in an adequate and permanent object. So that while Guido's "death-wound" was perhaps in reality nothing but the rebuff offered him by a prospective mistress, yet the sting of it, in a mind of Platonic habit, served at once to enforce the distinction between the ideal beauty, so full of sweetness and heavenly charm, which had tempted the soul out of his heart on its brief adventure, and the particular and real object against which the soul was dashed, and from which it returned bruised and troubled to its inward solitude.

So the meditative Guido represents his experience: a new planet swam into his ken radiant with every grace and virtue; yet all the magic of that lady lay in her resemblance to the mysterious Giovanna, the double of Beatrice, the ideal of the poet's imagination. The soul, at first, went out eagerly to the new love as to an image and embodiment of the old, but was afraid, and justly, to mention the ideal in the presence of the reality. There is always danger in doing that; it breaks the spell and reduces us again to the old and patient loyalty to the unseen. The present thing being so like the ideal we unhesitatingly pursue it: but we are quickly disappointed, and the soul returns sighing and mortally wounded, as the new object of passion fades away.

We may now understand somewhat better that strange combination of loyalty and disloyalty which we find in Dante. While the object of love is any particular thing, it excludes all others; but it includes all others as soon as it becomes a general ideal. All beauties attract by suggesting the ideal and then fail to satisfy by not fulfilling it. While Giovanna remained a woman, Guido, as his after life plainly showed, had no difficulty in forgetting her and in loving many others with a frank heart; but when Giovanna had become a name for the absolute ideal, that sovereign mistress could never be forgotten, and the thought of her subordinated every particular attachment and called the soul away from it. Compared with the ideal, every human perfection becomes a shadow and a deceit; every mortal passion leaves, as Keats has told us,

> *A heart high-sorrowful and cloyed,*
> *A burning forehead and a parching tongue.*

Such is the nature of idealisation. Like the Venus of Apelles, in which all known beauties were combined, the ideal is the union of all we prize in all creatures; and the mind that has once felt the irresistible compulsion to create this ideal and to believe in it has become incapable of unreserved love of anything else. The absolute is a jealous god; it is a consuming fire that blasts the affections upon which it feeds. For this reason the soul of Guido, in his sonnet, is mortally wounded by the shaft of that beauty which has awakened a vehement longing for perfection without being able to satisfy it. All things become to the worshipper of the ideal so many signs and symbols of what he seeks; like the votary who, kneeling now before one image and now before another, lets his incense float by all with a certain abstracted impartiality, because his aspiration mounts through them equally to the invisible God they alike represent.

Another aspect of the same process is well described by Shakespeare, in whom Italian influences count for much, when he says to the person he has chosen as the object of his idealisation:—

> *Thy bosom is endearèd with all hearts*
> *Which I, by lacking, have supposèd dead,*
> *And there reigns love and all love's loving parts*

99

And all those friends which I thought burièd.
How many a holy and obsequious tear
Hath dear religious love stolen from mine eye
As interest for the dead, which now appear
But things removed, which hidden in thee lie.
Thou art the grave where buried love doth live
Hung with the trophies of my lovers gone,
Who all their parts of me to thee did give:
That due of many now is thine alone.
Their images I loved I view in thee,
And thou, all they, hast all the all of me.

We need not, then, waste erudition in trying to prove whether Dante's Beatrice or Guido's Giovanna or any one else who has been the subject of the greater poetry of love, was a symbol or a reality. To poets and philosophers real things are themselves symbols. The child of seven whom Dante saw at the Florentine feast was, if you will, a reality. As such she is profoundly unimportant. To say that Dante loved her then and ever after is another way of saying that she was a symbol to him. That is the way with childish loves. Neither the conscious spell of the senses nor the affinities of taste and character can then be powerful, but the sense of loneliness and the vague need of loving may easily conspire with the innocence of the eyes to fix upon a single image and to make it the imaginary goal of all those instincts which as yet do not know themselves.

When with time these instincts become explicit and select their respective objects, if the inmost heart still remains unsatisfied, as it must in all profound or imaginative natures, the name and memory of that vague early love may well subsist as a symbol for the perfect good yet unattained. It is intelligible that as time goes on that image, grown thus consciously symbolic, should become interchangeable with the abstract method of pursuing perfection —that Beatrice, that is, should become the same as sacred theology. Having recognised that she was to his childish fancy what the ideals of religion were to his mature imagination, Dante intentionally fused the two, as every poet intentionally fuses the general and the particular, the universal and the personal. Beatrice thenceforth appeared, as Plato wished that our loves should, as a manifestation of absolute beauty and as an avenue of divine grace. Dante merely added his Christian humility and tenderness to the insight of the Pagan philosopher.

The tendency to impersonality, we see, is essential to the ideal. It could not fulfil its functions if it retained too many of the traits of any individual. A blind love, an unreasoning passion, is therefore inconsistent with the Platonic spirit, which is favourable rather to abstraction from persons and to admiration of qualities. These may, of course, be found in many individuals. Too much subjection to another personality makes the expression of our own impossible, and the ideal is nothing but a projection of the demands of our imagination. If the imagination is overpowered by too strong a fascination, by the absolute dominion of an alien influence, we form no ideal at all. We must master a passion before we can see its meaning.

For this reason, among others, we find so little Platonism in that poet in whom we might have expected to find most—I mean in Petrarch. Petrarch is musical, ingenious, learned, and passionate, but he is weak. His art is greater than his thought. In the quality of his mind there is nothing truly distinguished. The discipline of his long and hopeless love brings him little wisdom, little consolation. He is lachrymose and sentimental at the end as at the beginning, and his best dream of heaven, expressed, it is true, in entrancing verse, is only to hold his lady's hand and hear her voice. Sometimes, indeed, he repeats what he must have read and heard so often, and gives us his version of Plato in half a sonnet. Thus, for instance, speaking of his love for Laura, he says in one place:—

> *Hence comes the understanding of love's scope*
> *That seeking her to perfect good aspires,*
> *Accounting little what all flesh desires;*
> *And hence the spirit's happy pinions ope*
> *In flight impetuous to the heaven's choirs,*
> *Wherefore I walk already proud in hope.*

If we are looking, however, for more direct expressions of the idealism of feeling, of love, and the sense of beauty passing into religion, we shall do well to turn to another Italian, not so great a poet as Petrarch by any means, but a far greater man—to Michael Angelo. Michael Angelo justly regarded himself as essentially a sculptor, and said even of painting that it was not his art; his verses are therefore both laboured and rough. Yet they have been too much neglected, for they breathe the same pathos of strength, the same agony in hope, as his Titanic designs.

Like every Italian of culture in those days, Michael Angelo was in the habit of addressing little pieces to his friends, and of casting his thoughts or his prayers into the mould of a sonnet or a madrigal. Verse has a greater naturalness and a wider range among the Latin peoples than among the English; poetry and prose are less differentiated. In French, Italian, and Spanish, as in Latin itself, elegance and neatness of expression suffice for verse. The reader passes without any sense of incongruity or anti-climax from passion to reflection, from sentiment to satire, from flights of fancy to homely details: the whole has a certain human sincerity and intelligibility which weld it together. As the Latin languages are not composed of two diverse elements, as English is of Latin and German, so the Latin mind does not have two spheres of sentiment, one vulgar and the other sublime. All changes are variations on a single key, which is the key of intelligence. We must not be surprised, therefore, to find now a message to a friend, now an artistic maxim, now a bit of dialectic, and now a confession of sin, taking the form of verse and filling out the fourteen lines of a sonnet. On the contrary, we must look to these familiar compositions for the most genuine evidence of a man's daily thoughts.

We find in Michael Angelo's poems a few recurring ideas, or rather the varied expression of a single half æsthetic, half religious creed. The soul, he tells us in effect, is by nature made for God and for the enjoyment of divine beauty. All true beauty leads to the idea of perfection; the effort toward perfection is the burden of all art, which labours, therefore, with a superhuman and insoluble problem. All love, also, that does not lead to the love of God and merge into that love, is a long and hopeless torment; while the light of love is already the light of heaven, the fire of love is already the fire of hell. These are the thoughts that perpetually recur, varied now with a pathetic reference to the poet's weariness and old age, now with an almost despairing appeal for divine mercy, often with a powerful and rugged description of the pangs of love, and with a pious acceptance of its discipline. The whole is intense, exalted, and tragic, haunted by something of that profound terror, of that magnificent strength, which we admire in the figures of the

Sixtine Chapel, those noble agonies of beings greater than any we find in this world.

What, we may ask, is all this tragedy about? What great sorrow, what great love, had Michael Angelo or his giants that they writhe so supernaturally? As those decorative youths are sprinkled over the Sixtine vault, filled, we know not why, with we know not what emotion, so these scraps of verse, these sibylline leaves of Michael Angelo's, give us no reason for their passion. They tell no story; there seems to have been no story to tell. There is something impersonal and elusive about the subject and occasion of these poems. Attempts have been made to attribute them to discreditable passions, as also to a sentimental love for Vittoria Colonna. But the friendship with Vittoria Colonna was an incident of Michael Angelo's mature years; some of the sonnets and madrigals are addressed to her, but we cannot attribute to her influence the passion and sorrow that seem to permeate them all.

Perhaps there is less mystery in this than the curious would have us see in it. Perhaps the love and beauty, however base their primal incarnation, are really, as they think themselves, aspirations toward the Most High. In the long studies and weary journeys of the artist, in his mighty inspiration, in his intense love of the structural beauty of the human body, in his vicissitudes of fortune and his artistic disappointments, in his exalted piety, we may see quite enough explanation for the burden of his soul. It is not necessary to find vulgar causes for the extraordinary feelings of an extraordinary man. It suffices that life wore this aspect to him; that the great demands of his spirit so expressed themselves in the presence of his world. Here is a madrigal in which the Platonic theory of beauty is clearly stated:—

> For faithful guide unto my labouring heart
> Beauty was given me at birth,
> To be my glass and lamp in either art.
> Who thinketh otherwise misknows her worth,
> For highest beauty only gives me light
> To carve and paint aright.
> Rash is the thought and vain
> That maketh beauty from the senses grow.
> She lifts to heaven hearts that truly know,

> *But eyes grown dim with pain*
> *From mortal to immortal cannot go*
> *Nor without grace of God look up again.*

And here is a sonnet, called by Mr. Symonds "the heavenly birth of love and beauty." I borrow in part from his translation:—

> *My love's life comes not from this heart of mine.*
> *The love wherewith I love thee hath no heart,*
> *Turned thither whither no fell thoughts incline*
> *And erring human passion leaves no smart.*
> *Love, from God's bosom when our souls did part,*
> *Made me pure eye to see, thee light to shine,*
> *And I must needs, half mortal though thou art,*
> *In spite of sorrow know thee all divine.*
> *As heat in fire, so must eternity*
> *In beauty dwell; through thee my soul's endeavour*
> *Mounts to the pattern and the source of thee;*
> *And having found all heaven in thine eyes,*
> *Beneath thy brows my burning spirit flies*
> *There where I loved thee first to dwell for ever.*

Something of this kind may also be found in the verses of Lorenzo de' Medici, who, like Michael Angelo, was a poet only incidentally, and even thought it necessary to apologise in a preface for having written about love. Many of his compositions are, indeed, trivial enough, but his pipings will not seem vain to the severest philosopher when he finds them leading to strains like the following, where the thought rises to the purest sphere of tragedy and of religion:—

> *As a lamp, burning through the waning night,*
> *When the oil begins to fail that fed its fire*
> *Flares up, and in its dying waxes bright*
> *And mounts and spreads, the better to expire;*
> *So in this pilgrimage and earthly flight*
> *The ancient hope is spent that fed desire,*
> *And if there burn within a greater light*
> *'Tis that the vigil's end approacheth nigher.*
> *Hence thy last insult, Fortune, cannot move,*
> *Nor death's inverted torches give alarm;*

I see the end of wrath and bitter moan.
My fair Medusa into sculptured stone
Turns me no more, my Siren cannot charm.
Heaven draws me up to its supernal love.

From such spontaneous meditation Lorenzo could even pass to verses officially religious; but in them too, beneath the threadbare metaphors of the pious muse and her mystical paradoxes, we may still feel the austerity and firmness of reason. The following stanzas, for instance, taken from his *Laudi Spirituali,* assume a sublime meaning if we remember that the essence to which they are addressed, before being a celestial Monarch into whose visible presence any accident might usher us, was a general idea of what is good and an intransitive rational energy, indistinguishable from the truth of things.

O let this wretched life within me die
    That I may live in thee, my life indeed;
In thee alone, where dwells eternity,
    While hungry multitudes death's hunger feed.
I list within, and hark! Death's stealthy tread!
I look to thee, and nothing then is dead.

Then eyes may see a light invisible
    And ears may hear a voice without a sound,—
A voice and light not harsh, but tempered well,
    Which the mind wakens when the sense is drowned,
Till, wrapped within herself, the soul have flown
To that last good which is her inmost own.

When, sweet and beauteous Master, on that day,
    Reviewing all my loves with aching heart,
I take from each its bitter self away,
    The remnant shall be thou, their better part.
This perfect sweetness be his single store
Who seeks the good; this faileth nevermore.

A thirst unquenchable is not beguiled
    By draught on draught of any running river
    Whose fiery waters feed our pangs for ever,

> *But by a living fountain undefiled.*
> *O sacred well, I seek thee and were fain*
> *To drink; so should I never thirst again.*

Having before us these characteristic expressions of Platonic feeling, as it arose again in a Christian age, divorced from the accidental setting which Greek manners had given it, we may be better able to understand its essence. It is nothing else than the application to passion of that pursuit of something permanent in a world of change, of something absolute in a world of relativity, which was the essence of the Platonic philosophy. If we may give rein to the imagination in a matter which without imagination could not be understood at all, we may fancy Plato trying to comprehend the power which beauty exerted over his senses by applying to the objects of love that profound metaphysical distinction which he had learned to make in his dialectical studies—the distinction between the appearance to sense and the reality envisaged by the intellect, between the phenomenon and the ideal. The whole natural world had come to seem to him like a world of dreams. In dreams images succeed one another without other meaning than that which they derive from our strange power of recognition—a power which enables us somehow, among the most incongruous transformations and surroundings, to find again the objects of our waking life, and to name those absurd and unmannerly visions by the name of father or mother or by any other familiar name. As these resemblances to real things make up all the truth of our dream, and these recognitions all its meaning, so Plato thought that all the truth and meaning of earthly things was the reference they contained to a heavenly original. This heavenly original we remember and recognise even among the distortions, disappearances, and multiplications of its earthly copies.

This thought is easily applicable to the affections; indeed, it is not impossible that it was the natural transcendence of any deep glance into beauty, and the lessons in disillusion and idealism given by that natural metaphysician we call love, that first gave Plato the key to his general system. There is, at any rate, no sphere in which the supersensible is approached with so warm a feeling of its reality, in which the phenomenon is so transparent and so indifferent a symbol of something perfect and divine beyond. In love and beauty, if anywhere, even the common man thinks he has visitations from a better world, approaches to a lost happiness; a happiness never tasted by us in this world, and yet so natural, so expected, that we look for it at every turn of a corner, in every new face; we look for it with so much confidence, with so much depth of expectation, that we never quite overcome our disappointment that it is not found.

And it is not found,—no, never,—in spite of what we may think when we are first in love. Plato knew this well from his experience. He had had successful loves, or what the world calls such, but he could not fancy that these successes were more than provocations, more than hints of what the true good is. To have mistaken them for real happiness would have been to continue to dream. It would have shown as little comprehension of the heart's experience as the idiot shows of the experience of the senses when he is unable to put together impressions of his eyes and hands and to say, "Here is a table; here is a stool." It is by a parallel use of the understanding that we put together the impressions of the heart and the imagination and are able to say, "Here is absolute beauty: here is God." The impressions themselves have no permanence, no intelligible essence. As Plato said, they are never anything fixed but are always either becoming or ceasing to be what we think them. There must be, he tells us, an eternal and clearly definable object of which the visible appearances to us are the manifold semblance; now by one trait now by another the phantom before us lights up that vague and haunting idea, and makes us utter its name with a momentary sense of certitude and attainment.

Just so the individual beauties that charm our attention and enchain the soul have only a transitive existence; they are momentary visions, irrecoverable moods. Their object is unstable; we never can say what it is, it changes so quickly before our eyes. What is it that a mother loves in her child? Perhaps the babe not yet born, or the babe that grew long ago by her suffering and unrecognised care; perhaps the man to be or the youth that has been. What does a man love in a woman? The girl that is yet, perhaps, to be his, or the wife that once chose to give him her whole existence. Where, among all these glimpses, is the true object of love? It flies before us, it tempts us on, only to escape and turn to mock us from a new quarter. And yet nothing can concern us more or be more real to us than this mysterious good, since the pursuit of it gives our lives whatever they have of true earnestness and meaning, and the approach to it whatever they have of joy.

So far is this ideal, Plato would say, from being an illusion, that it is the source of the world, the power that keeps us in existence. But for it, we should be dead. A profound indifference, an initial torpor, would have kept us from ever opening our eyes, and we should have no world of business or pleasure, politics or science, to think about at all. We, and the whole universe, exist only by the passionate attempt to return to our perfection, by the radical need of losing ourselves again in God. That ineffable good is our natural possession; all we honour in this life is but the partial recovery of our birthright; every delightful thing is like a rift in the clouds through which we catch a glimpse of our native heaven. If that heaven seems so far away and the idea of it so dim and unreal, it is because we are so far from perfect, so much immersed in what is alien and destructive to the soul.

Thus the history of our loves is the record of our divine conversations, of our intercourse with heaven. It matters very little whether this history seems to us tragic or not. In one sense, all mortal loves are tragic because never is the creature we think we possess the true and final object of our love; this love must ultimately pass beyond that particular apparition, which is itself continually passing away and shifting all its lines and colours. As Heraclitus could never bathe twice in the same river, because its water had flowed away, so Plato could never look twice at the same face, for it had become another. But on the other hand the most unsuccessful passion cannot be a vain thing. More, perhaps, than if it had found an apparent satisfaction, it will reveal to us an object of infinite worth, and the flight of the soul, detached by it from the illusions of common life, will be more straight and steady toward the ultimate good.

Such, if we are not mistaken, is the lesson of Plato's experience and also of that of the Italian poets whom we have quoted. Is this experience something normal? Is it the rational outcome of our own lives? That is a question which each man must answer for himself. Our immediate object will have been attained if we have made more intelligible a tendency which is certainly very common among men, and not among the men least worthy of honour. It is the tendency to make our experience of love rational, as scientific thinking is a tendency to make rational our experience of the outer world. The theories of natural science are creations of human reason; they change with the growth of reason, and express the intellectual impulses of each nation and age. Theories about the highest good do the same; only being less applicable in practice, less controllable by experiment, they seldom attain the same distinctness and articulation. But there is nothing authoritative in those constructions of the intellect, nothing coercive except in so far as our own experience and reflection force us to accept them. Natural science is persuasive because it embodies the momentum of common sense and of the practical arts; it carries on their spontaneous processes by more refined but essentially similar methods. Moral science is persuasive under the same conditions, but these conditions are not so generally found in the minds of men. Their conscience is often superstitious and perfunctory; their imagination is usually either disordered or dull. There is little momentum in their lives which the moralist can rely upon to carry them onward toward rational ideals. Deprived of this support his theories fall to the ground; they must seem, to every man whose nature cannot elicit them from his own experience, empty verbiage and irrelevant dreams.

Nothing in the world of fact obliges us to agree with Michael Angelo when he says that eternity can no more be separated from beauty than heat from fire. Beauty is a thing we experience, a value we feel; but eternity is something problematical. It might well happen that beauty should exist for a while in our contemplation and that eternity should have nothing to do with it or with us. It might well happen that our affections, being the natural expression of our instincts in the family and in the state, should bind us for a while to the beings with whom life has associated us—a father, a lover, a child—and that these affections should gradually fade with the decay of our vitality, declining in the evening of life, and passing away when we surrender our breath, without leading us to any single and supreme good, to any eternal love. If, therefore, the thoughts and consolations we have been rehearsing have sounded to us extravagant or unnatural, we cannot justify them by attempting to prove the actual existence of their objects, by producing the absolute beauty or by showing where and how we may come face to face with God. We may well feel that beauty and love are clear and good enough without any such additional embodiments. We may take the world as it is, without feigning another, and study actual experience without postulating any that is hypothetical. We can welcome beauty for the pleasure it affords and love for the happiness it brings, without asking that these things should receive supernatural extensions.

But we should have studied Plato and his kindred poets to little purpose if we thought that by admitting all this we were rejecting more than the mythical element that was sometimes mixed with their ideal philosophy. Its essence is not touched by any acknowledgement of what seems true or probable in the realm of actual existence. Nothing is more characteristic of the Platonic mind than a complete indifference to the continuance of experience and an exclusive interest in its comprehension. If we wish to understand this classic attitude of reason, all we need do is to let reason herself instruct us. We do not need more data, but more mind. If we take the sights and the loves that our mortal limitations have allowed of, and surrender ourselves unreservedly to their natural eloquence; if we say to the spirit that stirs within them, "Be thou me, impetuous one"; if we become, as Michael Angelo says he was, all eyes to see or all heart to feel, then the force of our spiritual vitality, the momentum of our imagination, will carry us beyond ourselves, beyond an interest in our personal existence or eventual emotions, into the presence of a divine beauty and an eternal truth —things impossible to realise in experience, although necessarily envisaged by thought.

As the senses that perceive, in the act of perceiving assert an absolute reality in their object, as the mind that looks before and after believes in the existence of a past and a future which cannot now be experienced, so the imagination and the heart behold, when they are left free to expand and express themselves, an absolute beauty and a perfect love. Intense contemplation disentangles the ideal from the idol of sense, and a purified will rests in it as in the true object of worship. These are the oracles of reason, the prophecies of those profounder spirits who in the world of Nature are obedient unto death because they belong intrinsically to a world where death is impossible, and who can rise continually, by abstraction from personal sensibility, into identity with the eternal objects of rational life.

Such a religion must elude popular apprehension until it is translated into myths and cosmological dogmas. It is easier for men to fill out the life of the spirit by supplementing the facts of experience by other facts for which there is no evidence than it is for them to master the given facts and turn them to spiritual uses. Many can fight for a doubtful fact when they cannot perform a difficult idealisation. They trust, as all men must, to what they can see; they believe in things as their faculties represent things to them. By the same right, however, the rationaliser of experience believes in his visions; he rests, like the meanest of us, in the present object of his thought. So long as we live at all we must trust in something, at least in the coherence and permanence of the visible world and in the value of the objects of our own desires. And if we live nobly, we are under the same necessity of believing in noble things. However unreal, therefore, these Platonic intuitions may seem to those of us whose interests lie in other quarters, we may rest assured that these very thoughts would dominate our minds and these eternal companionships would cheer our desolation, if we had wrestled as manfully with the same passions and passed through the transmuting fire of as great a love.

CERVANTES

CERVANTES is known to the world as the author of *Don Quixote*, and although his other works are numerous and creditable, and his pathetic life is carefully recorded, yet it is as the author of *Don Quixote* alone that he deserves to be generally known or considered. Had his wit not come by chance on the idea of the Ingenious Hidalgo, Cervantes would never have attained his universal renown, even if his other works and the interest of his career should have sufficed to give him a place in the literary history of his country. Here, then, where our task is to present in miniature only what has the greatest and most universal value,* we may treat our author as playwrights are advised to treat their heroes, saying of him only what is necessary to the understanding of the single action with which we are concerned. This single action is the writing of *Don Quixote;* and what we shall try to understand is what there was in the life and environment of Cervantes that enabled him to compose that great book, and that remained imbedded in its characters, its episodes, and its moral.

There was in vogue in the Spain of the sixteenth century a species of romance called books of chivalry. They were developments of the legends dealing with King Arthur and the Knights of the Table Round, and their numerous descendants and emulators. These stories had appealed in the first place to what we should still think of as the spirit of chivalry: they were full of tourneys and single combats, desperate adventures and romantic loves. The setting was in the same vague and wonderful region as the Coast of Bohemia, where to the known mountains, seas, and cities that have poetic names, was added a prodigious number of caverns,

*This essay originally appeared in *Library of the World's Best Literature,* Vol. VI, edited by Charles Dudley Warner, New York, R. S. Pearle and J. A. Hill, 1897.

castles, islands, and forests of the romancer's invention. With time and popularity this kind of story had naturally intensified its characteristics until it had reached the greatest extravagance and absurdity, and combined in a way the unreality of the fairy tale with the bombast of the melodrama.

Cervantes had apparently read these books with avidity, and was not without a great sympathy with the kind of imagination they embodied. His own last and most carefully written book, the *Travails of Persiles and Sigismunda,* is in many respects an imitation of them; it abounds in savage islands, furious tyrants, prodigious feats of arms, disguised maidens whose discretion is as marvelous as their beauty, and happy deliverances from intricate and hopeless situations. His first book also, the *Galatea,* was an embodiment of a kind of pastoral idealism: sentimental verses being interspersed with euphuistic prose, the whole describing the lovelorn shepherds and heartless shepherdesses of Arcadia.

But while these books, which were the author's favorites among his own works, expressed perhaps Cervantes's natural taste and ambition, the events of his life and the real bent of his talent, which in time he came himself to recognize, drove him to a very different sort of composition. His family was ancient but impoverished, and he was forced throughout his life to turn his hand to anything that could promise him a livelihood. His existence was a continuous series of experiments, vexations, and disappointments. He adopted at first the profession of arms, and followed his colors as a private soldier upon several foreign expeditions. He was long quartered in Italy; he fought at Lepanto against the Turks, where among other wounds he received one that maimed his left hand, to the greater glory, as he tells us, of his right; he was captured by Barbary pirates and remained for five years a slave in Algiers; he was ransomed, and returned to Spain only to find official favors and recognitions denied him; and finally, at the age of thirty-seven, he abandoned the army for literature.

His first thought as a writer does not seem to have been to make direct use of his rich experience and varied observation; he was rather possessed by an obstinate longing for that poetic gift which, as he confesses in one place, Heaven had denied him. He began with the idyllic romance, the *Galatea,* already mentioned, and at various times during the rest of his life wrote poems, plays, and stories of a romantic and sentimental type. In the course of these labors, however, he struck one vein of much richer promise. It was what the Spanish call the *picaresque;* that is, the description of the life and character of rogues, pickpockets, vagabonds, and all those wretches and sorry wits that might be found about the highways, in the country inns, or in the slums of cities. Of this kind is much of what is best in his collected stories, the *Novelas Ejemplares.* The talent and the experience which he betrays in these amusing narratives were to be invaluable to him later as the author of *Don Quixote,* where they enabled him to supply a foil to the fine world of his poor hero's imagination.

We have now mentioned what were perhaps the chief elements of the preparation of Cervantes for his great task. They were a great familiarity with the romances of chivalry, and a natural liking for them; a life of honorable but unrewarded endeavor both in war and in the higher literature; and much experience of Vagabondia, with the art of taking down and reproducing in amusing profusion the typical scenes and languages of low life. Out of these elements a single spark, which we may attribute to genius, to chance, or to inspiration, was enough to produce a new and happy conception: that of a parody on the romances of chivalry, in which the extravagances of the fables of knighthood should be contrasted with the sordid realities of life. This is done by the ingenious device of representing a country gentleman whose naturally generous mind, unhinged by much reading of the books of chivalry, should lead him to undertake the office of knight-errant, and induce him to ride about the country clad in ancient armor, to right wrongs, to succor defenseless maidens, to kill giants, and to win empires at least as vast as that of Alexander.

This is the subject of *Don Quixote.* But happy as the conception is, it could not have produced a book of enduring charm and well-seasoned wisdom, had it not been filled in with a great number of amusing and lifelike episodes, and verified by two admirable figures, Don Quixote and Sancho Panza, characters at once intimately individual and truly universal.

Don Quixote at first appears to the reader, and probably appeared to the author as well, as primarily a madman,—a thin and gaunt old village squire, whose brain has been turned by the nonsense he has read and taken for gospel truth; and who is punished for his ridiculous mania by an uninterrupted series of beatings, falls, indignities, and insults. But the hero and the author together, with the ingenuity proper to madness and the inevitableness proper to genius, soon begin to disclose the fund of intelligence and ideal passion which underlies this superficial insanity. We see that Don Quixote is only mad north-north-west, when the wind blows from the quarter of his chivalrous preoccupation. At other times he shows himself a man of great goodness and fineness of wit; virtuous, courageous, courteous, and generous, and in fact the perfect ideal of a gentleman. When he takes, for instance, a handful of acorns from the goat-herds' table and begins a grandiloquent discourse upon the Golden Age, we feel how cultivated the man is, how easily the little things of life suggest to him the great things, and with what delight he dwells on what is beautiful and happy. The truth and pathos of the character become all the more compelling when we consider how naturally the hero's madness and calamities flow from this same exquisite sense of what is good.

The contrast to this figure is furnished by that of Sancho Panza, who embodies all that is matter-of-fact, gross, and plebeian. Yet he is willing to become Don Quixote's esquire, and by his credulity and devotion shows what an ascendency a heroic and enthusiastic nature can gain over the most sluggish of men. Sancho has none of the instincts of his master. He never read the books of chivalry or desired to right the wrongs of the world. He is naturally satisfied with his crust and his onions, if they can be washed down with enough bad wine. His good drudge of a wife never transformed herself in his fancy into a peerless Dulcinea. Yet Sancho follows his master into every danger, shares his discomfiture and the many blows that rain down upon him, and hopes to the end for the governorship of that Insula with which Don Quixote is some day to reward his faithful esquire.

As the madness of Don Quixote is humanized by his natural intelligence and courage, so the grossness and credulity of Sancho are relieved by his homely wit. He abounds in proverbs. He never fails to see the reality of a situation, and to protest doggedly against his master's visionary flights. He holds fast as long as he can to the evidence of his senses, and to his little weaknesses of flesh and spirit. But finally he surrenders to the authority of Don Quixote, and of the historians of chivalry, although not without a certain reluctance and some surviving doubts.

The character of Sancho is admirable for the veracity with which its details are drawn. The traits of the boor, the glutton, and the coward come most naturally to the surface upon occasion, yet Sancho remains a patient, good-natured peasant, a devoted servant, and a humble Christian. Under the cover of such lifelike incongruities, and of a pervasive humor, the author has given us a satirical picture of human nature not inferior, perhaps, to that furnished by Don Quixote himself. For instance: Don Quixote, after mending his helmet, tries its strength with a blow that smashes it to pieces. He mends it a second time, but now, without trial, deputes it to be henceforth a strong and perfect helmet. Sancho, when he is sent to bear a letter to Dulcinea, neglects to deliver it, and invents an account of his interview with the imaginary lady for the satisfaction of his master. But before long, by dint of repeating the story, he comes himself to believe his own lies. Thus self-deception in the knight is the ridiculous effect of courage, and in the esquire the not less ridiculous effect of sloth.

The adventures these two heroes encounter are naturally only such as travelers along the Spanish roads would then have been likely to come upon. The point of the story depends on the familiarity and commonness of the situations in which Don Quixote finds himself, so that the absurdity of his pretensions may be overwhelmingly shown. Critics are agreed in blaming the exceptions which Cervantes allowed himself to make to the realism of his scenes, where he introduced romantic tales into the narrative of the first part. The tales are in themselves unworthy of their setting, and contrary to the spirit of the whole book. Cervantes doubtless yielded here partly to his story-telling habits, partly to a fear of monotony in the uninterrupted description of Don Quixote's adventures. He avoided this mistake in the second part, and devised the visit to the Duke's palace, and the intentional sport there made of the hero, to give variety to the story.

More variety and more unity may still, perhaps, seem desirable in the book. The episodes are strung together without much coherence, and without any attempt to develop either the plot or the characters. Sancho, to be sure, at last tastes the governorship of his

Insula, and Don Quixote on his death-bed recovers his wits. But this conclusion, appropriate and touching as it is, might have come almost anywhere in the course of the story. The whole book has, in fact, rather the quality of an improvisation. The episodes suggest themselves to the author's fancy as he proceeds; a fact which gives them the same unexpectedness and sometimes the same incompleteness which the events of a journey naturally have. It is in the genius of this kind of narrative to be a sort of imaginary diary, without a general dramatic structure. The interest depends on the characters and the incidents alone; on the fertility of the author's invention, on the ingenuity of the turns he gives to the story, and on the incidental scenes and figures he describes.

When we have once accepted this manner of writing fiction—which might be called that of the novelist before the days of the novel—we can only admire the execution of *Don Quixote* as masterly in its kind. We find here an abundance of fancy that is never at a loss for some probable and interesting incident; we find a graphic power that makes living and unforgettable many a minor character, even if slightly sketched; we find the charm of the country rendered by little touches without any formal descriptions; and we find a humorous and minute reproduction of the manners of the time. All this is rendered in a flowing and easy style, abounding in both characterization and parody of diverse types of speech and composition; and the whole is still but the background for the figures of Don Quixote and Sancho, and for their pleasant discourse, the quality and savor of which is maintained to the end. These excellences unite to make the book one of the most permanently delightful in the world, as well as one of the most diverting. Seldom has laughter been so well justified as that which the reading of *Don Quixote* continually provokes; seldom has it found its causes in such genuine fancy, such profound and real contrast, and such victorious good-humor.

We sometimes wish, perhaps, that our heroes were spared some of their bruises, and that we were not asked to delight so much in promiscuous beatings and floggings. But we must remember that these three hundred years have made the European race much more sensitive to physical suffering. Our ancestors took that doubtful pleasure in the idea of corporal writhings which we still take in the description of the tortures of the spirit. The ideal of both

117

evils is naturally distasteful to a refined mind; but we admit more willingly the kind which habit has accustomed us to regard as inevitable, and which personal experience very probably has made an old friend.

Don Quixote has accordingly enjoyed a universal popularity, and has had the singular privilege of accomplishing the object for which it was written, which was to recall fiction from the extravagances of the books of chivalry to the study of real life. This is the simple object which Cervantes had and avowed. He was a literary man with literary interests, and the idea which came to him was to ridicule the absurdities of the prevalent literary mode. The rich vein which he struck in the conception of Don Quixote's madness and topsy-turvy adventures encouraged him to go on. The subject and the characters deepened under his hands, until from a parody of a certain kind of romances the story threatened to become a satire on human idealism. At the same time Cervantes grew fond of his hero, and made him, as we must feel, in some sort a representative of his own chivalrous enthusiasms and constant disappointments.

We need not, however, see in this transformation any deep-laid malice or remote significance. As the tale opened out before the author's fancy and enlisted his closer and more loving attention, he naturally enriched it with all the wealth of his experience. Just as he diversified it with pictures of common life and manners, so he weighted it with the burden of human tragedy. He left upon it an impress of his own nobility and misfortunes side by side with a record of his time and country. But in this there was nothing intentional. He only spoke out of the fullness of his heart. The highest motives and characters had been revealed to him by his own impulses, and the lowest by his daily experience.

There is nothing in the book that suggests a premeditated satire upon faith and enthusiasm in general. The author's evident purpose is to amuse, not to upbraid or to discourage. There is no bitterness in his pathos or despair in his disenchantment; partly because he retains a healthy fondness for this naughty world, and partly because his heart is profoundly and entirely Christian. He would have rejected with indignation an interpretation of his work that would see in it an attack on religion or even on chivalry. His birth and nurture had made him religious and chivalrous from the beginning, and he remained so by conviction to the end. He was still full of plans and hopes when death overtook him, but he greeted it with perfect simplicity, without lamentations over the past or anxiety for the future.

If we could have asked Cervantes what the moral of *Don Quixote* was to his own mind, he would have told us perhaps that it was this: that the force of idealism is wasted when it does not recognize the reality of things. Neglect of the facts of daily life made the absurdity of the romances of chivalry and of the enterprise of Don Quixote. What is needed is not, of course, that idealism should be surrendered, either in literature or in life; but that in both it should be made efficacious by a better adjustment to the reality it would transform.

Something of this kind would have been, we may believe, Cervantes's own reading of his parable. But when parables are such direct and full transcripts of life as is the story of Don Quixote, they offer almost as much occasion for diversity of interpretation as does the personal experience of men in the world. That the moral of *Don Quixote* should be doubtful and that each man should be tempted to see in it the expression of his own convictions, is after all the greatest possible encomium of the book. For we may infer that the truth has been rendered in it, and that men may return to it always, as to Nature herself, to renew their theories or to forget them, and to refresh their fancy with the spectacle of a living world.

HAMLET

THE GREATER figures of fiction, as behooves things destined to last, have usually had an evolution and a history. Like the immortal gods, they have taken vague shape in the popular mind and in anonymous legends before receiving their most memorable form at the hand of some supreme poet. Perhaps no small part of Shakespeare's eminence is due to his having adopted plots and characters already current, already sanctioned by a certain proved vitality and power to charm. This conservatism is one of the many bonds by which art, when successful, clings to the life of the world and sucks in strength parasitically through its practical functions. Shakespeare's need of being a playwright before he was a poet, his concern to produce a popular play, won an audience for him in the beginning and still enables him to hold the boards. When creative genius neglects to ally itself in this way to some public interest it hardly gives birth to works of wide or perennial influence. Imagination needs a soil in history, tradition, or human institutions, else its random growths are not significant enough and, like trivial melodies, go immediately out of fashion. A great poem needs to be built up and remodelled on some given foundation with materials already at hand. Even in those fables which, like that of *Don Quixote,* may seem to be casual and original thoughts, we can usually detect a certain stage of experimentation with the idea, a certain novitiate and self-discovery on its part. The hero's character does not come out at first in its ultimate shape; but the shape it comes in, taking root and branching out in the mind into growths that had never been expected, becomes the germ of what is finally accepted and given out to the public. The true ideal of the most airy things is discoverable only by experimental methods, and there is nothing to which the approach is more blind and tentative than to the heart.

For this reason readers of *Hamlet* should not be surprised if this most psychological of tragedies should turn out to be a product of gradual accretions, or if its hero, most spontaneous and individual of characters, should be an afterthought and a discovery. Shakespeare followed a classic precept in this romantic drama: he allowed the plot to suggest the characters, and conceived their motives and psychological movement only as an underpinning and satiric deepening for their known actions. The play is an ordinary story with an extraordinary elaboration. Not only did Shakespeare, as his practice was, borrow an old plot, but he apparently worked over a first version of his own play and "enlarged it to almost as much again as it was." The personage of Hamlet, no less than the episodes of the piece, shows traces of this expansion. Some of Hamlet's actions and speeches seem anterior to his true character. They apparently remain over from the old melodrama and mark the points neglected by the poet and left untransmuted by his intuition.

These survivals of cruder methods, if survivals they be, give a touch of positive incoherence to Hamlet's character, otherwise sufficiently complex. His behaviour, for instance, before the praying King, and the reasons he gives there for sparing the villain, are apparently a remnant of bombast belonging to the old story, far more Christian and conventional in its motives than Shakespeare's is. So the grotesque bout with Laertes in Ophelia's grave is perhaps a bit of old rodomontade left unexpunged. The disconcerting mixture of comic and ignoble elements in several crucial passages may be due to the same circumstance, as, for example, when Hamlet says of the Ghost, "Ah, ha, boy . . . Art there, truepenny? . . . You hear this fellow in the cellarage. . . . Old mole, canst work in the earth so fast?" or when he crowns the heart-rending closet scene with a bad pun: "Come, sir, to draw toward an end with you," as he draws out Polonius's body. These passages may contain remnants of that conventional farce which, as some think, was inherited by Elizabethan drama from the Middle Ages, when piety and obscenity, quaint simplicity and rant, could be jumbled together without offence. Yet this barbaric medley, surviving by chance or by inertia, is the occasion for the creation of a spirit that shall justify it, and shall express therein its own profound discord. The historical accidents that make these patches in the play are embodied and personified in a mind that can cover them all by its own complexity and dislocation. Each of these blots thus becomes a beauty, each of these accidents a piece of profound characterisation. In Hamlet's personality incoherent sentiments, due, in a genetic sense, to the imperfect recasting of a grotesque old story, are made attributable ideally to his habit of acting out a mood irresponsibly and of giving a mock expression to every successive intuition. Thus his false rhetoric before the praying King becomes characteristic, and may be taken to betray an inveterate vacillation which seizes on verbal excuses and plays with unreal sentiments in order to put off the moment of action. So at Ophelia's grave he may be said to exhibit his ingrained histrionic habit, his incapacity to control the inner dialogue or dream in his own mind, which continually carries him into fits of speech and action, sometimes incongruous with one another but always ingenious and fetched from the depths of a distracted and tender heart. So, too, his sardonic humour and nonsensical verbiage at the most tragic junctures may justify themselves ideally and seem to be deeply inspired. These wild starts suggest a mind inwardly rent asunder, a delicate genius disordered, such as we now learn that Hamlet's was, a mind that with infinite sensibility possessed no mastery over itself nor over things. Thus the least digested elements in the fable come, by a happy turn, to constitute its profoundest suggestion.

The Middle Ages and the Renaissance into which they finally burst had at once a decrepit and a juvenile character. They looked back with rather a doting and indiscriminate respect on the confused past, while at the same time they bubbled over with all manner of native mischief and fancy. In Gothic drama, as in Gothic architecture, we find bits of savage or classic antiquity, incongruities, afterthoughts, and accretions, old materials, precious or rude, built again into a new edifice. Yet these accepted and sanctified accidents make the charm and bewitching poetry of the work, for they have crystallised into a new style and a new structure; a historical junk-shop has become the temple of a new spirit. Its miscellaneous treasures, so heaped together, have acquired their own expression and pathos, and a certain unifying mystery has settled over the whole. The beauty and ideal import of a human work can thus come to resemble that of a landscape or of a living body; it can be felt instinctively by a certain assimilation as if to a mystical influence, without distinct discrimination of the elements involved.

Evidently the same thing happened to Shakespeare with his histrionic Prince that happened to Cervantes with his mad Knight: he fell in love with his hero. He caught in that figure, at first only grotesque and melodramatic, a suggestion of something noble, spiritual, and pathetic, and he devoted all his imaginative powers to developing that suggestion. He enriched the lines with all that reflection could furnish that was most pungent and poetical; he added the philosophic play of mind, gave free rein to soliloquy, insisted everywhere on what might seem keen and significant. At the same time he found pleasure in elaborating the story. He constructed, for instance, a young Hamlet, to stand behind the tragic hero, a witty, tender, and accomplished prince, to be overtaken by that cursed spite which he should prove incapable of turning aside. Here we have a piece of deliberate art. By numerous and well-chosen phrases scattered throughout the play, Shakespeare takes pains to evoke the image of a consummate and admirable nature, so that the charm and pathos of the tragedy which ruins it may be enhanced. In the young Hamlet we are asked to imagine the

Unmatched form and feature of blown youth,

The courtier's, soldier's, scholar's, eye, tongue, sword;
The expectancy and rose of the fair state,
The glass of fashion and the mould of form,
The observed of all observers!

We learn of his proficiency in fencing, his fondness for the stage, and his competence as a critic of it; he is attached enough to the university to prefer it to the court. He can adopt for a moment the affectations of clever people, and be enough of a prig "to hold it baseness to write fair"; but he writes fair, nevertheless. His "noble and most sovereign reason" pierces most things in the world, and among them philosophy (or, as we should say, science), of which he understands enough to see its limits. He knows how to humour and play with a fop no less than how to expose and transfix a flatterer, and he can be as contemptuous of foolish wordiness in a counsellor, as he can be courteous to sincerity in a humble artist. For comradeship he has a natural sense and is willing to drink deep with an old acquaintance; but for true intimacy he chooses the poor scholar and devoted friend, unworldly because capable of understanding the world, and shows in this choice his princely freedom and elevation of mind. And lest the last crown and flower of generous youth should be wanting, Hamlet is, of course, in love. Yet he is not without a soberer and more settled affection than that expressed in his fancy for the fair Ophelia; his deepest sentiment is a great love and admiration for the King, his father. On this natural piety in the young Hamlet, his new tragic life is to be grafted. By striking rudely in this quarter fate strikes not merely at his filial affection, but at his intellectual peace and at his confidence in justice. The wound is mortal and saps his moral being.

The hero, so conceived, is presented to us by the instrumentality of that same plot which had originally suggested his character. The beloved father dies suddenly, and to his son's natural grief at this loss is added the scandal of his mother's hasty second marriage. A heavy mood, filled with vague sinister suspicions, falls upon Hamlet. Presently, the supernatural comes upon the scene. Hamlet sees his father's ghost. He receives audible and explicit tidings of his mother's adultery and the murder of his father.

We might say that to see—or if the spiritualistic reader prefers, to call up—a ghost is a first sign of Hamlet's moral dissolution. It would be easy to rationalise this part of the story, and explain the Ghost as a sort of symbol or allegory. Hamlet's character and situation were well conceived to base such a hallucination upon. His prophetic soul might easily have cheated him with such a counterfeit presentment of its own suspicions. But Shakespeare was evidently content to take the Ghost literally, and expected his audience naturally to do the same. Although not visible to the Queen on its final appearance, the Ghost is seen by Horatio and others on several occasions. The report it gives of its torments corresponds to the popular and orthodox conception of Purgatory, so that a Christian public might accept this ghost as a possible wanderer from the other world. Had Shakespeare cared much about ghosts, or wished to give, as in *Macbeth,* a realistic picture of the shabby supernatural, Hamlet's Ghost might well have been a much less theological and conventional being. It might well have resem-

bled somewhat more the shade of Achilles in the *Odyssey*, which
is a beautiful idealisation of the spirits actually evoked by necro-
mancy in all ages, which are echoes of former existences in this
world, witless, fretful, sad, and unseizable. But such shades were
little cultivated in Shakespeare's day. The Church had no need for
them, and wished to preserve its ideal conception of the other
world from all empirical and pathological influences. Shakespeare's
Ghost is accordingly wholly, though inconsistently, conventional.
It is a Christian soul in Purgatory, which ought, in theological
strictness, to be a holy and redeemed soul, a phase of penitential
and spiritual experience; yet this soul fears to scent the morning
air, trembles at the cock-crow, and instigates the revenging of
crime by crime. That is, it is no Christian soul, but a heathen and
pathological spectre. It speaks, as Hamlet justly feels, by the ambiguous authority of hell and heaven at once. This hybrid personage, however, like the other anomalies in the play, comes to
have its expressive value. It unites in a single image various threads
of superstition actually tangled in the public mind. Ostensibly an
emissary from the other world, such as would be admissible by
a slightly heterodox Christian fancy, the Ghost is at the same time
an echo of popular fable and demonology, and withal a moral and
dramatic symbol, a definite *point d'appui* for the hero's morbid
impulses. If Hamlet had not been likely to imagine a Ghost,
Shakespeare would hardly have created one. There is affinity and
emotional congruity in the various mysteries gathered together
in this scene—the night, the sea, the hidden crime, the hero's metaphysical melancholy, and the budding purpose in him to enact
madness. Into this artful setting the Ghost falls naturally enough,
and, under the scenic spell of its presence, we do not stop to ask
which elements in that apparition are food for Hamlet's fancy,
and which are rather its products and expression.

The first effect of the Ghost's revelation is characteristic of
Hamlet's nature. He and the Ghost both insist on secrecy, as if
too much had already been done. Hamlet induces his fellow-
witnesses to swear to keep silence about the marvel they have
seen; he checks a natural impulse to repeat the Ghost's story; and
the Ghost himself, on its way to its subterranean torture-chamber,
echoes Hamlet's demand—"Swear, Swear"—in hollow and melodramatic accents. Why this fear to divulge the truth? Why this un-

necessary precaution and delay? Why this fantastic notion, at once imposing itself on the hero's mind, that there would be occasion for him to feign madness and put an antic disposition on? The simple truth is, that the play preëxists and imposes itself here on the poet, who is reduced to paving the way as best he can for the foregone complications. Had Hamlet forthwith communicated his mission to his friends and rushed with them to the banquet hall where the King was at that moment carousing, had he instantly dispatched the usurper and proclaimed himself king in his stead, there would have been no occasion for four more acts and for so much heart-searching soliloquy. The given plot is the starting-point, and its irrationality at this juncture, by which the comic effects of a feigned madness were secured for the playwright, must be accepted as a fundamental datum on which incidents and characters are alike built up.

Those who have maintained that Hamlet is really mad had this partial justification for their paradox, that Hamlet is irrational. He acts without reflection, as he reflects without acting. At the basis of all his ingenuity and reasoning, of his nimble wit and varied fooling, lies this act of inexplicable folly: that he conceals his discovery, postpones his vengeance before questioning its propriety, and descends with no motive to a grotesque and pitiful piece of dissimulation. This unreason is not madness, because his intellect remains clear, his discourse sound and comprehensive; but it is a sort of passionate weakness and indirection in his will, which mocks its own ends, strikes fantastic attitudes, and invents elaborate schemes of action useless for his declared purposes. The psychology of Hamlet is like that which some German metaphysicians have attributed to the Spirit of the World, which is the prey to its own perversity and to what is called romantic irony, so that it eternally pursues the good in a way especially designed never to attain it. In Hamlet, as in them, beneath this histrionic duplicity and earnestness about the unreal, there is a very genuine pathos. Such brilliant futility is really helpless and sick at heart. The clouded will which plays with all these artifices of thought would fain break its way to light and self-knowledge through this magic circle of sophistication. It is the tragedy of a soul buzzing in the glass prison of a world which it can neither escape nor understand, in which it flutters about without direction, without clear hope, and yet with many a keen pang, many a dire imaginary problem, and much exquisite music.

This morbid indirection of Hamlet's, in the given situation, yields the rest of the play. Its theme is a hidden crime met by a fantastic and incapable virtue. The hero's reaction takes various forms: his soliloquies and reflections, his moody and artful treatment of other persons, his plans and spurts of action. In soliloquy Hamlet is much the same from the beginning to the end of the piece. His philosophy learns little from events and consequently makes little progress. When he has still nothing more portentous to disturb him than his father's death and his mother's marriage, he already wishes that his too, too solid flesh should melt, and that the Everlasting had not laid His canon against self-slaughter. The uses of this world seem to him even then wholly weary, flat, stale, and unprofitable. This remains his habitual sentiment whenever he looks within, but he can meantime be won over at any moment to shrewd and satirical observation of things external. If the funeral baked meats coldly furnished forth the marriage tables, it is, he tells us, but thrift; nor is his habit of mind at all changed when, at the point of highest tension in his adventures, he stops to consider how a king may go a progress through the guts of a beggar, nor when, in a lull that precedes the last spasm of his destiny, he versifies the same theme:

> Imperious Cæsar, dead and turn'd to clay,
> Might stop a hole to keep the wind away:
> O, that the earth, which kept the world in awe,
> Should patch a wall to expel the winter's flaw!

This satirical humour, touching melancholy with the sting of absurdity, crops up everywhere. "I am too much in the sun," he says, with a bitter and jocular obscurity. "He is at supper: not where he eats but where he is eaten; a certain convocation of politic worms are e'en at him."

Reason in young men is an accomplishment rather than a vital function, and may be allowed to play pranks with respectable ideas and to seem capricious and even mad; but while enjoying this license and turning, as it were, somersaults in the air, reason remains by nature the organ of truth, and seizes every opportunity which its game affords to prick some sanctified bubble and aim some home-thrust at the foibles of the world. This sort of youthful roguery has a fine sincerity about it; under the sparkle of paradox it shows a loyal heart and a tongue not yet suborned to the praising of familiar or necessary evils. Nevertheless such idealism is lame because it cannot conceive a better alternative to the things it criticises. It stops at bickerings and lamentations which, although we cannot deny the ample warrant they have in experience, leave us disconcerted and in an unstable equilibrium, ready to revert, when imagination falters, to all our old platitudes and conventional judgments. Therefore, Hamlet's sad reflections have in the end the merit of humour rather than of wisdom. Their aptness is inconsequential. His sense for what is good and ideal is strong enough to raise him above worldliness and a gross optimism, but it is far too negative and poor to inspire creation in the imaginative sphere or better action in the world.

Hamlet's attitude towards the minor characters in the play is a source of perennial joy to spectators and readers. His words and manner to Polonius, Horatio, Rosencrantz, and Guildenstern, the players, the grave-diggers, the court messengers, are alike keen, kindly, witty, and noble. Since he is playing at madness he can allow his humour to be broader, his scorn franker, his fancy more wayward than they could well have been otherwise; yet in all mock disguises appears the same exquisite courtesy, even in that clever and cruel parrying of the King's treachery during the expedition to England. It is when we come to Hamlet's attitude towards the other chief figures—the Ghost, Ophelia, the Queen—that we observe a certain indistinctness and dispersion of mind, so that both the hero's character and the poet's intentions are, to say the least, less obvious. In the Ghost's presence Hamlet is overcome with feeling, in its absence with doubts. What he ostensibly wishes to have confirmed is the veracity of that witness, and the play-scene is arranged to obtain corroboration of this. Yet when that ostensible doubt is solved and the facts are beyond question, he is no more ready for action than before. He still feels a reluctance to kill the King, founded apparently no longer on doubts about his crime but on scruples or distaste in avenging it. The suspicious element in the Ghost was really less the testimony it gave than the behaviour it inspired, the mission of active vengeance which it seemed to lay on the kindly and meditative Prince. Such conduct was indeed conformable to tradition and barbarous practice, but it was opposed to the secret promptings of the hero's own mind. In his individual and free reflection he could find more grounds for suicide than for murder. When the Ghost appears there is room in Hamlet's heart only for filial affection, and horror at seeing his father in such a shape; but as the sensuous impression fades it passes into a doubtful and sinister obsession. Hamlet feels that he is leaving a duty unperformed and at the same time that he is being driven on by the devil. If his instinctive hesitation could have expressed itself theoretically he might perhaps have asked whether the treacherous murder of one innocent man could well be righted by more treachery and more murder, involving disaster to many innocent persons. Of course, neither a prosaic rationalism of this sort, nor foresight of what in that particular case was likely to ensue, could properly be expected in Hamlet; yet possibly some premonition of both existed in the poet's mind and gave Hamlet's hesitation that symbolic and moral import which we somehow feel it to possess. Conventional maxims, stock passions, and theological sanctions play very different rôles in different people's lives. In the vulgar they may serve to cloak the absence of genuine principles and of a fixed purpose of any kind. In noble minds they may cheapen the genuine intuitions which they come to clothe, and cause these minds to fall short of that clearness and generosity which they would have shown if they had found free and untrammelled expression. So Hamlet's whole entanglement with the Ghost, and with the crude morality of vengeance which the plot imposes upon him, fails to bring his own soul to a right utterance, and this stifling of his better potential mind is no small part of his tragedy. Or is it only a fond critic's illusion that makes us read that better idea into what is purely unconscious barbarism and a vacillation useful for theatrical purposes?

Towards his mother Hamlet maintains throughout the greater part of the play a wounded reserve appropriate to the situation. He speaks of her with sarcasm, but addresses her with curt respect. Only in the closet scene does he unbosom himself with a somewhat emphatic eloquence which shows touches of dignity and pathos; yet this scene, central as it is in the plot, hardly rises in power above the level of its neighbours. In comparison, for instance, the scenes with Ophelia are full of wonder and charm. There the poet's imagination flowers out, and Hamlet appears in all his originality and wild inspiration. Yet Ophelia and Hamlet's relation to her are incidental to the drama, while the Queen and her fate are essential to it. We may observe in general that Shakespeare's genius shines in the texture of his poems rather than in their structure, in imagery and happy strokes rather than in integrating ideas. His poetry plays about life like ivy about a house, and is more akin to landscape than to architecture. He feels no vocation to call the stones themselves to their ideal places and enchant the very substance and skeleton of the world. How blind to him, and to Hamlet, are all ultimate issues, and the sum total of things how unseizable! The heathen chaos enveloping everything is all the more sensible on account of the lovely natures which it engulfs. Ophelia, for instance, that slight and too flexible treble in the general dirge, turns it to favour and to prettiness. If she had been a casual ornamental figure, like Ariel, introduced only for its own sake, she would not have illustrated so well the main drift of the drama nor been herself so touching an apparition. She is closely bound up with the plot, and what is more important, with the emotion which it arouses; yet she is hardly necessary, and Hamlet's affection for her, though a real and congruent part of his experience, forms only an incidental and subordinate part of it. He loved Ophelia before the catastrophe came that unhinged his life; afterwards he remembers her, when he comes across her, as one might remember some tender episode of childhood. His feeling is sentiment rather than passion. He grows sentimental under the influence of her sensuous charm and of her innocence. "Here's metal more attractive," he says, in one place; and in another,

> Nymph, in thy orisons
> Be all my sins remember'd.

His love for her plays no part in his essential resolutions. She does not console him at all, even in his initial bereavement and first suspicions. The speeches in his first scene are not those of a man in love. His pleasure in Ophelia's presence, his interest in his own love, has been undone by enterprises of greater pith and moment. When face to face with her grief, he is not impelled to explain and appeal to her constancy and trust, or invite her to share his calamity. His impulse is merely to despair and throw the blame upon the world at large. "Get thee to a nunnery, go." "Why wouldst thou be a breeder of sinners?" There is doubtless a shade of jealousy in this cry, with a touch of tender solicitude to save and screen her from his own troubles. Yet the dominating sentiment is one of helpless regret. He is sorry, very sorry; but it does not occur to him that he can do anything or can find in Ophelia any resource or inspiration. His love, though sincere, seems to him now one of the frail treasures of his youth, blasted by destiny. It had never taken deep enough root in his soul to endure the blasts of fortune, and be, like his love for his father, one of the moving forces in his destiny itself.

Hamlet's positive and deliberate action is limited to two stratagems, one with the players, to catch the King's conscience, and one by which he makes Rosencrantz and Guildenstern suffer the fate prepared for himself in England. In both cases Hamlet betrays a sort of exuberance and wild delight. He feels the luxury of hitting home, the absolute joy of playing the game, without particular reference to the end in view. The speech in which he recounts his escape from shipboard and his counterfeiting the King's letter, positively bubbles over with high spirits and the sense of mastery. In the play scene, too, he is all vivacity and eager comments. He cannot suppress his tense excitement, and comes near defeating his plan by disclosing it prematurely. When the bubble has burst and his point is gained, he is incoherent in his exultation, in his relief at having discovered the worst, and his joy at having verified his expectations. If he acts seldom and with difficulty, it is not because he does not hugely enjoy action. Yet his delight is in the shimmer and movement of action rather than in its use; so that the weakness of his character appears just as much in his bursts of activity as in his long hesitations. He kills Polonius by accident, hoping that in a blind thrust through the arras he might turn out at last to have dispatched the King; and when, himself mortally wounded, he finally executes that long-meditated sentence, he can do so only by yielding to a sudden hysterical impulse. So consistently does unreason pursue him: an inexplicable crime is followed by a miraculous vision; that portent he meets by a senseless and too congenial pretence of madness; a successful stratagem confirms the King's guilt, but does not lead to exposure or punishment, rather to a passive reconciliation with him on Hamlet's part. Innocent persons meantime perish, and the end is a general but casual slaughter, amid treachery, misunderstandings, and ghastly confusions.

This picture of universal madness is relieved by the very finest and purest glints of wit, intelligence, and feeling. It is crammed with exquisite lines, and vivified by most interesting and moving characters in great variety, all drawn with masterly breadth, depth, and precision. Hamlet, in particular, as our analysis testifies, is more than a vivid dramatic figure, more than an unparalleled poetic vision. He lays bare the heart of a whole race, or, perhaps we should rather say, expresses a conflict to which every soul is more or less liable. There is a kind of initial earnestness in all life which in some people remains predominant; a certain soulfulness and idealism which the Germans attribute especially to themselves, but which they would probably recognise also in the deeper intuitions of English poetry. It is a mood proper to youth; and youth in a race (since there is no question of a shorter descent from Adam or his Darwinian rival) can only mean that at a given juncture sentiment, fancy, and dialectic have outrun external experience. Youth is far from implying less complexity than age or a meaner endowment, for youth, at least potentially, often has the advantage in these respects. Youth means only less complete adjustment of capacity to opportunity, of intelligence to practice and art. In a fertile mind such want of adjustment intensifies self-consciousness and, because so much that the mind is pregnant with remains unexpressed and untested, it produces a sense of vague profundity which is often an illusion. An unexpressed mind may be deep, but it is none the deeper for not exercising itself successfully on real things; and though it need not lack poetry or philosophy for being comparatively without experience, yet its poetry will tend to be irrelevant and fantastic, and its philosophy *a priori*. The former will show more airy richness than rational beauty, and the latter more ingenuity than wisdom. These characteristics, whether or not essential to the spirit of "the North," are unmistakably present in Hamlet's person. They render his moral being "dark, true, and tender." He is strong in his integrity and purity of purpose, but lost in floating emotion, perplexed by want of concentration and of self-knowledge. Here are immense endowment and strange incompetence, constant perspicacity and general confusion, entire virtue in the intention, and complete disaster in the result. An apt pupil of philosophy, of politics, of art, of love, Hamlet is master in nothing. The solution eludes him for every riddle and even for every plain question; and his vast consciousness is ignorant of its own function.

Compare with such a mind what may be called by contrast the mind of the East or South, the mind of fatigued and long-indoctrinated races, disillusioned, distinct, malicious, for the most part unblushingly subservient to interest, passion, or superstition (for this temperament is too worn and sceptical to think rebellion worth while), yet in its reflective phase detached and contemplative, able occasionally to despise all entanglements, to dominate the will, and to look truth in the eye without blinking.

If Shakespeare had intended to make his drama allegorical of this contrast, he could not have hit upon a better theme and title: Hamlet the Dane! How that name evokes the image of virgin and barbarous heroes standing on the horizon of the world! Their experience upon descending among the nations must have been quite like Hamlet's on finding himself suddenly in a perverse world. They, too, must have been burdened with longing, scornful of corruption, touched yet puzzled by Christianity, attracted yet wounded by civilisation. Although Shakespeare was troubled, of course, by no such thought of historic symbolism, and made Hamlet in all externals a prince of Queen Elizabeth's time, yet the assimilation would not on that account cease to be possible. It was at bottom no anachronism to give to a barbaric jewel an Elizabethan setting. The old Norseman's soul was uncontaminated by migration into a richer age and a milder air; in fact, the poet's nation had not, in spirit, outgrown or disowned its ancestry.

The ghost scenes in *Hamlet*—to return to them for a moment—are excellent examples of profound, ill-digested emotions breaking out fiercely against circumstances which are not well in hand, and which consequently are not met intelligently or successfully by the inspiration in question. This ghost is not like the deities that often appear in Greek tragedy, a *deus ex machina* coming to solve, in the light of serene thought and eternal interests, the tangled problems of the single life. On the contrary, this ghost is a party to the conflict, an instigator of sinister thoughts, a thing hatched in a nest of sorrows. Its scope is so exclusively personal that it may well seem the very coinage of the brain; yet it is ostensibly miraculous, noble, pathetic, veracious. It is at once a spectre and a suspicion, a physical marvel and an inward and authoritative voice. Our reason itself flits with this ghost through a night half mockery and half horror. We feel that not Hamlet the Dane but the human soul in its inmost depths is moonstruck and haunted. Poetry, in these wonderful scenes, does not entrance by presenting natural and heavenly harmonies so convincingly that the heart, too, begins to beat in unison with them; that might be the highest achievement of some classic poet. Here, when the deepest note is sounded, we can only cry, "O Hamlet! thou hast cleft my heart in twain." We wait to see the spectacle of things dissolved and exorcised. The fretted pipe has defied all earthly powers to play upon it, this too, too solid flesh has melted away, and the rest, as Hamlet says, is silence.

All this, however, is only half, and the less intentional half, of what comes before us in this unfathomable poem. The impression of utter gloom which the plot leaves when taken, so to speak, realistically, as if it were a picture of actual existences, is not the impression which it leaves when we take it as lyric poetry, as music, as an abstract representation of sundry moods and loyalties traversing a noble mind. The world which is here set before us may be grotesque and distracted; but we are not asked to be interested in that world. Had Hamlet himself been interested in it, he would have acted more rationally. It was not intelligence or courage that he lacked; it was practical conviction or sense for reality. Had he possessed this he would have turned his wits and sympathies towards improving the state of Denmark, as he turns them towards improving the player's art. In truth he cared nothing for the world; man pleased him not, no, nor woman, neither; and we may well abandon to its natural confusion a dream in which we do not believe. Had Hamlet tried to justify his temperament by expressing it in a philosophy, he would have been an idealist. He would have said that events were only occasions for exercising the spirit; they were nothing but imagined situations meant to elicit a certain play of mind. If a man's comments had been keen, if his heart had been tender, if his will had been upright and pure, the rest were nothing. The world might feign to be mad and put on an antic disposition; it was sane enough if it fulfilled its purpose and gave a man an opportunity to test his own mettle. Those idiocies and horrors which he lived among would have been in truth the flights of angels that bore him to his rest. At any rate, express it how we will, the sympathetic reader will instinctively feel that he should pass over lightly the experience which the play depicts and carry away from it only the moral feeling, the spiritual sentiment, which it calls forth in the characters. As the poet himself thought a violent and somewhat absurd fable not unworthy to support his richest verse and subtlest characterisations, so we must take the fabric of destiny, in this tragedy and in that, too, which we enact in the world, as it happens to be, and think the moral lights that flicker through it bright enough to redeem it.

We must remember that the modern mind, like the modern world, is compacted out of ruins, and that the fresh northern spirit, inducted into that Byzantine labyrinth which we call civilisation, feels a marked discord between its genius and its culture. The latter is alien and imperfectly grafted on the living stem from which it must draw its sap. Hence the most radical and excruciating experience of the romantic mind comes from just such hereditary incoherence, just such perplexity and half-feigned madness, just such obsession by artifices, as Hamlet presents to us in a tragic miniature. The deep interest of this figure lies accordingly in its affinity to the situation in which every romantic spirit must in a measure find itself. There is no richer or more exquisite monument to the failure of emotional good-will, and of intelligence inclined to embroider rather than to build. So absolute a feat of imagination cannot be ranked in comparison with other works, nor estimated by any standard of which it does not itself furnish the suggestion and type. It is rather to be studied and absorbed, to be made a part of our habitual landscape and mental furniture, lest we should miss much of what is deepest and rarest in human feeling. If we care to pass, however, from admiration of the masterpiece to reflection on the experience which it expresses, we see that here is no necessary human tragedy, no universal destiny or divine law. It is a picture of incidental unfitness, of a genius wasted for being plucked quite unripe from the sunny places of the world. In Hamlet our incoherent souls see their own image; in him romantic potentiality and romantic failure wears each its own feature. In him we see the gifts most congenial and appealing to us reduced to a pathetic impotence because of the disarray in which we are content to leave them.

THE ABSENCE OF RELIGION
IN SHAKESPEARE

W<small>E ARE</small> accustomed to think of the universality of Shakespeare as not the least of his glories. No other poet has given so many-sided an expression to human nature, or rendered so many passions and moods with such an appropriate variety of style, sentiment, and accent. If, therefore, we were asked to select one monument of human civilisation that should survive to some future age, or be transported to another planet to bear witness to the inhabitants there of what we have been upon earth, we should probably choose the works of Shakespeare. In them we recognise the truest portrait and best memorial of man. Yet the archaeologists of that future age, or the cosmographers of that other part of the heavens, after conscientious study of our Shakespearian autobiography, would misconceive our life in one important respect. They would hardly understand that man had had a religion.

There are, indeed, numerous exclamations and invocations in Shakespeare which we, who have other means of information, know to be evidences of current religious ideas. Shakespeare adopts these, as he adopts the rest of his vocabulary, from the society about him. But he seldom or never gives them their original value. When Iago says " *'sblood*," a commentator might add explanations which should involve the whole philosophy of Christian devotion; but this Christian sentiment is not in Iago's mind, nor in Shakespeare's, any more than the virtues of Heracles and his twelve labours are in the mind of every slave and pander that cries *"hercule"* in the pages of Plautus and Terence. Oaths are the fossils of piety. The geologist recognises in them the relics of a once active devotion, but they are now only counters and pebbles tossed about in the unconscious play of expression. The lighter and more constant their use, the less their meaning.

Only one degree more inward than this survival of a religious vocabulary in profane speech is the reference we often find in Shakespeare to religious institutions and traditions. There are monks, bishops, and cardinals; there is even mention of saints, although none is ever presented to us in person. The clergy, if they have any wisdom, have an earthly one. Friar Lawrence culls his herbs like a more benevolent Medea; and Cardinal Wolsey flings away ambition with a profoundly Pagan despair; his robe and his integrity to heaven are cold comfort to him. Juliet goes to shrift to arrange her love affairs, and Ophelia should go to a nunnery to forget hers. Even the chastity of Isabella has little in it that would have been out of place in Iphigenia. The metaphysical Hamlet himself sees a "true ghost," but so far reverts to the positivism that underlies Shakespeare's thinking as to speak soon after of that "undiscovered country from whose bourn no traveller returns."

There are only two or three short passages in the plays, and one sonnet, in which true religious feeling seems to break forth. The most beautiful of these passages is that in "Richard II," which commemorates the death of Mowbray, Duke of Norfolk:—

> *Many a time hath banished Norfolk fought*
> *For Jesu Christ in glorious Christian field,*
> *Streaming the ensign of the Christian cross*
> *Against black Pagans, Turks, and Saracens;*
> *And, toiled with works of war, retired himself*
> *To Italy; and there, at Venice, gave*
> *His body to that pleasant country's earth,*
> *And his pure soul unto his captain Christ,*
> *Under whose colours he had fought so long.*

This is tender and noble, and full of an indescribable chivalry and pathos, yet even here we find the spirit of war rather than that of religion, and a deeper sense of Italy than of heaven. More unmixed is the piety of Henry V after the battle of Agincourt:—

> *O God, thy arm was here;*
> *And not to us, but to thy arm alone,*
> *Ascribe we all!—When, without stratagem,*

138

> *But in plain shock and even play of battle,*
> *Was ever known so great and little loss,*
> *On one part and on the other?—Take it, God,*
> *For it is none but thine. . . .*
> *Come, go we in procession to the village,*
> *And be it death proclaimèd through our host,*
> *To boast of this, or take that praise from God,*
> *Which is his only. . . .*
>   *Do we all holy rites;*
> *Let there be sung* Non nobis *and* Te Deum.

This passage is certainly a true expression of religious feeling, and just the kind that we might expect from a dramatist. Religion appears here as a manifestation of human nature and as an expression of human passion. The passion, however, is not due to Shakespeare's imagination, but is essentially historical: the poet has simply not rejected, as he usually does, the religious element in the situation he reproduces.[1]

With this dramatic representation of piety we may couple another, of a more intimate kind, from the Sonnets:—

> *Poor soul, the centre of my sinful earth,*
> *Fooled by these rebel powers that thee array,*
> *Why dost thou pine within and suffer dearth,*
> *Painting thy outward walls so costly gay?*
> *Why so large cost, having so short a lease,*
> *Dost thou upon thy fading mansion spend?*
> *Shall worms, inheritors of this excess,*
> *Eat up thy charge? Is this thy body's end?*
> *Then, soul, live thou upon thy servant's loss,*
> *And let that pine to aggravate thy store;*
> *Buy terms divine by selling hours of dross,*
> *Within be fed, without be rich no more:*

---

[1]"And so aboute foure of the clocke in the afternoone, the Kynge when he saw no apparaunce of enemies, caused the retreite to be blowen, and gathering his army togither, gave thankes to almightie god for so happy a victory, causing his prelates and chapleines to sing this psalm, *In exitu Israell de Egipto,* and commandyng every man to kneele downe on the grounde at this verse; *Non nobis, domine, non nobis, sed nomini tuo da gloriam.* Which done, he caused *Te Deum,* with certain anthems, to be song, giving laud & praise to god, and not boasting of his owne force or any humaine power." HOLINSHED.

Then shalt thou feed on death, that feeds on men,
And death once dead, there's no more dying then.

This sonnet contains more than a natural religious emotion inspired by a single event. It contains reflection, and expresses a feeling not merely dramatically proper but rationally just. A mind that habitually ran into such thoughts would be philosophically pious; it would be spiritual. The Sonnets, as a whole, are spiritual; their passion is transmuted into discipline. Their love, which, whatever its nominal object, is hardly anything but love of beauty and youth in general, is made to triumph over time by a metaphysical transformation of the object into something eternal. At first this is the beauty of the race renewing itself by generation, then it is the description of beauty in the poet's verse, and finally it is the immortal soul enriched by the contemplation of that beauty. This noble theme is the more impressively rendered by being contrasted with another, with a vulgar love that by its nature refuses to be so transformed and transmuted. "Two loves," cries the poet, in a line that gives us the essence of the whole, "Two loves I have,—of comfort, and despair."

In all this depth of experience, however, there is still wanting any religious image. The Sonnets are spiritual, but, with the doubtful exception of the one quoted above, they are not Christian. And, of course, a poet of Shakespeare's time could not have found any other mould than Christianity for his religion. In our day, with our wide and conscientious historical sympathies, it may be possible for us to find in other rites and doctrines than those of our ancestors an expression of some ultimate truth. But for Shakespeare, in the matter of religion, the choice lay between Christianity and nothing. He chose nothing; he chose to leave his heroes and himself in the presence of life and of death with no other philosophy than that which the profane world can suggest and understand.

This positivism, we need hardly say, was not due to any grossness or sluggishness in his imagination. Shakespeare could be idealistic when he dreamed, as he could be spiritual when he reflected. The spectacle of life did not pass before his eyes as a mere phantasmagoria. He seized upon its principles; he became wise. Nothing can exceed the ripeness of his seasoned judgment, or the occasional breadth, sadness, and terseness of his reflection. The author of *Hamlet* could not be without metaphysical aptitude; *Macbeth* could not have been written without a sort of sibylline inspiration, or the Sonnets without something of the Platonic mind. It is all the more remarkable, therefore, that we should have to search through all the works of Shakespeare to find half a dozen passages that have so much as a religious sound, and that even these passages, upon examination, should prove not to be the expression of any deep religious conception. If Shakespeare had been without metaphysical capacity, or without moral maturity, we could have explained his strange insensibility to religion; but as it is, we must marvel at his indifference and ask ourselves what can be the causes of it. For, even if we should not regard the absence of religion as an imperfection in his own thought, we must admit it to be an incompleteness in his portrayal of the thought of others. Positivism may be a virtue in a philosopher, but it is a vice in a dramatist, who has to render those human passions to which the religious imagination has always given a larger meaning and a richer depth.

Those greatest poets by whose side we are accustomed to put Shakespeare did not forego this advantage. They gave us man with his piety and the world with its gods. Homer is the chief repository of the Greek religion, and Dante the faithful interpreter of the Catholic. Nature would have been inconceivable to them without the supernatural, or man without the influence and companionship of the gods. These poets live in a cosmos. In their minds, as in the mind of their age, the fragments of experience have fallen together into a perfect picture, like the bits of glass in a kaleidoscope. Their universe is a total. Reason and imagination have mastered it completely and peopled it. No chaos remains beyond, or, if it does, it is thought of with an involuntary shudder that soon passes into a healthy indifference. They have a theory of human life; they see man in his relations, surrounded by a kindred universe in which he fills his allotted place. He knows the meaning and issue of his life, and does not voyage without a chart.

Shakespeare's world, on the contrary, is only the world of human society. The cosmos eludes him; he does not seem to feel the need of framing that idea. He depicts human life in all its richness and variety, but leaves that life without a setting, and consequently without a meaning. If we asked him to tell us what is the significance of the passion and beauty he had so vividly displayed, and what is the outcome of it all, he could hardly answer in any other words than those he puts into the mouth of Macbeth:—

> To-morrow, and to-morrow, and to-morrow,
> Creeps in this petty pace from day to day,
> To the last syllable of recorded time;
> And all our yesterdays have lighted fools
> The way to dusty death. Out, out, brief candle!
> Life's but a walking shadow, a poor player
> That struts and frets his hour upon the stage
> And then is heard no more: it is a tale
> Told by an idiot, full of sound and fury,
> Signifying nothing.

How differently would Homer or Dante have answered that question! Their tragedy would have been illumined by a sense of the divinity of life and beauty, or by a sense of the sanctity of suffering and death. Their faith had enveloped the world of experience in a world of imagination, in which the ideals of the reason, of the fancy, and of the heart had a natural expression. They had caught in the reality the hint of a lovelier fable,—a fable in which that reality was completed and idealised, and made at once vaster in its extent and more intelligible in its principle. They had, as it were, dramatised the universe, and endowed it with the tragic unities. In contrast with such a luminous philosophy and so well-digested an experience, the silence of Shakespeare and his philosophical incoherence have something in them that is still heathen; something that makes us wonder whether the northern mind, even in him, did not remain morose and barbarous at its inmost core.

But before we allow ourselves such hasty and general inferences, we may well stop to consider whether there is not some simpler answer to our question. An epic poet, we might say, naturally deals with cosmic themes. He needs supernatural machinery because he depicts the movement of human affairs in their generality, as typified in the figures of heroes whose function it is to embody or to overcome elemental forces. Such a poet's world is fabulous, because his inspiration is impersonal. But the dramatist renders the concrete reality of life. He has no need of a superhuman setting for his pictures. Such a setting would destroy the vitality of his creations. His plots should involve only human actors and human motives: the *deus ex machina* has always been regarded as an interloper on his stage. The passions of man are his all-sufficient material; he should weave his whole fabric out of them.

To admit the truth of all this would not, however, solve our problem. The dramatist cannot be expected to put cosmogonies on the boards. Miracle-plays become dramatic only when they become human. But the supernatural world, which the playwright does not bring before the footlights, may exist nevertheless in the minds of his characters and of his audience. He may refer to it, appeal to it, and imply it, in the actions and in the sentiments he attributes to his heroes. And if the comparison of Shakespeare with Homer or Dante on the score of religious inspiration is invalidated by the fact that he is a dramatist while they are epic poets, a comparison may yet be instituted between Shakespeare and other dramatists, from which his singular insensibility to religion will as readily appear.

Greek tragedy, as we know, is dominated by the idea of fate. Even when the gods do not appear in person, or where the service or neglect of them is not the moving cause of the whole play,—as it is in the *Bacchæ* and the *Hippolytus* of Euripides,—still the deep conviction of the limits and conditions of human happiness underlies the fable. The will of man fulfils the decrees of Heaven. The hero manifests a higher force than his own, both in success and in failure. The fates guide the willing and drag the unwilling. There is no such fragmentary view of life as we have in our romantic drama, where accidents make the meaningless happiness or unhappiness of a supersensitive adventurer. Life is seen whole, although in miniature. Its boundaries and its principles are studied more than its incidents. The human, therefore, everywhere merges with the divine. Our mortality, being sharply defined and much insisted upon, draws the attention all the more to that eternity of Nature and of law in which it is embosomed. Nor is the fact of superhuman control left for our reflection to discover; it is emphatically asserted in those oracles on which so much of the action commonly turns.

When the Greek religion was eclipsed by the Christian, the

ancient way of conceiving the ultra-human relations of human life became obsolete. It was no longer possible to speak with sincerity of the oracles and gods, of Nemesis and ὕβρις. Yet for a long time it was not possible to speak in any other terms. The new ideas were without artistic definition, and literature was paralysed. But in the course of ages, when the imagination had had time and opportunity to develop a Christian art and a Christian philosophy, the dramatic poets were ready to deal with the new themes. Only their readiness in this respect surpassed their ability, at least their ability to please those who had any memory of the ancient perfection of the arts.

The miracle-plays were the beginning. Their crudity was extreme and their levity of the frankest; but they had still, like the Greek plays, a religious excuse and a religious background. They were not without dramatic power, but their offences against taste and their demands upon faith were too great for them to survive the Renaissance. Such plays as the *Polyeucte* of Corneille and the *Devocion de la Cruz* of Calderon, with other Spanish plays that might be mentioned, are examples of Christian dramas by poets of culture; but as a whole we must say that Christianity, while it succeeded in expressing itself in painting and in architecture, failed to express itself in any adequate drama. Where Christianity was strong, the drama either disappeared or became secular; and it has never again dealt with cosmic themes successfully, except in such hands as those of Goethe and Wagner, men who either neglected Christianity altogether or used it only as an incidental ornament, having, as they say, transcended it in their philosophy.

The fact is, that art and reflection have never been able to unite perfectly the two elements of a civilisation like ours, that draws its culture from one source and its religion from another. Modern taste has ever been, and still is, largely exotic, largely a revolution in favour of something ancient or foreign. The more cultivated a period has been, the more wholly it has reverted to antiquity for its inspiration. The existence of that completer world has haunted all minds struggling for self-expression, and interfered, perhaps, with the natural development of their genius. The old art which they could not disregard distracted them from the new ideal, and prevented them from embodying this ideal outwardly; while the same ideal, retaining their inward allegiance, made their revivals of ancient forms artificial and incomplete. The strange idea could thus gain admittance that art was not called to deal with everything; that its sphere was the world of polite conventions. The serious and the sacred things of life were to be left unexpressed and inarticulate; while the arts masqueraded in the forms of a Pagan antiquity, to which a triviality was at the same time attributed which in fact it had not possessed. This unfortunate separation of experience and its artistic expression betrayed itself in the inadequacy of what was beautiful and the barbarism of what was sincere.

When such are the usual conditions of artistic creation, we need not wonder that Shakespeare, a poet of the Renaissance, should have confined his representation of life to its secular aspects, and that his readers after him should rather have marvelled at the variety of the things of which he showed an understanding than have taken note of the one thing he overlooked. To omit religion was after all to omit what was not felt to be congenial to a poet's mind. The poet was to trace for us the passionate and romantic embroideries of life; he was to be artful and humane, and above all he was to be delightful. The beauty and charm of things had nothing any longer to do with those painful mysteries and contentions which made the temper of the pious so acrid and sad. In Shakespeare's time and country, to be religious already began to mean to be Puritanical; and in the divorce between the fulness of life on the one hand and the depth and unity of faith on the other, there could be no doubt to which side a man of imaginative instincts would attach himself. A world of passion and beauty without a meaning must seem to him more interesting and worthy than a world of empty principle and dogma, meagre, fanatical, and false. It was beyond the power of synthesis possessed by that age and nation to find a principle of all passion and a religion of all life.

This power of synthesis is indeed so difficult and rare that the attempt to gain it is sometimes condemned as too philosophical, and as tending to embarrass the critical eye and creative imagination with futile theories. We might say, for instance, that the absence of religion in Shakespeare was a sign of his good sense; that a healthy instinct kept his attention within the sublunary world; and that he was in that respect superior to Homer and to Dante. For, while they allowed their wisdom to clothe itself in fanciful forms, he gave us his in its immediate truth, so that he embodied what they signified. The supernatural machinery of their poems was, we might say, an accidental incumbrance, a traditional means of expression, which they only half understood, and which made their representation of life indirect and partly unreal. Shakespeare, on the other hand, had reached his poetical majority and independence. He rendered human experience no longer through symbols, but by direct imaginative representation. What I have treated as a limitation in him would, then, appear as the maturity of his strength.

There is always a class of minds in whom the spectacle of history produces a certain apathy of reason. They flatter themselves that they can escape defeat by not attempting the highest tasks. We need not here stop to discuss what value as truth a philosophical synthesis may hope to attain, nor have we to protest against the æsthetic preference for the sketch and the episode over a reasoned and unified rendering of life. Suffice it to say that the human race hitherto, whenever it has reached a phase of comparatively high development and freedom, has formed a conception of its place in Nature, no less than of the contents of its life; and that this conception has been the occasion of religious sentiments and practices; and further, that every art, whether literary or plastic, has drawn its favourite themes from this religious sphere. The poetic imagination has not commonly stopped short of the philosophical in representing a superhuman environment of man.

Shakespeare, however, is remarkable among the greater poets for being without a philosophy and without a religion. In his drama there is no fixed conception of any forces, natural or moral, dominating and transcending our mortal energies. Whether this characteristic be regarded as a merit or as a defect, its presence cannot be denied. Those who think it wise or possible to refrain from searching for general principles, and are satisfied with the successive empirical appearance of things, without any faith in their rational continuity or completeness, may well see in Shakespeare their natural prophet. For he, too, has been satisfied with the successive description of various passions and events. His world, like the earth before Columbus, extends in an indefinite plane which he is not tempted to explore.

Those of us, however, who believe in circumnavigation, and who think that both human reason and human imagination require a certain totality in our views, and who feel that the most important thing in life is the lesson of it, and its relation to its own ideal,—we can hardly find in Shakespeare all that the highest poet could give. Fulness is not necessarily wholeness, and the most profuse wealth of characterisation seems still inadequate as a picture of experience, if this picture is not somehow seen from above and reduced to a dramatic unity,—to that unity of meaning that can suffuse its endless details with something of dignity, simplicity, and peace. This is the imaginative power found in several poets we have mentioned,—the power that gives certain passages in Lucretius also their sublimity, as it gives sublimity to many passages in the Bible.

For what is required for theoretic wholeness is not this or that system but some system. Its value is not the value of truth, but that of victorious imagination. Unity of conception is an æsthetic merit no less than a logical demand. A fine sense of the dignity and pathos of life cannot be attained unless we conceive somehow its outcome and its relations. Without such a conception our emotions cannot be steadfast and enlightened. Without it the imagination cannot fulfil its essential function or achieve its supreme success. Shakespeare himself, had it not been for the time and place in which he lived, when religion and imagination blocked rather than helped each other, would perhaps have allowed more of a cosmic background to appear behind his crowded scenes. If the Christian in him was not the real man, at least the Pagan would have spoken frankly. The material forces of Nature, or their vague embodiment in some northern pantheon, would then have stood behind his heroes. The various movements of events would have appeared as incidents in a larger drama to which they had at least some symbolic relation. We should have been awed as well as saddened, and purified as well as pleased, by being made to feel the dependence of human accidents upon cosmic forces and their fated evolution. Then we should not have been able to say that Shakespeare was without a religion. For the effort of religion, says Goethe, is to adjust us to the inevitable; each religion in its way strives to bring about this consummation.

THE POETRY
OF BARBARISM

I.

It is an observation at first sight melancholy but in the end, perhaps, enlightening, that the earliest poets are the most ideal, and that primitive ages furnish the most heroic characters and have the clearest vision of a perfect life. The Homeric times must have been full of ignorance and suffering. In those little barbaric towns, in those camps and farms, in those shipyards, there must have been much insecurity and superstition. That age was singularly poor in all that concerns the convenience of life and the entertainment of the mind with arts and sciences. Yet it had a sense for civilisation. That machinery of life which men were beginning to devise appealed to them as poetical; they knew its ultimate justification and studied its incipient processes with delight. The poetry of that simple and ignorant age was, accordingly, the sweetest and sanest that the world has known; the most faultless in taste, and the most even and lofty in inspiration. Without lacking variety and homeliness, it bathed all things human in the golden light of morning; it clothed sorrow in a kind of majesty, instinct with both self-control and heroic frankness. Nowhere else can we find so noble a rendering of human nature, so spontaneous a delight in life, so uncompromising a dedication to beauty, and such a gift of seeing beauty in everything. Homer, the first of poets, was also the best and the most poetical.

From this beginning, if we look down the history of Occidental literature, we see the power of idealisation steadily decline. For while it finds here and there, as in Dante, a more spiritual theme and a subtler and riper intellect, it pays for that advantage by a more than equivalent loss in breadth, sanity, and happy vigour.

And if ever imagination bursts out with a greater potency, as in Shakespeare (who excels the patriarch of poetry in depth of passion and vividness of characterisation, and in those exquisite bubblings of poetry and humour in which English genius is at its best), yet Shakespeare also pays the price by a notable loss in taste, in sustained inspiration, in consecration, and in rationality. There is more or less rubbish in his greatest works. When we come down to our own day we find poets of hardly less natural endowment (for in endowment all ages are perhaps alike) and with vastly richer sources of inspiration; for they have many arts and literatures behind them, with the spectacle of a varied and agitated society, a world which is the living microcosm of its own history and presents in one picture many races, arts, and religions. Our poets have more wonderful tragedies of the imagination to depict than had Homer, whose world was innocent of any essential defeat, or Dante, who believed in the world's definitive redemption. Or, if perhaps their inspiration is comic, they have the pageant of mediæval manners, with its picturesque artifices and passionate fancies, and the long comedy of modern social revolutions, so illusory in their aims and so productive in their aimlessness. They have, moreover, the new and marvellous conception which natural science has given us of the world and of the conditions of human progress.

With all these lessons of experience behind them, however, we find our contemporary poets incapable of any high wisdom, incapable of any imaginative rendering of human life and its meaning. Our poets are things of shreds and patches; they give us episodes and studies, a sketch of this curiosity, a glimpse of that romance; they have no total vision, no grasp of the whole reality, and consequently no capacity for a sane and steady idealisation. The comparatively barbarous ages had a poetry of the ideal; they had visions of beauty, order, and perfection. This age of material elaboration has no sense for those things. Its fancy is retrospective, whimsical, and flickering; its ideals, when it has any, are negative and partial; its moral strength is a blind and miscellaneous vehemence. Its poetry, in a word, is the poetry of barbarism.

This poetry should be viewed in relation to the general moral crisis and imaginative disintegration of which it gives a verbal echo; then we shall avoid the injustice of passing it over as insignificant, no less than the imbecility of hailing it as essentially glorious and successful. We must remember that the imagination of our race has been subject to a double discipline. It has been formed partly in the school of classic literature and polity, and partly in the school of Christian piety. This duality of inspiration, this contradiction between the two accepted methods of rationalising the world, has been a chief source of that incoherence, that romantic indistinctness and imperfection, which largely characterise the products of the modern arts. A man cannot serve two masters; yet the conditions have not been such as to allow him wholly to despise the one or wholly to obey the other. To be wholly Pagan is impossible after the dissolution of that civilisation which had seemed universal, and that empire which had believed itself eternal. To be wholly Christian is impossible for a similar reason, now that the illusion and cohesion of Christian ages is lost, and for the further reason that Christianity was itself fundamentally eclectic. Before it could succeed and dominate men even for a time, it was obliged to adjust itself to reality, to incorporate many elements of Pagan wisdom, and to accommodate itself to many habits and passions at variance with its own ideal.

In these latter times, with the prodigious growth of material life in elaboration and of mental life in diffusion, there has supervened upon this old dualism a new faith in man's absolute power, a kind of return to the inexperience and self-assurance of youth. This new inspiration has made many minds indifferent to the two traditional disciplines; neither is seriously accepted by them, for the reason, excellent from their own point of view, that no discipline whatever is needed. The memory of ancient disillusions has faded with time. Ignorance of the past has bred contempt for the lessons which the past might teach. Men prefer to repeat the old experiment without knowing that they repeat it.

I say advisedly ignorance of the past, in spite of the unprecedented historical erudition of our time; for life is an art not to be learned by observation, and the most minute and comprehensive studies do not teach us what the spirit of man should have learned by its long living. We study the past as a dead object, as a ruin, not as an authority and as an experiment. One reason why history was less interesting to former ages was that they were less conscious of separation from the past. The perspective of time was less clear because the synthesis of experience was more complete. The mind does not easily discriminate the successive phases of an action in which it is still engaged; it does not arrange in a temporal series the elements of a single perception, but posits them all together as constituting a permanent and real object. Human nature and the life of the world were real and stable objects to the apprehension of our forefathers; the actors changed, but not the characters or the play. Men were then less studious of derivations because they were more conscious of identities. They thought of all reality as in a sense contemporary, and in considering the maxims of a philosopher or the style of a poet, they were not primarily concerned with settling his date and describing his environment. The standard by which they judged was eternal; the environment in which man found himself did not seem to them subject of any essential change.

To us the picturesque element in history is more striking because we feel ourselves the children of our own age only, an age which, being itself singular and revolutionary, tends to read its own character into the past, and to regard all other periods as no less fragmentary and effervescent than itself. The changing and the permanent elements are, indeed, everywhere present, and the bias of the observer may emphasise the one or the other as it will: the only question is whether we find the significance of things in their variations or in their similarities.

Now the habit of regarding the past as effete and as merely a stepping-stone to something present or future, is unfavourable to any true apprehension of that element in the past which was vital and which remains eternal. It is a habit of thought that destroys the sense of the moral identity of all ages, by virtue of its very insistence on the mechanical derivation of one age from another. Existences that cause one another exclude one another; each is alien to the rest inasmuch as it is the product of new and different conditions. Ideas that cause nothing unite all things by giving them a common point of reference and a single standard of value.

The classic and the Christian systems were both systems of ideas, attempts to seize the eternal morphology of reality and describe its unchanging constitution. The imagination was summoned thereby to contemplate the highest objects, and the essence of things being thus described, their insignificant variations could retain little importance and the study of these variations might well seem superficial. Mechanical science, the science of causes, was accordingly neglected, while the science of values, with the arts that express these values, was exclusively pursued. The reverse has now occurred and the spirit of life, innocent of any rationalising discipline and deprived of an authoritative and adequate method of expression, has relapsed into miscellaneous and shallow exuberance. Religion and art have become short-winded. They have forgotten the old maxim that we should copy in order to be copied and remember in order to be remembered. It is true that the multiplicity of these incompetent efforts seems to many a compensation for their ill success, or even a ground for asserting their absolute superiority. Incompetence, when it flatters the passions, can always find a greater incompetence to approve of it. Indeed, some people would have regarded the Tower of Babel as the best academy of eloquence on account of the variety of oratorical methods prevailing there.

It is thus that the imagination of our time has relapsed into barbarism. But discipline of the heart and fancy is always so rare a thing that the neglect of it need not be supposed to involve any very terrible or obvious loss. The triumphs of reason have been few and partial at any time, and perfect works of art are almost unknown. The failure of art and reason, because their principle is ignored, is therefore hardly more conspicuous than it was when their principle, although perhaps acknowledged, was misunderstood or disobeyed. Indeed, to one who fixes his eye on the ideal goal, the greatest art often seems the greatest failure, because it alone reminds him of what it should have been. Trivial stimulations coming from vulgar objects, on the contrary, by making us forget altogether the possibility of a deep satisfaction, often succeed in interesting and in winning applause. The pleasure they give us is so brief and superficial that the wave of essential disappointment which would ultimately drown it has not time to rise from the heart.

The poetry of barbarism is not without its charm. It can play with sense and passion the more readily and freely in that it does not aspire to subordinate them to a clear thought or a tenable attitude of the will. It can impart the transitive emotions which it expresses; it can find many partial harmonies of mood and fancy; it can, by virtue of its red-hot irrationality, utter wilder cries, surrender itself and us to more absolute passion, and heap up a more indiscriminate wealth of images than belong to poets of seasoned experience or of heavenly inspiration. Irrational stimulation may tire us in the end, but it excites us in the beginning; and how many conventional poets, tender and prolix, have there not been, who tire us now without ever having excited anybody? The power to stimulate is the beginning of greatness, and when the barbarous poet has genius, as he well may have, he stimulates all the more powerfully on account of the crudity of his methods and the recklessness of his emotions. The defects of such art—lack of distinction, absence of beauty, confusion of ideas, incapacity permanently to please—will hardly be felt by the contemporary public, if once its attention is arrested; for no poet is so undisciplined that he will not find many readers, if he finds readers at all, less disciplined than himself.

These considerations may perhaps be best enforced by applying them to two writers of great influence over the present generation who seem to illustrate them on different planes—Robert Browning and Walt Whitman. They are both analytic poets—poets who seek to reveal and express the elemental as opposed to the conventional; but the dissolution has progressed much farther in Whitman than in Browning, doubtless because Whitman began at a much lower stage of moral and intellectual organisation; for the good will to be radical was present in both. The elements to which Browning reduces experience are still passions, characters, persons; Whitman carries the disintegration further and knows nothing but moods and particular images. The world of Browning is a world of history with civilisation for its setting and with the conventional passions for its motive forces. The world of Whitman is innocent of these things and contains only far simpler and more chaotic elements. In him the barbarism is much more pronounced; it is, indeed, avowed, and the "barbaric yawp" is sent "over the roofs of the world" in full consciousness of its inarticulate character; but in Browning the barbarism is no less real though disguised by a literary and scientific language, since the passions of civilised life with which he deals are treated as so many "barbaric yawps," complex indeed in their conditions, puffings of an intricate engine, but aimless in their vehemence and mere ebullitions of lustiness in adventurous and profoundly ungoverned souls.

Irrationality on this level is viewed by Browning with the same satisfaction with which, on a lower level, it is viewed by Whitman; and the admirers of each hail it as the secret of a new poetry which pierces to the quick and awakens the imagination to a new and genuine vitality. It is in the rebellion against discipline, in the abandonment of the ideals of classic and Christian tradition, that this rejuvenation is found. Both poets represent, therefore, and are admired for representing, what may be called the poetry of barbarism in the most accurate and descriptive sense of this word. For the barbarian is the man who regards his passions as their own excuse for being; who does not domesticate them either by understanding their cause or by conceiving their ideal goal. He is the man who does not know his derivations nor perceive his tendencies, but who merely feels and acts, valuing in his life its force and its filling, but being careless of its purpose and its form. His delight is in abundance and vehemence; his art, like his life, shows an exclusive respect for quantity and splendour of materials. His scorn for what is poorer and weaker than himself is only surpassed by his ignorance of what is higher.

II. WALT WHITMAN

The works of Walt Whitman offer an extreme illustration of this phase of genius, both by their form and by their substance. It was the singularity of his literary form—the challenge it threw to the conventions of verse and of language—that first gave Whitman notoriety: but this notoriety has become fame, because those incapacities and solecisms which glare at us from his pages are only the obverse of a profound inspiration and of a genuine courage. Even the idiosyncrasies of his style have a side which is not mere perversity or affectation; the order of his words, the procession of his images, reproduce the method of a rich, spontaneous, absolutely lazy fancy. In most poets such a natural order is modified by various governing motives—the thought, the metrical form, the echo of other poems in the memory. By Walt Whitman these conventional influences are resolutely banished. We find the swarms of men and objects rendered as they might strike the retina in a sort of waking dream. It is the most sincere possible confession of the lowest—I mean the most primitive—type of perception. All ancient poets are sophisticated in comparison and give proof of longer intellectual and moral training. Walt Whitman has gone back to the innocent style of Adam, when the animals filed before him one by one and he called each of them by its name.

In fact, the influences to which Walt Whitman was subject were as favourable as possible to the imaginary experiment of beginning the world over again. Liberalism and transcendentalism both harboured some illusions on that score; and they were in the air which our poet breathed. Moreover he breathed this air in America, where the newness of the material environment made it easier to ignore the fatal antiquity of human nature. When he afterward became aware that there was or had been a world with a history, he studied that world with curiosity and spoke of it not without a certain shrewdness. But he still regarded it as a foreign world and imagined, as not a few Americans have done, that his own world was a fresh creation, not amenable to the same laws as the old. The difference in the conditions blinded him, in his merely sensuous apprehension, to the identity of the principles.

His parents were farmers in central Long Island and his early years were spent in that district. The family seems to have been not too prosperous and somewhat nomadic; Whitman himself drifted through boyhood without much guidance. We find him now at school, now helping the labourers at the farms, now wandering along the beaches of Long Island, finally at Brooklyn working in an apparently desultory way as a printer and sometimes as a writer for a local newspaper. He must have read or heard something, at this early period, of the English classics; his style often betrays the deep effect made upon him by the grandiloquence of the Bible, of Shakespeare, and of Milton. But his chief interest, if we may trust his account, was already in his own sensations. The aspects of Nature, the forms and habits of animals, the sights of cities, the movement and talk of common people, were his constant delight. His mind was flooded with these images, keenly felt and afterward to be vividly rendered with bold strokes of realism and imagination.

Many poets have had this faculty to seize the elementary aspects of things, but none has had it so exclusively; with Whitman the surface is absolutely all and the underlying structure is without interest and almost without existence. He had had no education and his natural delight in imbibing sensations had not been trained to the uses of practical or theoretical intelligence. He basked in the sunshine of perception and wallowed in the stream of his own sensibility, as later at Camden in the shallows of his favourite brook. Even during the civil war, when he heard the drum-taps so clearly, he could only gaze at the picturesque and terrible aspects of the struggle, and linger among the wounded day after day with a canine devotion; he could not be aroused either to clear thought or to positive action. So also in his poems; a multiplicity of images pass before him and he yields himself to each in turn with absolute passivity. The world has no inside; it is a phantasmagoria of continuous visions, vivid, impressive, but monotonous and hard to distinguish in memory, like the waves of the sea or the decorations of some barbarous temple, sublime only by the infinite aggregation of parts.

This abundance of detail without organisation, this wealth of perception without intelligence and of imagination without taste, makes the singularity of Whitman's genius. Full of sympathy and receptivity, with a wonderful gift of graphic characterisation and an occasional rare grandeur of diction, he fills us with a sense of the individuality and the universality of what he describes—it is a drop in itself yet a drop in the ocean. The absence of any principle of selection or of a sustained style enables him to render aspects of things and of emotion which would have eluded a trained writer. He is, therefore, interesting even where he is grotesque or perverse. He has accomplished, by the sacrifice of almost every other good quality, something never so well done before. He has approached common life without bringing in his mind any higher standard by which to criticise it; he has seen it, not in contrast with an ideal, but as the expression of forces more indeterminate and elementary than itself; and the vulgar, in this cosmic setting, has appeared to him sublime.

There is clearly some analogy between a mass of images without structure and the notion of an absolute democracy. Whitman, inclined by his genius and habits to see life without relief or organisation, believed that his inclination in this respect corresponded with the spirit of his age and country, and that Nature and society, at least in the United States, were constituted after the fashion of his own mind. Being the poet of the average man, he wished all

157

men to be specimens of that average, and being the poet of a fluid
Nature, he believed that Nature was or should be a formless flux.
This personal bias of Whitman's was further encouraged by the
actual absence of distinction in his immediate environment. Surrounded by ugly things and common people, he felt himself happy,
ecstatic, overflowing with a kind of patriarchal love. He accordingly came to think that there was a spirit of the New World which
he embodied, and which was in complete opposition to that of the
Old, and that a literature upon novel principles was needed to
express and strengthen this American spirit.

Democracy was not to be merely a constitutional device for the
better government of given nations, not merely a movement for
the material improvement of the lot of the poorer classes. It was
to be a social and a moral democracy and to involve an actual
equality among all men. Whatever kept them apart and made it
impossible for them to be messmates together was to be discarded.
The literature of democracy was to ignore all extraordinary gifts
of genius or virtue, all distinction drawn even from great passions
or romantic adventures. In Whitman's works, in which this new
literature is foreshadowed, there is accordingly not a single character nor a single story. His only hero is Myself, the "single separate person," endowed with the primary impulses, with health, and
with sensitiveness to the elementary aspects of Nature. The perfect
man of the future, the prolific begetter of other perfect men, is to
work with his hands, chanting the poems of some future Walt,
some ideally democratic bard. Women are to have as nearly as
possible the same character as men: the emphasis is to pass from
family life and local ties to the friendship of comrades and the
general brotherhood of man. Men are to be vigorous, comfortable,
sentimental, and irresponsible.

This dream is, of course, unrealised and unrealisable, in America as elsewhere. Undeniably there are in America many suggestions of such a society and such a national character. But the
growing complexity and fixity of institutions necessarily tends to
obscure these traits of a primitive and crude democracy. What
Whitman seized upon as the promise of the future was in reality
the survival of the past. He sings the song of pioneers, but it is in
the nature of the pioneer that the greater his success the quicker
must be his transformation into something different. When Whit-

158

man made the initial and amorphous phase of society his ideal, he became the prophet of a lost cause. That cause was lost, not merely when wealth and intelligence began to take shape in the American Commonwealth, but it was lost at the very foundation of the world, when those laws of evolution were established which Whitman, like Rousseau, failed to understand. If we may trust Mr. Herbert Spencer, these laws involve a passage from the homogeneous to the heterogeneous, and a constant progress at once in differentiation and in organisation—all, in a word, that Whitman systematically deprecated or ignored. He is surely not the spokesman of the tendencies of his country, although he describes some aspects of its past and present condition: nor does he appeal to those whom he describes, but rather to the *dilettanti* he despises. He is regarded as representative chiefly by foreigners, who look for some grotesque expression of the genius of so young and prodigious a people.

Whitman, it is true, loved and comprehended men; but this love and comprehension had the same limits as his love and comprehension of Nature. He observed truly and responded to his observation with genuine and pervasive emotion. A great gregariousness, an innocent tolerance of moral weakness, a genuine admiration for bodily health and strength, made him bubble over with affection for the generic human creature. Incapable of an ideal passion, he was full of the milk of human kindness. Yet, for all his acquaintance with the ways and thoughts of the common man of his choice, he did not truly understand him. For to understand people is to go much deeper than they go themselves; to penetrate to their characters and disentangle their inmost ideals. Whitman's insight into man did not go beyond a sensuous sympathy; it consisted in a vicarious satisfaction in their pleasures, and an instinctive love of their persons. It never approached a scientific or imaginative knowledge of their hearts.

Therefore Whitman failed radically in his dearest ambition: he can never be a poet of the people. For the people, like the early races whose poetry was ideal, are natural believers in perfection. They have no doubts about the absolute desirability of wealth and learning and power, none about the worth of pure goodness and pure love. Their chosen poets, if they have any, will be always those who have known how to paint these ideals in lively even if in gaudy colours. Nothing is farther from the common people than the corrupt desire to be primitive. They instinctively look toward a more exalted life, which they imagine to be full of distinction and pleasure, and the idea of that brighter existence fills them with hope or with envy or with humble admiration.

If the people are ever won over to hostility to such ideals, it is only because they are cheated by demagogues who tell them that if all the flowers of civilisation were destroyed its fruits would become more abundant. A greater share of happiness, people think, would fall to their lot could they destroy everything beyond their own possible possessions. But they are made thus envious and ignoble only by a deception: what they really desire is an ideal good for themselves which they are told they may secure by depriving others of their preëminence. Their hope is always to enjoy perfect satisfaction themselves; and therefore a poet who loves the picturesque aspects of labour and vagrancy will hardly be the poet of the poor. He may have described their figure and occupation, in neither of which they are much interested; he will not have read their souls. They will prefer to him any sentimental story-teller, any sensational dramatist, any moralising poet; for they are hero-worshippers by temperament, and are too wise or too unfortunate to be much enamoured of themselves or of the conditions of their existence.

Fortunately, the political theory that makes Whitman's principle of literary prophecy and criticism does not always inspire his chants, nor is it presented, even in his prose works, quite bare and unadorned. In *Democratic Vistas* we find it clothed with something of the same poetic passion and lighted up with the same flashes of intuition which we admire in the poems. Even there the temperament is finer than the ideas and the poet wiser than the thinker. His ultimate appeal is really to something more primitive and general than any social aspirations, to something more elementary than an ideal of any kind. He speaks to those minds and to those moods in which sensuality is touched with mysticism. When the intellect is in abeyance, when we would "turn and live with the animals, they are so placid and self-contained," when we are weary of conscience and of ambition, and would yield ourselves for a while to the dream of sense, Walt Whitman is a welcome companion. The images he arouses in us, fresh, full of light and health and of a kind of frankness and beauty, are prized all the more at such a time because they are not choice, but drawn perhaps from a hideous and sordid environment. For this circumstance makes them a better means of escape from convention and from that fatigue and despair which lurk not far beneath the surface of conventional life. In casting off with self-assurance and a sense of fresh vitality the distinctions of tradition and reason a man may feel, as he sinks back comfortably to a lower level of sense and instinct, that he is returning to Nature or escaping into the infinite. Mysticism makes us proud and happy to renounce the work of intelligence, both in thought and in life, and persuades us that we become divine by remaining imperfectly human. Walt Whitman gives a new expression to this ancient and multiform tendency. He feels his own cosmic justification and he would lend the sanction of his inspiration to all loafers and holiday-makers. He would be the congenial patron of farmers and factory hands in their crude pleasures and pieties, as Pan was the patron of the shepherds of Arcadia: for he is sure that in spite of his hairiness and animality, the gods will acknowledge him as one of themselves and smile upon him from the serenity of Olympus.

III. ROBERT BROWNING

If we would do justice to Browning's work as a human document, and at the same time perceive its relation to the rational ideals of the imagination and to that poetry which passes into religion, we must keep, as in the case of Whitman, two things in mind. One is the genuineness of the achievement, the sterling quality of the vision and inspiration; these are their own justification when we approach them from below and regard them as manifesting a more direct or impassioned grasp of experience than is given to mildly blatant, convention-ridden minds. The other thing to remember is the short distance to which this comprehension is carried, its failure to approach any finality, or to achieve a recognition even of the traditional ideals of poetry and religion.

In the case of Walt Whitman such a failure will be generally felt; it is obvious that both his music and his philosophy are those of a barbarian, nay, almost of a savage. Accordingly there is need of dwelling rather on the veracity and simple dignity of his thought and art, on their expression of an order of ideas latent in all better experience. But in the case of Browning it is the success that is obvious to most people. Apart from a certain superficial grotesqueness to which we are soon accustomed, he easily arouses and engages the reader by the pithiness of his phrase, the volume of his passion, the vigour of his moral judgment, the liveliness of his historical fancy. It is obvious that we are in the presence of a great writer, of a great imaginative force, of a master in the expression of emotion. What is perhaps not so obvious, but no less true, is that we are in the presence of a barbaric genius, of a truncated imagination, of a thought and an art inchoate and ill-digested, of a volcanic eruption that tosses itself quite blindly and ineffectually into the sky.

The points of comparison by which this becomes clear are perhaps not in every one's mind, although they are merely the elements of traditional culture, æsthetic and moral. Yet even without reference to ultimate ideals, one may notice in Browning many superficial signs of that deepest of all failures, the failure in rationality and the indifference to perfection. Such a sign is the turgid style, weighty without nobility, pointed without naturalness or precision. Another sign is the "realism" of the personages, who, quite like men and women in actual life, are always displaying traits of character and never attaining character as a whole. Other hints might be found in the structure of the poems, where the dramatic substance does not achieve a dramatic form; in the metaphysical discussion, with its confused prolixity and absence of result; in the moral ideal, where all energies figure without their ultimate purposes; in the religion, which breaks off the expression of this life in the middle, and finds in that suspense an argument for immortality. In all this, and much more that might be recalled, a person coming to Browning with the habits of a cultivated mind might see evidence of some profound incapacity in the poet; but more careful reflection is necessary to understand the nature of this incapacity, its cause, and the peculiar accent which its presence gives to those ideas and impulses which Browning stimulates in us.

There is the more reason for developing this criticism (which might seem needlessly hostile and which time and posterity will doubtless make in their own quiet and decisive fashion) in that Browning did not keep within the sphere of drama and analysis, where he was strong, but allowed his own temperament and opinions to vitiate his representation of life, so that he sometimes turned the expression of a violent passion into the last word of what he thought a religion. He had a didactic vein, a habit of judging the spectacle he evoked and of loading the passions he depicted with his visible sympathy or scorn.

Now a chief support of Browning's popularity is that he is, for many, an initiator into the deeper mysteries of passion, a means of escaping from the moral poverty of their own lives and of feeling the rhythm and compulsion of the general striving. He figures, therefore, distinctly as a prophet, as a bearer of glad tidings, and it is easy for those who hail him as such to imagine that, knowing the labour of life so well, he must know something also of its fruits, and that in giving us the feeling of existence, he is also giving us its meaning. There is serious danger that a mind gathering from his pages the raw materials of truth, the unthreshed harvest of reality, may take him for a philosopher, for a rationaliser of what he describes. Awakening may be mistaken for enlightenment, and the galvanising of torpid sensations and impulses for wisdom.

Against such fatuity reason should raise her voice. The vital and historic forces that produce illusions of this sort in large groups of men are indeed beyond the control of criticism. The ideas of passion are more vivid than those of memory, until they become memories in turn. They must be allowed to fight out their desperate battle against the laws of Nature and reason. But it is worth while in the meantime, for the sake of the truth and of a just philosophy, to meet the varying though perpetual charlatanism of the world with a steady protest. As soon as Browning is proposed to us as a leader, as soon as we are asked to be not the occasional patrons of his art, but the pupils of his philosophy, we have a right to express the radical dissatisfaction which we must feel, if we are rational, with his whole attitude and temper of mind.

The great dramatists have seldom dealt with perfectly virtuous characters. The great poets have seldom represented mythologies that would bear scientific criticism. But by an instinct which constituted their greatness they have cast these mixed materials furnished by life into forms congenial to the specific principles of their art, and by this transformation they have made acceptable in the æsthetic sphere things that in the sphere of reality were evil or imperfect: in a word, their works have been beautiful as works of art. Or, if their genius exceeded that of the technical poet and rose to prophetic intuition, they have known how to create ideal characters, not possessed, perhaps, of every virtue accidentally needed in this world, but possessed of what is ideally better, of internal greatness and perfection. They have also known how to select and reconstruct their mythology so as to make it a true interpretation of moral life. When we read the maxims of Iago, Falstaff, or Hamlet, we are delighted if the thought strikes us as true, but we are not less delighted if it strikes us as false. These characters are not presented to us in order to enlarge our capacities of passion nor in order to justify themselves as processes of redemption; they are there, clothed in poetry and imbedded in plot, to entertain us with their imaginable feelings and their interesting errors. The poet, without being especially a philosopher, stands by virtue of his superlative genius on the plane of universal reason, far above the passionate experience which he overlooks and on which he reflects; and he raises us for the moment to his own level, to send us back again, if not better endowed for practical life, at least not unacquainted with speculation.

With Browning the case is essentially different. When his heroes are blinded by passion and warped by circumstance, as they almost always are, he does not describe the fact from the vantage-ground of the intellect and invite us to look at it from that point of view. On the contrary, his art is all self-expression or satire. For the most part his hero, like Whitman's, is himself; not appearing, as in the case of the American bard, *in puris naturalibus*, but masked in all sorts of historical and romantic finery. Sometimes, however, the personage, like Guido in *The Ring and the Book* or the "frustrate ghosts" of other poems, is merely a Marsyas, shown flayed and quivering to the greater glory of the poet's ideal Apollo. The impulsive utterances and the crudities of most of the speakers are passionately adopted by the poet as his own. He thus perverts what might have been a triumph of imagination into a failure of reason.

This circumstance has much to do with the fact that Browning, in spite of his extraordinary gift for expressing emotion, has hardly produced works purely and unconditionally delightful. They not only portray passion, which is interesting, but they betray it, which is odious. His art was still in the service of the will. He had not attained, in studying the beauty of things, that detachment of the phenomenon, that love of the form for its own sake, which is the secret of contemplative satisfaction. Therefore, the lamentable accidents of his personality and opinions, in themselves no worse than those of other mortals, passed into his art. He did not seek to elude them: he had no free speculative faculty to dominate them by. Or, to put the same thing differently, he was too much in earnest in his fictions, he threw himself too unreservedly into his creations. His imagination, like the imagination we have in dreams, was merely a vent for personal preoccupations. His art was inspired by purposes less simple and universal than the ends of imagination itself. His play of mind consequently could not be free or pure. The creative impulse could not reach its goal or manifest in any notable degree its own organic ideal.

We may illustrate these assertions by considering Browning's treatment of the passion of love, a passion to which he gives great prominence and in which he finds the highest significance.

Love is depicted by Browning with truth, with vehemence, and with the constant conviction that it is the supreme thing in life. The great variety of occasions in which it appears in his pages and the different degrees of elaboration it receives, leave it always of the same quality—the quality of passion. It never sinks into sensuality; in spite of its frequent extreme crudeness, it is always, in Browning's hands, a passion of the imagination, it is always love. On the other hand it never rises into contemplation: mingled as it may be with friendship, with religion, or with various forms of natural tenderness, it always remains a passion; it always remains a personal impulse, a hypnotisation, with another person for its object or its cause. Kept within these limits it is represented, in a series of powerful sketches, which are for most readers the gems of the Browning gallery, as the last word of experience, the highest phase of human life.

> *The woman yonder, there's no use in life*
> *But just to obtain her! Heap earth's woes in one*
> *And bear them—make a pile of all earth's joys*
> *And spurn them, as they help or help not this;*
> *Only, obtain her!*

When I do come, she will speak not, she will stand,
 Either hand
On my shoulder, give her eyes the first embrace
 Of my face,
Ere we rush, ere we extinguish sight and speech
 Each on each. . . .
O heart, O blood that freezes, blood that burns!
 Earth's returns
For whole centuries of folly, noise, and sin—
 Shut them in—
With their triumphs and their follies and the rest.
 Love is best.

In the piece called *In a Gondola* the lady says to her lover:—

 Heart to heart
And lips to lips! Yet once more, ere we part,
Clasp me and make me thine, as mine thou art.

And he, after being surprised and stabbed in her arms, replies:—

It was ordained to be so, sweet!—and best
Comes now, beneath thine eyes, upon thy breast:
Still kiss me! Care not for the cowards; care
Only to put aside thy beauteous hair
My blood will hurt! The Three I do not scorn
To death, because they never lived, but I
Have lived indeed, and so— (yet one more kiss)—
 can die.

We are not allowed to regard these expressions as the cries of souls blinded by the agony of passion and lust. Browning unmistakably adopts them as expressing his own highest intuitions. He so much admires the strength of this weakness that he does not admit that it is a weakness at all. It is with the strut of self-satisfaction, with the sensation, almost, of muscular Christianity, that he boasts of it through the mouth of one of his heroes, who is explaining to his mistress the motive of his faithful services as a minister of the queen:—

 She thinks there was more cause
In love of power, high fame, pure loyalty?

Perhaps she fancies men wear out their lives
Chasing such shades. . . .
I worked because I want you with my soul.

Readers of the fifth chapter of this volume* need not be reminded here of the contrast which this method of understanding
love offers to that adopted by the real masters of passion and imagination. They began with that crude emotion with which Browning ends; they lived it down, they exalted it by thought, they ex-
tracted the pure gold of it in a long purgation of discipline and
suffering. The fierce paroxysm which for him is heaven, was for
them the proof that heaven cannot be found on earth, that the
value of experience is not in experience itself but in the ideals
which it reveals. The intense, voluminous emotion, the sudden,
overwhelming self-surrender in which he rests was for them the
starting-point of a life of rational worship, of an austere and impersonal religion, by which the fire of love, kindled for a moment by
the sight of some creature, was put, as it were, into a censer, to burn
incense before every image of the Highest Good. Thus love ceased
to be a passion and became the energy of contemplation: it diffused
over the universe, natural and ideal, that light of tenderness and
that faculty of worship which the passion of love often is first to
quicken in a man's breast.

Of this art, recommended by Plato and practised in the Christian Church by all adepts of the spiritual life, Browning knew
absolutely nothing. About the object of love he had no misgivings.
What could the object be except somebody or other? The important thing was to love intensely and to love often. He remained in
the phenomenal sphere: he was a lover of experience; the ideal
did not exist for him. No conception could be farther from his
thought than the essential conception of any rational philosophy,
namely, that feeling is to be treated as raw material for thought,
and that the destiny of emotion is to pass into objects which shall
contain all its value while losing all its formlessness. This transformation of sense and emotion into objects agreeable to the intellect, into clear ideas and beautiful things, is the natural work of
reason; when it has been accomplished very imperfectly, or not at
all, we have a barbarous mind, a mind full of chaotic sensations,

*I.e. the essay "Platonic Love In Some Italian Poets."

167

objectless passions, and undigested ideas. Such a mind Browning's was, to a degree remarkable in one with so rich a heritage of civilisation.

The nineteenth century, as we have already said, has nourished the hope of abolishing the past as a force while it studies it as an object; and Browning, with his fondness for a historical stage setting and for the gossip of history, rebelled equally against the Pagan and the Christian discipline. The "Soul" which he trusted in was the barbarous soul, the "Spontaneous Me" of his half-brother Whitman. It was a restless personal impulse, conscious of obscure depths within itself which it fancied to be infinite, and of a certain vague sympathy with wind and cloud and with the universal mutation. It was the soul that might have animated Attila and Alaric when they came down into Italy, a soul not incurious of the tawdriness and corruption of the strange civilisation it beheld, but incapable of understanding its original spirit; a soul maintaining in the presence of that noble, unappreciated ruin all its own lordliness and energy, and all its native vulgarity.

Browning, who had not had the education traditional in his own country, used to say that Italy had been his university. But it was a school for which he was ill prepared, and he did not sit under its best teachers. For the superficial ferment, the worldly passions, and the crimes of the Italian Renaissance he had a keen interest and intelligence. But Italy has been always a civilised country, and beneath the trappings and suits of civilisation which at that particular time it flaunted so gayly, it preserved a civilised heart to which Browning's insight could never penetrate. There subsisted in the best minds a trained imagination and a cogent ideal of virtue. Italy had a religion, and that religion permeated all its life, and was the background without which even its secular art and secular passions would not be truly intelligible. The most commanding and representative, the deepest and most appealing of Italian natures are permeated with this religious inspiration. A Saint Francis, a Dante, a Michael Angelo, breathe hardly anything else. Yet for Browning these men and what they represented may be said not to have existed. He saw, he studied, and he painted a decapitated Italy. His vision could not mount so high as her head.

One of the elements of that higher tradition which Browning

was not prepared to imbibe was the idealisation of love. The passion he represents is lava hot from the crater, in no way moulded, smelted, or refined. He had no thought of subjugating impulses into the harmony of reason. He did not master life, but was mastered by it. Accordingly the love he describes has no wings; it issues in nothing. His lovers "extinguish sight and speech, each on each"; sense, as he says elsewhere, drowning soul. The man in the gondola may well boast that he can die; it is the only thing he can properly do. Death is the only solution of a love that is tied to its individual object and inseparable from the alloy of passion and illusion within itself. Browning's hero, because he has loved intensely, says that he has lived; he would be right, if the significance of life were to be measured by the intensity of the feeling it contained, and if intelligence were not the highest form of vitality. But had that hero known how to love better and had he had enough spirit to dominate his love, he might perhaps have been able to carry away the better part of it and to say that he could not die; for one half of himself and of his love would have been dead already and the other half would have been eternal, having fed—

> *On death, that feeds on men;*
> *And death once dead, there's no more dying then.*

The irrationality of the passions which Browning glorifies, making them the crown of life, is so gross that at times he cannot help perceiving it.

> *How perplexed*
> *Grows belief! Well, this cold clay clod*
> *Was man's heart:*
> *Crumble it, and what comes next? Is it God?*

Yes, he will tell us. These passions and follies, however desperate in themselves and however vain for the individual, are excellent as parts of the dispensation of Providence:—

> *Be hate that fruit or love that fruit,*
> *It forwards the general deed of man,*
> *And each of the many helps to recruit*
> *The life of the race by a general plan,*
> *Each living his own to boot.*

169

If we doubt, then, the value of our own experience, even perhaps of our experience of love, we may appeal to the interdepend-
ence of goods and evils in the world to assure ourselves that, in
view of its consequences elsewhere, this experience was great and
important after all. We need not stop to consider this supposed
solution, which bristles with contradictions; it would not satisfy
Browning himself, if he did not back it up with something more
to his purpose, something nearer to warm and transitive feeling.
The compensation for our defeats, the answer to our doubts, is
not to be found merely in a proof of the essential necessity and
perfection of the universe; that would be cold comfort, especially
to so uncontemplative a mind. No: that answer, and compensation
are to come very soon and very vividly to every private bosom.
There is another life, a series of other lives, for this to happen in.
Death will come, and—

> *I shall thereupon*
> *Take rest, ere I be gone*
> *Once more on my adventure brave and new,*
> *Fearless and unperplexed,*
> *When I wage battle next,*
> *What weapons to select, what armour to endue.*
>
> *For sudden the worst turns the best to the brave,*
> *The black minute's at end,*
> *And the element's rage, the fiend-voices that rave*
> *Shall dwindle, shall blend,*
> *Shall change, shall become first a peace out of pain,*
> *Then a light, then thy breast,*
> *O thou soul of my soul! I shall clasp thee again*
> *And with God be the rest!*

Into this conception of continued life Browning has put, as a
collection of further passages might easily show, all the items furnished by fancy or tradition which at the moment satisfied his
imagination—new adventures, reunion with friends, and even,
after a severe strain and for a short while, a little peace and quiet.
The gist of the matter is that we are to live indefinitely, that all
our faults can be turned to good, all our unfinished business set-

tled, and that therefore there is time for anything we like in this world and for all we need in the other. It is in spirit the direct opposite of the philosophic maxim of regarding the end, of taking care to leave a finished life and a perfect character behind us. It is the opposite, also, of the religious *memento mori*, of the warning that the time is short before we go to our account. According to Browning, there is no account: we have an infinite credit. With an unconscious and characteristic mixture of heathen instinct with Christian doctrine, he thinks of the other world as heaven, but of the life to be led there as of the life of Nature.

Aristotle observes that we do not think the business of life worthy of the gods, to whom we can only attribute contemplation; if Browning had had the idea of perfecting and rationalising this life rather than of continuing it indefinitely, he would have followed Aristotle and the Church in this matter. But he had no idea of anything eternal; and so he gave, as he would probably have said, a filling to the empty Christian immortality by making every man busy in it about many things. And to the irrational man, to the boy, it is no unpleasant idea to have an infinite number of days to live through, an infinite number of dinners to eat, with an infinity of fresh fights and new love-affairs, and no end of last rides together.

But it is a mere euphemism to call this perpetual vagrancy a development of the soul. A development means the unfolding of a definite nature, the gradual manifestation of a known idea. A series of phases, like the successive leaps of a water-fall, is no development. And Browning has no idea of an intelligible good which the phases of life might approach and with reference to which they might constitute a progress. His notion is simply that the game of life, the exhilaration of action, is inexhaustible. You may set up your tenpins again after you have bowled them over, and you may keep up the sport for ever. The point is to bring them down as often as possible with a master-stroke and a big bang. That will tend to invigorate in you that self-confidence which in this system passes for faith. But it is unmeaning to call such an exercise heaven, or to talk of being "with God" in such a life, in any sense in which we are not with God already and under all circumstances. Our destiny would rather be, as Browning himself expresses it in

171

a phrase which Attila or Alaric might have composed, "bound dizzily to the wheel of change to slake the thirst of God."

Such an optimism and such a doctrine of immortality can give no justification to experience which it does not already have in its detached parts. Indeed, those dogmas are not the basis of Browning's attitude, not conditions of his satisfaction in living, but rather overflowings of that satisfaction. The present life is presumably a fair average of the whole series of "adventures brave and new" which fall to each man's share; were it not found delightful in itself, there would be no motive for imagining and asserting that it is reproduced *in infinitum*. So too if we did not think that the evil in experience is actually utilised and visibly swallowed up in its good effects, we should hardly venture to think that God could have regarded as a good something which has evil for its condition and which is for that reason profoundly sad and equivocal. But Browning's philosophy of life and habit of imagination do not require the support of any metaphysical theory. His temperament is perfectly self-sufficient and primary; what doctrines he has are suggested by it and are too loose to give it more than a hesitant expression; they are quite powerless to give it any justification which it might lack on its face.

It is the temperament, then, that speaks; we may brush aside as unsubstantial, and even as distorting, the web of arguments and theories which it has spun out of itself. And what does the temperament say? That life is an adventure, not a discipline; that the exercise of energy is the absolute good, irrespective of motives or of consequences. These are the maxims of a frank barbarism; nothing could express better the lust of life, the dogged unwillingness to learn from experience, the contempt for rationality, the carelessness about perfection, the admiration for mere force, in which barbarism always betrays itself. The vague religion which seeks to justify this attitude is really only another outburst of the same irrational impulse.

In Browning this religion takes the name of Christianity, and identifies itself with one or two Christian ideas arbitrarily selected; but at heart it has far more affinity to the worship of Thor or of Odin than to the religion of the Cross. The zest of life becomes a cosmic emotion; we lump the whole together and cry, "Hurrah for the Universe!" A faith which is thus a pure matter of lustiness and inebriation rises and falls, attracts or repels, with the ebb and flow of the mood from which it springs. It is invincible because unseizable; it is as safe from refutation as it is rebellious to embodiment. But it cannot enlighten or correct the passions on which it feeds. Like a servile priest, it flatters them in the name of Heaven. It cloaks irrationality in sanctimony; and its admiration for every bluff folly, being thus justified by a theory, becomes a positive fanaticism, eager to defend any wayward impulse.

Such barbarism of temper and thought could hardly, in a man of Browning's independence and spontaneity, be without its counterpart in his art. When a man's personal religion is passive, as Shakespeare's seems to have been, and is adopted without question or particular interest from the society around him, we may not observe any analogy between it and the free creations of that man's mind. Not so when the religion is created afresh by the private imagination; it is then merely one among many personal works of art, and will naturally bear a family likeness to the others. The same individual temperament, with its limitations and its bias, will appear in the art which has appeared in the religion. And such is the case with Browning. His limitations as a poet are the counterpart of his limitations as a moralist and theologian; only in the poet they are not so regrettable. Philosophy and religion are nothing if not ultimate; it is their business to deal with general principles and final aims. Now it is in the conception of things fundamental and ultimate that Browning is weak; he is strong in the conception of things immediate. The pulse of the emotion, the bobbing up of the thought, the streaming of the reverie—these he can note down with picturesque force or imagine with admirable fecundity.

Yet the limits of such excellence are narrow, for no man can safely go far without the guidance of reason. His long poems have no structure—for that name cannot be given to the singular mechanical division of *The Ring and the Book*. Even his short poems have no completeness, no limpidity. They are little torsos made broken so as to stimulate the reader to the restoration of their missing legs and arms. What is admirable in them is pregnancy of phrase, vividness of passion and sentiment, heaped-up scraps of observation, occasional flashes of light, occasional beauties of versification,—all like

the quick sharp scratch
And blue spurt of a lighted match.

There is never anything largely composed in the spirit of pure beauty, nothing devotedly finished, nothing simple and truly just. The poet's mind cannot reach equilibrium; at best he oscillates between opposed extravagances; his final word is still a *boutade,* still an explosion. He has no sustained nobility of style. He affects with the reader a confidential and vulgar manner, so as to be more sincere and to feel more at home. Even in the poems where the effort at impersonality is most successful, the dramatic disguise is usually thrown off in a preface, epilogue or parenthesis. The author likes to remind us of himself by some confidential wink or genial poke in the ribs, by some little interlarded sneer. We get in these tricks of manner a taste of that essential vulgarity, that indifference to purity and distinction, which is latent but pervasive in all the products of this mind. The same disdain of perfection which appears in his ethics appears here in his verse, and impairs its beauty by allowing it to remain too often obscure, affected, and grotesque.

Such a correspondence is natural: for the same powers of conception and expression are needed in fiction, which, if turned to reflection, would produce a good philosophy. Reason is necessary to the perception of high beauty. Discipline is indispensable to art. Work from which these qualities are absent must be barbaric; it can have no ideal form and must appeal to us only through the sensuousness and profusion of its materials. We are invited by it to lapse into a miscellaneous appreciativeness, into a subservience to every detached impression. And yet, if we would only reflect even on these disordered beauties, we should see that the principle by which they delight us is a principle by which an ideal, an image of perfection, is inevitably evoked. We can have no pleasure or pain, nor any preference whatsoever, without implicitly setting up a standard of excellence, an ideal of what would satisfy us there. To make these implicit ideals explicit, to catch their hint, to work out their theme, and express clearly to ourselves and to the world what they are demanding in the place of the actual—that is the labour of reason and the task of genius. The two cannot be divided. Clarification of ideas and disentanglement of values are as

174

essential to æsthetic activity as to intelligence. A failure of reason is a failure of art and taste.

The limits of Browning's art, like the limits of Whitman's, can therefore be understood by considering his mental habit. Both poets had powerful imaginations, but the type of their imaginations was low. In Whitman imagination was limited to marshalling sensations in single file; the embroideries he made around that central line were simple and insignificant. His energy was concentrated on that somewhat animal form of contemplation, of which, for the rest, he was a great, perhaps an unequalled master. Browning rose above that level; with him sensation is usually in the background; he is not particularly a poet of the senses or of ocular vision. His favourite subject-matter is rather the stream of thought and feeling in the mind; he is the poet of soliloquy. Nature and life as they really are, rather than as they may appear to the ignorant and passionate participant in them, lie beyond his range. Even in his best dramas, like *A Blot in the 'Scutcheon* or *Colombe's Birthday*, the interest remains in the experience of the several persons as they explain it to us. The same is the case in *The Ring and the Book*, the conception of which, in twelve monstrous soliloquies, is a striking evidence of the poet's predilection for this form.

The method is, to penetrate by sympathy rather than to portray by intelligence. The most authoritative insight is not the poet's or the spectator's, aroused and enlightened by the spectacle, but the various heroes' own, in their moment of intensest passion. We therefore miss the tragic relief and exaltation, and come away instead with the uncomfortable feeling that an obstinate folly is apparently the most glorious and choiceworthy thing in the world. This is evidently the poet's own illusion, and those who do not happen to share it must feel that if life were really as irrational as he thinks it, it would be not only profoundly discouraging, which it often is, but profoundly disgusting, which it surely is not; for at least it reveals the ideal which it fails to attain.

This ideal Browning never disentangles. For him the crude experience is the only end, the endless struggle the only ideal, and the perturbed "Soul" the only organon of truth. The arrest of his intelligence at this point, before it has envisaged any rational object, explains the arrest of his dramatic art at soliloquy. His immersion in the forms of self-consciousness prevents him from dramatising the real relations of men and their thinkings to one another, to Nature, and to destiny. For in order to do so he would have had to view his characters from above (as Cervantes did, for instance), and to see them not merely as they appeared to themselves, but as they appear to reason. This higher attitude, however, was not only beyond Browning's scope, it was positively contrary to his inspiration. Had he reached it, he would no longer have seen the universe through the "Soul," but through the intellect, and he would not have been able to cry, "How the world is made for each one of us!" On the contrary, the "Soul" would have figured only in its true conditions, in all its ignorance and dependence, and also in its essential teachableness, a point against which Browning's barbaric wilfulness particularly rebelled. Rooted in his persuasion that the soul is essentially omnipotent and that to live hard can never be to live wrong, he remained fascinated by the march and method of self-consciousness, and never allowed himself to be weaned from that romantic fatuity by the energy of rational imagination, which prompts us not to regard our ideas as mere filling of a dream, but rather to build on them the conception of permanent objects and overruling principles, such as Nature, society, and the other ideals of reason. A full-grown imagination deals with these things, which do not obey the laws of psychological progression, and cannot be described by the methods of soliloquy.

We thus see that Browning's sphere, though more subtle and complex than Whitman's, was still elementary. It lay far below the spheres of social and historical reality in which Shakespeare moved; far below the comprehensive and cosmic sphere of every great epic poet. Browning did not even reach the intellectual plane of such contemporary poets as Tennyson and Matthew Arnold, who, whatever may be thought of their powers, did not study consciousness for itself, but for the sake of its meaning and of the objects which it revealed. The best things that come into a man's consciousness are the things that take him out of it—the rational things that are independent of his personal perception and of his personal existence. These he approaches with his reason, and they, in the same measure, endow him with their immortality. But precisely these things—the objects of science and of the constructive imagination —Browning always saw askance, in the outskirts of his field of vision, for his eye was fixed and riveted on the soliloquising Soul.

And this Soul being, to his apprehension, irrational, did not give itself over to those permanent objects which might otherwise have occupied it, but ruminated on its own accidental emotions, on its love-affairs, and on its hopes of going on so ruminating for ever.

The pathology of the human mind—for the normal, too, is pathological when it is not referred to the ideal—the pathology of the human mind is a very interesting subject, demanding great gifts and great ingenuity in its treatment. Browning ministers to this interest, and possesses this ingenuity and these gifts. More than any other poet he keeps a kind of speculation alive in the now large body of sentimental, eager-minded people, who no longer can find in a definite religion a form and language for their imaginative life. That this service is greatly appreciated speaks well for the ineradicable tendency in man to study himself and his destiny. We do not deny the achievement when we point out its nature and limitations. It does not cease to be something because it is taken to be more than it is.

In every imaginative sphere the nineteenth century has been an era of chaos, as it has been an era of order and growing organisation in the spheres of science and of industry. An ancient doctrine of the philosophers asserts that to chaos the world must ultimately return. And what is perhaps true of the cycles of cosmic change is certainly true of the revolutions of culture. Nothing lasts for ever: languages, arts, and religions disintegrate with time. Yet the perfecting of such forms is the only criterion of progress; the destruction of them the chief evidence of decay. Perhaps fate intends that we should have, in our imaginative decadence, the consolation of fancying that we are still progressing, and that the disintegration of religion and the arts is bringing us nearer to the protoplasm of sensation and passion. If energy and actuality are all that we care for, chaos is as good as order, and barbarism as good as discipline —better, perhaps, since impulse is not then restrained within any bounds of reason or beauty. But if the powers of the human mind are at any time adequate to the task of digesting experience, clearness and order inevitably supervene. The moulds of thought are imposed upon Nature, and the conviction of a definite truth arises together with the vision of a supreme perfection. It is only at such periods that the human animal vindicates his title of rational. If such an epoch should return, people will no doubt retrace our present gropings with interest and see in them gradual approaches to their own achievement. Whitman and Browning might well figure then as representatives of our time. For the merit of being representative cannot be denied them. The mind of our age, like theirs, is choked with materials, emotional, and inconclusive. They merely aggravate our characteristics, and their success with us is due partly to their own absolute strength and partly to our common weakness. If once, however, this imaginative weakness could be overcome, and a form found for the crude matter of experience, men might look back from the height of a new religion and a new poetry upon the present troubles of the spirit; and perhaps even these things might then be pleasant to remember.

HINTS OF EGOTISM
IN GOETHE

To take what views we will of things, if things will barely suffer us to take them, and then to declare that the things are mere terms in the views we take of them—that is transcendentalism. All transcendentalists are preoccupied with the self, but not all are egotists. Some regard as a sad disability this limitation of their knowledge to what they have created; they are humble, and almost ashamed to be human, and to possess a mind that must cut them off hopelessly from all reality. On the other hand there are many instinctive egotists who are not transcendentalists, either because their attention has not been called to this system, or because they discredit all speculation, or because they see clearly that the senses and the intellect, far from cutting us off from the real things that surround us, have the function of adjusting our action to them and informing our mind about them. Such an instinctive egotist does not allege that he creates the world by willing and thinking it, yet he is more interested in his own sensations, fancies, and preferences than in the other things in the world. The attention he bestows on things seems to him to bathe in light their truly interesting side. What he chiefly considers is his own experience—what he cared for first, what second, what he thinks to-day, what he will probably think to-morrow, what friends he has had, and how they have lost their charm, what religions he has believed in, and in general what contributions the universe has made to him and he to the universe. His interest in personality need not be confined to his own; he may have a dramatic imagination, and may assign their appropriate personality to all other people; every situation he hears of or invents may prompt him to conceive the thrilling passions and pungent thoughts of some *alter ego,* in whom latent sides of his own nature may be richly expressed. And impersonal things, too, may fascinate him, when he feels that they stir his genius fruitfully; and he will be the more ready to scatter his favours broadcast in that what concerns him is not any particular truth or person (things which might prove jealous and exclusive), but rather the exercise of his own powers of universal sympathy.

Something of this sort seems to appear in Goethe; and although his contact with philosophical egotism was but slight, and some of his wise maxims are incompatible with it, yet his romanticism, his feeling for development in everything, his private life, the nebulous character of his religion, and some of his most important works, like *Faust* and *Wilhelm Meister,* are all so full of the spirit of German philosophy, that it would be a pity not to draw some illustration for our subject from so pleasant a source.

There are hints of egotism in Goethe, but in Goethe there are hints of everything, and it would be easy to gather an imposing mass of evidence to the effect that he was not like the transcendentalists, but far superior to them. For one thing he was many-sided, not encyclopædic; he went out to greet the variety of things, he did not pack it together. He did not even arrange the phases of his experience (as he did those of Faust) in an order supposed to be a progress, although, as the commentators on *Faust* inform us, not a progress in mere goodness. Hegel might have *understood* all these moral attitudes, and described them in a way not meant to appear satirical; but he would have criticised and demolished them, and declared them obsolete—all but the one at which he happened to stop. Goethe *loved* them all; he hated to outgrow them, and if involuntarily he did so, at least he still honoured the feelings that he had lost. He kept his old age genial and green by that perennial love. In order to hold his head above water and be at peace in his own heart, he did not need to be a Christian, a pagan, or an epicurean; yet he lent himself unreservedly, in imagination, to Christianity, paganism, and sensuality—three things your transcendental egotist can never stomach: each in its way would impugn his self-sufficiency.

Nevertheless the sympathies of Goethe were only romantic or æsthetic; they were based on finding in others an interesting variation from himself, an exotic possibility, rather than an identity

with himself in thought or in fate. Christianity was an atmosphere
necessary to certain figures, that of Gretchen, for instance, who
would have been frankly vulgar without it; paganism was a learned
masque, in which one could be at once distinguished and emanci-
pated; and sensuality was a sentimental and scientific licence in
which the free mind might indulge in due season. The sympathy
Goethe felt with things was that of a lordly observer, a traveller, a
connoisseur, a philanderer; it was egotistical sympathy.

Nothing, for instance, was more romantic in Goethe than his
classicism. His *Iphigenie* and his *Helena* and his whole view of
antiquity were full of the pathos of distance. That pompous sweetness, that intense moderation, that moral somnambulism were too
intentional; and Goethe felt it himself. In *Faust*, after Helen has
evaporated, he makes the hero revisit his native mountains and
revert to the thought of Gretchen. It is a wise home-coming, because that craze for classicism which Helen symbolised alienated
the mind from real life and led only to hopeless imitations and
lackadaisical poses. Gretchen's garden, even the *Walpurgisnacht,*
was in truth more classical. This is only another way of saying that
in the attempt to be Greek the truly classical was missed even by
Goethe, since the truly classical is not foreign to anybody. It is
precisely that part of tradition and art which does not alienate us
from our own life or from nature, but reveals them in all their
depth and nakedness, freed from the fashions and hypocrisies of
time and place. The effort to reproduce the peculiarities of antiquity is a proof that we are not its natural heirs, that we do not
continue antiquity instinctively. People can mimic only what they
have not absorbed. They reconstruct and turn into an archæological masquerade only what strikes them as outlandish. The genuine
inheritors of a religion or an art never dream of reviving it; its an-
tique accidents do not interest them, and its eternal substance they
possess by nature.

The Germans are not in this position in regard to the ancients.
Whether sympathetic like Goethe, or disparaging like Burckhardt,
or both at once, like Hegel, they have seen in antiquity its local
colour, its mannerisms, its documents, and above all its contrasts
with the present. It was not so while the traditions of antiquity
were still living and authoritative. But the moderns, and especially
the Germans, have not a humble mind. They do not go to school

with the Greeks unfeignedly, as if Greek wisdom might possibly be true wisdom, a pure expression of experience and reason, valid essentially for us. They prefer to take that wisdom for a phase of sentiment, of course outgrown, but still enabling them to reconstruct learnedly the image of a fascinating past. This is what they call giving vitality to classical studies, turning them into *Kulturgeschichte*. This is a vitality lent by the living to the dead, not one drawn by the young and immature from a perennial fountain. In truth classical studies were vital only so long as they were still authoritative morally and set the standard for letters and life. They became otiose and pedantic when they began to serve merely to recover a dead past in its trivial detail, and to make us grow sentimental over its remoteness, its beauty, and its ruins.

How much freer and surer was Goethe's hand when it touched the cord of romanticism! How perfectly he knew the heart of the romantic egotist! The romantic egotist sets no particular limits to the range of his interests and sympathies; his programme, indeed, is to absorb the whole world. He is no wounded and disappointed creature, like Byron, that takes to sulking and naughtiness because things taste bitter in his mouth. He finds good and evil equally digestible. The personal egotism of Byron or of Musset after all was humble; it knew how weak it was in the universe. But absolute egotism in Goethe, as in Emerson, summoned all nature to minister to the self: all nature, if not actually compelled to this service by a human creative fiat, could at least be won over to it by the engaging heroism of her favourite child. In his warm pantheistic way Goethe felt the swarming universal life about him; he had no thought of dragooning it all, as sectarians and nationalists would, into vindicating some particular creed or nation. Yet that fertile and impartial universe left each life free and in uncensored competition with every other life. Each creature might feed blamelessly on all the others and become, if it could, the focus and epitome of the world. The development of self was the only duty, if only the self was developed widely and securely enough, with insight, calmness, and godlike irresponsibility.

Goethe exhibited this principle in practice more plainly, perhaps, than in theory. His family, his friends, his feelings were so many stepping-stones in his moral career; he expanded as he left

them behind. His love-affairs were means to the fuller realisation
of himself. Not that his love-affairs were sensual or his infidelities
callous; far from it. They often stirred him deeply and unsealed
the springs of poetry in his heart; that was precisely their function.
Every tender passion opened before him a primrose path into
which his inexorable genius led him to wander. If in passing he
must tread down some flower, that was a great sorrow to him; but
perhaps that very sorrow and his inevitable remorse were the most
needful and precious elements in the experience. Every pathetic
sweetheart in turn was a sort of Belgium to him; he violated her
neutrality with a sigh; his heart bled for her innocent sufferings,
and he never said afterwards in self-defence, like the German
Chancellor, that she was no better than she should be. But he
must press on. His beckoning destiny, the claims of his spiritual
growth, compelled him to sacrifice her and to sacrifice his own
lacerated feelings on the altar of duty to his infinite self. Indeed,
so truly supreme was this vocation that universal nature too, he
thought, was bound to do herself some violence in his behalf and
to grant him an immortal life, that so noble a process of self-
expansion might go on for ever.

Goethe's perfect insight into the ways of romantic egotism appears also in *Faust*, and not least in the latter parts of it, which
are curiously prophetic. If the hero of that poem has a somewhat
incoherent character, soft, wayward, emotional, yet at the same
time stubborn and indomitable, that circumstance only renders
him the fitter vehicle for absolute Will, a metaphysical entity whose
business is to be vigorous and endlessly energetic while remaining perfectly plastic. Faust was at first a scholar, fervid and grub-
bing, but so confused and impatient that he gave up science for
magic. Notwithstanding the shams of professional people which
offended him, a private and candid science was possible, which
might have brought him intellectual satisfaction; and the fact
would not have escaped him if he had been a simple lover of
truth. But absolute Will cannot be restricted to any single interest, much less to the pursuit of a frigid truth in which it cannot
believe; for the Will would not be absolute if it recognised any
truth which it had to discover; it can recognise and love only the
truth that it makes. Its method of procedure, we are told, consists

in first throwing out certain assumptions, such perhaps as that everything must have a cause or that life and progress must be everlasting; and the truth is then whatever conforms to these assumptions. But since evidently these assumptions might be utterly false, it is clear that what interests absolute Will is not truth at all, but only orthodoxy. A delightful illustration of this is given by Faust when, emulating Luther for a moment, he undertakes to translate the first verse of Saint John—that being the Gospel that impresses him most favourably. The point is not prosaically to discover what the Evangelist meant, but rather what he must and shall have meant. *The Word* will never do; *the Sense* would be somewhat better; but *In the beginning was Force* would have even more to recommend it. Suddenly, however, what absolute Will demands flashes upon him, and he writes down contentedly: *In the beginning was the Deed:*

> *Auf einmal seh' ich Rat*
> *Und schreibe getröst: Im Anfang war die That!*

Yet even in this exciting form, the life of thought cannot hold him long. He aches to escape from it; not that his knowledge of the sciences, as well as his magic, will not accompany him through life; he will not lose his acquired art nor his habit of reflection, and in this sense his career is really a progress, in that his experience accumulates; but the living interest is always something new. He turns to miscellaneous adventures, not excluding love; from that he passes to imperial politics, a sad mess, thence to sentimental classicism, rather an unreality, and finally to war, to public works, to trade, to piracy, to colonisation, and to clearing his acquired estates of tiresome old natives, who insist on ringing church bells and are impervious to the new *Kultur*. These public enterprises he finds more satisfying, perhaps only because he dies in the midst of them.

Are these hints of romantic egotism in Goethe mere echoes of his youth and of the ambient philosophy, echoes which he would have rejected if confronted with them in an abstract and doctrinal form, as he rejected the system of Fichte? Would he not have judged Schopenhauer more kindly? Above all, what would he have thought of Nietzsche, his own wild disciple? No doubt he would have wished to buttress and qualify in a thousand ways that faith

in absolute Will which they emphasised so exclusively, Schopenhauer in metaphysics and Nietzsche in morals. But the same faith
was a deep element in his own genius, as in that of his country, and
he would hardly have disowned it.

SHELLEY: OR THE POETIC VALUE
OF REVOLUTIONARY PRINCIPLES

IT IS possible to advocate anarchy in criticism as in politics, and
there is perhaps nothing coercive to urge against a man who maintains that any work of art is good enough, intrinsically and incom-
mensurably, if it pleased anybody at any time for any reason. In
practice, however, the ideal of anarchy is unstable. Irrefutable
by argument, it is readily overcome by nature. It melts away before the dogmatic operation of the anarchist's own will, as soon
as he allows himself the least creative endeavour. In spite of the
infinite variety of what is merely possible, human nature and will
have a somewhat definite constitution, and only what is harmonious with their actual constitution can long maintain itself in
the moral world. Hence it is a safe principle in the criticism of art
that technical proficiency, and brilliancy of fancy or execution,
cannot avail to establish a great reputation. They may dazzle for
a moment, but they cannot absolve an artist from the need of having an important subject-matter and a sane humanity.

If this principle is accepted, however, it might seem that certain artists, and perhaps the greatest, might not fare well at our
hands. How would Shelley, for instance, stand such a test? Every
one knows the judgment passed on Shelley by Matthew Arnold,
a critic who evidently relied on this principle, even if he preferred to speak only in the name of his personal tact and literary
experience. Shelley, Matthew Arnold said, was "a beautiful and
ineffectual angel, beating his wings in a luminous void in vain."
In consequence he declared that Shelley was not a classic, especially
as his private circle had had an unsavoury morality, to be expressed only by the French word *sale*, and as moreover Shelley

himself occasionally showed a distressing want of the sense of humour, which could only be called *bête*. These strictures, if a bit incoherent, are separately remarkably just. They unmask essential weaknesses not only in Shelley, but in all revolutionary people. The life of reason is a heritage and exists only through tradition. Half of it is an art, an adjustment to an alien reality, which only a long experience can teach: and even the other half, the inward inspiration and ideal of reason, must be also a common inheritance in the race, if people are to work together or so much as to understand one another. Now the misfortune of revolutionists is that they are disinherited, and their folly is that they wish to be disinherited even more than they are. Hence, in the midst of their passionate and even heroic idealisms, there is commonly a strange poverty in their minds, many an ugly turn in their lives, and an ostentatious vileness in their manners. They wish to be the leaders of mankind, but they are wretched representatives of humanity. In the concert of nature it is hard to keep in tune with oneself if one is out of tune with everything.

We should not then be yielding to any private bias, but simply noting the conditions under which art may exist and may be appreciated, if we accepted the classical principle of criticism and asserted that substance, sanity, and even a sort of pervasive wisdom are requisite for supreme works of art. On the other hand—who can honestly doubt it?—the rebels and individualists are the men of direct insight and vital hope. The poetry of Shelley in particular is typically poetical. It is poetry divinely inspired; and Shelley himself is perhaps no more ineffectual or more lacking in humour than an angel properly should be. Nor is his greatness all a matter of æsthetic abstraction and wild music. It is a fact of capital importance in the development of human genius that the great revolution in Christendom against Christianity, a revolution that began with the Renaissance and is not yet completed, should have found angels to herald it, no less than that other revolution did which began at Bethlehem; and that among these new angels there should have been one so winsome, pure, and rapturous as Shelley. How shall we reconcile these conflicting impressions? Shall we force ourselves to call the genius of Shelley second rate because it was revolutionary, and shall we attribute all enthusiasm for him to literary affectation or political prejudice? Or shall we rather abandon the orthodox principle that an important subject-matter and a sane spirit are essential to great works? Or shall we look for a different issue out of our perplexity, by asking if the analysis and comprehension are not perhaps at fault which declare that these things are not present in Shelley's poetry? This last is the direction in which I conceive the truth to lie. A little consideration will show us that Shelley really has a great subject-matter— what ought to be; and that he has a real humanity—though it is humanity in the seed, humanity in its internal principle, rather than in those deformed expressions of it which can flourish in the world.

Shelley seems hardly to have been brought up; he grew up in the nursery among his young sisters, at school among the rude boys, without any affectionate guidance, without imbibing any religious or social tradition. If he received any formal training or correction, he instantly rejected it inwardly, set it down as unjust and absurd, and turned instead to sailing paper boats, to reading romances or to writing them, or to watching with delight the magic of chemical experiments. Thus the mind of Shelley was thoroughly disinherited; but not, like the minds of most revolutionists, by accident and through the niggardliness of fortune, for few revolutionists would be such if they were heirs to a baronetcy. Shelley's mind disinherited itself out of allegiance to itself, because it was too sensitive and too highly endowed for the world into which it had descended. It rejected ordinary education, because it was incapable of assimilating it. Education is suitable to those few animals whose faculties are not completely innate, animals that, like most men, may be perfected by experience because they are born with various imperfect alternative instincts rooted equally in their system. But most animals, and a few men, are not of this sort. They cannot be educated, because they are born complete. Full of predeterminate intuitions, they are without intelligence, which is the power of seeing things as they are. Endowed with a specific, unshakable faith, they are impervious to experience: and as they burst the womb they bring ready-made with them their final and only possible system of philosophy.

Shelley was one of these spokesmen of the *a priori*, one of these nurslings of the womb, like a bee or a butterfly; a dogmatic, inspired, perfect, and incorrigible creature. He was innocent and cruel, swift and wayward, illuminated and blind. Being a finished child of nature, not a joint product, like most of us, of nature, history, and society, he abounded miraculously in his own clear sense, but was obtuse to the droll, miscellaneous lessons of fortune. The cannonade of hard, inexplicable facts that knocks into most of us what little wisdom we have left Shelley dazed and sore, perhaps, but uninstructed. When the storm was over, he began chirping again his own natural note. If the world continued to confine and obsess him, he hated the world, and gasped for freedom. Being incapable of understanding reality, he revelled in creating world after world in idea. For his nature was not merely pre-determined and obdurate, it was also sensitive, vehement, and fertile. With the soul of a bird, he had the senses of a man-child; the instinct of the butterfly was united in him with the instinct of the brooding fowl and of the pelican. This winged spirit had a heart. It darted swiftly on its appointed course, neither expecting nor understanding opposition; but when it met opposition it did not merely flutter and collapse; it was inwardly outraged, it protested proudly against fate, it cried aloud for liberty and justice.

The consequence was that Shelley, having a nature preformed but at the same time tender, passionate, and moral, was exposed to early and continual suffering. When the world violated the ideal which lay so clear before his eyes, that violation filled him with horror. If to the irrepressible gushing of life from within we add the suffering and horror that continually checked it, we shall have in hand, I think, the chief elements of his genius.

Love of the ideal, passionate apprehension of what ought to be, has for its necessary counterpart condemnation of the actual, wherever the actual does not conform to that ideal. The spontaneous soul, the soul of the child, is naturally revolutionary; and when the revolution fails, the soul of the youth becomes naturally pessimistic. All moral life and moral judgment have this deeply romantic character; they venture to assert a private ideal in the face of an intractable and omnipotent world. Some moralists begin by feeling the attraction of untasted and ideal perfection. These, like Plato, excel in elevation, and they are apt to despise rather than to reform the world. Other moralists begin by a revolt against the actual, at some point where they find the actual particularly galling. These excel in sincerity; their purblind conscience is urgent, and they are reformers in intent and sometimes even in action. But the ideals they frame are fragmentary and shallow, often mere provisional vague watchwords, like liberty, equality, and fraternity; they possess no positive visions or plans for moral life as a whole, like Plato's *Republic*. The utopian or visionary moralists are often rather dazed by this wicked world; being well-intentioned but impotent, they often take comfort in fancying that the ideal they pine for is already actually embodied on earth, or is about to be embodied on earth in a decade or two, or at least is embodied eternally in a sphere immediately above the earth, to which we shall presently climb, and be happy for ever.

Lovers of the ideal who thus hastily believe in its reality are called idealists, and Shelley was an idealist in almost every sense of that hard-used word. He early became an idealist after Berkeley's fashion, in that he discredited the existence of matter and embraced a psychological or (as it was called) intellectual system of the universe. In his drama *Hellas* he puts this view with evident approval into the mouth of Ahasuerus:

> *This whole*
> *Of suns and worlds and men and beasts and flowers,*
> *With all the silent or tempestuous workings*
> *By which they have been, are, or cease to be,*
> *Is but a vision;—all that it inherits*
> *Are motes of a sick eye, bubbles and dreams.*
> *Thought is its cradle and its grave; nor less*
> *The future and the past are idle shadows*
> *Of thought's eternal flight—they have no being:*
> *Nought is but that which feels itself to be.*

But Shelley was even more deeply and constantly an idealist after the manner of Plato; for he regarded the good as a magnet (inexplicably not working for the moment) that draws all life and motion after it; and he looked on the types and ideals of things as on eternal realities that subsist, beautiful and untarnished, when the glimmerings that reveal them to our senses have died away. From the infinite potentialities of beauty in the abstract, articulate mind draws certain bright forms—the Platonic ideas— "the gathered rays which are reality," as Shelley called them: and it is the light of these ideals cast on objects of sense that lends to these objects some degree of reality and value, making out of them "lovely apparitions, dim at first, then radiant . . . the progeny immortal of painting, sculpture, and rapt poesy."

The only kind of idealism that Shelley had nothing to do with is the kind that prevails in some universities, that Hegelian idealism which teaches that perfect good is a vicious abstraction, and maintains that all the evil that has been, is, and ever shall be is indispensable to make the universe as good as it possibly could be. In this form, idealism is simply contempt for all ideals, and a hearty adoration of things as they are; and as such it appeals mightily to the powers that be, in church and in state; but in that capacity it would have been as hateful to Shelley as the powers that be always were, and as the philosophy was that flattered them. For his moral feeling was based on suffering and horror at what is actual, no less than on love of a visioned good. His conscience was, to a most unusual degree, at once elevated and sincere. It was inspired in equal measure by prophecy and by indignation. He was carried away in turn by enthusiasm for what his ethereal and fertile fancy pictured as possible, and by detestation of the reality forced upon him instead. Hence that extraordinary moral fervour which is the soul of his poetry. His imagination is no playful undirected kaleidoscope; the images, often so tenuous and metaphysical, that crowd upon him, are all sparks thrown off at white heat, embodiments of a fervent, definite, unswerving inspiration. If we think that the *Cloud* or the *West Wind* or the *Witch of the Atlas* are mere fireworks, poetic dust, a sort of *bataille des fleurs* in which we are pelted by a shower of images —we have not understood the passion that overflows in them, as any long-nursed passion may, in any of us, suddenly overflow in an unwonted profusion of words. This is a point at which Francis Thompson's understanding of Shelley, generally so perfect, seems to me to go astray. The universe, Thompson tells us, was Shelley's box of toys. "He gets between the feet of the horses of the sun. He stands in the lap of patient Nature, and twines her loosened tresses after a hundred wilful fashions, to see how she will look nicest in his song." This last is not, I think, Shelley's motive; it is not the truth about the spring of his genius. He undoubtedly shatters the world to bits, but only to build it nearer to the heart's desire, only to make out of its coloured fragments some more Elysian home for love, or some more dazzling symbol for that infinite beauty which is the need—the profound, aching, imperative need—of the human soul. This recreative impulse of the poet's is not wilful, as Thompson calls it· it is moral. Like the *Sensitive Plant*

> *It loves even like Love,—its deep heart is full;*
> *It desires what it has not, the beautiful.*

The question for Shelley is not at all what will look nicest in his song; that is the preoccupation of mincing rhymesters, whose well is soon dry. Shelley's abundance has a more generous source; it springs from his passion for picturing what would be best, not in the picture, but in the world. Hence, when he feels he has pictured or divined it, he can exclaim:

> *The joy, the triumph, the delight, the madness,*
> *The boundless, overflowing, bursting gladness,*
> *The vaporous exultation, not to be confined!*
> *Ha! Ha! the animation of delight,*
> *Which wraps me like an atmosphere of light,*
> *And bears me as a cloud is borne by its own wind!*

To match this gift of bodying forth the ideal Shelley had his vehement sense of wrong; and as he seized upon and recast all images of beauty, to make them more perfectly beautiful, so, to vent his infinite horror of evil, he seized on all the worst images of crime or torture that he could find, and recast them so as to reach the quintessence of distilled badness. His pictures of war, famine, lust, and cruelty are, or seem, forced, although perhaps, as in the *Cenci*, he might urge that he had historical warrant for his descriptions, far better historical warrant, no doubt, than the beauty and happiness actually to be found in the world could give him for his *Skylark*, his *Epipsychidion*, or his *Prometheus*. But to exaggerate good is to vivify, to enhance our sense of moral coherence and beautiful naturalness; it is to render things more graceful, intelligible, and congenial to the spirit which they ought to serve. To aggravate evil, on the contrary, is to darken counsel—already dark enough—and the want of truth to nature in this pessimistic sort of exaggeration is not compensated for by any advantage.

The violence and, to my feeling, the wantonness of these invectives—for they are invectives in intention and in effect—may have seemed justified to Shelley by his political purpose. He was thirsting to destroy kings, priests, soldiers, parents, and heads of colleges—to destroy them, I mean, in their official capacity; and the exhibition of their vileness in all its diabolical purity might serve to remove scruples in the half-hearted. We, whom the nineteenth century has left so tender to historical rights and historical beauties, may wonder that a poet, an impassioned lover of the beautiful, could have been such a leveller, and such a vandal in his theoretical destructiveness. But here the legacy of the eighteenth century was speaking in Shelley, as that of the nineteenth is speaking in us: and moreover, in his own person, the very fertility of imagination could be a cause of blindness to the past and its contingent sanctities. Shelley was not left standing aghast, like a Philistine, before the threatened destruction of all traditional order. He had, and knew he had, the seeds of a far lovelier order in his own soul; there he found the plan or memory of a perfect commonwealth of nature ready to rise at once on the ruins of this sad world, and to make regret for it impossible.

So much for what I take to be the double foundation of Shelley's genius, a vivid love of ideal good on the one hand, and on the other, what is complementary to that vivid love, much suffering and horror at the touch of actual evils. On this double foundation he based an opinion which had the greatest influence on his poetry, not merely on the subject-matter of it, but also on the exuberance and urgency of emotion which suffuses it. This opinion was that all that caused suffering and horror in the world could be readily destroyed: it was the belief in perfectibility.

An animal that has rigid instincts and an *a priori* mind is probably very imperfectly adapted to the world he comes into: his organs cannot be moulded by experience and use; unless they are fitted by some miraculous pre-established harmony, or by natural selection, to things as they are, they will never be reconciled with them, and an eternal war will ensue between what the animal needs, loves, and can understand and what the outer reality offers. So long as such a creature lives—and his life will be difficult and short—events will continually disconcert and puzzle him; everything will seem to him unaccountable, inexplicable, unnatural.

He will not be able to conceive the real order and connection of things sympathetically, by assimilating his habits of thought to their habits of evolution. His faculties being innate and unadaptable will not allow him to correct his presumptions and axioms; he will never be able to make nature the standard of naturalness. What contradicts his private impulses will seem to him to contradict reason, beauty, and necessity. In this paradoxical situation he will probably take refuge in the conviction that what he finds to exist is an illusion, or at least not a fair sample of reality. Being so perverse, absurd, and repugnant, the given state of things must be, he will say, only accidental and temporary. He will be sure that his own *a priori* imagination is the mirror of all the eternal proprieties, and that as his mind can move only in one predetermined way, things cannot be prevented from moving in that same way save by some strange violence done to their nature. It would be easy, therefore, to set everything right again: nay, everything must be on the point of righting itself spontaneously. Wrong, of its very essence, must be in unstable equilibrium. The conflict between what such a man feels ought to exist and what he finds actually existing must, he will feel sure, end by a speedy revolution in things, and by the removal of all scandals; that it should end by the speedy removal of his own person, or by such a revolution in his demands as might reconcile him to existence, will never occur to him; or, if the thought occurs to him, it will seem too horrible to be true.

Such a creature cannot adapt himself to things by education, and consequently he cannot adapt things to himself by industry. His choice lies absolutely between victory and martyrdom. But at the very moment of martyrdom, martyrs, as is well known, usually feel assured of victory. The *a priori* spirit will therefore be always a prophet of victory, so long as it subsists at all. The vision of a better world at hand absorbed the Israelites in exile, St. John the Baptist in the desert, and Christ on the cross. The martyred spirit always says to the world it leaves, "This day thou shalt be with me in paradise."

In just this way, Shelley believed in perfectibility. In his latest poems—in *Hellas*, in *Adonais*—he was perhaps a little inclined to remove the scene of perfectibility to a metaphysical region, as the Christian church soon removed it to the other world. Indeed, an earth really made perfect is hardly distinguishable from a post-humous heaven: so profoundly must everything in it be changed, and so angel-like must every one in it become. Shelley's earthly paradise, as described in *Prometheus* and in *Epipsychidion,* is too festival-like, too much of a mere culmination, not to be fugitive: it cries aloud to be translated into a changeless and metaphysical heaven, which to Shelley's mind could be nothing but the realm of Platonic ideas, where "life, like a dome of many-coloured glass," no longer "stains the white radiance of eternity." But the age had been an age of revolution and, in spite of disappointments, retained its faith in revolution; and the young Shelley was not satisfied with a paradise removed to the intangible realms of poetry or of religion; he hoped, like the old Hebrews, for a paradise on earth. His notion was that eloquence could change the heart of man, and that love, kindled there by the force of reason and of example, would transform society. He believed, Mrs. Shelley tells us, "that mankind had only to will that there should be no evil, and there would be none." And she adds: "That man could be so perfectionised as to be able to expel evil from his own nature, and from the greater part of creation, was the cardinal point of his system." This cosmic extension of the conversion of men reminds one of the cosmic extension of the Fall conceived by St. Augustine; and in the *Prometheus* Shelley has allowed his fancy, half in symbol, half in glorious physical hyperbole, to carry the warm contagion of love into the very bowels of the earth, and even the moon, by reflection, to catch the light of love, and be alive again.

Shelley, we may safely say, did not understand the real constitution of nature. It was hidden from him by a cloud, all woven of shifting rainbows and bright tears. Only his emotional haste made it possible for him to entertain such opinions as he did entertain; or rather, it was inevitable that the mechanism of nature, as it is in its depths, should remain in his pictures only the shadowiest of backgrounds. His poetry is accordingly a part of the poetry of illusion; the poetry of truth, if we have the courage to hope for such a thing, is reserved for far different and yet unborn poets. But it is only fair to Shelley to remember that the moral being of mankind is as yet in its childhood; all poets play with images not understood; they touch on emotions sharply, at random, as in a dream;

they suffer each successive vision, each poignant sentiment, to evaporate into nothing, or to leave behind only a heart vaguely softened and fatigued, a gentle languor, or a tearful hope. Every modern school of poets, once out of fashion, proves itself to have been sadly romantic and sentimental. None has done better than to spangle a confused sensuous pageant with some sparks of truth, or to give it some symbolic relation to moral experience. And this Shelley has done as well as anybody: all other poets also have been poets of illusion. The distinction of Shelley is that his illusions are so wonderfully fine, subtle, and palpitating; that they betray passions and mental habits so singularly generous and pure. And why? Because he did not believe in the necessity of what is vulgar, and did not pay that demoralising respect to it, under the title of fact or of custom, which it exacts from most of us. The past seemed to him no valid precedent, the present no final instance. As he believed in the imminence of an overturn that should make all things new, he was not checked by any divided allegiance, by any sense that he was straying into the vapid or fanciful, when he created what he justly calls "Beautiful idealisms of moral excellence."

That is what his poems are fundamentally—the *Skylark,* and the *Witch of the Atlas,* and the *Sensitive Plant* no less than the grander pieces. He infused into his gossamer world the strength of his heroic conscience. He felt that what his imagination pictured was a true symbol of what human experience should and might pass into. Otherwise he would have been aware of playing with idle images; his poetry would have been mere millinery and his politics mere business; he would have been a worldling in art and in morals. The clear fire, the sustained breath, the fervent accent of his poetry are due to his faith in his philosophy. As Mrs. Shelley expressed it, he "had no care for any of his poems that did not emanate from the depths of his mind, and develop some high and abstruse truth." Had his poetry not dealt with what was supreme in his own eyes, and dearest to his heart, it could never have been the exquisite and entrancing poetry that it is. It would not have had an adequate subject-matter, as, in spite of Matthew Arnold, I think it had; for nothing can be empty that contains such a soul. An angel cannot be ineffectual if the standard of efficiency is moral; he is what all other things bring about, when

196

they are effectual. And a void that is alive with the beating of luminous wings, and of a luminous heart, is quite sufficiently peopled. Shelley's mind was angelic not merely in its purity and fervour, but also in its moral authority, in its prophetic strain. What was conscience in his generation was life in him.

The mind of man is not merely a sensorium. His intelligence is not merely an instrument for adaptation. There is a germ within, a nucleus of force and organisation, which can be unfolded, under favourable circumstances, into a perfection inwardly determined. Man's constitution is a fountain from which to draw an infinity of gushing music, not representing anything external, yet not unmeaning on that account, since it represents the capacities and passions latent in him from the beginning. These potentialities, however, are no oracles of truth. Being innate they are arbitrary; being *a priori* they are subjective; but they are good principles for fiction, for poetry, for morals, for religion. They are principles for the true expression of man, but not for the true description of the universe. When they are taken for the latter, fiction becomes deception, poetry illusion, morals fanaticism, and religion bad science. The orgy of delusion into which we are then plunged comes from supposing the *a priori* to be capable of controlling the actual, and the innate to be a standard for the true. That rich and definite endowment which might have made the distinction of the poet, then makes the narrowness of the philosopher. So Shelley, with a sort of tyranny of which he does not suspect the possible cruelty, would impose his ideal of love and equality upon all creatures; he would make enthusiasts of clowns and doves of vultures. In him, as in many people, too intense a need of loving excludes the capacity for intelligent sympathy. His feeling cannot accommodate itself to the inequalities of human nature: his good-will is a geyser, and will not consent to grow cool, and to water the flat and vulgar reaches of life. Shelley is blind to the excellences of what he despises, as he is blind to the impossibility of realising what he wants. His sympathies are narrow as his politics are visionary, so that there is a certain moral incompetence in his moral intensity. Yet his abstraction from half of life, or from nine-tenths of it, was perhaps necessary if silence and space were to be won in his mind for its own upwelling, ecstatic harmonies. The world we have always with us, but such spirits we have not always. And the spirit has fire enough within to make a second stellar universe.

An instance of Shelley's moral incompetence in moral intensity is to be found in his view of selfishness and evil. From the point of view of pure spirit, selfishness is quite absurd. As a contemporary of ours has put it: "It is so evident that it is better to secure a greater good for A than a lesser good for B that it is hard to find any still more evident principle by which to prove this. And if A happens to be some one else, and B to be myself, that cannot affect the question." It is very foolish not to love your neighbour as yourself, since his good is no less good than yours. Convince people of this—and who can resist such perfect logic?—and *presto* all property in things has disappeared, all jealousy in love, and all rivalry in honour. How happy and secure every one will suddenly be, and how much richer than in our mean, blind, competitive society! The single word love—and we have just seen that love is a logical necessity—offers an easy and final solution to all moral and political problems. Shelley cannot imagine why this solution is not accepted, and why logic does not produce love. He can only wonder and grieve that it does not; and since selfishness and ill-will seem to him quite gratuitous, his ire is aroused; he thinks them unnatural and monstrous. He could not in the least understand evil, even when he did it himself; all villainy seemed to him wanton, all lust frigid, all hatred insane. All was an abomination alike that was not the lovely spirit of love.

Now this is a very unintelligent view of evil; and if Shelley had had time to read Spinoza—an author with whom he would have found himself largely in sympathy—he might have learned that nothing is evil in itself, and that what is evil in things is not due to any accident in creation, nor to groundless malice in man. Evil is an inevitable aspect which things put on when they are struggling to preserve themselves in the same habitat, in which there is not room or matter enough for them to prosper equally side by side. Under these circumstances the partial success of any creature—say, the cancer-microbe—is an evil from the point of view of those other creatures—say, men—to whom that success is a defeat. Shelley sometimes half perceived this inevitable tragedy. So he says of the fair lady in the *Sensitive Plant*:

> *All killing insects and gnawing worms,*
> *And things of obscene and unlovely forms,*

She bore in a basket of Indian woof,
Into the rough woods far aloof—
In a basket of grasses and wild flowers full,
The freshest her gentle hands could pull
For the poor banished insects, whose intent,
Although they did ill, was innocent.

Now it is all very well to ask cancer-microbes to be reasonable, and go feed on oak-leaves, if the oak-leaves do not object; oak-leaves might be poison for them, and in any case cancer-microbes cannot listen to reason; they must go on propagating where they are, unless they are quickly and utterly exterminated. And fundamentally men are subject to the same fatality exactly; they cannot listen to reason unless they are reasonable; and it is unreasonable to expect that, being animals, they should be reasonable exclusively. Imagination is indeed at work in them, and makes them capable of sacrificing themselves for any idea that appeals to them, for their children, perhaps, or for their religion. But they are not more capable of sacrificing themselves to what does not interest them than the cancer-microbes are of sacrificing themselves to men.

When Shelley marvels at the perversity of the world, he shows his ignorance of the world. The illusion he suffers from is constitutional, and such as larks and sensitive plants are possibly subject to in their way: what he is marvelling at is really that anything should exist at all not a creature of his own moral disposition. Consequently the more he misunderstands the world and bids it change its nature, the more he expresses his own nature: so that all is not vanity in his illusion, nor night in his blindness. The poet sees most clearly what his ideal is; he suffers no illusion in the expression of his own soul. His political utopias, his belief in the power of love, and his cryingly subjective and inconstant way of judging people are one side of the picture; the other is his lyrical power, wealth, and ecstasy. If he had understood universal nature, he would not have so glorified in his own. And his own nature was worth glorifying; it was, I think, the purest, tenderest, richest, most rational nature ever poured forth in verse. I have not read in any language such a full expression of the unadulterated instincts of the mind. The world of Shelley is that which the vital monad within many of us—I will not say within all, for who shall set bounds to the variations of human nature?—the world which the vital monad within many of us, I say, would gladly live in if it could have its way.

Matthew Arnold said that Shelley was not quite sane; and certainly he was not quite sane, if we place sanity in justness of external perception, adaptation to matter, and docility to the facts; but his lack of sanity was not due to any internal corruption; it was not even an internal eccentricity. He was like a child, like a Platonic soul just fallen from the Empyrean; and the child may be dazed, credulous, and fanciful; but he is not mad. On the contrary, his earnest playfulness, the constant distraction of his attention from observation to day-dreams, is the sign of an inward order and fecundity appropriate to his age. If children did not see visions, good men would have nothing to work for. It is the soul of observant persons, like Matthew Arnold, that is apt not to be quite sane and whole inwardly, but somewhat warped by familiarity with the perversities of real things, and forced to misrepresent its true ideal, like a tree bent by too prevalent a wind. Half the fertility of such a soul is lost, and the other half is denaturalised. No doubt, in its sturdy deformity, the practical mind is an instructive and not unpleasing object, an excellent, if somewhat pathetic, expression of the climate in which it is condemned to grow, and of its dogged clinging to an ingrate soil; but it is a wretched expression of its innate possibilities. Shelley, on the contrary, is like a palm-tree in the desert or a star in the sky; he is perfect in the midst of the void. His obtuseness to things dynamic—to the material order—leaves his whole mind free to develop things æsthetic after their own kind; his abstraction permits purity, his playfulness makes room for creative freedom, his ethereal quality is only humanity having its way.

We perhaps do ourselves an injustice when we think that the heart of us is sordid; what is sordid is rather the situation that cramps or stifles the heart. In itself our generative principle is surely no less fertile and generous than the generative principle of crystals or flowers. As it can produce a more complex body, it is capable of producing a more complex mind; and the beauty and life of this mind, like that of the body, is all predetermined in the seed. Circumstances may suffer the organism to develop, or prevent it from doing so; they cannot change its plan without making it ugly and deformed. What Shelley's mind draws from the outside,

200

its fund of images, is like what the germ of the body draws from the outside, its food—a mass of mere materials to transform and reorganise. With these images Shelley constructs a world determined by his native genius, as the seed organises out of its food a predetermined system of nerves and muscles. Shelley's poetry shows us the perfect but naked body of human happiness. What clothes circumstances may compel most of us to add may be a necessary concession to climate, to custom, or to shame; they can hardly add a new vitality or any beauty comparable to that which they hide.

When the soul, as in Shelley's case, is all goodness, and when the world seems all illegitimacy and obstruction, we need not wonder that *freedom* should be regarded as a panacea. Even if freedom had not been the idol of Shelley's times, he would have made an idol of it for himself. "I never could discern in him," says his friend Hogg, "any more than two principles. The first was a strong, irrepressible love of liberty. . . . The second was an equally ardent love of toleration . . . and . . . an intense abhorrence of persecution." We all fancy nowadays that we believe in liberty and abhor persecution; but the liberty we approve of is usually only a variation in social compulsions, to make them less galling to our latest sentiments than the old compulsions would be if we retained them. Liberty of the press and liberty to vote do not greatly help us in living after our own mind, which is, I suppose, the only positive sort of liberty. From the point of view of a poet, there can be little essential freedom so long as he is forbidden to live with the people he likes, and compelled to live with the people he does not like. This, to Shelley, seemed the most galling of tyrannies; and free love was, to his feeling, the essence and test of freedom. Love must be spontaneous to be a spiritual bond in the beginning and it must remain spontaneous if it is to remain spiritual. To be bound by one's past is as great a tyranny to pure spirit as to be bound by the sin of Adam, or by the laws of Artaxerxes; and those of us who do not believe in the possibility of free love ought to declare frankly that we do not, at bottom, believe in the possibility of freedom.

> *I never was attached to that great sect*
> *Whose doctrine is that each one should select,*
> *Out of the crowd, a mistress or a friend*

And all the rest, though fair and wise, commend
To cold oblivion; though it is the code
Of modern morals, and the beaten road
Which those poor slaves with weary footsteps tread
Who travel to their home among the dead
By the broad highway of the world, and so
With one chained friend, perhaps a jealous foe,
The dreariest and the longest journey go.
True love in this differs from gold and clay,
That to divide is not to take away.
Love is like understanding that grows bright
Gazing on many truths. . . . Narrow
The heart that loves, the brain that contemplates,
The life that wears, the spirit that creates
One object and one form, and builds thereby
A sepulchre for its eternity!

The difficulties in reducing this charming theory of love to practice are well exemplified in Shelley's own life. He ran away with his first wife not because she inspired any uncontrollable passion, but because she declared she was a victim of domestic oppression and threw herself upon him for protection. Nevertheless, when he discovered that his best friend was making love to her, in spite of his free-love principles, he was very seriously annoyed. When he presently abandoned her, feeling a spiritual affinity in another direction, she drowned herself in the Serpentine: and his second wife needed all her natural sweetness and all her inherited philosophy to reconcile her to the waves of Platonic enthusiasm for other ladies which periodically swept the too sensitive heart of her husband. Free love would not, then, secure freedom from complications; it would not remove the present occasion for jealousy, reproaches, tragedies, and the dragging of a lengthening chain. Freedom of spirit cannot be translated into freedom of action; you may amend laws, and customs, and social entanglements, but you will still have them; for this world is a lumbering mechanism and not, like love, a plastic dream. Wisdom is very old and therefore often ironical, and it has long taught that it is well for those who would live in the spirit to keep as clear as possible of the world: and that marriage, especially a free-love marriage, is a snare for poets. Let them endure to love freely, hopelessly, and infinitely, after the manner of Plato and Dante, and even of Goethe, when Goethe really loved: that exquisite sacrifice will improve their verse, and it will not kill them. Let them follow in the traces of Shelley when he wrote in his youth: "I have been most of the night pacing a church-yard. I must now engage in scenes of strong interest. . . . I expect to gratify some of this insatiable feeling in poetry. . . . I slept with a loaded pistol and some poison last night, but did not die." Happy man if he had been able to add, "And did not marry!"

Last among the elements of Shelley's thought I may perhaps mention his atheism. Shelley called himself an atheist in his youth; his biographers and critics usually say that he was, or that he became, a pantheist. He was an atheist in the sense that he denied the orthodox conception of a deity who is a voluntary creator, a legislator, and a judge; but his aversion to Christianity was not founded on any sympathetic or imaginative knowledge of it; and a man who preferred the *Paradiso* of Dante to almost any other poem, and preferred it to the popular *Inferno* itself, could evidently be attracted by Christian ideas and sentiment the moment they were presented to him as expressions of moral truth rather than as gratuitous dogmas. A pantheist he was in the sense that he felt how fluid and vital this whole world is; but he seems to have had no tendency to conceive any conscious plan or logical necessity connecting the different parts of the whole; so that rather than a pantheist he might be called a panpsychist; especially as he did not subordinate morally the individual to the cosmos. He did not surrender the authority of moral ideals in the face of physical necessity, which is properly the essence of pantheism. He did the exact opposite; so much so that the chief characteristic of his philosophy is its Promethean spirit. He maintained that the basis of moral authority was internal, diffused among all individuals; that it was the natural love of the beautiful and the good wherever it might spring, and however fate might oppose it.

> *To suffer . . .*
> *To forgive . . .*
> *To defy Power . . .*
> *To love and bear; to hope, still hope creates*
> *From its own wreck the thing it contemplates;*

> *Neither to change, nor falter, nor repent;*
> *This . . . is to be*
> *Good, great and joyous, beautiful and free.*

Shelley was also removed from any ordinary atheism by his truly speculative sense for eternity. He was a thorough Platonist. All metaphysics perhaps is poetry, but Platonic metaphysics is good poetry, and to this class Shelley's belongs. For instance:

> *The pure spirit shall flow*
> *Back to the burning fountain whence it came,*
> *A portion of the eternal, which must glow*
> *Through time and change, unquenchably the same.*
> *Peace, peace! he is not dead, he doth not sleep!*
> *He hath awakened from the dream of life.*
> *'Tis we who, lost in stormy visions, keep*
> *With phantoms an unprofitable strife.*
>
> *He is made one with Nature. There is heard*
> *His voice in all her music, from the moan*
> *Of thunder, to the song of night's sweet bird.*
>
> *He is a portion of the loveliness*
> *Which once he made more lovely.*
>
> *The splendours of the firmament of time*
> *May be eclipsed, but are extinguished not:*
> *Like stars to their appointed height they climb,*
> *And death is a low mist which cannot blot*
> *The brightness it may veil. When lofty thought*
> *Lifts a young heart above its mortal lair,*
> *. . . the dead live there.*

Atheism or pantheism of this stamp cannot be taxed with being gross or materialistic; the trouble is rather that it is too hazy in its sublimity. The poet has not perceived the natural relation between facts and ideals so clearly or correctly as he has felt the moral relation between them. But his allegiance to the intuition which defies, for the sake of felt excellence, every form of idolatry or cowardice wearing the mask of religion—this allegiance is itself the purest religion; and it is capable of inspiring the sweetest and most absolute poetry. In daring to lay bare the truths of fate, the poet creates for himself the subtlest and most heroic harmonies; and he is comforted for the illusions he has lost by being made incapable of desiring them.

We have seen that Shelley, being unteachable, could never put together any just idea of the world: he merely collected images and emotions, and out of them made worlds of his own. His poetry accordingly does not well express history, nor human character, nor the constitution of nature. What he unrolls before us instead is, in a sense, fantastic; it is a series of landscapes, passions, and cataclysms such as never were on earth, and never will be. If you are seriously interested only in what belongs to earth you will not be seriously interested in Shelley. Literature, according to Matthew Arnold, should be criticism of life, and Shelley did not criticise life; so that his poetry had no solidity. But is life, we may ask, the same thing as the circumstances of life on earth? Is the spirit of life, that marks and judges those circumstances, itself nothing? Music is surely no description of the circumstances of life; yet it is relevant to life unmistakably, for it stimulates by means of a torrent of abstract movements and images the formal and emotional possibilities of living which lie in the spirit. By so doing music becomes a part of life, a congruous addition, a parallel life, as it were, to the vulgar one. I see no reason, in the analogies of the natural world, for supposing that the circumstances of human life are the only circumstances in which the spirit of life can disport itself. Even on this planet, there are sea-animals and air-animals, ephemeral beings and self-centered beings, as well as persons who can grow as old as Matthew Arnold, and be as fond as he was of classifying other people. And beyond this planet, and in the interstices of what our limited senses can perceive, there are probably many forms of life not criticised in any of the books which Matthew Arnold said we should read in order to know the best that has been thought and said in the world. The future, too, even among men, may contain, as Shelley puts it, many "arts, though unimagined, yet to be." The divination of poets cannot, of course, be expected to reveal any of these hidden regions as they actually exist or will exist; but what would be the advantage of revealing them? It could only be what the advantage of criticising human life would be also, to improve subsequent life indirectly by turning it towards attainable goods, and is it not as important a thing to improve life directly and in the present, if one has the gift, by enriching rather than criticising it? Besides, there is need of fixing the ideal by which criticism is to be guided. If you have no image of happiness or beauty or perfect goodness before you, how are you to judge what portions of life are important, and what rendering of them is appropriate?

Being a singer inwardly inspired, Shelley could picture the ideal goals of life, the ultimate joys of experience, better than a discursive critic or observer could have done. The circumstances of life are only the bases or instruments of life: the fruition of life is not in retrospect, not in description of the instruments, but in expression of the spirit itself, to which those instruments may prove useful; as music is not a criticism of violins, but a playing upon them. This expression need not resemble its ground. Experience is diversified by colours that are not produced by colours, sounds that are not conditioned by sounds, names that are not symbols for other names, fixed ideal objects that stand for ever-changing material processes. The mind is fundamentally lyrical, inventive, redundant. Its visions are its own offspring, hatched in the warmth of some favourable cosmic gale. The ambient weather may vary, and these visions be scattered; but the ideal world they pictured may some day be revealed again to some other poet similarly inspired; the possibility of restoring it, or something like it, is perpetual. It is precisely because Shelley's sense for things is so fluid, so illusive, that it opens to us emotionally what is a serious scientific probability; namely, that human life is not all life, nor the landscape of earth the only admired landscape in the universe; that the ancients who believed in gods and spirits were nearer the virtual truth (however anthropomorphically they may have expressed themselves) than any philosophy or religion that makes human affairs the centre and aim of the world. Such moral imagination is to be gained by sinking into oneself, rather than by observing remote happenings, because it is at its heart, not at its finger-tips, that the human soul touches matter, and is akin to whatever other centres of life may people the infinite.

For this reason the masters of spontaneity, the prophets, the inspired poets, the saints, the mystics, the musicians are welcome and most appealing companions. In their simplicity and abstraction from the world they come very near the heart. They say little and help much. They do not picture life, but have life, and give it. So we may say, I think, of Shelley's magic universe what he said of Greece; if it

> *Must be*
> *A wreck, yet shall its fragments re-assemble,*
> *And build themselves again impregnably*
> *In a diviner clime,*
> *To Amphionic music, on some cape sublime*
> *Which frowns above the idle foam of time.*

"Frowns," says Shelley rhetorically, as if he thought that something timeless, something merely ideal, could be formidable, or could threaten existing things with any but an ideal defeat. Tremendous error! Eternal possibilities may indeed beckon; they may attract those who instinctively pursue them as a star may guide those who wish to reach the place over which it happens to shine. But an eternal possibility has no material power. It is only one of an infinity of other things equally possible intrinsically, yet most of them quite unrealisable in this world of blood and mire. The realm of eternal essences rains down no Jovian thunderbolts, but only a ghostly Uranian calm. There is no frown there; rather, a passive and universal welcome to any who may have in them the will and the power to climb. Whether any one has the will depends on his material constitution, and whether he has the power depends on the firm texture of that constitution and on circumstances happening to be favourable to its operation. Otherwise what the rebel or the visionary hails as his ideal will be no picture of his destiny or of that of the world. It will be, and will always remain, merely a picture of his heart. This picture, indestructible in its ideal essence, will mirror also the hearts of those who may share, or may have shared, the nature of the poet who drew it. So purely ideal and so deeply human are the visions of Shelley. So truly does he deserve the epitaph which a clear-sighted friend wrote upon his tomb: *cor cordium,* the heart of hearts.

LEOPARDI

T HIS BOOK* speaks for itself. To the gallery of romantic poets of
the early nineteenth century it adds for the English-speaking
reader a life-like portrait of Leopardi. I have no competence and
no wish to retouch the picture, painted as it is with a fine perception of character and a deep knowledge of Italy, yet without
surrendering the English point of view that serves to frame the
perspectives in and to bring out the colours.

There is only one thing that the purely English reader may
miss, because it is only communicable to those who have some
familiarity with the Italian language and some sympathy with the
classic temperament: I mean the poignant accent, the divine elevation of this poet. The student, the writer, the sufferer, the wanderer was only Conte Giacomo Leopardi, but the poet was Orpheus
himself. Long passages are fit to repeat in lieu of prayers through
all the watches of the night. How shall I express their quality?
Suppose you were held up in some minor Italian town where by
chance an itinerant company was to perform *Il Trovatore*. Suppose that having nothing better to do you strolled into the theatre,
resigned in advance to a meagre stage-setting, a harsh orchestra,
a prima donna past her prime, a rhetorical little tenor saving his
breath for the gymnastic prodigy of his final high note. But suppose also that, having found things in general much as you expected, suddenly you heard, coming from behind the wings, an
unexampled heavenly voice, a voice pure as moonlight, rich as
sorrow, firm as truth, singing *Solo in terra*. Alone on earth that
voice might indeed seem, and far from earth it would carry you;
and no matter how commonplace the singer might look, or even

Leopardi by Iris Origo, Oxford University Press, 1935, of which this essay was
originally the Foreword.

ridiculous, when he stepped before the footlights, if ever that sheer music sounded again, there would be something not himself that sang and something not yourself that listened.

I speak of voice and of music, but that is only a metaphor. What works the miracle in Leopardi is far from being mere sound or diction or the enigmatic suggestion of strange words. His versification is remarkable only when a divine afflatus blows through it, which is not always. This afflatus is intellectual, this music is a flood of thoughts. We are transported out of ourselves ascetically, by the vision of truth. Leopardi lived in a romantic tower, a dismal, desolate ruin; but through the bars of his prison he beheld the same classic earth and Olympian sky that had been visible to Homer, Pindar, and Sophocles. The world is always classical, the truth of human destiny is always clear, if only immersion in our animal cares does not prevent us from seeing it. Lifting the eyes would be so easy, yet it is seldom done; and when a rapt poet compels us to do so, we are arrested, we are rebuked, we are delivered.

The misfortunes of Leopardi were doubtless fortunate for his genius. Every classic poet has his romantic accent, corresponding with the scope of his intuition and the degree of harmony or conflict that the vision of the truth creates in his heart. In Leopardi this vision was saturated with anguish; narrowed by it, no doubt, but not distorted. The white heat of his anguish burned all anguish away, and cleared the air. Beneath the glorious monotony of the stars he saw the universal mutation of earthly things, and their vanity, yet also, almost everywhere, the beginning if not the fullness of beauty; and this intuition, at once rapturous and sad, liberated him from the illusions of the past and from those of the future.

DICKENS

I F CHRISTENDOM should lose everything that is now in the melting-pot, human life would still remain amiable and quite adequately human. I draw this comforting assurance from the pages of Dickens. Who could not be happy in his world? Yet there is nothing essential to it which the most destructive revolution would be able to destroy. People would still be as different, as absurd, and as charming as are his characters; the springs of kindness and folly in their lives would not be dried up. Indeed, there is much in Dickens which communism, if it came, would only emphasise and render universal. Those schools, those poorhouses, those prisons, with those surviving shreds of family life in them, show us what in the coming age (with some sanitary improvements) would be the nursery and home of everybody. Everybody would be a waif, like Oliver Twist, like Smike, like Pip, and like David Copperfield; and amongst the agents and underlings of social government, to whom all these waifs would be entrusted, there would surely be a goodly sprinkling of Pecksniffs, Squeers's, and Fangs; whilst the Fagins would be everywhere commissioners of the people. Nor would there fail to be, in high places and in low, the occasional sparkle of some Pickwick or Cherryble Brothers or Sam Weller or Mark Tapley; and the voluble Flora Finchings would be everywhere in evidence, and the strong-minded Betsey Trotwoods in office. There would also be, among the inefficient, many a Dora and Agnes and Little Emily—with her charm but without her tragedy, since this is one of the things which the promised social reform would happily render impossible; I mean, by removing all the disgrace of it. The only element in the world of Dickens which would become obsolete would be the setting, the atmosphere of material instrumentalities and arrangements, as travelling by coach is obsolete; but travelling by rail, by motor, or by airship will emotionally be much the same thing. It is worth noting how such instrumentalities, which absorb modern life, are admired and enjoyed by Dickens, as they were by Homer. The poets ought not to be afraid of them; they exercise the mind congenially, and can be played with joyfully. Consider the black ships and the chariots of Homer, the coaches and river-boats of Dickens, and the aeroplanes of to-day; to what would an unspoiled young mind turn with more interest? Dickens tells us little of English sports, but he shares the sporting nature of the Englishman, to whom the whole material world is a playing-field, the scene giving ample scope to his love of action, legality, and pleasant achievement. His art is to sport according to the rules of the game, and to do things for the sake of doing them, rather than for any ulterior motive.

It is remarkable, in spite of his ardent simplicity and openness of heart, how insensible Dickens was to the greater themes of the human imagination—religion, science, politics, art. He was a waif himself, and utterly disinherited. For example, the terrible heritage of contentious religions which fills the world seems not to exist for him. In this matter he was like a sensitive child, with a most religious disposition, but no religious ideas. Perhaps, properly speaking, he had no *ideas* on any subject; what he had was a vast sympathetic participation in the daily life of mankind; and what he saw of ancient institutions made him hate them, as needless sources of oppression, misery, selfishness, and rancour. His one political passion was philanthropy, genuine but felt only on its negative, reforming side; of positive utopias, or enthusiasms we hear nothing. The political background of Christendom is only, so to speak, an old faded back-drop for his stage; a castle, a frigate, a gallows, and a large female angel with white wings standing above an orphan by an open grave—a decoration which has to serve for all the melodramas in his theatre, intellectually so provincial and poor. Common life as it is lived was varied and lovable enough for Dickens, if only the pests and cruelties could be removed from it. Suffering wounded him, but not vulgarity; whatever pleased his senses and whatever shocked them filled his mind alike with romantic wonder, with the endless delight of observation. Vulgarity —and what can we relish, if we recoil at vulgarity?—was innocent and amusing; in fact, for the humourist, it was the spice of life. There was more piety in being human than in being pious. In reviving Christmas, Dickens transformed it from the celebration of a metaphysical mystery into a feast of overflowing simple kindness and good cheer; the church bells were still there—in the orchestra; and the angels of Bethlehem were still there—painted on the back-curtain. Churches, in his novels, are vague, desolate places where one has ghastly experiences, and where only the pew-opener is human; and such religious and political conflicts as he depicts in *Barnaby Rudge* and in *A Tale of Two Cities* are street brawls and prison scenes and conspiracies in taverns, without any indication of the contrasts in mind or interests between the opposed parties. Nor had Dickens any lively sense for fine art, classical tradition, science, or even the manners and feelings of the upper classes in his own time and country: in his novels we may almost say there is no army, no navy, no church, no sport, no distant travel, no daring adventure, no feeling for the watery wastes and the motley nations of the planet, and—luckily, with his notion of them—no lords and ladies. Even love of the traditional sort is hardly in Dickens's sphere—I mean the soldierly passion in which a rather rakish gallantry was sobered by devotion, and loyalty rested on pride. In Dickens love is sentimental or benevolent or merry or sneaking or canine; in his last book he was going to describe a love that was passionate and criminal; but love for him was never chivalrous, never poetical. What he paints most tragically is a quasi-paternal devotion in the old to the young, the love of Mr. Peggotty for Little Emily, or of Solomon Gills for Walter Gay. A series of shabby little adventures, such as might absorb the interest of an average youth, were romantic enough for Dickens.

I say he was disinherited, but he inherited the most terrible negations. Religion lay on him like the weight of the atmosphere, sixteen pounds to the square inch, yet never noticed nor mentioned. He lived and wrote in the shadow of the most awful prohibitions. Hearts petrified by legality and falsified by worldliness offered, indeed, a good subject for a novelist, and Dickens availed himself of it to the extent of always contrasting natural goodness and happiness with whatever is morose; but his morose people were wicked, not virtuous in their own way; so that the protest of his temperament against his environment never took a radical form nor went back to first principles. He needed to feel, in his writing, that he was carrying the sympathies of every man with him. In him conscience was single, and he could not conceive how it could ever be divided in other men. He denounced scandals without exposing shams, and conformed willingly and scrupulously to the proprieties. Lady Dedlock's secret, for instance, he treats as if it were the sin of Adam, remote, mysterious, inexpiable. Mrs. Dombey is not allowed to deceive her husband except by pretending to deceive him. The seduction of Little Emily is left out altogether, with the whole character of Steerforth, the development of which would have been so important in the moral experience of David Copperfield himself. But it is not public prejudice alone that plays the censor over Dickens's art; his own kindness and even weakness of heart act sometimes as marplots. The character of Miss Mowcher, for example, so brilliantly introduced, was evidently intended to be shady, and to play a very important part in the story; but its original in real life, which was recognised, had to be conciliated, and the sequel was omitted and patched up with an apology—itself admirable—for the poor dwarf. Such a sacrifice does honour to Dickens's heart; but artists should meditate on their works in time, and it is easy to remove any too great likeness in a portrait by a few touches making it more consistent than real people are apt to be; and in this case, if the little creature had been really guilty, how much more subtle and tragic her apology for herself might have been, like that of the bastard Edmund in *King Lear*! So, too, in *Dombey and Son*, Dickens could not bear to let Walter Gay turn out badly, as he had been meant to do, and to break his uncle's heart as well as the heroine's; he was accordingly transformed into a stage hero miraculously saved from shipwreck, and Florence was not allowed to reward the admirable Toots, as she should have done, with her trembling hand. But Dickens was no free artist; he had more genius than taste, a warm fancy not aided by a thorough understanding of complex characters. He worked under pressure, for money and applause, and often had to cheapen in execution what his inspiration had so vividly conceived.

What, then, is there left, if Dickens has all these limitations? In our romantic disgust we might be tempted to say, Nothing.

But in fact almost everything is left, almost everything that counts in the daily life of mankind, or that by its presence or absence can determine whether life shall be worth living or not; because a simple good life is worth living, and an elaborate bad life is not. There remain in the first place eating and drinking; relished not bestially, but humanly, jovially, as the sane and exhilarating basis for everything else. This is a sound English beginning; but the immediate sequel, as the England of that day presented it to Dickens, is no less delightful. There is the ruddy glow of the hearth; the sparkle of glasses and brasses and well-scrubbed pewter; the savoury fumes of the hot punch, after the tingle of the wintry air; the coaching-scenes, the motley figures and absurd incidents of travel; the changing sights and joys of the road. And then, to balance this, the traffic of ports and cities, the hubbub of crowded streets, the luxury of shop-windows and of palaces not to be entered; the procession of the passers-by, shabby or ludicrously genteel; the dingy look and musty smell of their lodgings; the labyrinth of back-alleys, courts, and mews, with their crying children, and scolding old women, and listless, half-drunken loiterers. These sights, like fables, have a sort of moral in them to which Dickens was very sensitive; the important airs of nobodies on great occasions, the sadness and preoccupation of the great as they hasten by in their mourning or on their pressing affairs; the sadly comic characters of the tavern; the diligence of shop-keepers, like squirrels turning in their cages; the children peeping out everywhere like grass in an untrodden street; the charm of humble things, the nobleness of humble people, the horror of crime, the ghastliness of vice, the deft hand and shining face of virtue passing through the midst of it all; and finally a fresh wind of indifference and change blowing across our troubles and clearing the most lurid sky.

I do not know whether it was Christian charity or naturalistic insight, or a mixture of both (for they are closely akin) that attracted Dickens particularly to the deformed, the half-witted, the abandoned, or those impeded or misunderstood by virtue of some singular inner consecration. The visible moral of these things, when brutal prejudice does not blind us to it, comes very near to true philosophy; one turn of the screw, one flash of reflection, and we have understood nature and human morality and the relation between them.

In his love of roads and wayfarers, of river-ports and wharves and the idle or sinister figures that lounge about them, Dickens was like Walt Whitman; and I think a second Dickens may any day appear in America, when it is possible in that land of hurry to reach the same degree of saturation, the same unquestioning pleasure in the familiar facts. The spirit of Dickens would be better able to do justice to America than was that of Walt Whitman; because America, although it may seem nothing but a noisy nebula to the impressionist, is not a nebula but a concourse of very distinct individual bodies, natural and social, each with its definite interest and story. Walt Whitman had a sort of transcendental philosophy which swallowed the universe whole, supposing there was a universal spirit in things identical with the absolute spirit that observed them; but Dickens was innocent of any such clap-trap, and remained a true spirit in his own person. Kindly and clear-sighted, but self-identical and unequivocally human, he glided through the slums like one of his own little heroes, uncontaminated by their squalor and confusion, courageous and firm in his clear allegiances amid the flux of things, a pale angel at the Carnival, his heart aflame, his voice always flute-like in its tenderness and warning. This is the true relation of spirit to existence, not the other which confuses them; for this earth (I cannot speak for the universe at large) has no spirit of its own, but brings forth spirits only at certain points, in the hearts and brains of frail living creatures, who like insects flit through it, buzzing and gathering what sweets they can; and it is the spaces they traverse in this career, charged with their own moral burden, that they can report on or describe, not things rolling on to infinity in their vain tides. To be hypnotised by that flood would be a heathen idolatry. Accordingly Walt Whitman, in his comprehensive democratic vistas, could never see the trees for the wood, and remained incapable, for all his diffuse love of the human herd, of ever painting a character or telling a story; the very things in which Dickens was a master. It is this life of the individual, as it may be lived in a given nation, that determines the whole value of that nation to the poet, to the moralist, and to the judicious historian. But for the excellence of the typical single life, no nation deserves to be remembered more than the sands of the sea; and America will not be a success, if every American is a failure.

Dickens entered the theatre of this world by the stage door; the shabby little adventures of the actors in their private capacity replace for him the mock tragedies which they enact before a dreaming public. Mediocrity of circumstances and mediocrity of soul forever return to the centre of his stage; a more wretched or a grander existence is sometimes broached, but the pendulum soon swings back, and we return, with the relief with which we put on our slippers after the most romantic excursion, to a golden mediocrity—to mutton and beer, and to love and babies in a suburban villa with one frowsy maid. Dickens is the poet of those acres of yellow brick streets which the traveller sees from the railway viaducts as he approaches London; they need a poet, and they deserve one, since a complete human life may very well be lived there. Their little excitements and sorrows, their hopes and humours are like those of the Wooden Midshipman in *Dombey and Son;* but the sea is not far off, and the sky—Dickens never forgets it—is above all those brief troubles. He had a sentiment in the presence of this vast flatness of human fates, in spite of their individual pungency, which I think might well be the dominant sentiment of mankind in the future; a sense of happy freedom in littleness, an open-eyed reverence and religion without words. This universal human anonymity is like a sea, an infinitive democratic desert, chock-full and yet the very image of emptiness, with nothing in it for the mind, except, as the Moslems say, the presence of Allah. Awe is the counterpart of humility—and this is perhaps religion enough. The atom in the universal vortex ought to be humble; he ought to see that, materially, he doesn't much matter, and that morally his loves are merely his own, without authority over the universe. He can admit without obloquy that he is what he is; and he can rejoice in his own being, and in that of all other things in so far as he can share it sympathetically. The apportionment of existence and of fortune is in Other Hands; his own portion is contentment, vision, love, and laughter.

Having humility, that most liberating of sentiments, having a true vision of human existence and joy in that vision, Dickens had in a superlative degree the gift of humour, of mimicry, of unrestrained farce. He was the perfect comedian. When people say Dickens exaggerates, it seems to me they can have no eyes and no ears. They probably have only *notions* of what things and people are; they accept them conventionally, at their diplomatic value. Their minds run on in the region of discourse, where there are masks only and no faces, ideas and no facts; they have little sense for those living grimaces that play from moment to moment upon the countenance of the world. The world is a perpetual caricature of itself; at every moment it is the mockery and the contradiction of what it is pretending to be. But as it nevertheless intends all the time to be something different and highly dignified, at the next moment it corrects and checks and tries to cover up the absurd thing it was; so that a conventional world, a world of masks, is superimposed on the reality, and passes in every sphere of human interest for the reality itself. Humour is the perception of this illusion, the fact allowed to pierce here and there through the convention, whilst the convention continues to be maintained, as if we had not observed its absurdity. Pure comedy is more radical, cruder, in a certain sense less human; because comedy throws the convention over altogether, revels for a moment in the fact, and brutally says to the notions of mankind, as if it slapped them in the face, There, take that! That's what you really are! At this the polite world pretends to laugh, not tolerantly as it does at humour, but a little angrily. It does not like to see itself by chance in the glass, without having had time to compose its features for demure self-contemplation. "What a bad mirror," it exclaims; "it must be concave or convex; for surely I never looked like that. Mere caricature, farce, and horse play. Dickens exaggerates; *I* never was so sentimental as that; *I* never saw anything so dreadful; *I* don't believe there were ever any people like Quilp, or Squeers, or Serjeant Buzfuz." But the polite world is lying; there *are* such people; we are such people ourselves in our true moments, in our veritable impulses; but we are careful to stifle and to hide those moments from ourselves and from the world; to purse and pucker ourselves into the mask of our conventional personality; and so simpering, we profess that it is very coarse and inartistic of Dickens to undo our life's work for us in an instant, and remind us of what we are. And as to other people, though we may allow that considered superficially they are often absurd, we do not wish to dwell on their eccentricities, nor to mimic them. On the contrary, it is good manners to look away quickly, to suppress a smile, and to say to ourselves that the ludicrous figure in the street is not at all comic, but a dull ordinary Christian, and that it is foolish to give any importance to the fact that its hat has blown off, that it has slipped on an orange-peel and unintentionally sat on the pavement, that it has a pimple on its nose, that its one tooth projects over its lower lip, that it is angry with things in general, and that it is looking everywhere for the penny which it holds tightly in its hand. That may fairly represent the moral condition of most of us at most times; but we do not want to think of it; we do not want to see; we gloss the fact over; we console ourselves before we are grieved, and reassert our composure before we have laughed. We are afraid, ashamed, anxious to be spared. What displeases us in Dickens is that he does not spare us; he mimics things to the full; he dilates and exhausts and repeats; he wallows. He is too intent on the passing experience to look over his shoulder, and consider whether we have not already understood, and had enough. He is not thinking of us; he is obeying the impulse of the passion, the person, or the story he is enacting. This faculty, which renders him a consummate comedian, is just what alienated from him a later generation in which people of taste were æsthetes and virtuous people were higher snobs; they wanted a mincing art, and he gave them copious improvisation, they wanted analysis and development, and he gave them absolute comedy. I must confess, though the fault is mine and not his, that sometimes his absoluteness is too much for me. When I come to the death of Little Nell, or to What the Waves were always Saying, or even to the incorrigible perversities of the pretty Dora, I skip. I can't take my liquor neat in such draughts, and my inner man says to Dickens, Please don't. But then I am a coward in so many ways! There are so many things in this world that I skip, as I skip the undiluted Dickens! When I reach Dover on a rough day, I wait there until the Channel is smoother; am I not travelling for pleasure? But my prudence does not blind me to the admirable virtue of the sailors that cross in all weathers, nor even to the automatic determination of the sea-sick ladies, who might so easily have followed my example, if they were not the slaves of their railway tickets and of their labelled luggage. They are loyal to their tour, and I to my philosophy. Yet as wrapped in my great-coat and sure of a good dinner, I pace the windy pier and soliloquise, I feel the superiority of the bluff tar, glad of breeze, stretching a firm arm to the unsteady passenger, and watching with a masterful thrill of emotion the home cliffs receding and the foreign coasts ahead. It is only courage (which Dickens had without knowing it) and universal kindness (which he knew he had) that are requisite to nerve us for a true vision of this world. And as some of us are cowards about crossing the Channel, and others about "crossing the bar," so almost everybody is a coward about his own humanity. We do not consent to be absurd, though absurd we are. We have no fundamental humility. We do not wish the moments of our lives to be caught by a quick eye in their grotesque initiative, and to be pilloried in this way before our own eyes. For that reason we don't like Dickens, and don't like comedy, and don't like the truth. Dickens could don the comic mask with innocent courage; he could wear it with a grace, ease, and irresistible vivacity seldom given to men. We must go back for anything like it to the very greatest comic poets, to Shakespeare or to Aristophanes. Who else, for instance, could have penned this:

> "It was all Mrs. Bumble. She *would* do it," urged Mr. Bumble; first looking round to ascertain that his partner had left the room.
>
> "That is no excuse," replied Mr. Brownlow. "You were present on the occasion of the destruction of these trinkets, and indeed are the more guilty of the two, in the eye of the law; for the law supposes that your wife acts under your direction."
>
> "If the law supposes that," said Mr. Bumble, squeezing his hat emphatically in both hands, "the law is a ass, a idiot. If that's the eye of the law, the law is a bachelor; and the worse I wish the law is, that his eye may be opened by experience—by experience."
>
> Laying great stress on the repetition of these two words, Mr. Bumble fixed his hat on very tight, and putting his hands in his pockets, followed his helpmate downstairs.

This is high comedy; the irresistible, absurd, intense dream of the old fool, personifying the law in order to convince and to punish it. I can understand that this sort of thing should not be common in English literature, nor much relished; because pure comedy is scornful, merciless, devastating, holding no door open to anything beyond. Cultivated English feeling winces at this brutality, although the common people love it in clowns and in puppet shows; and I think they are right. Dickens, who surely was tender enough, had so irresistible a comic genius that it carried him beyond the gentle humour which most Englishmen possess to the absolute grotesque reality. Squeers, for instance, when he sips the wretched dilution which he has prepared for his starved and shivering little pupils, smacks his lips and cries: "Here's richness!" It is savage comedy; humour would come in if we understood (what Dickens does not tell us) that the little creatures were duly impressed and thought the thin liquid truly delicious. I suspect that English sensibility prefers the humour and wit of Hamlet to the pure comedy of Falstaff; and that even in Aristophanes it seeks consolation in the lyrical poetry for the flaying of human life in the comedy itself. Tastes are free; but we should not deny that in merciless and rollicking comedy life is caught in the act. The most grotesque creatures of Dickens are not exaggerations or mockeries of something other than themselves; they arise because nature generates them, like toadstools; they exist because they can't help it, as we all do. The fact that these perfectly self-justified beings are absurd appears only by comparison, and from outside; circumstances, or the expectations of other people, make them ridiculous and force them to contradict themselves; but in nature it is no crime to be exceptional. Often, but for the savagery of the average man, it would not even be a misfortune. The sleepy fat boy in *Pickwick* looks foolish; but in himself he is no more foolish, nor less solidly self-justified, than a pumpkin lying on the ground. Toots seems ridiculous; and we laugh heartily at his incoherence, his beautiful waistcoats, and his extreme modesty; but when did anybody more obviously grow into what he is because he couldn't grow otherwise? So with Mr. Pickwick, and Sam Weller, and Mrs. Gamp, and Micawber, and all the rest of this wonderful gallery; they are ridiculous only by accident, and in a context in which they never intended to appear. If Oedipus and Lear and Cleopatra do not seem ridiculous, it is only because tragic reflection has taken them out of the context in which, in real life, they would have figured. If we saw them as facts, and not as emanations of a poet's dream, we should laugh at them till doomsday; what grotesque presumption, what silly whims, what mad contradiction of the simplest realities! Yet we should not laugh at them without feeling how real their griefs were; as real and terrible as the griefs of children and of dreams.

But facts, however serious inwardly, are always absurd outwardly; and the just critic of life sees both truths at once, as Cervantes did in *Don Quixote*. A pompous idealist who does not see the ridiculous in *all* things is the dupe of his sympathy and abstraction; and a clown, who does not see that these ridiculous creatures are living quite in earnest, is the dupe of his egotism. Dickens saw the absurdity, and understood the life; I think he was a good philosopher.

It is usual to compare Dickens with Thackeray, which is like comparing the grape with the gooseberry; there are obvious points of resemblance, and the gooseberry has some superior qualities of its own; but you can't make red wine of it. The wine of Dickens is of the richest, the purest, the sweetest, the most fortifying to the blood; there is distilled in it, with the perfection of comedy, the perfection of morals. I do not mean, of course, that Dickens appreciated all the values that human life has or might have; that is beyond any man. Even the greatest philosophers, such as Aristotle, have not always much imagination to conceive forms of happiness or folly other than those which their age or their temperament reveals to them; their insight runs only to discovering the *principle* of happiness, that it is spontaneous life of any sort harmonised with circumstances. The sympathies and imagination of Dickens, vivid in their sphere, were no less limited in range; and of course it was not his business to find philosophic formulas; nevertheless I call his the perfection of morals for two reasons: that he put the distinction between good and evil in the right place, and that he felt this distinction intensely. A moralist might have excellent judgment, he might see what sort of life is spontaneous in a given being and how far it may be harmonised with circumstances, yet his heart might remain cold, he might not suffer nor rejoice with the suffering or joy he foresaw. Humanitarians like Bentham and Mill, who talked about the greatest happiness of the greatest number, might conceivably be moral prigs in their own persons, and they might have been chilled to the bone in their theoretic love of mankind, if they had had the wit to imagine in what, as a matter of fact, the majority would place their happiness. Even if their theory had been correct (which I think it was in intention, though not in statement) they would then not have been perfect moralists, because their maxims would not have expressed their hearts. In expressing their hearts, they ought to have embraced one of those forms of "idealism" by which men fortify themselves in their bitter passions or in their helpless commitments; for they do not wish mankind to be happy in its own way, but in theirs. Dickens was not one of those moralists who summon every man to do himself the greatest violence so that he may not offend them, nor defeat their ideals. Love of the good of others is something that shines in every page of Dickens with a truly celestial splendour. How entirely limpid is his sympathy with life—a sympathy uncontaminated by dogma or pedantry or snobbery or bias of any kind! How generous is this keen, light spirit, how pure this open heart! And yet, in spite of this extreme sensibility, not the least wobbling; no deviation from a just severity of judgment, from an uncompromising distinction between white and black. And this happens as it ought to happen; sympathy is not checked by a flatly contrary prejudice or commandment, by some categorical imperative irrelevant to human nature; the check, like the cheer, comes by tracing the course of spontaneous impulse amid circumstances that inexorably lead it to success or to failure. There is a bed to this stream, freely as the water may flow; when it comes to this precipice it must leap, when it runs over these pebbles it must sing, and when it spreads into that marsh it must become livid and malarial. The very sympathy with human impulse quickens in Dickens the sense of danger; his very joy in joy makes him stern to what kills it. How admirably drawn are his surly villains! No rhetorical vilification of them, as in a sermon; no exaggeration of their qualms or fears; rather a sense of how obvious and human all their courses seem from their own point of view; and yet no sentimental apology for them, no romantic worship of rebels in their madness or crime. The pity of it, the waste of it all, are seen not by a second vision but by the same original vision which revealed the lure and the drift of the passion. Vice is a monster here of such sorry mien, that the longer we see it the more we deplore it; that other sort of vice which Pope found so seductive was perhaps only some innocent impulse artificially suppressed, and called a vice because it broke out inconveniently and displeased the company. True vice is human nature strangled by the suicide of attempting the impossible. Those so self-justified villains of Dickens never elude their fates.

Bill Sikes is not let off, neither is Nancy; the oddly benevolent Magwitch does not escape from the net, nor does the unfortunate young Richard Carstone, victim of the Circumlocution Office. The horror and ugliness of their fall are rendered with the hand of a master; we see here, as in the world, that in spite of the romanticists it is not virtue to rush enthusiastically along any road. I think Dickens is one of the best friends mankind has ever had. He has held the mirror up to nature, and of its reflected fragments has composed a fresh world, where the men and women differ from real people only in that they live in a literary medium, so that all ages and places may know them. And they are worth knowing, just as one's neighbours are, for their picturesque characters and their pathetic fates. Their names should be in every child's mouth; they ought to be adopted members of every household. Their stories cause the merriest and the sweetest chimes to ring in the fancy, without confusing our moral judgment or alienating our interest from the motley commonplaces of daily life. In every English-speaking home, in the four quarters of the globe, parents and children will do well to read Dickens aloud of a winter's evening; they will love winter, and one another, and God the better for it. What a wreath that will be of ever-fresh holly, thick with bright berries, to hang to this poet's memory—the very crown he would have chosen.

EMERSON

THOSE WHO knew Emerson, or who stood so near to his time and to his circle that they caught some echo of his personal influence, did not judge him merely as a poet or philosopher, nor identify his efficacy with that of his writings. His friends and neighbours, the congregations he preached to in his younger days, the audiences that afterward listened to his lectures, all agreed in a veneration for his person which had nothing to do with their understanding or acceptance of his opinions. They flocked to him and listened to his word, not so much for the sake of its absolute meaning as for the atmosphere of candour, purity, and serenity that hung about it, as about a sort of sacred music. They felt themselves in the presence of a rare and beautiful spirit, who was in communion with a higher world. More than the truth his teaching might express, they valued the sense it gave them of a truth that was inexpressible. They became aware, if we may say so, of the ultra-violet rays of his spectrum, of the inaudible highest notes of his gamut, too pure and thin for common ears.

This effect was by no means due to the possession on the part of Emerson of the secret of the universe, or even of a definite conception of ultimate truth. He was not a prophet who had once for all climbed his Sinai or his Tabor, and having there beheld the transfigured reality, descended again to make authoritative report of it to the world. Far from it. At bottom he had no doctrine at all. The deeper he went and the more he tried to grapple with fundamental conceptions, the vaguer and more elusive they became in his hands. Did he know what he meant by Spirit or the "Over-Soul"? Could he say what he understood by the terms, so constantly on his lips, Nature, Law, God, Benefit, or Beauty? He could not, and the consciousness of that incapacity was so lively within him that he never attempted to give articulation to his philosophy. His finer instinct kept him from doing that violence to his inspiration.

The source of his power lay not in his doctrine, but in his temperament, and the rare quality of his wisdom was due less to his reason than to his imagination. Reality eluded him; he had neither diligence nor constancy enough to master and possess it; but his mind was open to all philosophic influences, from whatever quarter they might blow; the lessons of science and the hints of poetry worked themselves out in him to a free and personal religion. He differed from the plodding many, not in knowing things better, but in having more ways of knowing them. His grasp was not particularly firm, he was far from being, like a Plato or an Aristotle, past master in the art and the science of life. But his mind was endowed with unusual plasticity, with unusual spontaneity and liberty of movement—it was a fairyland of thoughts and fancies. He was like a young god making experiments in creation: he blotched the work, and always began again on a new and better plan. Every day he said, "Let there be light," and every day the light was new. His sun, like that of Heraclitus, was different every morning.

What seemed, then, to the more earnest and less critical of his hearers a revelation from above was in truth rather an insurrection from beneath, a shaking loose from convention, a disintegration of the normal categories of reason in favour of various imaginative principles, on which the world might have been built, if it had been built differently. This gift of revolutionary thinking allowed new aspects, hints of wider laws, premonitions of unthought-of fundamental unities to spring constantly into view. But such visions were necessarily fleeting, because the human mind had long before settled its grammar, and discovered, after much groping and many defeats, the general forms in which experience will allow itself to be stated. These general forms are the principles of common sense and positive science, no less imaginative in their origin than those notions which we now call transcendental, but grown prosaic, like the metaphors of common speech, by dint of repetition.

Yet authority, even of this rational kind, sat lightly upon Emerson. To reject tradition and think as one might have thought if no man had ever existed before was indeed the aspiration of the Transcendentalists, and although Emerson hardly regarded himself as a member of that school, he largely shared its tendency and passed for its spokesman. Without protesting against tradition, he smilingly eluded it in his thoughts, untamable in their quiet irresponsibility. He fled to his woods or to his "pleached garden," to be the creator of his own worlds in solitude and freedom. No wonder that he brought thence to the tightly conventional minds of his contemporaries a breath as if from paradise. His simplicity in novelty, his profundity, his ingenuous ardour must have seemed to them something heavenly, and they may be excused if they thought they detected inspiration even in his occasional thin paradoxes and guileless whims. They were stifled with conscience and he brought them a breath of Nature; they were surfeited with shallow controversies and he gave them poetic truth.

Imagination, indeed, is his single theme. As a preacher might under every text enforce the same lessons of the gospel, so Emerson traces in every sphere the same spiritual laws of experience—compensation, continuity, the self-expression of the Soul in the forms of Nature and of society, until she finally recognises herself in her own work and sees its beneficence and beauty. His constant refrain is the omnipotence of imaginative thought; its power first to make the world, then to understand it, and finally to rise above it. All Nature is an embodiment of our native fancy, all history a drama in which the innate possibilities of the spirit are enacted and realised. While the conflict of life and the shocks of experience seem to bring us face to face with an alien and overwhelming power, reflection can humanise and rationalise that power by conceiving its laws; and with this recognition of the rationality of all things comes the sense of their beauty and order. The destruction which Nature seems to prepare for our special hopes is thus seen to be the victory of our impersonal interests. To awaken in us this spiritual insight, an elevation of mind which is at once an act of comprehension and of worship, to substitute it for lower passions and more servile forms of intelligence—that is Emerson's constant effort. All his resources of illustration, observation, and rhetoric are used to deepen and clarify this sort of wisdom.

Such thought is essentially the same that is found in the German romantic or idealistic philosophers, with whom Emerson's affinity is remarkable, all the more as he seems to have borrowed little or nothing from their works. The critics of human nature, in the eighteenth century, had shown how much men's ideas depend on their predispositions, on the character of their senses and the habits of their intelligence. Seizing upon this thought and exaggerating it, the romantic philosophers attributed to the spirit of man the omnipotence which had belonged to God, and felt that in this way they were reasserting the supremacy of mind over matter and establishing it upon a safe and rational basis.

The Germans were great system-makers, and Emerson cannot rival them in the sustained effort of thought by which they sought to reinterpret every sphere of being according to their chosen principles. But he surpassed them in an instinctive sense of what he was doing. He never represented his poetry as science, nor countenanced the formation of a new sect that should nurse the sense of a private and mysterious illumination, and relight the fagots of passion and prejudice. He never tried to seek out and defend the universal implications of his ideas, and never wrote the book he had once planned on the law of compensation, foreseeing, we may well believe, the sophistries in which he would have been directly involved. He fortunately preferred a fresh statement on a fresh subject. A suggestion once given, the spirit once aroused to speculation, a glimpse once gained of some ideal harmony, he chose to descend again to common sense and to touch the earth for a moment before another flight. The faculty of idealisation was itself what he valued. Philosophy for him was rather a moral energy flowering into sprightliness of thought than a body of serious and defensible doctrines. In practising transcendental speculation only in this poetic and sporadic fashion, Emerson retained its true value and avoided its greatest danger. He secured the freedom and fertility of his thought and did not allow one conception of law or one hint of harmony to sterilise the mind and prevent the subsequent birth within it of other ideas, no less just and imposing than their predecessors. For we are not dealing at all in such a philosophy with matters of facts or with such verifiable truths as exclude their opposites. We are dealing only with imagination, with the art of conception, and with the various forms in which reflection, like a poet, may compose and recompose human experience.

A certain disquiet mingled, however, in the minds of Emerson's contemporaries with the admiration they felt for his purity and genius. They saw that he had forsaken the doctrines of the Church; and they were not sure whether he held quite unequivocally any doctrine whatever. We may not all of us share the concern for orthodoxy which usually caused this puzzled alarm: we may understand that it was not Emerson's vocation to be definite and dogmatic in religion any more than in philosophy. Yet that disquiet will not, even for us, wholly disappear. It is produced by a defect which naturally accompanies imagination in all but the greatest minds. I mean disorganisation. Emerson not only conceived things in new ways, but he seemed to think the new ways might cancel and supersede the old. His imagination was to invalidate the understanding. That inspiration which should come to fulfil seemed too often to come to destroy. If he was able so constantly to stimulate us to fresh thoughts, was it not because he demolished the labour of long ages of reflection? Was not the startling effect of much of his writing due to its contradiction to tradition and to common sense?

So long as he is a poet and in the enjoyment of his poetic license, we can blame this play of mind only by a misunderstanding. It is possible to think otherwise than as common sense thinks; there are other categories beside those of science. When we employ them we enlarge our lives. We add to the world of fact any number of worlds of the imagination in which human nature and the eternal relations of ideas may be nobly expressed. So far our imaginative fertility is only a benefit: it surrounds us with the congenial and necessary radiation of art and religion. It manifests our moral vitality in the bosom of Nature.

But sometimes imagination invades the sphere of understanding and seems to discredit its indispensable work. Common sense, we are allowed to infer, is a shallow affair: true insight changes all that. When so applied, poetic activity is not an unmixed good. It loosens our hold on fact and confuses our intelligence, so that we forget that intelligence has itself every prerogative of imagination, and has besides the sanction of practical validity. We are made to believe that since the understanding is something human and conditioned, something which might have been different, as the senses might have been different, and which we may yet, so to speak, get behind—therefore the understanding ought to be abandoned. We long for higher faculties, neglecting those we have, we yearn for intuition, closing our eyes upon experience. We become mystical.

Mysticism, as we have said, is the surrender of a category of thought because we divine its relativity. As every new category, however, must share this reproach, the mystic is obliged in the end to give them all up, the poetic and moral categories no less than the physical, so that the end of his purification is the atrophy of his whole nature, the emptying of his whole heart and mind to make room, as he thinks, for God. By attacking the authority of the understanding as the organon of knowledge, by substituting itself for it as the herald of a deeper truth, the imagination thus prepares its own destruction. For if the understanding is rejected because it cannot grasp the absolute, the imagination and all its works—art, dogma, worship—must presently be rejected for the same reason. Common sense and poetry must both go by the board, and conscience must follow after: for all these are human and relative. Mysticism will be satisfied only with the absolute, and as the absolute, by its very definition, is not representable by any specific faculty, it must be approached through the abandonment of all. The lights of life must be extinguished that the light of the absolute may shine, and the possession of everything in general must be secured by the surrender of everything in particular.

The same diffidence, however, the same constant renewal of sincerity which kept Emerson's flights of imagination near to experience, kept his mysticism also within bounds. A certain mystical tendency is pervasive with him, but there are only one or two subjects on which he dwells with enough constancy and energy of attention to make his mystical treatment of them pronounced. One of these is the question of the unity of all minds in the single soul of the universe, which is the same in all creatures; another is the question of evil and of its evaporation in the universal harmony of things. Both these ideas suggest themselves at certain turns in every man's experience, and might receive a rational formulation. But they are intricate subjects, obscured by many emotional prejudices, so that the labour, impartiality, and precision which would be needed to elucidate them are to be looked for in scholastic rather than in inspired thinkers, and in Emerson least of all. Before these problems he is alternately ingenuous and rhapsodical, and in both moods equally helpless. Individuals no doubt exist, he says to himself. But, ah! Napoleon is in every schoolboy. In every squatter in the western prairies we shall find an owner—

> *Of Cæsar's hand and Plato's brain,*
> *Of Lord Christ's heart, and Shakespeare's strain.*

But how? we may ask. Potentially? Is it because any mind, were it given the right body and the right experience, were it made over, in a word, into another mind, would resemble that other mind to the point of identity? Or is it that our souls are already so largely similar that we are subject to many kindred promptings and share many ideals unrealisable in our particular circumstances? But then we should simply be saying that if what makes men different were removed, men would be indistinguishable, or that, in so far as they are now alike, they can understand one another by summoning up their respective experiences in the fancy. There would be no mysticism in that, but at the same time, alas, no eloquence, no paradox, and, if we must say the word, no nonsense.

On the question of evil, Emerson's position is of the same kind. There is evil, of course, he tells us. Experience is sad. There is a crack in everything that God has made. But, ah! the laws of the universe are sacred and beneficent. Without them nothing good could arise. All things, then, are in their right places and the universe is perfect above our querulous tears. Perfect? we may ask. But perfect from what point of view, in reference to what ideal? To its own? To that of a man who renouncing himself and all naturally dear to him, ignoring the injustice, suffering, and impotence in the world, allows his will and his conscience to be hypnotised by the spectacle of a necessary evolution, and lulled into cruelty by the pomp and music of a tragic show? In that case the evil is not explained, it is forgotten; it is not cured, but condoned. We have surrendered the category of the better and the worse, the deepest foundation of life and reason; we have become mystics on the one subject on which, above all others, we ought to be men.

Two forces may be said to have carried Emerson in this mystical direction; one, that freedom of his imagination which we have already noted, and which kept him from the fear of self-contradiction; the other the habit of worship inherited from his clerical ancestors and enforced by his religious education. The spirit of conformity, the unction, the loyalty even unto death inspired by the religion of Jehovah, were dispositions acquired by too long a discipline and rooted in too many forms of speech, of thought, and of worship for a man like Emerson, who had felt their full force, ever to be able to lose them. The evolutions of his abstract opinions left that habit unchanged. Unless we keep this circumstance in mind, we shall not be able to understand the kind of elation and sacred joy, so characteristic of his eloquence, with which he propounds laws of Nature and aspects of experience which, viewed in themselves, afford but an equivocal support to moral enthusiasm. An optimism so persistent and unclouded as his will seem at variance with the description he himself gives of human life, a description coloured by a poetic idealism, but hardly by an optimistic bias.

We must remember, therefore, that this optimism is a pious tradition, originally justified by the belief in a personal God and in a providential government of affairs for the ultimate and positive good of the elect, and that the habit of worship survived in Emerson as an instinct after those positive beliefs had faded into a recognition of "spiritual laws." We must remember that Calvinism had known how to combine an awe-struck devotion to the Supreme Being with no very roseate picture of the destinies of mankind, and for more than two hundred years had been breeding in the stock from which Emerson came a willingness to be, as the phrase is, "damned for the glory of God."

What wonder, then, that when, for the former inexorable dispensation of Providence, Emerson substituted his general spiritual and natural laws, he should not have felt the spirit of worship fail within him? On the contrary, his thought moved in the presence of moral harmonies which seemed to him truer, more beautiful, and more beneficent than those of the old theology. An independent philosopher would not have seen in those harmonies an object of worship or a sufficient basis for optimism. But he was not an independent philosopher, in spite of his belief in independence. He inherited the problems and the preoccupations of the theology from which he started, being in this respect like the German idealists, who, with all their pretence of absolute metaphysics, were in reality only giving elusive and abstract forms to traditional theology. Emerson, too, was not primarily a philosopher, but a Puritan mystic with a poetic fancy and a gift for observation and epigram, and he saw in the laws of Nature, idealised by his imagination, only a more intelligible form of the divinity he had always recognised and adored. His was not a philosophy passing into a religion, but a religion expressing itself as a philosophy and veiled, as at its setting it descended the heavens, in various tints of poetry and science.

If we ask ourselves what was Emerson's relation to the scientific and religious movements of his time, and what place he may claim in the history of opinion, we must answer that he belonged very little to the past, very little to the present, and almost wholly to that abstract sphere into which mystical or philosophic aspiration has carried a few men in all ages. The religious tradition in which he was reared was that of Puritanism, but of a Puritanism which, retaining its moral intensity and metaphysical abstraction, had minimised its doctrinal expression and become Unitarian. Emerson was indeed the Psyche of Puritanism, "the latest-born and fairest vision far" of all that "faded hierarchy." A Puritan whose religion was all poetry, a poet whose only pleasure was thought, he showed in his life and personality the meagreness, the constraint, the frigid and conscious consecration which belonged to his clerical ancestors, while his inmost impersonal spirit ranged abroad over the fields of history and Nature, gathering what ideas it might, and singing its little snatches of inspired song.

The traditional element was thus rather an external and unessential contribution to Emerson's mind; he had the professional tinge, the decorum, the distinction of an old-fashioned divine; he had also the habit of writing sermons, and he had the national pride and hope of a religious people that felt itself providentially chosen to establish a free and godly commonwealth in a new world. For the rest, he separated himself from the ancient creed of the community with a sense rather of relief than of regret. A literal belief in Christian doctrines repelled him as unspiritual, as manifesting no understanding of the meaning which, as allegories, those doctrines might have to a philosophic and poetical spirit. Although as a clergyman he was at first in the habit of referring to the Bible and its lessons as to a supreme authority, he had no instinctive sympathy with the inspiration of either the Old or the New Testament; in Hafiz or Plutarch, in Plato or Shakespeare, he found more congenial stuff.

While he thus preferred to withdraw, without rancour and without contempt, from the ancient fellowship of the church, he assumed an attitude hardly less cool and deprecatory toward the enthusiasms of the new era. The national ideal of democracy and freedom had his entire sympathy; he allowed himself to be drawn into the movement against slavery; he took a curious and smiling interest in the discoveries of natural science and in the material progress of the age. But he could go no farther. His contemplative nature, his religious training, his dispersed reading, made him stand aside from the life of the world, even while he studied it with benevolent attention. His heart was fixed on eternal things, and he was in no sense a prophet for his age or country. He belonged by nature to that mystical company of devout souls that recognise no particular home and are dispersed throughout history, although not without intercommunication. He felt his affinity to the Hindoos and the Persians, to the Platonists and the Stoics. Like them he remains "a friend and aider of those who would live in the spirit." If not a star of the first magnitude, he is certainly a fixed star in the firmament of philosophy. Alone as yet among Americans, he may be said to have won a place there, if not by the originality of his thought, at least by the originality and beauty of the expression he gave to thoughts that are old and imperishable.

PENITENT ART

Art is like a charming woman who once had her age of innocence in the nursery, when she was beautiful without knowing it, being wholly intent on what she was making or telling or imagining.

Then she has had a season of passion and vanity, when having discovered how beautiful she was, she decked herself out in all possible pomp and finery, invented fashion after fashion to keep admiration alive, and finally began to put on rouge and false hair and too much scent, in the hope of still being a belle at seventy.

But it sometimes happens, during her long decline, that she hears a call to repentance, and thinks of being converted. Naturally, such a fine lady cannot give up her carriage; she is obliged occasionally to entertain her old friends at dinner, and to be seen now and then at the opera. Habit and the commitments she has in the world, where no function is complete without her, are too strong for her to be converted suddenly, or altogether; but henceforth something in her, in her most sensitive and thoughtful hours, upbraids her for the hollowness of her old airs and graces. It is really a sorry business, this perpetual pretence of being important and charming and charmed and beautiful.

Art seems to be passing at present through a lenten mood of this sort. Not all art, of course: somebody must still manufacture official statues and family portraits, somebody must design apartment houses, clubs, churches, skyscrapers, and stations. Visible through the academic framework of these inevitable objects, there is often much professional learning and judgment; there is even, sometimes, a hint of poetic life, or a suggestion of exotic beauty. In Mr. Sargent's painting, for instance, beneath the photographic standards of the studio, we often catch a satirical intention, or a

234

philosophic idea, or love of the sensuous qualities in the model
and in the accessories; a technical echo of Velasquez and Goya,
though without plastic vitality or dramatic ease; a sort of Van
Dyck, as it were, for the days of Edward VII; the dreadful lapse in
refinement not being greater, perhaps, than is requisite for the
documentary value of a true mirror of fashion in the later age.
Taste of the old honest worldly sort is far from dead; it is found
still in milliners and designers of fashionable garments, of furniture and ornaments. All this luxurious traditional art is as far as
possible from repentance. Yet as the Magdalene was potentially a
saint—perhaps always a saint really—so the most meretricious con-
trivances in the arts may sometimes include and betray the very
principle of redemption, which is love; in this case the love of
beauty. For example, here is the Russian ballet, doubling the dose
of luxurious stimulation in every direction, erotic, tragic, historical, and decorative; yet see how it glides at times into simplicity, and in spite of all the paraphernalia of expert æstheticism,
issues in forms of unmistakably penitent art, like pure colour and
caricature.

I call pure colour and caricature penitent art, because it is only
disappointment in other directions that drives artists back to these
primary effects. By an austere and deliberate abstinence from
everything that naturally tempts them, they achieve in this way
a certain peace; but they would far rather have found it by genuinely recovering their naïveté. Sensuous splendour and caricature
would then have seemed to them not the acme of abstract art, but
the obvious truth of things; they would have doted on puppets
and pantomime as a child dotes on dolls, without ever noticing
how remote they are from reality. In the nineteenth century some
romantic artists, poets, and philosophers actually tried being re-
baptised, hoping that a fresh dip in the Jordan might rejuvenate
them; but it was of no use. The notion of *recovering innocence*
is a contradiction in terms; conversion can only initiate a non-
natural life of grace; death must intervene before corruption can
put on incorruption. That age was accordingly an age of revivals,
of antiquaries, nothing in art and religion but retrospective; it was
progressive only in things material and in the knowledge of them.
Even its philosophical idealism and psychology were meant to be
historical and descriptive of facts, literary and egotistical as the

view of the facts might be. Romanticism thought it was exquisitely sensitive to the spirit of remote things, but in reality it was sensitive only to material perspectives, to costume and stage-setting; it grew sentimental over legends and ruins, and being moonstruck, thought it was imbibing the spirit of the past. But the past had not been consciously romantic; what the ancients actually thought and felt was understood much better before the nineteenth century than since; for formerly they were regarded simply as men, essentially contemporary—which comes much nearer the truth. Of course, the passion that can drive people to such earnest affectations must be itself genuine. Keats or Ruskin or Oscar Wilde had abundant vitality and expressed, each in his studied archaism, the profound helplessness that beset him; but what was vital in them was some sensuous or moral or revolutionary instinct of their own, such as in Shelley had existed pure; only in them it was contorted by their terrible preoccupation with being early, or rich, or choice. They were hypnotised by dead beauty; and not having invention nor influence enough to remodel their own age, they fled from it to exotic delights, sometimes primitive, sometimes luxurious, sometimes religious, and sometimes all these things at once. Similarly the revivals in architecture and in the minor crafts expressed a genuine love of colour, ornament, and beauty; they gave the snobbish middle classes a taste of cheap luxury; they could sip culture in a teacup. Yet the particular fashions revived were unstable; each successive affectation had hardly ceased to seem exquisite when it began to look foolish. Art at best is subject to fashion, because there is a margin of arbitrary variation in its forms, even when their chief lines are determined by their function; but in revived art fashion is all; it is a fancy-dress, unsatisfying even in the glamour of the ballroom, which we are positively ashamed to be seen in in the morning.

Fortunately revivals now seem to be over. Ruins and museums are interesting to the antiquary; they stir the historical imagination, and dazzle us here and there with some ray of living beauty, like that of a jewel; but they cannot supply inspiration. In art, in poetry, unless you become as a little child you cannot enter the kingdom of heaven. Little children are what artists and poets are now striving hard to be; little children who instead of blowing a tin trumpet blow by chance through a whole orchestra, but with the same emotion as the child; or who, instead of daubing a geometrical skeleton with a piece of chalk, can daub a cross-eyed cross-section of the entire spectrum or a compound fracture of a nightmare. Such is Cubism: by no means an inexpert or meaningless thing. Before you can compose a chaos or paint the unnamable, you must train yourself to a severe abstention from all practical habits of perception; you must heroically suppress the understanding. The result, when the penance is genuinely performed, has a very deep and recondite charm; you revert to what the spinal column might feel if it had a separate consciousness, or to what the retina might see if it could be painlessly cut off from the brain; lights, patterns, dynamic suggestions, sights and memories fused together, hypnotic harmonies such as may visit a vegetative or even mineral sensibility; you become a thousand prisms and mirrors reflecting one another. This is one kind of æsthetic repentance. Vain, vain, it says to itself, was the attempt to depict or beautify external objects; let material things be what they will; what are they to the artist? Nature has the urgency of life, which art cannot rival; it has the lure, the cruelty, of actual existence, where all is sin and confusion and vanity, a hideous strife of forms devouring one another, in which all are mutilated and doomed. What is that to the spirit? Let it confess its own impotence in that field, and abandon all attempts to observe or preserve what are called *things:* let it devote itself instead to cleansing the inside of the cup, to purifying its sensibility, which is after all what nature plays upon when she seems to us to be beautiful. Perhaps in that way spirit may abstract the gold of beauty and cast the dross away —all that alloy of preoccupation with material forms and external events and moral sentiments and vain animal adventures which has so long distracted the misguided artist, when he could paint the whole world and had lost his own soul. It is always the play of sensibility, and nothing else, that lends interest to external themes; and it was an evil obsession with alien things that dragged sensibility into a slavery to things which stifled and degraded it: *salvation lies in emancipating the medium.*

To renounce representation, or be representative only by accident, is accordingly one sort of penitent art; but there is another sort, more humble and humourous. This second sort makes no attempt to resist the impulse to observe and to express external things. It does not proudly imagine that the medium, which is the human contribution to representation, can be sufficient unto itself. On the contrary, in its sensuous orchestration it is content to be rudimentary, to work in clay or in wood, and to dress in homespun. It is all feeling, all childlike tenderness, all sense of life. Persons and animals fascinate it. At the same time, warned by the fate of explicit poets and realistic painters, it does not attempt, in its portraiture, to give more than a pregnant hint, some large graphic sign, some profound caricature. Don't be rhetorical, it says; don't try to be exhaustive; all that is worth saying can be said in words of one syllable. Look long, and be brief. It is not in their material entirety and detail that things penetrate to the soul, but in their simple large identity, as a child knows his mother, nurse, or dog. Fresh inchoate forms, voices draped in mantles, people the mind, and return to it in dreams. Monsters and dwarfs were the first gods; the half, said a Greek proverb, is better than the whole. The implicit is alone important where life is concerned: nothing is more eloquent than an abstract posture, an immovable single gesture. Let art abandon reproduction and become indication. If it threatens thereby to become caricature, know that profound art can never be anything else. If men, when seen truly, take on the aspect of animals or puppets, it is because they are animals and puppets at bottom. But all caricature need not be unkind; it may be tender, or even sublime. The distortion, the single emphasis, the extreme simplification may reveal a soul which rhetoric and self-love had hidden in a false rationality. The absurd is the naked truth, the pathetic appeal of sheer fact, attempting to come into existence, like a featherless chick peeping out of its eggshell. All this pompous drapery of convention was a disguise; strip it away. Do not make maps of your images; make companions of them, make idols. Be reticent, emphatic, moody, bold; *salvation lies in caricature.*

Accustomed as they are to revivals, some critics have called this form of æsthetic penance a revival of savage art; but the mood is reversed. Savages were never rudimentary on purpose; they were not experimenting in the distortion or simplification of forms; much less, of course, did they voluntarily eliminate all representation of objects in order to deepen sensibility for the medium. They simply painted as well as they could. We have got far be-

yond that. Penitent art, childish as it may seem at times, is a refinement, perhaps an over-refinement; it is not so much crude or
incompetent, as ascetic or morbid. It is also sometimes a little
vulgar; because one of the forms of caricature and self-revelation
is to be brutal, to flaunt what is out of place, what spoils the picture. Tragedy used to be noble; there is a new refinement in seeing how often it is ignoble; there is a second tragedy in that. Perhaps what we regard at first sight as a terrible decline in art may
be sometimes the awakening of this sort of self-scorn. See how
ugly I am, it cries, how brutish, common, and deformed! There
are remains of sculpture and paintings of the late Roman Empire
in some respects like our latest experiments. The decorative splendour (which was very marked) is lost; we miss the coloured mar-
bles, the gold, the embroideries, the barbaric armour and jewels;
but the stunted pathetic human figures remain in crowds. It seems
that the spirit had no joy in man any more; it hid him in hieratic
garments or pityingly recorded his gregarious misery. He was a
corpse laid out in pontifical vestments. We too are dying; but in
nature the death of one thing is commonly the birth of another.
Instead of decorating a Byzantine sanctuary, our artists do penance
in a psychological desert, studying their own sensations, the mysteries of sheer light and sound; and as music was long ago divorced
from poetry and instrumental music from singing, so a luxurious
but strident art is detaching itself from everything but its own
medium. This on the decorative side; in representation the same
retrenchment stops at another level. Representation too has a
psychological medium; fancy must create the images which the
observer or reproducer of things conceives to be their forms. These
images are not the forms of things at all; not only is their perspective created by the observer, but their character, when it is truly
considered, is amazingly summary, variable, and fantastic—a mere
wraith, a mere hint, a mere symbol. What we suppose we see,
what we *say* things look like, is rather an inventory, collected in
memory and language, of many successive observations; it is discursive study, registered perhaps in discursive painting. But as the
total composition never was nor ever could be a living image, so
its parts are not images any longer; in being arrested they have
acquired new boundaries and lost half their primitive essence. We
may paint the things we see, we cannot arrest the images by which

239

we see them; all we can do—if the images and not the things are what interest us—is to paint something that, by some occult trick of optics, may revive the image in some particular; and then, although the picture when studied discursively may not resemble the thing at all, it may bring back to us, as it were by scent, the feeling which the thing originally gave us; and we may say that it has caught the *spirit* of the thing. It is the medium that in such a case animates the object, and seems to obscure it; and this medium which we call sense in so far as things affect us through it, we call spirit in so far as it modifies our view of the things. The more we transform things in seeing them, the more we seem to spiritualise them and turn them into forms of our own sensibility, regarding the living image in us as the dramatic essence of the object. It is the business of science to correct this illusion; but the penitent artist—who has taken refuge in the spirit and is not striving to stretch his apprehension into literal tuth, since the effort to depict things discursively has proved a vain and arid ambition—the penitent artist is content with the rhythms, echoes, or rays which things awaken within him; and in proportion as these reverberations are actually renewed, the poem remains a cry, the story a dream, the building a glimpse, the portrait a caricature.

PROUST ON
ESSENCES

N o NOVELIST," writes Mr. Desmond MacCarthy, "has ever done such complete justice (as has Proust) to the great fact that all things pass and change." Yet this complete absorption in the flux of sensations, and abstention from all judgments about their causes or their relative values, leads Proust in the end to a very remarkable perception: that the flux of phenomena is after all accidental to them, and that the positive reality in each is not the fact that it appears or disappears, but rather the intrinsic quality which it manifests, an eternal essence which may appear and disappear a thousand times. Such an essence, when it is talked about, may seem mysterious and needlessly invented, but when noticed it is the clearest and least doubtful of things—the only sort of thing, indeed, that can ever be observed with direct and exhaustive clearness. An essence is simply the recognisable character of any object or feeling, all of it that can actually be possessed in sensation or recovered in memory, or transcribed in art, or conveyed to another mind. All that was intrinsically real in past time is accordingly recoverable. The hopeless flux and the temporal order of things are not ultimately interesting; they belong merely to the material occasions on which essences recur, or to the flutterings of attention, hovering like a moth about lights which are eternal.

A beautiful and impassioned confession of this discovery will be found in the last volume of Proust's great work, the second *Le Temps Retrouvé*, pp. 14–23. Speaking of the vivid recovery of things long past, he says:

> Ces diverses impressions bienheureuses . . . avaient entre elles ceci de commun, que je les éprouvais à la fois dans le moment

actuel et dans un moment éloigné . . . L'être qui alors goûtait en moi cette impression la goûtait en ce qu'elle avait de commun dans un jour ancien et maintenant, dans ce qu'elle avait d'extra-temporel, un être qui n'apparaissait que . . . dans le seul milieu où il pût vivre, jouir de l'essence des choses, c'est à dire, en dehors du temps. . . . Cet être là n'était jamais venu à moi, ne s'était jamais manifesté, qu'en dehors de l'action, de la jouissance im-médiate, chaque fois que le miracle d'une analogie m'avait fait échapper au présent. Seul il avait le pouvoir de me faire retrouver les jours anciens, le Temps Perdu, devant quoi les efforts de ma mémoire et de mon intelligence échouaient toujours. . . . J'avais pu trouver le monde et la vie ennuyeux parce que je les jugeais d'après des souvenirs sans vérité, alors que j'avais un tel appétit de vivre maintenant qui venait de renaître en moi . . . un véri-table moment du passé.

Rien qu'un moment du passé? Beaucoup plus, peut-être; quel-que chose qui, commun à la fois au passé et au présent, est beau-coup plus essentiel qu'eux deux.

L'être qui était rené en moi . . . ne se nourrit que de l'essence des choses, en elle seulement il trouve sa subsistance, ses délices. . . . Qu'un bruit, qu'une odeur, déjà entendu et respirée jadis le soient de nouveau, à la fois dans le présent et dans le passé, réels sans être actuels, idéaux sans être abstraits, aussitôt l'essence permanente et habituellement cachée des choses se trouve libérée et notre vrai moi . . . s'éveille, s'anime en recevant la céleste nourriture qui lui est apportée. . . . Cette contemplation, quoi-que d'éternité, était fugitive. Et pourtant je sentais que le plaisir qu'elle m'avait donné à de rares intervalles dans ma vie, était le seul qui fût fécond et véritable. Le signe de l'irréalité des autres ne se montre-t-il pas assez, soit dans leur impossibilité à nous satis-faire . . . soit dans la tristesse qui suit leur satisfaction? . . . Aussi cette contemplation de l'essence des choses, j'étais main-tenant décidé à m'attacher à elle, à la fixer . . . Et si je faisais la récapitulation des déceptions de ma vie, en tant que vécue, qui me faisait croire que sa réalité devait résider ailleurs qu'en l'ac-tion . . . je sentais bien que la déception du voyage, la déception de l'amour, n'étaient pas des déceptions différentes, mais l'aspect varié que prend, selon le fait auquel il s'applique, l'impuissance que nous avons à nous réaliser, dans la jouissance matérielle, dans l'action effective.[1]

[1]"These various happy impressions . . . had this in common, namely, that I felt them as if they were occurring simultaneously in the present moment and in some

No wonder that a sensibility so exquisite and so voluminous as that of Proust, filled with endless images and their distant reverberations, could be rescued from distraction only by finding certain repetitions or rhymes in this experience. He was a tireless husbandman of memory, gathering perhaps more poppies than corn; and the very fragility and worthlessness of the weeds collected may have led him to appreciate their presence only when lost, and their harsh scent only when recovered. Thus he required two phenomena to reveal to him one essence, as if essences needed to appear a second time in order to appear at all. A mind less volatile and less retentive, but more concentrated and loyal, might easily have discerned the eternal essence in any single momentary fact. It might also have felt the scale of values imposed on things by human nature, and might have been carried towards some by

---

distant past. . . . The person within me who was at that moment enjoying the impression enjoyed in it the qualities it possessed which were common to both an earlier day and the present moment, qualities which were independent of all considerations of time; and this person came into play only . . . in the . . . environment in which he could live and enjoy the essence of things, that is to say, entirely outside of time. . . . That person had never come to me, never manifested himself, except independently of all immediate activity, all immediate enjoyment, whenever the miracle of a resemblance with things past enabled me to escape out of the present. He alone had the power to make me recapture bygone days, times past, which had always balked the efforts of my memory and my intelligence. . . . I found society and even life tiresome . . . because I appraised them on the basis of false impressions of the past, whereas in reality I had now such an eager desire to live that an actual moment from the past had just been revived within me on three distinct occasions.

"Merely a moment from the past? Much more than that, perhaps; something which, common to both past and present, is far more essential than either.

"The being that was called to life again in me . . . draws its sustenance only from the essence of things, in that alone does it find its nourishment and its delight. . . . Let a sound already heard or an odour caught in bygone years be sensed anew, simultaneously in the present and the past, real without being of the present moment, ideal but not abstract, and immediately the permanent essence of things, usually concealed, is set free and our true self . . . awakes, takes on fresh life as it receives the celestial nourishment brought to it. . . . This contemplation, although part of eternity, was transitory. And yet I felt that the pleasure it had bestowed on me at rare intervals in my life was the only one that was fecund and real. Is not the indication of the unreality of the others sufficiently evident either in their inability to satisfy us . . . or in the despondency that follows whatever satisfaction they may give? . . . And so I was decided to consecrate myself to this study of the essence of things, to establish its true nature. . . . And if I recapitulated the disappointments in my life, as far as it had been lived, which led me to believe that its real essence must lie somewhere else than in action . . . I came to realise clearly that disappointment in a journey and disappointment in a love affair were not different in themselves but merely the different aspects assumed in varying situations by our inability to find our real selves in physical enjoyment or material activity." (*The Past Recaptured*, pp. 196–204, trans. Blossom.)

an innate love and away from others by a quick repulsion: something which in Proust is remarkably rare. Yet this very inhumanity and innocent openness, this inclination to be led on by endlessly rambling perception, makes his testimony to the reality of essences all the more remarkable. We could not have asked for a more competent or a more unexpected witness to the fact that life as it flows is so much time wasted, and that nothing can ever be recovered or truly possessed save under the form of eternity which is also, as he tells us, the form of art.

That Proust was endowed with a great power of intuition appears also in his style, since an adequate rendering of intuition in words must necessarily be diffuse and many-sided, and must invite to many a postscript and much reconsideration. The evanescent and immediate cannot be defined or traced or analysed: it must be re-evoked by suggestion. And here a scrupulous psychological critic might express a doubt: Is it likely that any given essence should be ever re-evoked exactly? Doubtless, similar events often recur: the same bell strikes the same hours, and the old head shakes in the same old way. But the observer is seldom or never in exactly the same mood, or capable of an intuition equally keen and pure. The repetition of similar events is common: the recurrence of a given essence in a living mind is rare, and perhaps impossible. Much iteration of the stimulus may, indeed, be requisite before there is any relevant intuition at all. How many times may we not hear, or even repeat, a phrase, before its meaning flashes upon us? How many years may we not be daily passing a monument, before its proportions and composition are at last perceived? The earlier impressions may not have been wholly wasted: they may have prepared the ground, and may help to deepen and fix the intuition when it comes at last. But the persuasion that this new intuition is not new, and that we have had it in exactly this form before, is probably an illusion; the well-known illusion of the déjà-vu. In any case, the mere feeling of recognition is no evidence of recurrence: on the contrary, the fact that two terms are compared and identified in intuition proves of itself that they are both given at once: and if a long-lost instance of this given essence seems to have lodged before in some past moment, the reason lies in the mechanism of memory, of belief, and of arrested reaction. The essence attributed to the past moment must be given

now, else it could not be attributed. It is not found by inspection
in two facts of different dates—something psychologically impossible—and then abstracted from them. It is given spontaneously,
in the present flow of sensibility, as in a waking dream: and it
seems to be reduplicated only because it is attributed both to a
present and to a past object, conceived to exist apart.

The important point, however, is not how intuition is reached,
but that when reached it reveals an essence belonging of itself
neither here nor there, but undated and eternal. Such essences
are set over against existence everywhere and at all times, and it
remains for existence, if it will, to embody their forms or to give
attention to them, so that they may become evident to living
spirits. And a living spirit finds a great joy in conceiving them, not
because they are all beautiful or true, but because in conceiving
them it is liberated from the pressure of ulterior things, energises
perfectly, and simply conceives.

THE LAST PURITAN

(selections)

O N PRINCIPLE it would seem futile as well as egotistical for an author to explain himself and tell the public what they ought to think of him. He has once for all surrendered his work to their jurisdiction, and even surrendered his own person and private history, which they are now at liberty, if they choose, to make an object of investigation or conjecture: and he cannot be sure, when he thinks their praise or censure to be ill grounded, that after all they may not be right: for who is man, especially histrionic rhetorical man, to see the truth of his own doings?

Nevertheless, in respect to *The Last Puritan* I have been asked for explanations; and in the *Prologue* and *Epilogue* I have already given the critics some hints: rashly, perhaps, since sometimes they have taken advantage of my frankness to exaggerate my limitations. For instance, when I say that my characters all speak my language and are in some sense masks for my own spirit, that is no reason for assuming without examination that they must be a philosopher's puppets and not "living." On the contrary, if these characters are expressions of actual experience, and only dressed, like an actor on the stage, for their several parts, they ought to be all the more profoundly alive, being impersonations of the soul and not sketches taken by a social tourist. When a man has lived as long as I have with his characters—forty-five years—they seem to him to speak and act of their own free will, and without prompting. No doubt this only happens because they are parts of himself; yet these parts were originally contrasted and spontaneous potentialities within him, and by no means vehicles for his own later conventional personality or approved thoughts. If the book

246

is something of a monologue, it is nevertheless *acted* throughout. The *Prologue* and *Epilogue* (and also Oliver's college essay, which has deceived some people) are integral parts of the fable, and written in character, even when, for a moment, that character is a stage-presentation of myself. Indeed, what I am now adding in this Preface, though an afterthought and spoken before the curtain, is also composed for the public, and is no innocent aside. This commentary therefore remains, like the rest of the book, subject to revaluation and suspicion on the critic's part. In fact, I am more confident of uttering sincerely the sentiments of my characters than of describing justly their place in my own mind. Self-criticism and autobiography, no matter how sincere, are far from being naturally truthful. They belong to a peculiarly treacherous and double-dyed species of the subjective. Perhaps if, as Aristotle tells us, poetry is essentially truer than history, one reason may be that fiction, by an avowed artifice, redresses the balance of selfish illusion, and satirically exposes the dark labyrinths of self-deception to the light of day.

People ask: How much in the story of your Last Puritan have you drawn from real life, and how much is invented? I reply: Nothing is wholly historical, nothing is wholly imaginary. In the first page of the *Prologue* I have taken pains to establish my privilege of hopelessly mixing the two: many of the threads are real but the tapestry is a dream. I actually lived in Paris at the place and time indicated, and in that half scholastic, half cosmopolitan atmosphere. More than one young friend of my Harvard days has rung the bell of that apartment in the Avenue de l'Observatoire, and come to dine with me at a restaurant. Howard Sturgis, too, was really a cousin of my family's, and lived at Windsor, as I describe him: but his halcyon days fell in the 1890's, a little earlier than the events of my story. I laugh at anachronisms, when they are not incongruities. All these real details, however, are transfigured in my fancy and made to dance as they never danced in reality by the imaginary presence of Mario Van de Weyer. Oliver and Mario are the original personages of my fable. In them converge sundry potentialities which from my earliest youth I felt in myself or divined in other people: potentialities not realisable together in a single person, nor perhaps realisable at all in the modern world. Both these figures were self-composed, by an accumulation of kindred traits, as legendary figures take shape in tradition. They were not psychological manikins, contrived intentionally, but true heroes, imposing themselves upon me with the authority of a moral force.

I call this book *A Memoir in the Form of a Novel*, because it was never planned as a story with an artificial dramatic unity, but was meant from the beginning to be the chronicle, half satirical, half poetic, of a sentimental education. In the early 1890's, when I had returned to Harvard to teach but still lived among undergraduates, it occurred to me to contrast the moral development of two friends, one gay and the other demure, who should be drawn in opposite directions, such as to test their mutual affection and lend it a tragic touch. But I soon found that college life hardly afforded occasions even for the slightest comedy. The canvas would have to be filled in with humorous details about the boys' background and families. *How They Lived* was indeed the title which I gave to my first sketches; but the original moral theme tended to be submerged in those miscellaneous episodes, my dominant interest turned to other projects, and the novel lay dormant for years, until the war of 1914, and fresh contacts with university life, now at Oxford, suggested to me how the whole story might be unified and brought to a head.

Meantime a tragic circumstance in the American scene had aroused my special attention: the early death of five or six young Harvard poets in the 1880's and 1890's, all more or less friends of mine, whose unanimous collapse I could not attribute to accident. To what insoluble conflict between the world and the spirit could such failure be due? As I revolved this doubt, the whole nature and history of Oliver began to grow clearer in my mind. My dead friends had all had philosophic keenness and moral fervour; they had all been fearless and independent in mind; but none of them seemed to have found matter fitted for his energies, or to have had the intellectual power requisite to dominate his circumstances and turn what might be unfavourable in them into a triumph of expression. Here, then, was the essential tragedy of the late-born Puritan, made concrete in several instances and illustrated before my eyes. This, added to a certain aridity, difficulty, and confusion which I could feel in the spirits of the elder New England worthies, and in my remarkable teachers and colleagues at Harvard, supplied moral substance for those sketches of manners and types which I could draw from observation.

Old Bostonians will recognise the originals of my Nathaniel Alden and Caleb Wetherbee: yet even these figures have not been copied literally from nature, but caricatured and recomposed with an eye to the general theme of my story. Moreover, the original of Nathaniel had no younger half-brother; and the mania for collecting bad paintings belonged not to him but to a different and more amiable old gentleman. Caleb also had not one original but two; and the one who changed his religion had not turned Catholic but Buddhist. For Peter Alden and his wife the models were legion, like those for the Van de Weyer family in New York. Even in the case of Oliver, originals might be found for some of his personal traits or family circumstances. But I paint no full-length portraits from life: I fuse as many sympathetic intuitions as possible into a fiction which might have been actualised as easily as any actual experience, and perhaps more tellingly. My sources for the whole American scene—Oliver's inner life excepted—were diffused widely and observed somewhat externally; for though I was perfectly at home in that life and immensely interested in it, having lived and gone to school in Boston through all the most important years of boyhood and youth, yet I found myself in that world by force of peculiar circumstances of which I felt the strangeness. It always seemed to me a strained, kindly, humorous, somehow fleshless world. Spain, of which I say nothing in this book, was after all my real country: when I went back there, or came across stray Spanish people, I was not happier or better pleased, but decidedly less comfortable physically and morally: yet that old passive passionate way of living, that religion, those very faults and disillusions seemed to me somehow more human, more classical, than all this slavish diligence in modern duties. I could not help feeling that what dominated America was a passing fever, a heresy, a forced enthusiasm, not really satisfying the heart and destined to end in emptiness.

Entirely different was my sentiment towards England and the genesis of my English characters. In England I have never had any home or legitimate stamping-ground, such as my mother's connections through her first marriage had given me in Boston. Perhaps for that very reason my affection for England has always been romantic. From my first prolonged visit in 1887 to the outbreak of the war, when I lived there for five consecutive years, England was the Mecca of my yearly pilgrimage. Physically and morally, I found myself there even more comfortable than in America; all strain was relaxed; the eye and the ear were softly flattered; the imagination was stirred by living remnants of mediaeval Christendom; and something wholesome and Spartan in the air seemed to neutralise the affectations and crotchets of the inhabitants. I could wander about the country in leisurely enchantment. I could live with my scattered but familiar friends in perfect half-silent sympathy. My English characters in this book—I don't know with what success—are therefore evoked poetically. Except Jim Darnley—who though entirely transformed in externals has been recognised by those who knew him most intimately—they are not so much drawn from particular persons as created for me by the landscape, by the voices, by the atmosphere of cool domesticity and indomitable private religion. There was something primitive and sacred here, for instance in the sentiment of my friend Robert Bridges, that escaped me, but that I revered: something at once Spartan, Christian, and feudal, yet merged in the English mist with a profound naturalism, as if the Druid also had survived in the modern man of letters. Was not this the fulness and the happy decline and self-transformation of that very spirit which in my American friends died so hard, or was so cruelly dispersed amongst irrelevant cares?

This brings us back to my hero, who is the hero and martyr of a spiritual crisis. Not all my readers have understood that what we may call Oliver's failures were due to his superiority, not to his inferiority. In the first place, he did not fail altogether, but without breaking away from a social order which violated all his instincts he succeeded in maintaining a perfect integrity and sweetness. He never sought praise, pleasure, or riches. He was faithful in everything and cherished everybody, even his mother, as much as was humanly possible. Charity and insight in him entirely killed personal resentment and even tamed his instinctive moral ferocity. False comforts and false loves never deceived him, so profound was his allegiance to a chivalrous sincerity. Yet he was not perfect; his capacity for perfection was moral only. One is not with impunity an heir to all the Puritans. A certain hardness and egotism limited his comprehension even of the people and things that attracted him most; and with the clearest theoretical intelligence he could sometimes act stupidly. If a thing seemed to him right, he could not admit that other people would perhaps object to it. And in himself he could not be happy. Natural perfection, the witchery of the moment, the irresponsible courage of young life, though he felt their charm, could never win him over to complete acquiescence and inward peace. He had been hamstrung by circumstances. Naturally a spiritual man, he had neither the force nor the time to break through and live victoriously in the spirit.

Satirical reasons are given in the *Prologue,* from Mario's point of view, for calling Oliver the last Puritan, but I had other reasons also in mind. In him puritanism was exhausted, and on the other hand it was surpassed. It was exhausted as a reforming political force, with a secret aggressive worldliness inspiring its iconoclasms. Oliver was "the third sloppy wash in the family teapot," and had neither the robustness to militate in that dubious cause nor the coarseness of fibre to live happy under that domination. But spiritually he was a born puritan, and more thoroughly distilled and refined than his ancestors. If in him the metaphysical austerity of the seventeenth century reappeared atavistically, his late birth relieved him of any horrid uncertainty about the truth of traditional myths and dogmas. Like the Stoics and like Spinoza he found his moral demands face to face with a universe that inspired but did not sanction them. The sea, the stars, the heathen, his own father and his dearest friends set up no such standards as were imposed on him by his sovereign conscience: sovereign over him, not over them. And though this diversity of allegiance condemned him to a secret solitude, he was too rational and generous to blame them, or to think them wrong. If anything, he envied them a little; sighed, like a young heir to a throne, at the limitations imposed on him by privilege: and he admired the grace and alacrity with which Mario, for instance, could rise, without asking questions, to the crest of each successive wave.

Yet Mario, too, like Oliver, was late-born. The two were differently aristocratic, and belonged to the past rather than to the future. Only Mario, being less serious and more adaptable, could make the best of his good luck, and sail before the wind without pretending to have any firm hold on reality. He was healthy and

therefore bold, humble and therefore facile. His ability to laugh
at everything, including himself, made it easy for him to put up
with the mixed loose world in which he lived, and positively to
enjoy it: easier, too, than for Oliver, much easier, to put up with
himself. People may lead cheerful and prosperous lives, and make
wonderful companions, if they can put up with everything.

Oliver was neither humble nor facile; but was he healthy? I
have given various indications to the contrary, on which the dis-
cerning reader will not ask me to insist. I am willing that amateur
pathologists should call Oliver degenerate. But that is not the end
of the story. He was a spiritual man, with a divine vocation. On
different occasions, Irma, Caleb Wetherbee, and the Vicar compare
him with Christ. Now a divine vocation is a devastating thing; and
it makes no ultimate difference whether you attribute poetically
the mortification and withering up of the flesh to a touch of celestial fire, or cynically regard a high spiritual temperature as an
effect of disease. Either way, the spirit burns unquenchably: and
the secret of Oliver's tragedy is missed by those amiable critics who
write to me that their own sons were just like him, but turned out
splendidly; or that if only he had noticed how much nicer Maud
was than Edith, or if Rose had only been less offish and wilful, all
would have been well, and Oliver might have spent a gloriously
useful life in the service of humanity. That is what his mother
would have said. I know how readily many young men with Puritan traditions can be harnessed to the public coach; and perhaps
their hereditary uprightness helps to leaven business, and to make
them personally nicer than other Babbitts. But this solution, which
Oliver in his helplessness actually foresaw and was willing sadly
to accept as his human duty, could never have satisfied him, as it
satisfies the normal fleshly and worldly man, who cares for nothing
beyond. For in Oliver there was something else: an inner inhibition intercepted and waylaid him, as it were, in all his actions,
without availing to redirect his life. He proved inapt, not only in
love-making, but even in those studies, sports, and friendships on
which he had prided himself most. His great error was that he
tried to be commonplace. His vocation remained vague: he had
not the insight or the courage to make it definite. In vain the Vicar
reminded him that Christ had not been a soldier or an athlete or

a lover of women or a merchant or a statesman or even (though the Vicar did not say so) a professor of philosophy or a believing Christian. All these sweets are at last bitter to the spirit. Buddha, at the first glimpse of the truth of life, had abandoned his throne and his young wife and child, to meditate on the fourfold root of suffering and preach the way of salvation. Poor Oliver too was ready for every sacrifice: he was what the rich young man in the Gospel would have been if he had offered to sell his goods and give to the poor, but then had found no cross to take up, no Jesus to follow, and no way of salvation to preach.

It is thought sad to come to an end early, or to come to an end at all; but such sadness is only the foiled sympathy of body with body, when motion ceases, and the flesh that was warm and living has grown stiff and cold. To the spirit, on the contrary, it is glorious to have finished all there was to do. It would be distressing rather to be tossed about perpetually from impulse to impulse, where nothing definite could ever be accomplished, nothing achieved. What was sad about Oliver was not that he died young or was stopped by accident, but that he stopped himself, not trusting his inspiration: so that he knew "the pity, not the joy, of love," the severity of intellect and not its glory.

CRITICAL EXCERPTS

. . . "Why haven't you any American books?"

"Haven't we?" Peter murmured, apparently surprised. "Didn't we have *Moby Dick* in the *Hesperus?*"

"Yes," Jim replied, "and there's also Walt Whitman."

"But mother says nobody reads Walt Whitman except foreigners. I thought he was English."

Oliver wondered at the loud laughter that greeted this confession. He might have made a mistake, but why so much merriment?

"But he's the great, the best, the only American poet," Jim burst out, "the only one truly American. Do you mean that you've never read him?"

"Oliver has been brought up on the classics, and Walt Whitman isn't yet counted among them, at least not in our family. No reason why Oliver shouldn't read those effusions, but I don't think he will like them. I don't read them myself: so that, as far as we three are concerned, Oliver's mother is quite right. Only the Englishman reads Walt Whitman."

"But you have read him, only you choose to disparage all great poetry."

"I confess I don't care for poetry that is long-winded and over-bearing, poetry that fumes and preaches. The poetry of western nations is chiefly rhetoric—eloquence in metre. So Shakespeare in the long speeches, though not in the songs, nor always in the sonnets. I think it is useless to try to beautify things in general, and that is what all speechifying poets do. Walt Whitman no less than the others. When a rhetorician composes long poems about God or Satan or the Universe or Agricultural Labours or Love or Liberty or Revolution, I don't say he may not propound important truths, although I doubt it, or that his moral sentiments may not seem edifying to people of his own sect; but I say he is not a poet. He carries a load. His Pegasus is a pack-ass with wings attached that flap in time as he plods along. Consecutive and progressive eloquence is all very well; and a political flambeau may pass from hand to hand and start a universal conflagration. But poetry is something secret and pure, some magical perception lighting up the mind for a moment, like reflections in the water, playful and fugitive. Your true poet catches the charm of something or anything, dropping the thing itself. His feeling is rapturous, mocking, musical, sad; above all, it is involuntary."

Jim had disappeared to work out his observations. Didn't he know by heart what the Doctor was going to say? But he returned for a moment and emphatically laid the *Leaves of Grass* on Oliver's knee. "There you are. Read a bit and judge for yourself."

There was a book-mark in the volume, which opened of itself at a passage heavily scored in the margin. *I could turn and live with the animals, they are so placid. . . . They do not weep for their sins. They do not make me sick discussing their duty to God.*

Dope, thought Oliver, himself a little somnolent in the noon-day heat and the soft air, *dope* in another form. A lazy refusal to look backward, or to look ahead. A hatred of reason, a hatred of sacrifice. The lilies of the field. Work wasn't worth while. Work wasn't necessary. Why should his father object to this sort of *dope?* And he read aloud a part of the passage.

"Don't you like that?"

"I like the first three words: *I could turn.* Deeply felt, they would mean conversion, repentance. They might have been spoken by Buddha or by John the Baptist."

"But you don't like the rest?"

"I should have liked it well enough if he had said he could turn and *no longer* live with the animals, they are so restless and merciless and ferocious, possessed with a mania for munching grass and gnawing bones and nosing one another, when they don't make me sick saying they are God's chosen people, doing God's work. But Walt Whitman is as superficial as Rousseau. He doesn't see that human conventions are products of nature, that morality and religion and science express or protect animal passions: and that he couldn't possibly be more like an animal than by living like other men. His rebellion is no conversion, no deliverance. He pretends to turn—for it is largely affectation—only from the more refined devices of mankind to a ruder and more stupid existence. He is like Marie Antoinette playing the shepherdess." . . .

*　　*　　*

. . . "Oliver has had a German governess who is a priestess of the Goethe cult. What does she call it? Realistic idealism, romantic classicism, or pantheistic individualism?"

"She calls it simply philosophy," Oliver replied, feeling that his father was frivolous and his Papist cousin hopelessly prejudiced. "She says that philosophy is always outgrowing its own systems, and that Goethe had outgrown all the philosophies up to his day, but that we haven't yet outgrown his, because it sums up all our science."

"Don't let the Germans cheat you, my boy," Cousin Caleb began, horribly grinning. "They are greater bluffers at philosophy than any smart Yankee ever was at the game of poker. Their manipulations of history are always different and always scandalous. It is all a play of wilful arbitrary perspectives, hiding what you please, and joining what you please. Nothing else is required for them to pose as the latest leaders in the march of thought. Blow, blow, thou Zeitgeist; thou art not so unkind as the truth would be to these self-advertising prophets. Yet they are good teachers, Oliver, because they have the true workman's respect for his tools: they put you through the mill; there is as much humility in the grist of their brew as there is pride and impudence in the froth of it. Learn to burrow with them; learn to love your work; but come often out of that Nibelungen smithy into the sun. The passions of those quarrelsome tinkers are ridiculous, and their ultimate conclusions are worthless.

"Goethe at least was not a professor, though he talked a little like one at times. He was a great man; could be a lyric singer at one moment and a primitive naturalist at the next, poring over prismatic colours and volcanic stones like an innocent savage. But he also knew the world; he was very learned; and he lived in a somewhat manageable society, where his personal initiative told, and he could become the Napoleon of letters. But what a diabolical guide for the soul! Worse than Voltaire, worse than Rousseau, more fundamentally immoral, more insidiously dissolute and in-vertebrate. I said he knew the world: but he worshipped the world —worshipped nature, and life, and society, and convention or whatever else we call the world—which proves that, at bottom, he *didn't* know the world. He was taken in by it; he sold his soul to it, like his blackguard of a Faust. He was convinced that there was nothing else to do; that to sell your soul to the world was salvation; and he put religion on the stage like a ballet, to crown irreligion, and give it a final blessing with the trombones at full blast, and the angels singing hallelujah. Could a mind be fundamentally more vulgar? Worse than Walt Whitman slapping his hairy breast in the Brooklyn Ferry and saying, 'What a good man am I!' Goethe, in-stead, having married his cook and got his title of nobility, lounges in his western-easterly divan and affably offers you, in a golden snuff-box, the dust of worldly wisdom and the ashes of his soul."

Oliver laughed, laughed with a flush of excitement and merri-ment that quite transformed him, as if his old head on young shoulders had suddenly opened fresh communications with the vascular system. "Oh, if only Fräulein could hear that! How she would stare! She wouldn't understand one word of it."

"But *you* understand," Cousin Caleb cried triumphantly, glar-ing at Oliver with the globular eyes of an ogre. "I can see that *you* understand."

"Yes, I think I understand. Goethe was what you call a heathen. He said we must renounce, but he didn't. He gulped the whole thing down."

"Except the best things, Oliver. He renounced *them*. He had no taste for *them*, and no room."

"But I don't see how you can think him worse than Walt Whitman. In Walt Whitman, as far as I can see, there's only rigmarole. But in Goethe there is the Rathskellar in Leipsic and Faust's study and Mephisto and Gretchen and Mignon and Götz von Berlichingen and Egmont."

"Admirable, capital, true!" the old monster exclaimed with enthusiasm. "Our young Daniel knows what he likes. Goethe belonged to the great line of pictorial artists: Shakespeare, Raphael, Rubens, down to Dickens and Victor Hugo. Romantic illustration, picture-books, creations. Goethe created Mephistopheles, he painted Gretchen; but his love-lorn ladies and gentlemen and his philosophy were only for his own time. Faust himself, without Mephistopheles, would be a ninny; and therefore the great mind of Goethe decided that all good would be insipid without evil, and that the world is moved not by love of God but by love of woman. Was there ever a coxcomb on so grand a scale?"

There was a general laugh in which Caleb Wetherbee himself joined. But Oliver was too deeply stirred for laughter.

"Cousin Caleb," he said, leaning over towards the old wizard, who no longer seemed a repulsive stranger, "then you agree that Faust was never really saved at all? It's what I keep telling Fräulein. He had sold his soul to the devil in dead earnest, and he never repented. That *Himmelfahrt* at the end shouldn't have been put in: it's just a frill; and Goethe was inconsistent."

"What? At your age you've seen through that trick, which has taken in the wise and the learned? Yet it's clear enough, and I don't think Goethe meant to deceive. He supposed that nobody would be so stupid as not to understand. Of course there was nothing but life in this world. What better salvation could you hope for? What worse damnation could you fear? Of course it was right to sell your soul to the devil, as it had been right for Adam and Eve to eat the apple, because otherwise there wouldn't have been any pagan Greeks or any romantic Germans or any Wolfgang von Goethe. Life wouldn't be worth living, you see, if it weren't reckless and sinful."

"Then," Oliver persisted, still flushed with excitement, "then the *Prologue in Heaven*, too, would be nothing but a bad joke. Fräulein says there's the deepest wisdom in it, and the secret of life, but I say it's Old King Cole poking the devil in the ribs and telling him to keep the ball rolling."

"Who is this boy of yours, Peter," Cousin Caleb cried, "who is this boy of yours that sits here disputing among the doctors and putting us all to shame?"

"But I'm more than twelve years old," Oliver observed demurely. "I'm almost seventeen." And he wondered why the old man laughed. The gospels to him were a German storybook, and he felt sincerely modest.

His father, still smiling, had taken up the conversation in a changed tone.

"When Professor Norton says that Goethe was not a gentleman, I suppose we must all agree with him. But what does that matter? Very soon nobody will know what a gentleman was, unless he reads up the gentleman-concept in some German book of *Kulturgeschichte*. But as to Goethe being a heathen, you can't say, Caleb, that he despised the human heart, can you?"

"Despised it? No; he cultivated it, as my monks do their peaches against a sunny brick wall. He watched each prize heart ripen, and admired its velvety texture and colours richly fused. He was a connoisseur in hearts. But he didn't trust the heart, not even his own heart in his warmest love-affairs. He never probed the heart for its ultimate, its eternal object of love, in order to worship that object at all costs. Certainly he was no gentleman. He could never say yes to the heart, and he could never say no to the world." . . .

*　　*　　*

. . . What better theme than *Hamlet* for orchestration by young emotions, when the world still surprises us for being so wrong and transports us by being so beautiful? *Hamlet* provokes speculation, and without speculation, without wonder raising afresh the most baffling ultimate questions, the fervid confabulations of youth would not be complete. Philosophy is a romantic field into which chivalrous young souls must canter out bravely, to challenge the sinister shadows of failure and death. The sublimity of the issue establishes a sort of sporting fellowship even among opposite minds, and the green battlefield draws them together more than their contrary colours can avail to separate them. Oliver had read *Hamlet* carefully in the schoolroom and had learned from Fräulein

Schlote all that Goethe in *Wilhelm Meister* has to say about the play and the hero. Jim hadn't read Shakespeare at all, but he had seen *Hamlet* played once before at the Old Vic, and knew what he thought of it. It was, he confided to Oliver, by way of excuse for what he was about to hear, a rum old play, full of bombast and absurdities, but with a lot of topping lines in it that everybody had heard quoted. They were just the sort of thing that a clever chap like the hero might get off, but he was rather a muff at love and at politics, saw a ghost, and pretended to be mad in order to hide the fact that he was a quitter.

Oliver eagerly refuted these ignorant heresies, yet couldn't help chuckling at them. They gave him an occasion to maul their ridiculous author, and call him a fleshly brute without one glimmer of poetry in his soul. Hamlet, Oliver explained, was perfectly brave and firm when once sure of being right; but he had a tremendous intellect, tremendously pure and superior to all cut-and-dried opinions of ordinary people and even of science. This was what rendered him unfit for the everyday world. He wouldn't play his part whole-heartedly in human society, because he saw how one-sided and wicked were all the principles that governed it. The spirit in him, Goethe had said, burst through vulgar conventions as a young growing oak would burst through a little fancy flower-pot, if you had planted it there. One reason why Hamlet feigned to be mad was that he was aching to publish many a truth which it might have been rude to mention if he had seemed to be sane. When he tells Ophelia to go to a nunnery, it is his true mind that is breaking through. In this scene Oliver thought that Forbes Robertson had made a mistake. He had looked knowingly over his shoulder, to where the King and Polonius were hiding behind the arras, as much as to say that now he would put an antic disposition on expressly to deceive them. But why choose this moment, and precisely the antics that would break Ophelia's heart? Had Hamlet no insight and no tenderness? Surely, in Ophelia's presence, he didn't give a fig for those two old sneaking blackguards. He was thinking of Ophelia exclusively, and he spoke as he did, not because he didn't love her, but just because he loved and idealised her so much that he hated the idea of having her crushed and vulgarised in such a horrible mess as he now saw the world to be. At the cost of his own happiness, if he survived at all, he wished to save her from

all the awful things that may happen to a woman when she marries
and has children. He wanted to save her from everything coarsen-
ing, from everything degrading. Rather than that, he was willing
to seem cruel to her now and to let her think him a heartless beast
or a madman.

"Perhaps," said Jim with a paternal smile, "*perhaps* you know
what you are talking about. It's mysticism. My old Pater drops into
it sometimes in his sermons. When people fail in the world—and
Hamlet had been cheated out of the crown and hadn't the pluck to
resent it—they always say the world isn't a fit place to live in. But
it's all bally rot about Ophelia. Hamlet had to jilt Ophelia in the
play, so that she might go mad and scatter flowers and drown herself in the village pond, and make a lovely popular melodrama. Of
course Hamlet wouldn't have behaved like that, if you stop and
think; but you mustn't stop and think. You must be impressed.
The talk about a nasty world and living pure in a nunnery was
just the cant of those days. Every pulpit rang with it; as if one of
your intellectual cads nowadays, after seducing a girl, said, 'So
sorry, my dear. Can't marry. Believe in eugenics, and the doctors
say I'm consumptive.' It's just window-dressing to keep himself in
countenance while he sneaks away. If you took it seriously, you
ought to go yourself into old Wetherbee's tame monastery, and
never marry."

"Nonsense," cried Oliver a little ruffled. His smouldering Prot-
estantism had been blown upon, and there was an indignant spark.
He knew it was his duty to marry some day, as it was his duty to
go to college and to play football and to choose a profession. Fortunately the duty of marrying didn't come round at a fixed date like
the other duties, and he needn't think of it yet for years and years.
But what an insult to suppose that he would flinch from it when
the time came. "Of course," he went on aloud, blushing a little because unaccountably he remembered the first time he had un-
dressed in Jim's presence, on the deck of the *Black Swan*, and how
silly he had been about it, "of course, I shall get married some day.
The world has to be kept going, like a ship in mid-ocean. It would
be cowardly for a sailor to jump overboard, after having signed on
for the whole voyage, just because he was sick of it, like that en-
gineer of yours. Why on earth did he quit? Of course, a man might

die, like the mate—what did you say the mate died of?—or he might feel utterly unfit, like Hamlet, morally paralysed and overwhelmed, and might confess he was beaten. But *I* don't mean to be beaten. *I* don't see my grandfather's ghost, although he *was* murdered; and when I'm engaged, *I* sha'n't go and say to the dear thing: 'Get thee to a nunnery—because everything is so sad and I have tuberculosis.' " . . .

EPILOGUE

Fifteen years and more had elapsed since Mario Van de Weyer had first urged me to write this biography. We were still almost neighbours, but no longer in Paris. Different motives had prompted each of us to shift his centre to Rome, he more than ever in the current of the world and I more than ever out of it. We seldom met. Our acquaintance had passed into that serene crepuscular phase in which nothing more is demanded, and every past episode is affectionately folded in the cedar-chest of memory, to be shaken out on occasion together with the fragrance of time long past. At length I was able to send him a rough draft of these pages, composed at odd moments in the intervals of other work. He knew that, like the Pope, I accepted no invitations and paid no visits; but I asked him, after he had had time to dip into my manuscript, to come some fine day to lunch with me at the Pincio and tell me his impressions.

Accordingly we sat one early afternoon, basking the oblique warmth of the wintry sun, yet sheltered overhead by evergreen oak and ilex from the naked glare of the sky.

In respect to this novel, as I called it, I explained how insecure I had felt all these years, like an old schoolmaster for the first time in the saddle, at one moment innocently elated, and at the next in total distress. This wasn't my métier. However, I had got back alive to the stable, and safely dismounted. I stood again with both feet on my own ground; and I could laugh with him at my foolish excursion, if he pronounced it ridiculous.

My friend smiled amiably, looked about as if in doubt which of various observations to make first, and then said nothing.

Naturally he couldn't tell me outright to put the whole thing in the fire; but I was curious to know the grounds of his judgment.

"For instance," I said, "what of the characters, and in the first place of your own? Are you satisfied with your portrait?"

"It's no portrait; or so flattered that nobody would recognise it. You exaggerate enormously my favour with the fair sex. I wasn't different from any other young spark."

"You were more of a Don Juan than you now choose to remember. But you needn't disown your past. You are all of a piece, and your evolution has been natural. Don't you remember saying to Oliver that you wished to be a Knight of Malta? He thought the notion whimsical, but you have done even better. Gallantry in a gentleman passes easily into chivalry, and chivalry into religion."

"With my father-in-law's position at the Vatican," he replied colouring a little, "the thing came of itself."

"No, no. It wasn't mere nepotism; rather the outward sign of an inward grace. Your modernness sucks in all the sap of the past, like the modernness of the new Italy; and any future worth having will spring from men like you, not from weedy intellectuals or self-inhibited puritans. Fortune will never smile on those who disown the living forces of nature. You can well afford to let an old philosopher here and there anticipate death and live as much as possible in eternity. The truth cannot help triumphing at the last judgment. Perhaps it cannot triumph before. Perhaps, while life lasts, in order to reconcile mankind with reality, fiction in some directions may be more needful than truth. You are at home in the grand tradition. With the beautiful Donna Laura and your charming children, you will hand on the torch of true civilisation; or rather, in this classic Italy, you have little need of tradition or torches. You have blood within and sunlight above, and are true enough to the past in being true to yourselves."

"Yes. We are frankly animal—but to return to your book. Besides over-glorifying my peccadilloes, you almost turn me into a clever chap, which I never was. You put into my mouth a lot of good things of your own, or of Howard Sturgis's, or of other friends of yours. Moreover, in general, you make us all talk in your own philosophical style, and not in the least as we actually jabber. Your women are too intelligent, and your men also. There is clairvoyance in every quarter; whereas in the real world we are all unjust to one another and deceived about ourselves."

"Granted, granted," said I, delighted that at last the ball was rolling merrily. "I hardly see anybody, and I don't know how people talk. But that doesn't matter for my purpose. If I had been absolutely true to life, half my possible readers wouldn't have understood me. I wasn't composing a philological document in which future antiquarians might study the dialects and slang of the early twentieth century. I have made you all speak the lingo natural to myself, as Homer made all his heroes talk in Ionian hexameters. Fiction is poetry, poetry is inspiration, and every word should come from the poet's heart, not out of the mouths of other people. If here and there I have hinted at a characteristic idiom, it's not for the sake of the idiom but for the sake of the character or the mood. Even in the simplest of us passion and temperament have a rich potential rhetoric that never finds utterance; and all the resources of a poet's language are requisite to convey not what his personages would have been likely to say, but what they were really feeling. So with the characters themselves, I am not photographing real people and changing their names. On the contrary, wherever discretion permits, I keep the real names and the real places, just as Homer does. Real names have a wonderful atmosphere. But I recast, I re-live, I entirely transform the characters. They are creatures of imagination. Imagination! We are of imagination all compact. You know how energetically I reject the old axiom that sights and sounds exist in the material world, and somehow cause us to perceive them. Sights and sounds are products of the organism; they are forms of imagination; and all the treasures of experience are nothing but spontaneous fictions provoked by the impacts of material things. How foolish, then, should I have been in my own eyes to reject the images which you and my other friends have excited within me, when I have no other pigments at my disposal with which to paint mankind! And if we were not all clairvoyant at bottom, how should we ever recognise clairvoyance in others? Though an image must be only an image, it may be more or less suitable and proper: how much poetic truth, for instance, is there in my picture of Oliver himself?"

"More than in your picture of me. You knew him well. But you idealise him, and make him too complex. You introduce something Freudian into him which I never saw a sign of: fixations, transferences, inhibitions, or whatever else you call them. To my mind, he was perfectly normal, only a little vague and undeveloped. He required a lot of time to mobilise his forces."

"Yes," I interrupted, "because his forces were very great and drawn from a vast territory."

"Perhaps: but then why do you make him so much more intelligent than he seemed? You endow him with altogether too much insight. In reality he was simply bewildered. There was a fundamental darkness within him, a long arctic night, as in all Nordics."

"But isn't the arctic night very brilliant? And after the *aurora borealis* isn't there an arctic day, no less prolonged? I think there is no great truth that sensitive Nordics don't sometimes discover: only they don't stick to their best insights. They don't recognise the difference between a great truth and a speculative whim, and they wander off again into the mist, empty-handed and puzzle-headed. As to moral complications in Oliver, you must allow me my diagnosis. He was the child of an elderly and weary man, and of a thin-spun race; from his mother he got only his bigness and athleticism, which notoriously don't wear well. A moral nature burdened and overstrung, and a critical faculty fearless but helplessly subjective—isn't that the true tragedy of your ultimate Puritan? However, suppose I am wrong about the facts. Shall I tear the book up, or will it do as a fable?"

"As a fable you may publish it. It's all your invention; but perhaps there's a better philosophy in it than in your other books."

"How so?"

"Because now you're not arguing or proving or criticising anything, but painting a picture. The trouble with you philosophers is that you misunderstand your vocation. You ought to be poets, but you insist on laying down the law for the universe, physical and moral, and are vexed with one another because your inspirations are not identical."

"Are you accusing me of dogmatism? Do I demand that everybody should agree with me?"

"Less loudly, I admit, than most philosophers. Yet when you profess to be describing a fact, you can't help antagonising those who take a different view of it, or are blind altogether to that sort of object. In this novel, on the contrary, the argument is dramatised, the views become human persuasions, and the presentation is all the truer for not professing to be true. You have said it somewhere yourself, though I may misquote the words: After life is over and the world has gone up in smoke, what realities might the spirit in us still call its own without illusion save the form of those very illusions which have made up our story?"

TRAGIC PHILOSOPHY

In comparing a passage from *Macbeth* with one from the *Paradiso*, Mr. T. S. Eliot tells us that poetically the two are equally good, but that the philosophy in Shakespeare is inferior. By what standard, I am tempted to ask, may the poetic value of different types of poetry in different languages be declared equal? By the equal satisfaction, perhaps, that fills the critic's mind? But the total allegiance of a mature person, his total joy in anything, can hardly be independent of his developed conscience and his sense for ultimate realities. He cannot be utterly enchanted by what he feels to be trivial or false. And if he is not utterly enchanted, how should he recognise the presence of the supremely beautiful? Two passages could hardly be pronounced equal in poetic force if the ultimate suggestions of the one were felt to be inferior to those of the other.

Admitting, then, that poetry expressing an inferior philosophy would to that extent be inferior poetry, we may ask this further question: In what respect other than truth may philosophies be called inferior or superior? Perhaps in being more or less poetical or religious, more or less inspired? Sometimes a philosophy may spring up imaginatively, and in that sense may be inspired rather than strictly reasoned or observed, as the myths of Plato are inspired; but nobody would call such inspired philosophy *superior* unless he felt it to spring from the total needs and total wisdom of the heart; and in that case he would certainly believe, or at least hope, that this superior philosophy was true. How then should the poetic expression of this inspired philosophy not be conspicuously superior as poetry, and more utterly enchanting, than the expression of any other philosophy?

Let me postpone generalities, and turn to the passages in question.

266

Lady Macbeth is dead. Macbeth foresees his own end. All the prophecies flattering his ambition have been fulfilled, and after the mounting horror of his triumph he stands at the brink of ruin. Surveying the whole in a supreme moment, he consents to his destiny.

> *Tomorrow, and tomorrow and tomorrow*
> *Creeps in this petty pace from day to day*
> *To the last syllable of recorded time;*
> *And all our yesterdays have lighted fools*
> *The way to dusty death. Out, out, brief candle!*
> *Life's but a walking shadow; a poor player*
> *That struts and frets his hour upon the stage,*
> *And then is heard no more. It is a tale*
> *Told by an idiot, full of sound and fury,*
> *Signifying nothing.*

Mr. Eliot says that this philosophy is derived from Seneca; and it is certain that in Seneca's tragedies, if not in his treatises, there is a pomp of diction, a violence of pose, and a suicidal despair not unlike the tone of this passage. But would Seneca ever have said that life signifies nothing? It signified for him the universal reign of law, of reason, of the will of God. Fate was inhuman, it was cruel, it excited and crushed every finite wish; yet there was something in man that shared that disdain for humanity, and triumphed in that ruthless march of order and necessity. Something superior, not inferior, Seneca would have said; something that not only raised the mind into sympathy with the truth of nature and the decrees of heaven, but that taught the blackest tragedy to sing in verse. The passions in foreseeing their defeat became prophets, in remembering it became poets; and they created the noblest beauties by defying and transcending death.

In Seneca this tragic philosophy, though magnificent, seems stilted and forced; it struts rhetorically like an army of hoplites treading down the green earth. He was the last of ancient tragedians, the most aged and withered in his titanic strength; but all his predecessors, from Homer down, had proclaimed the same tragic truths, softened but not concealed by their richer medium. Some of them, like Virgil, had rendered those truths even more poignant precisely by being more sensitive to the loveliness of perishable things. After all, the same inhuman power that crushes us, breeds us and feeds us; life and death are but two aspects of the same natural mutation, the same round of seed-time and harvest. And if all human passions must be fugitive, they need not all be unamiable: some are merry in their prime, and even smile at their own fading. An accident of ritual led the ancients to divide tragedy sharply from comedy; I think it has been a happy return to nature in modern dramatists and novelists to intermingle the two. Comic episodes abound in the most tragic experience, if only we have the wit to see them; and even the tragic parts are in reality relieved by all sorts of compensations that stimulate our sense of life and prompt us to high reflection. What greater pleasure than a tear that pays homage to something beautiful and deepens the sense of our own profundity?

Not every part of this classic philosophy re-echoes in the pessimism of Macbeth. Shakespeare was not expressing, like Seneca, a settled doctrine of his own or of his times. Like an honest miscellaneous dramatist, he was putting into the mouths of his different characters the sentiments that, for the moment, were suggested to him by their predicaments. Macbeth, who is superstitious and undecided, storms excessively when he storms; there is something feverish and wild in his starts of passion, as there is something delicate in his perceptions. Shakespeare could give rein in such a character to his own subtle fancy in diction and by-play, as well as in the main to the exaggerated rhetoric proper to a stage where everybody was expected to declaim, to argue, and to justify sophistically this or that extravagant impulse. So at this point in *Macbeth*, where Seneca would have unrolled the high maxims of orthodox Stoicism, Shakespeare gives us the humours of his distracted hero; a hero nonplussed, confounded, stultified in his own eyes, a dying gladiator, a blinded lion at bay. And yet intellectually —and this is the tragedy of it—Macbeth is divinely human, rational enough to pause and survey his own agony, and see how brutish, how insignificant, it is. He sees no escape, no alternative; he cannot rise morally above himself; his philosophy is that there is no philosophy, because, in fact, he is incapable of any.

Shakespeare was a professional actor, a professional dramatist; his greatness lay there, and in the gift of the gab: in that exuberance and joy in language which everybody had in that age, but he supremely. The Renaissance needed no mastering living religion, no mastering living philosophy. Life was gayer without them. Philosophy and religion were at best like travels and wars, matters for the adventurer to plunge into, or for the dramatist to describe; never in England or for Shakespeare central matters even in that capacity, but mere conventions or tricks of fancy or moods in individuals. Even in a Hamlet, a Prospero or a Jaques, in a Henry VI or an Isabella, the poet feels no inner loyalty to the convictions he rehearses; they are like the cap and bells of his fools; and possibly if he had been pressed by some tiresome friend to propound a personal philosophy, he might have found in his irritation nothing else to fall back upon than the animal despair of Macbeth. Fortunately we may presume that burgherly comfort and official orthodoxy saved him from being unreasonably pressed.

That which a mastering living philosophy or religion can be, we may see at once by turning to the passage from Dante. In the lowest circle of Paradise, that of the inconstant moon, dwells the spirit of Piccarda, a lady who, having once been a nun but having been carried off and married by force, when later she became a widow preferred to continue her life in the world rather than return to her convent. Dante asks her if those who dwell in this part of Heaven ever desire to go higher, so as to see more and to love more. And she replies, No: for the essence of religious love is union with the order of creation. Perfect happiness would be impossible, if we were not perfectly happy in what God has given us; and in his will is our peace.

> *Frate, la nostra volontà quieta*
> *Virtù di carità, che fa volerne*
> *Sol quel ch'avemo, e d'altro non ci asseta*
> *Se disiassimo esser più superne,*
> *Foran discordi li nostri disiri*
> *Dal voler di colui che qui ne cerne;*
> *Che vedrai non capere in questi giri,*
> *S'essere in carità è qui necesse,*
> *E se la sua natura ben rimiri.*
> *Anzi è formale ad esto beato esse*
> *Tenersi dentro a la divina voglia,*

Per ch'una fansi nostre voglie stesse;
Si che, come noi sem di soglia in soglia
  Per questo regno, a tutto il regno piace
  Com' a lo re ch'a suo voler ne invoglia.
E'n la sua volontade è nostra pace:
  Ell'è quel mare al qual tutto si move
  Ciò ch'ella cria e che natura face.
Chiaro mi fu allor come ogni dove
  In cielo è paradiso, etsi la grazia
  Del sommo ben d'un modo non vi piove.

I questioned at the beginning whether the poetic value of unlike things could be pronounced equal: and if now I compare this
whole passage with the passage from *Macbeth* I find that to my
sense they are incommensurable. Both are notable passages, if that
is all that was meant; but they belong to different poetic worlds,
appealing to and developing different sides of the mind. And there
is more than disparity between these two worlds; there is con-
trariety and hostility between them, in as much as each professes
to include and to subordinate the other, and in so doing to annul
its tragic dignity and moral finality. For the mood of Macbeth,
religion and philosophy are insane vapours; for the mood of Dante,
Macbeth is possessed by the devil. There is no possible common
ground, no common criterion of truth, and no common criterion
even of taste or beauty. We might at best say that both poets succeed in conveying what they wish to convey, and that in that sense
their skill is equal: but I hardly think this is true in fact, because
in Shakespeare the medium is rich and thick and more important
than the idea; whereas in Dante the medium is as unvarying and
simple as possible, and meant to be transparent. Even in this
choice passage, there are stretches of pure scholastic reasoning, not
poetical at all to our sensuous and romantic apprehension; yet the
studious and rapt poet feels himself carried on those wings of logic
into a paradise of truth, where choir answers choir, and everything is beautiful. A clear and transparent medium is admirable,
when we love what we have to say; but when what we have to say
is nothing previously definite, expressiveness depends on stirring
the waters deeply, suggesting a thousand half-thoughts, and letting
the very unutterableness of our passion become manifest in our

disjointed words. The medium then becomes dominant: but can this be called success in expression? It is rather success in making an impression, if the reader is impressed; and this effect seems essentially incomparable with that of pure lucidity and tireless exact versification in one chosen form. To our insecure, distracted, impatient minds, the latter hardly seems poetry.

Voltaire said that Dante's reputation was safe, because nobody read him. Nowadays that is hardly true; all superior persons read him a little, or read a great deal about him. He sets tempting problems for professional critics and antiquarians, and he appeals to archaistic taste, that flies for refuge into the fourth dimension, to everything that seems pure and primitive. But as living poetry, as a mould and stimulus for honest feeling, is Dante for us at all comparable to Shakespeare? Shakespeare, in passages such as this from *Macbeth,* is orchestrated. He trills away into fancy: what was daylight a moment ago, suddenly becomes a candle: we are not thinking or reasoning, we are dreaming. He needs but to say "all our yesterdays," and presently the tedium of childhood, the tedium of labour and illnesss, the vacancy of friendships lost, rise like vague ghosts before us, and fill us with a sense of the unreality of all that once seemed most real. When he mentions "a poor player" we think at once of the poet himself, because our minds are biographical and our sympathies novelesque; we feel the misery and the lurid contrasts of a comedian's life; and the existence that just now seemed merely vain, now seems also tempestuous and bitter. And the rhythms help; the verse struts and bangs, holds our attention suspended, obliges our thoughts to become rhetorical, and brings our declamation round handsomely to a grand finale. We should hardly have found courage in ourselves for so much passion and theatricality; but we bless Shakespeare for enabling us still to indulge in such emotions, and to relieve ourselves of a weight that we hardly knew we were carrying.

Nothing of the sort in the Italian: the simplest language, the humble vernacular, made pungent and to us often obscure only by an excess of concision and familiarity, or by allusions to events then on everybody's tongue. Dante allows his personal fortunes and hatreds to crop out in many places, perhaps quickening the interest of the modern gossip-loving reader. Yet these are incidental indiscretions, which the poet's own conscience might have regarded as blemishes. His work as a whole, and in intention, is that of a consecrated mind. A single thread of thought guides him; the eye is focussed on pure truth, on human wills illustrating the divine laws against which they profess to rebel; hell in the heart of earth, and earth enveloped in celestial harmonies. No occasion, as in modern edifying works, to avoid mentioning things unpleasant or to explain them away. Every detail is noted, not bashfully or apologetically but with zest; when anything is wicked, its wickedness is exhibited and proved for our instruction. We learn the scientific complexity of the moral world, all plain facts, demonstrable truths, principles undoubted and certified. Mastered and chastened by this divine dispensation, what need should we feel of verbal opulence or lurid rhetoric? Not one rare epithet, not one poetic plum; instead, a childlike intellectual delight in everything being exact, limpid, and duly named, and dovetailed perfectly into everything else. Each word, each rhyme, files dutifully by in procession, white verses, three abreast, like choristers, holding each his taper and each singing in turn his appointed note. But what sweetness in this endless fugue, what simple exactitude, what devout assurance; and how unanimously these humble voices, often harsh and untutored if taken singly, rise together into a soaring canticle! The poetry, you might say, of industrious children, careful to make no mistake, but having nothing of their own to say, or not daring to say it. And indeed Dante's mind is busy, learned, and intense; exact even in allegory, as in a sort of heraldry; yet this very minuteness and pedantry are the work of love. Never was heart more tender or subtle or passionate; only that its intensity is all turned towards metaphysical joys, and transferred to an inward spiritual heaven.

I doubt whether either the beauty or the weakness of such poetry can be understood without understanding the nature of religion, as neither religious people nor irreligious people are likely to do; not the irreligious, because of insensibility, and not the religious, because of delusion. Still, a disinterested student, say of the origins of Christianity, ought to understand. Religion is not essentially a supplement to common knowledge or natural affection on the same level as the latter: it is not essentially a part of rational life, adjusted however gropingly to cosmic or social influences, and expressing them and their effect. Religion is rather a second life, native to the soul, developed there independently of all evidence, like a waking dream: not like dreams coming in sleep and composed largely of distorted waking impressions, but an autonomous other life, such as we have also in music, in games, and in imaginative love. In religion the soul projects out of her own impulses, especially when these are thwarted, the conditions under which she will regard herself as living. If she needs salvation, she will posit a saviour; if the thought of death offends her, she will posit resurrection or even immortality; if she is troubled at the injustice of fortune, she will posit previous crimes or original sins of her own, to explain her misery. If in general she wishes to impose her will where she is impotent, she will utter that will in prayers or imprecations, and posit an invisible power inclined to listen, and able to help.

Now such an inner fountain of life and thought is evidently akin to poetic inspiration. As in poetry, so in religion, imagination evokes a more or less systematic invisible world in which the passions latent in the soul may work themselves out dramatically. Yet there are differences. The profane poet is by instinct a naturalist. He loves landscape, he loves love, he loves the humour and pathos of earthly existence. But the religious prophet loves none of these things. It is precisely because he does not love them that he cultivates in himself, and summons the world to cultivate, a second more satisfying life, more deeply rooted, as he imagines, in the nature of things. Earthly images therefore interest him only as symbols and metaphors, or as themes for denunciation. He is hardly a poet in the ordinary sense, except in so far as (like Milton, for instance) he may owe a double allegiance, and be a profane poet altogether when he is a poet at all. Religion is often professed and intellectually accepted without ever having flowered in the soul, or being suspected to have any kinship with poetry. It may have withered into a forced and angry metaphysics or semi-political party doctrine, poetically deplorable.

The opposite is the case in Dante, whose poetry is essentially religious, as his religion is essentially poetical. We are in the presence of an overpowering inspiration, become traditional, become also learned and quasi-scientific, but still kindled by moral passion and fertile in poetic ideas. The Hebrew prophets had begun by denouncing that which was and proclaiming that which should be; but that which should be could evidently never become actual without a miracle and a total revolution in the world; so that prophecy turned to eschatology and to expectation of a Messiah. At this point pagan streams of inspiration began to mingle with the Hebraic stream. Perhaps the Messiah had already come. Perhaps he was to be no conquering monarch, but a god in disguise. Perhaps he had been crucified, as the spirit is always crucified. Perhaps his kingdom was not of this world. Were there not reports that Jesus, who had been crucified, had been seen, risen from the dead? Would he not surely come again with glory in the clouds of heaven? Transfigured by this new spiritual faith, many current legends and maxims were ascribed to Jesus, and beautifully set down in the Gospels. The fathers worked out the theology. The saints repeated the miracles and explored all the phases of ascetic and mystical experience. Nothing remained but for Dante, with exquisite fidelity and minuteness, to paint a total picture of the Christian universe. The whole substance of that universe was poetry; only the details could threaten to become prosaic; but this danger was removed, in the more important places, by Dante's extraordinary sensitiveness. He had had a revelation of his own in childhood, interrupted later by the false glare of the world, but finally restored in the form of religious wisdom and consecration. The fresh dew of poetry and love trembled upon everything. Indeed, for our modern feeling the picture is too imaginative, too visionary, soaked too much in emotion. In spite of the stern historical details, when we rub our eyes and shake off the spell, the whole thing seems childishly unreal. We can understand why Mr. Eliot feels this to be a "superior" philosophy; but how can he fail to see that it is false?

Inspiration has a more intimate value than truth and one more unmistakably felt by a sensitive critic, since inspiration marks a sort of spring-tide in the life of some particular creature, whereas truth impassively maps the steady merciless stretches of creation at large. Inspiration has a kind of truth of its own, truth to the soul; and this sincerity in intuition, however private and special it might be, would never conflict with the truth of things, if inspiration were content to be innocently free and undogmatic, as in music or lyric poetry. The inmost vegetative impulses of life might then come to perfect flower, feeling and celebrating their own reality without pretending to describe or command reality beyond, or giving any hostages to fortune. But unfortunately animals cannot long imitate the lilies of the field. Where life is adventurous, combative and prophetic, inspiration must be so too. Ideas, however spontaneous, will then claim to be knowledge of ulterior facts, and will be in constant danger of being contradicted by the truth. Experience, from being lyrical, will become tragic; for what is tragedy but the conflict between inspiration and truth? From within or, as we may fancy, from above, some passionate hope takes shape in the mind. We fall in love or hear a voice from heaven; new energies seem to leap up within us; a new life begins crowding the old life out, or making it seem dreary or wicked. Even when inspiration is not moral, but merely poetical, it kindles a secret fire and an inner light that put vulgar sunshine to shame. Yet not for long, nor for ever; unless we passionately shut ourselves up in the *camera obscura* of our first inspiration, and fear the darkness of other lights. The more profound and voluminous that first inspiration was, the more complete at last will be our astonishment and despair. We shall cry with *Le Cid:*

> *Percé jusques au fond du cœur*
> *D'une atteinte imprévue aussi bien que mortelle . . .*
> *Je demeure immobile, et mon âme abattue*
> *Cède au coup qui me tue.*

Tragedy must end in death: for any immortality which the poet or his hero may otherwise believe in is irrelevant to the passion that has absorbed him. That passion, at least, dies, and all he cares for dies with it. The possibility of ulterior lives or alien interests destined in future to agitate the world makes no difference to this drama in this soul; and the mention of those irrelevant sequels to this ruin, and to this tragic acceptance of ruin, would tinkle with a ghastly mockery at this supreme moment, when a man is entering eternity, his measure taken, his heart revealed, and his pride entire.

These considerations may help us to understand why Shakespeare, although Christianity was at hand, and Seneca, although a Platonic philosophy was at hand, based like Christianity on moral inspiration, nevertheless stuck fast in a disillusioned philosophy which Mr. Eliot thinks inferior. They stuck fast in the facts of life. They had to do so, whatever may have been their private religious convictions, because they were dramatists addressing the secular mind and concerned with the earthly career of passionate individuals, of inspired individuals, whose inspirations contradicted the truth and were shattered by it. This defeat, together with a proud and grandiloquent acceptance of it, is final for the tragic poet. His philosophy can build only on such knowledge of the world as the world can give. Even in the seventeenth century, when Christian orthodoxy was most severe, most intellectual, and most dominant, also most courtly and presentable to the worldly mind, Christianity was nevertheless strictly banished from the stage, except in a few expressly religious plays written for young ladies. Both Christian and pagan personages talked and felt throughout like thoroughly unregenerate mortals. To have allowed religion to shift the scenes, override the natural passions of men, and reverse the moral of the story, would have seemed an intolerable anticlimax.

Nor does even Dante, who calls his vision a comedy, really escape this tragic reality. Existence is indeed a comedy, in that it is a series of episodes, each blind and inconclusive, though often merry enough, but all having their fulfilment beyond themselves, in a cosmic music which they help to make without knowing it. Nonetheless, the individual souls in Dante's hell and heaven speak the language of tragedy, either in desperate pride or in devout self-surrender. In either case, in eternity, they have no further hopes, fears, or ambitions. Their lives *there* are simply the full knowledge of what their lives had been *here*. If the *Divine Comedy* had not had in it this sublime note of recollection, if it had attempted to describe new adventures and fanciful Utopias succeeding one another *ad infinitum*, it would not have been divine at all, but only a romantic medley like the second part of *Faust*. In Dante the hurly-burly is rounded out into a moral tale, into a joyful tragedy, with that sense of finality, of eternity, which Christian eschatology had always preserved.

I can think of only one tragedy in which religion might well play a leading part, and that is the tragedy of religion itself. The point would be to show that a second life of pure inspiration, freely bred in the soul out of moral impulses, must sooner or later confront the cold truth. The illusions then surrendered would not lose their poetic value, since their source would remain alive in the soul; and the element of deception involved might disappear insensibly, as it did in paganism, yielding with a good grace to an impartial philosophy. Such a philosophy need not be in the least hostile to inspiration. There is inspiration wherever there is mind. The sensuous images and the categories of thought on which common knowledge relies are themselves poetic and wholly original in form, being products of a kind of inspiration in the animal organism. But they are controlled in their significance and application by experiment in the field of action. Higher fictions are more loosely controlled by the experience of the heart. They are less readily revived or communicated. They flare up into passionate prophecies, take themselves for revealed truths, and come more often to a tragic end.

PART III

Critical Theory

THE ELEMENTS AND
FUNCTION OF POETRY

I F A critic, in despair of giving a serious definition of poetry, should be satisfied with saying that poetry is metrical discourse, he would no doubt be giving an inadequate account of the matter, yet not one of which he need be ashamed or which he should regard as superficial. Although a poem be not made by counting of syllables upon the fingers, yet "numbers" is the most poetical synonym we have for verse, and "measure" the most significant equivalent for beauty, for goodness, and perhaps even for truth. Those early and profound philosophers, the followers of Pythagoras, saw the essence of all things in number, and it was by weight, measure, and number, as we read in the Bible, that the Creator first brought Nature out of the void. Every human architect must do likewise with his edifice; he must mould his bricks or hew his stones into symmetrical solids and lay them over one another in regular strata, like a poet's lines.

Measure is a condition of perfection, for perfection requires that order should be pervasive, that not only the whole before us should have a form, but that every part in turn should have a form of its own, and that those parts should be coördinated among themselves as the whole is coördinated with the other parts of some greater cosmos. Leibnitz lighted in his speculations upon a conception of organic nature which may be false as a fact, but which is excellent as an ideal; he tells us that the difference between living and dead matter, between animals and machines, is that the former are composed of parts that are themselves organic, every portion of the body being itself a machine, and every portion of that machine still a machine, and so *ad infinitum;* whereas, in artificial

281

bodies the organisation is not in this manner infinitely deep. Fine Art, in this as in all things, imitates the method of Nature and makes its most beautiful works out of materials that are themselves beautiful. So that even if the difference between verse and prose consisted only in measure, that difference would already be analogous to that between jewels and clay.

The stuff of language is words, and the sensuous material of words is sound; if language therefore is to be made perfect, its materials must be made beautiful by being themselves subjected to a measure, and endowed with a form. It is true that language is a symbol for intelligence rather than a stimulus to sense, and accordingly the beauties of discourse which commonly attract attention are merely the beauties of the objects and ideas signified; yet the symbols have a sensible reality of their own, a euphony which appeals to our senses if we keep them open. The tongue will choose those forms of utterance which have a natural grace as mere sound and sensation; the memory will retain these catches, and they will pass and repass through the mind until they become types of instinctive speech and standards of pleasing expression.

The highest form of such euphony is song; the singing voice gives to the sounds it utters the thrill of tonality,—a thrill itself dependent, as we know, on the numerical proportions of the vibrations that it includes. But this kind of euphony and sensuous beauty, the deepest that sounds can have, we have almost wholly surrendered in our speech. Our intelligence has become complex, and language, to express our thoughts, must commonly be more rapid, copious, and abstract than is compatible with singing. Music at the same time has become complex also, and when united with words, at one time disfigures them in the elaboration of its melody, and at another overpowers them in the volume of its sound. So that the art of singing is now in the same plight as that of sculpture,—an abstract and conventional thing surviving by force of tradition and of an innate but now impotent impulse, which under simpler conditions would work itself out into the proper forms of those arts. The truest kind of euphony is thus denied to our poetry. If any verses are still set to music, they are commonly the worst only, chosen for the purpose by musicians of specialised sensibility and inferior intelligence, who seem to be attracted only by tawdry effects of rhetoric and sentiment.

When song is given up, there still remains in speech a certain sensuous quality, due to the nature and order of the vowels and consonants that compose the sounds. This kind of euphony is not neglected by the more dulcet poets, and is now so studied in some quarters that I have heard it maintained by a critic of relative authority that the beauty of poetry consists entirely in the frequent utterance of the sound of "j" and "sh," and the consequent copious flow of saliva in the mouth. But even if saliva is not the whole essence of poetry, there is an unmistakable and fundamental diversity of effect in the various vocalisation of different poets, which becomes all the more evident when we compare those who use different languages. One man's speech, or one nation's, is compact, crowded with consonants, rugged, broken with emphatic beats; another man's, or nation's, is open, tripping, rapid, and even. So Byron, mingling in his boyish fashion burlesque with exquisite sentiment, contrasts English with Italian speech:—

> *I love the language, that soft bastard Latin*
> *Which melts like kisses from a female mouth*
> *And sounds as if it should be writ on satin*
> *With syllables which breathe of the sweet South,*
> *And gentle liquids gliding all so pat in*
> *That not a single accent seems uncouth,*
> *Like our harsh Northern whistling, grunting guttural*
> *Which we're obliged to hiss and spit and sputter all.*

And yet these contrasts, strong when we compare extreme cases, fade from our consciousness in the actual use of a mother-tongue. The function makes us unconscious of the instrument, all the more as it is an indispensable and almost invariable one. The sense of euphony accordingly attaches itself rather to another and more variable quality; the tune, or measure, or rhythm of speech. The elementary sounds are prescribed by the language we use, and the selection we may make among those sounds is limited; but the arrangement of words is still undetermined, and by casting our speech into the moulds of metre and rhyme we can give it a heightened power, apart from its significance. A tolerable definition of poetry, on its formal side, might be found in this: that poetry is speech in which the instrument counts as well as the meaning— poetry is speech for its own sake and for its own sweetness. As common windows are intended only to admit the light, but painted windows also to dye it, and to be an object of attention in themselves as well as a cause of visibility in other things, so, while the purest prose is a mere vehicle of thought, verse, like stained glass, arrests attention in its own intricacies, confuses it in its own glories, and is even at times allowed to darken and puzzle in the hope of casting over us a supernatural spell.

Long passages in Shelley's *Revolt of Islam* and Keats' *Endymion* are poetical in this sense; the reader gathers, probably, no definite meaning, but is conscious of a poetic medium, of speech euphonious and measured, and redolent of a kind of objectless passion which is little more than the sensation of the movement and sensuous richness of the lines. Such poetry is not great; it has, in fact, a tedious vacuity, and is unworthy of a mature mind; but it is poetical, and could be produced only by a legitimate child of the Muse. It belongs to an apprenticeship, but in this case the apprenticeship of genius. It bears that relation to great poems which scales and aimless warblings bear to great singing—they test the essential endowment and fineness of the organ which is to be employed in the art. Without this sensuous background and ingrained predisposition to beauty, no art can reach the deepest and most exquisite effects; and even without an intelligible superstructure these sensuous qualities suffice to give that thrill of exaltation, that suggestion of an ideal world, which we feel in the presence of any true beauty.

The sensuous beauty of words and their utterance in measure suffice, therefore, for poetry of one sort—where these are there is something unmistakably poetical, although the whole of poetry, or the best of poetry, be not yet there. Indeed, in such works as *The Revolt of Islam* or *Endymion* there is already more than mere metre and sound; there is the colour and choice of words, the fanciful, rich, or exquisite juxtaposition of phrases. The vocabulary and the texture of the style are precious; affected, perhaps, but at any rate refined.

This quality, which is that almost exclusively exploited by the Symbolist, we may call euphuism—the choice of coloured words and rare and elliptical phrases. If great poets are like architects and sculptors, the euphuists are like goldsmiths and jewellers; their work is filigree in precious metals, encrusted with glowing stones.

Now euphuism contributes not a little to the poetic effect of the tirades of Keats and Shelley; if we wish to see the power of versification without euphuism we may turn to the tirades of Pope, where metre and euphony are displayed alone, and we have the outline or skeleton of poetry without the filling.

> *In spite of pride, in erring reason's spite,*
> *One truth is clear, Whatever is, is right.*

We should hesitate to say that such writing was truly poetical; so that some euphuism would seem to be necessary as well as metre, to the formal essence of poetry.

An example of this sort, however, takes us out of the merely verbal into the imaginative region; the reason that Pope is hardly poetical to us is not that he is inharmonious,—not to a defect of euphony,—but that he is too intellectual and has an excess of mentality. It is easier for words to be poetical without any thought, when they are felt merely as sensuous and musical, than for them to remain so when they convey an abstract notion,—especially if that notion be a tart and frigid sophism, like that of the couplet just quoted. The pyrotechnics of the intellect then take the place of the glow of sense, and the artifice of thought chills the pleasure we might have taken in the grace of expression.

If poetry in its higher reaches is more philosophical than history, because it presents the memorable types of men and things apart from unmeaning circumstances, so in its primary substance and texture poetry is more philosophical than prose because it is nearer to our immediate experience. Poetry breaks up the trite conceptions designated by current words into the sensuous qualities out of which those conceptions were originally put together. We name what we conceive and believe in, not what we see; things, not images; souls, not voices and silhouettes. This naming, with the whole education of the senses which it accompanies, subserves the uses of life; in order to thread our way through the labyrinth of objects which assault us, we must make a great selection in our sensuous experience; half of what we see and hear we must pass over as insignificant, while we piece out the other half with such an ideal complement as is necessary to turn it into a fixed and well-ordered world. This labour of perception and understanding, this spelling of the material meaning of experience is enshrined in our work-a-day language and ideas; ideas which are literally poetic in the sense that they are "made" (for every conception in an adult mind is a fiction), but which are at the same time prosaic because they are made economically, by abstraction, and for use.

When the child of poetic genius, who has learned this intellectual and utilitarian language in the cradle, goes afield and gathers for himself the aspects of Nature, he begins to encumber his mind with the many living impressions which the intellect rejected, and which the language of the intellect can hardly convey; he labours with his nameless burden of perception, and wastes himself in aimless impulses of emotion and reverie, until finally the method of some art offers a vent to his inspiration, or to such part of it as can survive the test of time and the discipline of expression.

The poet retains by nature the innocence of the eye, or recovers it easily; he disintegrates the fictions of common perception into their sensuous elements, gathers these together again into chance groups as the accidents of his environment or the affinities of his temperament may conjoin them; and this wealth of sensation and this freedom of fancy, which make an extraordinary ferment in his ignorant heart, presently bubble over into some kind of utterance.

The fulness and sensuousness of such effusions bring them nearer to our actual perceptions than common discourse could come; yet they may easily seem remote, overloaded, and obscure to those accustomed to think entirely in symbols, and never to be interrupted in the algebraic rapidity of their thinking by a moment's pause and examination of heart, nor ever to plunge for a moment into that torrent of sensation and imagery over which the bridge of prosaic associations habitually carries us safe and dry to some conventional act. How slight that bridge commonly is, how much an affair of trestles and wire, we can hardly conceive until we have trained ourselves to an extreme sharpness of introspection. But psychologists have discovered, what laymen generally will confess, that we hurry by the procession of our mental images as we do by the traffic of the street, intent on business, gladly forgetting the noise and movement of the scene and looking only for the corner we would turn or the door we would enter. Yet in our alertest moment the depths of the soul are still dreaming; the real world stands drawn in bare outline against a background of chaos and unrest. Our logical thoughts dominate experience only as the parallels and meridians make a checker-board of the sea. They guide our voyage without controlling the waves, which toss for ever in spite of our ability to ride over them to our chosen ends. Sanity is a madness put to good uses; waking life is a dream controlled.

Out of the neglected riches of this dream the poet fetches his wares. He dips into the chaos that underlies the rational shell of the world and brings up some superfluous image, some emotion dropped by the way, and reattaches it to the present object; he reinstates things unnecessary, he emphasises things ignored, he paints in again into the landscape the tints which the intellect has allowed to fade from it. If he seems sometimes to obscure a fact, it is only because he is restoring an experience. We may observe this process in the simplest cases. When Ossian, mentioning the sun, says it is round as the shield of his fathers, the expression is poetical. Why? Because he has added to the word sun, in itself sufficient and unequivocal, other words, unnecessary for practical clearness, but serving to restore the individuality of his perception and its associations in his mind. There is no square sun with which the sun he is speaking of could be confused; to stop and call it round is a luxury, a halting in the sensation for the love of its form. And to go on to tell us, what is wholly impertinent, that the shield of his fathers was round also, is to invite us to follow the chance wanderings of his fancy, to give us a little glimpse of the stuffing of his own brain, or, we might almost say, to turn over the patterns of his embroidery and show us the loose threads hanging out on the wrong side. Such an escapade disturbs and interrupts the true vision of the object, and a great poet, rising to a perfect conception of the sun and forgetting himself, would have disdained to make it; but it has a romantic and pathological interest, it restores an experience, and is in that measure poetical. We have been made to halt at the sensation, and to penetrate for a moment into its background of dream.

But it is not only thoughts or images that the poet draws in this way from the store of his experience, to clothe the bare form of conventional objects: he often adds to these objects a more subtle ornament, drawn from the same source. For the first element which the intellect rejects in forming its ideas of things is the emotion which accompanies the perception; and this emotion is the first thing the poet restores. He stops at the image, because he stops to enjoy. He wanders into the by-paths of association because the by-paths are delightful. The love of beauty which made him give measure and cadence to his words, the love of harmony which made him rhyme them, reappear in his imagination and make him select there also the material that is itself beautiful, or capable of assuming beautiful forms. The link that binds together the ideas, sometimes so wide apart, which his wit assimilates, is most often the link of emotion; they have in common some element of beauty or of horror.

The poet's art is to a great extent the art of intensifying emotions by assembling the scattered objects that naturally arouse them. He sees the affinities of things by seeing their common affinities with passion. As the guiding principle of practical thinking is some interest, so that only what is pertinent to that interest is selected by the attention; as the guiding principle of scientific thinking is some connection of things in time or space, or some identity of law; so in poetic thinking the guiding principle is often a mood or a quality of sentiment. By this union of disparate things having a common overtone of feeling, the feeling is itself evoked in all its strength; nay, it is often created for the first time, much as by a new mixture of old pigments Perugino could produce the unprecedented limpidity of his colour, or Titian the unprecedented glow of his. Poets can thus arouse sentiments finer than any which they have known, and in the act of composition become discoverers of new realms of delightfulness and grief. Expression is a misleading term which suggests that something previously known is rendered or imitated; whereas the expression is itself an original fact, the values of which are then referred to the thing expressed, much as the honours of a Chinese mandarin are attributed retroactively to his parents. So the charm which a poet, by his art of combining images and shades of emotion, casts over a scene or an action, is attached to the principal actor in it, who gets the benefit of the setting furnished him by a well-stocked mind.

The poet is himself subject to this illusion, and a great part of what is called poetry, although by no means the best part of it, consists in this sort of idealisation by proxy. We dye the world of our own colour; by a pathetic fallacy, by a false projection of sentiment, we soak Nature with our own feeling, and then celebrate her tender sympathy with our moral being. This aberration, as we see in the case of Wordsworth, is not inconsistent with a high development of both the faculties which it confuses,—I mean vision and feeling. On the contrary, vision and feeling, when most abundant and original, most easily present themselves in this undivided form. There would be need of a force of intellect which poets rarely possess to rationalise their inspiration without diminishing its volume: and if, as is commonly the case, the energy of the dream and the passion in them is greater than that of the reason, and they cannot attain true propriety and supreme beauty in their works, they can, nevertheless, fill them with lovely images and a fine moral spirit.

The pouring forth of both perceptive and emotional elements in their mixed and indiscriminate form gives to this kind of imagination the directness and truth which sensuous poetry possesses on a lower level. The outer world bathed in the hues of human feeling, the inner world expressed in the forms of things,— that is the primitive condition of both before intelligence and the prosaic classification of objects have abstracted them and assigned them to their respective spheres. Such identifications, on which a certain kind of metaphysics prides itself also, are not discoveries of profound genius; they are exactly like the observation of Ossian that the sun is round and that the shield of his fathers was round too; they are disintegrations of conventional objects, so that the original associates of our perceptions reappear; then the thing and the emotion which chanced to be simultaneous are said to be one, and we return, unless a better principle of organisation is substituted for the principle abandoned, to the chaos of a passive animal consciousness, where all is mixed together, projected together, and felt as an unutterable whole.

The pathetic fallacy is a return to that early habit of thought by which our ancestors peopled the world with benevolent and malevolent spirits; what they felt in the presence of objects they took to be a part of the objects themselves. In returning to this natural confusion, poetry does us a service in that she recalls and consecrates those phases of our experience which, as useless to the understanding of material reality, we are in danger of forgetting altogether. Therein is her vitality, for she pierces to the quick and

289

shakes us out of our servile speech and imaginative poverty; she reminds us of all we have felt, she invites us even to dream a little, to nurse the wonderful spontaneous creations which at every waking moment we are snuffing out in our brain. And the indulgence is no mere momentary pleasure; much of its exuberance clings afterward to our ideas; we see the more and feel the more for that exercise; we are capable of finding greater entertainment in the common aspects of Nature and life. When the veil of convention is once removed from our eyes by the poet, we are better able to dominate any particular experience and, as it were, to change its scale, now losing ourselves in its infinitesimal texture, now in its infinite ramifications.

If the function of poetry, however, did not go beyond this recovery of sensuous and imaginative freedom, at the expense of disrupting our useful habits of thought, we might be grateful to it for occasionally relieving our numbness, but we should have to admit that it was nothing but a relaxation; that spiritual discipline was not to be gained from it in any degree, but must be sought wholly in that intellectual system that builds the science of Nature with the categories of prose. So conceived, poetry would deserve the judgment passed by Plato on all the arts of flattery and entertainment; it might be crowned as delightful, but must be either banished altogether as meretricious or at least confined to a few forms and occasions where it might do little harm. The judgment of Plato has been generally condemned by philosophers, although it is eminently rational, and justified by the simplest principles of morals. It has been adopted instead, although unwittingly, by the practical and secular part of mankind, who look upon artists and poets as inefficient and brainsick people under whose spell it would be a serious calamity to fall, although they may be called in on feast days as an ornament and luxury together with the cooks, hairdressers, and florists.

Several circumstances, however, might suggest to us the possibility that the greatest function of poetry may be still to find. Plato, while condemning Homer, was a kind of poet himself; his quarrel with the followers of the Muse was not a quarrel with the goddess; and the good people of Philistia, distrustful as they may be of profane art, pay undoubting honour to religion, which is a kind of poetry as much removed from their sphere as the midnight revels upon Mount Citheron, which, to be sure, were also religious in their inspiration. Why, we may ask, these apparent inconsistencies? Why do our practical men make room for religion in the background of their world? Why did Plato, after banishing the poets, poetise the universe in his prose? Because the abstraction by which the world of science and of practice is drawn out of our experience, is too violent to satisfy even the thoughtless and vulgar; the ideality of the machine we call Nature, the conventionality of the drama we call the world, are too glaring not to be somehow perceived by all. Each must sometimes fall back upon the soul; he must challenge this apparition with the thought of death; he must ask himself for the mainspring and value of his life. He will then remember his stifled loves; he will feel that only his illusions have ever given him a sense of reality, only his passions the hope and the vision of peace. He will read himself through and almost gather a meaning from his experience; at least he will half believe that all he has been dealing with was a dream and a symbol, and raise his eyes toward the truth beyond.

This plastic moment of the mind, when we become aware of the artificiality and inadequacy of what common sense perceives, is the moment of poetic opportunity,—an opportunity, we may hasten to confess, which is generally missed. The strain of attention, the concentration and focussing of thought on the unfamiliar immediacy of things, usually brings about nothing but confusion. We are dazed, we are filled with a sense of unutterable things, luminous yet indistinguishable, many yet one. Instead of rising to imagination, we sink into mysticism.

To accomplish a mystical disintegration is not the function of any art; if any art seems to accomplish it, the effect is only incidental, being involved, perhaps, in the process of constructing the proper object of that art, as we might cut down trees and dig them up by the roots to lay the foundations of a temple. For every art looks to the building up of something. And just because the world built up by common sense and natural science is an inadequate world (a skeleton which needs the filling of sensation before it can live), therefore the moment when we realise its inadequacy is the moment when the higher arts find their opportunity. When the world is shattered to bits they can come and "build it nearer to the heart's desire."

The great function of poetry, which we have not yet directly mentioned, is precisely this: to repair to the material of experience, seizing hold of the reality of sensation and fancy beneath the surface of conventional ideas, and then out of that living but indefinite material to build new structures, richer, finer, fitter to the primary tendencies of our nature, truer to the ultimate possibilities of the soul. Our descent into the elements of our being is then justified by our subsequent freer ascent toward its goal; we revert to sense only to find food for reason; we destroy conventions only to construct ideals.

Such analysis for the sake of creation is the essence of all great poetry. Science and common sense are themselves in their way poets of no mean order, since they take the material of experience and make out of it a clear, symmetrical, and beautiful world; the very propriety of this art, however, has made it common. Its figures have become mere rhetoric and its metaphors prose. Yet, even as it is, a scientific and mathematical vision has a higher beauty than the irrational poetry of sensation and impulse, which merely tickles the brain, like liquor, and plays upon our random, imaginative lusts. The imagination of a great poet, on the contrary, is as orderly as that of an astronomer, and as large; he has the naturalist's patience, the naturalist's love of detail and eye trained to see fine gradations and essential lines; he knows no hurry; he has no pose, no sense of originality; he finds his effects in his subject, and his subject in his inevitable world. Resembling the naturalist in all this, he differs from him in the balance of his interests; the poet has the concreter mind; his visible world wears all its colours and retains its indwelling passion and life. Instead of studying in experience its calculable elements, he studies its moral values, its beauty, the openings it offers to the soul: and the cosmos he constructs is accordingly an ideal theatre for the spirit in which its noblest potential drama is enacted and its destiny resolved.

This supreme function of poetry is only the consummation of the method by which words and imagery are transformed into verse. As verse breaks up the prosaic order of syllables and subjects them to a recognisable and pleasing measure, so poetry breaks up the whole prosaic picture of experience to introduce into it a rhythm more congenial and intelligible to the mind. And in both these cases the operation is essentially the same as that by which, in an intermediate sphere, the images rejected by practical thought, and the emotions ignored by it, are so marshalled as to fill the mind with a truer and intenser consciousness of its memorable experience. The poetry of fancy, of observation, and of passion moves on this intermediate level; the poetry of mere sound and virtuosity is confined to the lower sphere; and the highest is reserved for the poetry of the creative reason. But one principle is present throughout,—the principle of Beauty,—the art of assimilating phenomena, whether words, images, emotions, or systems of ideas, to the deeper innate cravings of the mind.

Let us now dwell a little on this higher function of poetry and try to distinguish some of its phases.

The creation of characters is what many of us might at first be tempted to regard as the supreme triumph of the imagination. If we abstract, however, from our personal tastes and look at the matter in its human and logical relations, we shall see, I think, that the construction of characters is not the ultimate task of poetic fiction. A character can never be exhaustive of our materials: for it exists by its idiosyncrasy, by its contrast with other natures, by its development of one side, and one side only, of our native capacities. It is, therefore, not by characterisation as such that the ultimate message can be rendered. The poet can put only a part of himself into any of his heroes, but he must put the whole into his noblest work. A character is accordingly only a fragmentary unity; fragmentary in respect to its origin,—since it is conceived by enlargement, so to speak, of a part of our own being to the exclusion of the rest,—and fragmentary in respect to the object it presents, since a character must live in an environment and be appreciated by contrast and by the sense of derivation. Not the character, but its effects and causes, is the truly interesting thing. Thus in master poets, like Homer and Dante, the characters, although well drawn, are subordinate to the total movement and meaning of the scene. There is indeed something pitiful, something comic, in any comprehended soul; souls, like other things, are only definable by their limitations. We feel instinctively that it would be insulting to speak of any man to his face as we should speak of him in his absence, even if what we say is in the way of praise: for absent he is a character understood, but present he is a force respected.

In the construction of ideal characters, then, the imagination is

busy with material,—particular actions and thoughts,—which suggest their unification in persons; but the characters thus conceived
can hardly be adequate to the profusion of our observations, nor
exhaustive, when all personalities are taken together, of the interest
of our lives. Characters are initially imbedded in life, as the gods
themselves are originally imbedded in Nature. Poetry must, therefore, to render all reality, render also the background of its figures,
and the events that condition their acts. We must place them in
that indispensable environment which the landscape furnishes to
the eye and the social medium to the emotions.

The visible landscape is not a proper object for poetry. Its elements, and especially the emotional stimulation which it gives,
may be suggested or expressed in verse; but landscape is not
thereby represented in its proper form; it appears only as an element and associate of moral unities. Painting, architecture, and
gardening, with the art of stage setting, have the visible landscape
for their object, and to those arts we may leave it. But there is a
sort of landscape larger than the visible, which escapes the synthesis
of the eye; it is present to that topographical sense by which we
always live in the consciousness that there is a sea, that there are
mountains, that the sky is above us, even when we do not see it,
and that the tribes of men, with their different degrees of blame-
lessness, are scattered over the broad-backed earth. This cosmic
landscape poetry alone can render, and it is no small part of the
art to awaken the sense of it at the right moment, so that the object
that occupies the centre of vision may be seen in its true lights,
coloured by its wider associations, and dignified by its felt affinities
to things permanent and great. As the Italian masters were wont
not to paint their groups of saints about the Virgin without enlarging the canvas, so as to render a broad piece of sky, some mountains and rivers, and nearer, perhaps, some decorative pile; so the
poet of larger mind envelops his characters in the atmosphere of
Nature and history, and keeps us constantly aware of the world in
which they move.

The distinction of a poet—the dignity and humanity of his
thought—can be measured by nothing, perhaps, so well as by the
diameter of the world in which he lives; if he is supreme, his vision,
like Dante's, always stretches to the stars. And Virgil, a supreme
poet sometimes unjustly belittled, shows us the same thing in an-

other form; his landscape is the Roman universe, his theme the sacred springs of Roman greatness in piety, constancy, and law. He has not written a line in forgetfulness that he was a Roman; he loves country life and its labours because he sees in it the origin and bulwark of civic greatness; he honours tradition because it gives perspective and momentum to the history that ensues; he invokes the gods, because they are symbols of the physical and moral forces by which Rome struggled to dominion.

Almost every classic poet has the topographical sense; he swarms with proper names and allusions to history and fable; if an epithet is to be thrown in anywhere to fill up the measure of a line, he chooses instinctively an appellation of place or family; his wine is not red, but Samian; his gorges are not deep, but are the gorges of Hæmus; his songs are not sweet, but Pierian. We may deride their practice as conventional, but they could far more justly deride ours as insignificant. Conventions do not arise without some reason, and genius will know how to rise above them by a fresh appreciation of their rightness, and will feel no temptation to overturn them in favour of personal whimsies. The ancients found poetry not so much in sensible accidents as in essential forms and noble associations; and this fact marks very clearly their superior education. They dominated the world as we no longer dominate it, and lived, as we are too distracted to live, in the presence of the rational and the important.

A physical and historical background, however, is of little moment to the poet in comparison with that other environment of his characters,—the dramatic situations in which they are involved. The substance of poetry is, after all, emotion; and if the intellectual emotion of comprehension and the mimetic one of impersonation are massive, they are not so intense as the appetites and other transitive emotions of life; the passions are the chief basis of all interests, even the most ideal, and the passions are seldom brought into play except by the contact of man with man. The various forms of love and hate are only possible in society, and to imagine occasions in which these feelings may manifest all their inward vitality is the poet's function,—one in which he follows the fancy of every child, who puffs himself out in his day-dreams into an endless variety of heroes and lovers. The thrilling adventures which he craves demand an appropriate theatre; the glorious emotions with which he bubbles over must at all hazards find or feign their correlative objects.

But the passions are naturally blind, and the poverty of the imagination, when left alone, is absolute. The passions may ferment as they will, they never can breed an idea out of their own energy. This idea must be furnished by the senses, by outward experience, else the hunger of the soul will gnaw its own emptiness for ever. Where the seed of sensation has once fallen, however, the growth, variations, and exuberance of fancy may be unlimited. Only we still observe (as in the child, in dreams, and in the poetry of ignorant or mystical poets) that the intensity of inwardly generated visions does not involve any real increase in their scope or dignity. The inexperienced mind remains a thin mind, no matter how much its vapours may be heated and blown about by natural passion. It was a capital error in Fichte and Schopenhauer to assign essential fertility to the will in the creation of ideas. They mistook, as human nature will do, even when at times it professes pessimism, an ideal for a reality: and because they saw how much the will clings to its objects, how it selects and magnifies them, they imagined that it could breed them out of itself. A man who thinks clearly will see that such self-determination of a will is inconceivable, since what has no external relation and no diversity of structure cannot of itself acquire diversity of functions. Such inconceivability, of course, need not seem a great objection to a man of impassioned inspiration; he may even claim a certain consistency in positing, on the strength of his preference, the inconceivable to be a truth.

The alleged fertility of the will is, however, disproved by experience, from which metaphysics must in the end draw its analogies and plausibility. The passions discover, they do not create, their occasions; a fact which is patent when we observe how they seize upon what objects they find, and how reversible, contingent, and transferable the emotions are in respect to their objects. A doll will be loved instead of a child, a child instead of a lover, God instead of everything. The differentiation of the passions, as far as consciousness is concerned, depends on the variety of the objects of experience,—that is, on the differentiation of the senses and of the environment which stimulates them.

When the "infinite" spirit enters the human body, it is determined to certain limited forms of life by the organs which it wears; and its blank potentiality becomes actual in thought and deed, according to the fortunes and relations of its organism. The ripeness of the passions may thus precede the information of the mind and lead to groping in by-paths without issue; a phenomenon which appears not only in the obscure individual whose abnormalities the world ignores, but also in the starved, half-educated genius that pours the whole fire of his soul into trivial arts or grotesque superstitions. The hysterical forms of music and religion are the refuge of an idealism that has lost its way; the waste and failures of life flow largely in those channels. The carnal temptations of youth are incidents of the same maladaptation, when passions assert themselves before the conventional order of society can allow them physical satisfaction, and long before philosophy or religion can hope to transform them into fuel for its own sacrificial flames.

Hence flows the greatest opportunity of fiction. We have, in a sense, an infinite will; but we have a limited experience, an experience sadly inadequate to exercise that will either in its purity or its strength. To give form to our capacities nothing is required but the appropriate occasion; this the poet, studying the world, will construct for us out of the materials of his observations. He will involve us in scenes which lie beyond the narrow lane of our daily ploddings; he will place us in the presence of important events, that we may feel our spirit rise momentarily to the height of his great argument. The possibilities of love or glory, of intrigue and perplexity, will be opened up before us; if he gives us a good plot, we can readily furnish the characters, because each of them will be the realisation of some stunted potential self of our own. It is by the plot, then, that the characters will be vivified, because it is by the plot that our own character will be expanded into its latent possibilities.

The description of an alien character can serve this purpose only very imperfectly; but the presentation of the circumstances in which that character manifests itself will make description unnecessary, since our instinct will supply all that is requisite for the impersonation. Thus it seems that Aristotle was justified in making the plot the chief element in fiction: for it is by virtue of the plot that the characters live, or, rather, that we live in them, and by virtue of the plot accordingly that our soul rises to that imaginative activity by which we tend at once to escape from the personal life and to realise its ideal. This idealisation is, of course, partial and merely relative to the particular adventure in which we imagine ourselves engaged. But in some single direction our will finds self-expression, and understands itself; runs through the career which is ignorantly coveted, and gathers the fruits and the lesson of that enterprise.

This is the essence of tragedy: the sense of the finished life, of the will fulfilled and enlightened: that purging of the mind so much debated upon, which relieves us of pent-up energies, transfers our feelings to a greater object, and thus justifies and entertains our dumb passions, detaching them at the same time for a moment from their accidental occasions in our earthly life. An episode, however lurid, is not a tragedy in this nobler sense, because it does not work itself out to the end; it pleases without satisfying, or shocks without enlightening. This enlightenment, I need hardly say, is not a matter of theory or of moral maxims; the enlightenment by which tragedy is made sublime is a glimpse into the ultimate destinies of our will. This discovery need not be an ethical gain—Macbeth and Othello attain it as much as Brutus and Hamlet—it may serve to accentuate despair, or cruelty, or indifference, or merely to fill the imagination for a moment without much affecting the permanent tone of the mind. But without such a glimpse of the goal of a passion the passion has not been adequately read, and the fiction has served to amuse us without really enlarging the frontiers of our ideal experience. Memory and emotion have been played upon, but imagination has not brought anything new to the light.

The dramatic situation, however, gives us the environment of a single passion, of life in one of its particular phases; and although a passion, like Romeo's love, may seem to devour the whole soul, and its fortunes may seem to be identical with those of the man, yet much of the man, and the best part of him, goes by the board in such a simplification. If Leonardo da Vinci, for example, had met in his youth with Romeo's fate, his end would have been no more ideally tragic than if he had died at eighteen of a fever; we should be touched rather by the pathos of what he had missed, than by the sublimity of what he had experienced. A passion like

298

Romeo's compared with the ideal scope of human thought and emotion, is a thin dream, a pathological crisis.

Accordingly Aristophanes, remembering the original religious and political functions of tragedy, blushes to see upon the boards a woman in love. And we should readily agree with him, but for two reasons,—one, that we abstract too much, in our demands upon art, from nobility of mind, and from the thought of totality and proportion; the other, that we have learned to look for a symbolic meaning in detached episodes, and to accept the incidental emotions they cause, because of their violence and our absorption in them, as in some sense sacramental and representative of the whole. Thus the picture of an unmeaning passion, of a crime without an issue, does not appear to our romantic apprehension as the sorry farce it is, but rather as a true tragedy. Some have lost even the capacity to conceive of a true tragedy, because they have no idea of a cosmic order, of general laws of life, or of an impersonal religion. They measure the profundity of feeling by its intensity, not by its justifying relations; and in the radical disintegration of their spirit, the more they are devoured the more they fancy themselves fed. But the majority of us retain some sense of a meaning in our joys and sorrows, and even if we cannot pierce to their ultimate object, we feel that what absorbs us here and now has a merely borrowed or deputed power; that it is a symbol and foretaste of all reality speaking to the whole soul. At the same time our intelligence is too confused to give us any picture of that reality, and our will too feeble to marshal our disorganised loves into a religion consistent with itself and harmonious with the comprehended universe. A rational ideal eludes us, and we are the more inclined to plunge into mysticism.

Nevertheless, the function of poetry, like that of science, can only be fulfilled by the conception of harmonies that become clearer as they grow richer. As the chance note that comes to be supported by a melody becomes in that melody determinate and necessary, and as the melody, when woven into a harmony, is explicated in that harmony and fixed beyond recall; so the single emotion, the fortuitous dream, launched by the poet into the world of recognisable and immortal forms, looks in that world for its ideal supports and affinities. It must find them or else be blown back among the ghosts. The highest ideality is the comprehension of the real. Poetry is not at its best when it depicts a further possible experience, but when it initiates us, by feigning something which as an experience is impossible, into the meaning of the experience which we have actually had.

The highest example of this kind of poetry is religion; and although disfigured and misunderstood by the simplicity of men who believe in it without being capable of that imaginative interpretation of life in which its truth consists, yet this religion is even then often beneficent, because it colours life harmoniously with the ideal. Religion may falsely represent the ideal as a reality, but we must remember that the ideal, if not so represented, would be despised by the majority of men, who cannot understand that the value of things is moral, and who therefore attribute to what is moral a natural existence, thinking thus to vindicate its importance and value. But value lies in meaning, not in substance; in the ideal which things approach, not in the energy which they embody.

The highest poetry, then, is not that of the versifiers, but that of the prophets, or of such poets as interpret verbally the visions which the prophets have rendered in action and sentiment rather than in adequate words. That the intuitions of religion are poetical, and that in such intuitions poetry has its ultimate function, are truths of which both religion and poetry become more conscious the more they advance in refinement and profundity. A crude and superficial theology may confuse God with the thunder, the mountains, the heavenly bodies, or the whole universe; but when we pass from these easy identifications to a religion that has taken root in history and in the hearts of men, and has come to flower, we find its objects and its dogmas purely ideal, transparent expressions of moral experience and perfect counterparts of human needs. The evidence of history or of the senses is left far behind and never thought of; the evidence of the heart, the value of the idea, are alone regarded.

Take, for instance, the doctrine of transubstantiation. A metaphor here is the basis of a dogma, because the dogma rises to the same subtle region as the metaphor, and gathers its sap from the same soil of emotion. Religion has here rediscovered its affinity with poetry, and in insisting on the truth of its mystery it unconsciously vindicates the ideality of its truth. Under the accidents of bread and wine lies, says the dogma, the substance of Christ's body, blood, and divinity. What is that but to treat facts as an appearance, and their ideal import as a reality? And to do this is the very essence of poetry, for which everything visible is a sacrament —an outward sign of that inward grace for which the soul is thirsting.

In this same manner, where poetry rises from its elementary and detached expressions in rhythm, euphuism, characterisation, and story-telling, and comes to the consciousness of its highest function, that of portraying the ideals of experience and destiny, then the poet becomes aware that he is essentially a prophet, and either devotes himself, like Homer or Dante, to the loving expression of the religion that exists, or like Lucretius or Wordsworth, to the heralding of one which he believes to be possible. Such poets are aware of their highest mission; others, whatever the energy of their genius, have not conceived their ultimate function as poets. They have been willing to leave their world ugly as a whole, after stuffing it with a sufficient profusion of beauties. Their contemporaries, their fellow-countrymen for many generations, may not perceive this defect, because they are naturally even less able than the poet himself to understand the necessity of so large a harmony. If he is short-sighted, they are blind, and his poetic world may seem to them sublime in its significance, because it may suggest some partial lifting of their daily burdens and some partial idealisation of their incoherent thoughts.

Such insensibility to the highest poetry is no more extraordinary than the corresponding indifference to the highest religion; nobility and excellence, however, are not dependent on the suffrage of half-baked men, but on the original disposition of the clay and the potter; I mean on the conditions of the art and the ideal capacities of human nature. Just as a note is better than a noise because, its beats being regular, the ear and brain can react with pleasure on that regularity, so all the stages of harmony are better than the confusion out of which they come, because the soul that perceives that harmony welcomes it as the fulfilment of her natural ends. The Pythagoreans were therefore right when they made number the essence of the knowable world, and Plato was right when he said harmony was the first condition of the highest good. The good man is a poet whose syllables are deeds and make a harmony in

Nature. The poet is a rebuilder of the imagination, to make a harmony in that. And he is not a complete poet if his whole imagination is not attuned and his whole experience composed into a single symphony.

For his complete equipment, then, it is necessary, in the first place, that he sing; that his voice be pure and well pitched, and that his numbers flow; then, at a higher stage, his images must fit with one another; he must be euphuistic, colouring his thoughts with many reflected lights of memory and suggestion, so that their harmony may be rich and profound; again, at a higher stage, he must be sensuous and free, that is, he must build up his world with the primary elements of experience, not with the conventions of common sense or intelligence; he must draw the whole soul into his harmonies, even if in doing so he disintegrates the partial systematisations of experience made by abstract science in the categories of prose. But finally, this disintegration must not leave the poet weltering in a chaos of sense and passion; it must be merely the ploughing of the ground before a new harvest, the kneading of the clay before the modelling of a more perfect form. The expression of emotion should be rationalised by derivation from character and by reference to the real objects that arouse it—to Nature, to history, and to the universe of truth; the experience imagined should be conceived as a destiny, governed by principles, and issuing in the discipline and enlightenment of the will. In this way alone can poetry become an interpretation of life and not merely an irrelevant excursion into the realm of fancy, multiplying our images without purpose, and distracting us from our business without spiritual gain.

If we may then define poetry, not in the formal sense of giving the minimum of what may be called by that name, but in the ideal sense of determining the goal which it approaches and the achievement in which all its principles would be fulfilled, we may say that poetry is metrical and euphuistic discourse, expressing thought which is both sensuous and ideal.

Such is poetry as a literary form; but if we drop the limitation to verbal expression, and think of poetry as that subtle fire and inward light which seems at times to shine through the world and to touch the images in our minds with ineffable beauty, then poetry is a momentary harmony in the soul amid stagnation or conflict,— a glimpse of the divine and an incitation to a religious life.

Religion is poetry become the guide of life, poetry substituted for science or supervening upon it as an approach to the highest reality. Poetry is religion allowed to drift, left without points of application in conduct and without an expression in worship and dogma; it is religion without practical efficacy and without metaphysical illusion. The ground of this abstractness of poetry, however, is usually only its narrow scope; a poet who plays with an idea for half an hour, or constructs a character to which he gives no profound moral significance, forgets his own thought, or remembers it only as a fiction of his leisure, because he has not dug his well deep enough to tap the subterraneous springs of his own life. But when the poet enlarges his theatre and puts into his rhapsodies the true visions of his people and of his soul, his poetry is the consecration of his deepest convictions, and contains the whole truth of his religion. What the religion of the vulgar adds to the poet's is simply the inertia of their limited apprehension, which takes literally what he meant ideally, and degrades into a false extension of this world on its own level what in his mind was a true interpretation of it upon a moral plane.

This higher plane is the sphere of significant imagination, of relevant fiction, of idealism become the interpretation of the reality it leaves behind. Poetry raised to its highest power is then identical with religion grasped in its inmost truth; at their point of union both reach their utmost purity and beneficence, for then poetry loses its frivolity and ceases to demoralise, while religion surrenders its illusions and ceases to deceive.

SPEECH AND
SIGNIFICATION

SOUNDS WELL FITTED TO BE SYMBOLS

Music rationalises sound, but a more momentous rationalising of sound is seen in language. Language is one of the most useful of things, yet the greater part of it still remains (what it must all have been in the beginning) useless and without ulterior significance. The musical side of language is its primary and elementary side. Man is endowed with vocal organs so plastic as to emit a great variety of delicately varied sounds; and by good fortune his ear has a parallel sensibility, so that much vocal expression can be registered and confronted by auditory feeling. It has been said that man's pre-eminence in nature is due to his possessing hands; his modest participation in the ideal world may similarly be due to his possessing tongue and ear. For when he finds shouting and vague moaning after a while fatiguing, he can draw a new pleasure from uttering all sorts of labial, dental, and guttural sounds. Their rhythms and oppositions can entertain him, and he can begin to use his lingual gamut to designate the whole range of his perceptions and passions.

Here we touch upon one of the great crises in creation. As nutrition at first established itself in the face of waste, and reproduction in the face of death, so representation was able, by help of vocal symbols, to confront that dispersion inherent in experience, which is something in itself ephemeral. Merely to associate one thing with another brings little gain; and merely to have added a vocal designation to fleeting things—a designation which of course would have been taken for a part of their essence—would in itself have encumbered phenomena without rendering them in any way more docile to the will. But the encumbrance in this instance proved to be a wonderful preservative and means of comparison. It actually gave each moving thing its niche and cenotaph in the eternal. For the universe of vocal sounds was a field, like that of colour or number, in which the elements showed relations and transitions easy to dominate. It was a key-board over which attention could run back and forth, eliciting many implicit harmonies. Henceforth when various sounds had been idly associated with various things, and identified with them, the things could, by virtue of their names, be carried over mentally into the linguistic system; they could be manipulated there ideally, and vicariously preserved in representation. Needless to say that the things themselves remained unchanged all the while in their efficacy and mechanical succession, just as they remain unchanged in those respects when they pass for the mathematical observer into their measure or symbol; but as this reduction to mathematical form makes them calculable, so their earlier reduction to words rendered them comparable and memorable, first enabling them to figure in discourse at all.

LANGUAGE HAS A STRUCTURE INDEPENDENT OF THINGS

Language had originally no obligation to subserve an end which we may sometimes measure it by now, and depute to be its proper function, namely, to stand for things and adapt itself perfectly to their structure. In language as in every other existence idealism precedes realism, since it must be a part of nature living its own life before it can become a symbol for the rest and bend to external control. The vocal and musical medium is, and must always remain, alien to the spatial. What makes terms correspond and refer to one another is a relation eternally disparate from the relation of propinquity or derivation between existences. Yet when sounds were attached to an event or emotion, the sounds became symbols for that disparate fact. The net of vocal relations caught that natural object as a cobweb might catch a fly, without destroying or changing it. The object's quality passed to the word at the same time that the word's relations enveloped the object; and thus a new weight and significance was added to sound, previously nothing but a dull music. A conflict at once established itself between the drift proper to the verbal medium and that proper to the designated things; a conflict which the whole history of language and thought has embodied and which continues to this day.

WORDS, REMAINING IDENTICAL, SERVE TO IDENTIFY THINGS THAT CHANGE

Suppose an animal going down to a frozen river which he had previously visited in summer. Marks of all sorts would awaken in him an old train of reactions; he would doubtless feel premonitions of satisfied thirst and the splash of water. On finding, however, instead of the fancied liquid, a mass of something like cold stone, he would be disconcerted. His active attitude would be pulled up short and contradicted. In his fairyland of faith and magic the old river would have been simply annihilated, the dreamt-of water would have become a vanished ghost, and this ice for the moment the hard reality. He would turn away and live for a while on other illusions. When this shock was overgrown by time and it was summer again, the original habit might, however, reassert itself once more. If he revisited the stream, some god would seem to bring back something from an old familiar world; and the chill of that temporary estrangement, the cloud that for a while had made the good invisible, would soon be gone and forgotten.

If we imagine, on the contrary, that this animal could speak and had from the first called his haunt *the river*, he would have repeated its name on seeing it even when it was frozen, for he had not failed to recognise it in that guise. The variation afterwards noticed, upon finding it hard, would seem no total substitution, but a *change;* for it would be the same river, once flowing, that was now congealed. An identical word, covering all the identical qualities in the phenomena and serving to abstract them, would force the inconsistent qualities in those phenomena to pass for accidents; and the useful proposition could at once be framed that the same river may be sometimes free and sometimes frozen.

LANGUAGE THE DIALECTICAL GARMENT OF FACTS

This proposition is true, yet it contains much that is calculated to offend a scrupulous dialectician. Its language and categories are not purely logical, but largely physical and representative. The notion that what changes nevertheless endures is a remarkable hybrid. It arises when rigid ideal terms are imposed on evanescent existence. Feelings, taken alone, would show no identities; they would be lost in changing, or be woven into the infinite feeling of change. Notions, taken alone, would allow no lapse, but would merely lead attention about from point to point over an eternal system of relations. Power to understand the world, logical or scientific mastery of existence, arises only by the forced and conventional marriage of these two essences, when the actual flux is ideally suspended and an ideal harness is loosely flung upon things. For this purpose words are an admirable instrument. They have dialectical relations based on an ideal import, or tendency to definition, which makes their essence their signification; yet they can be freely bandied about and applied for a moment to the ambiguous things that pass through existence.

WORDS ARE WISE MEN'S COUNTERS

Had men been dumb, an exchange and circulation of images need not have been wanting, and associations might have arisen between ideals in the mind and corresponding reactive habits in the body. What words add is not power of discernment or action, but a medium of intellectual exchange. Language is like money, without which specific relative values may well exist and be felt, but cannot be reduced to a common denominator. And as money must have a certain intrinsic value of its own in order that its relation to other values may be stable, so a word, by which a thing is represented in discourse, must be a part of that thing's context, an ingredient in the total apparition it is destined to recall. Words, in their existence, are no more universal than gold by nature is a worthless standard of value in other things. Words are a material accompaniment of phenomena, at first an idle accompaniment, but one which happens to subserve easily a universal function. Some other element in objects might conceivably have served for a common denominator between them; but words, just by virtue of their adventitious, detachable status, and because they are so easily compared and manipulated in the world of sound, were singularly well fitted for this office. They are not vague, as any common quality abstracted from things would necessarily become; and though vagueness is a quality only too compatible with perception, so that vague ideas can exist without end, this vagueness is not what makes them universal in their functions. It is one thing to perceive an ill-determined form and quite another to attribute to it a precise general predicate. Words, distinct in their own category and perfectly recognisable, can accordingly perform very well the function of embodying a universal; for they can be identified in turn with many particulars and yet remain throughout particular themselves.

NOMINALISM RIGHT IN PSYCHOLOGY AND REALISM IN LOGIC

The psychology of nominalism is undoubtedly right where it insists that every image is particular and every term, in its existential aspect, a *flatum vocis;* but nominalists should have recognised that images may have any degree of vagueness and generality when measured by a conceptual standard. A figure having obviously three sides and three corners may very well be present to the mind when it is impossible to say whether it is an equilateral or a rectangular triangle. Functional or logical universality lies in another sphere altogether, being a matter of intent and not of existence. When we say that "universals alone exist in the mind" we mean by "mind" something unknown to Berkeley; not a bundle of psychoses nor an angelic substance, but quick intelligence, the faculty of discourse. Predication is an act, understanding a spiritual and transitive operation: its existential basis may well be counted in psychologically and reduced to a stream of immediate presences; but its meaning can be caught only by another meaning, as life only can exemplify life. Vague or general images are as little universal as sounds are; but a sound better than a flickering abstraction can serve the intellect in its operation of comparison and synthesis. Words are therefore the body of discourse, of which the soul is understanding.

LITERATURE MOVES BETWEEN THE EXTREMES OF MUSIC
AND DENOTATION

The categories of discourse are in part merely representative, in part merely grammatical, and in part attributable to both spheres.

308

Euphony and phonetic laws are principles governing language without any reference to its meaning; here speech is still a sort of music. At the other extreme lies that ultimate form of prose which we see in mathematical reasoning or in a telegraphic style, where absolutely nothing is rhetorical and speech is denuded of every feature not indispensable to its symbolic rôle. Between these two extremes lies the broad field of poetry, or rather of imaginative or playful expression, where the verbal medium is a medium indeed, having a certain transparency, a certain reference to independent facts, but at the same time elaborates the fact in expressing it, and endows it with affinities alien to its proper nature. A pun is a grotesque example of such diremption, where ambiguities belonging only to speech are used to suggest impossible substitutions in ideas. Less frankly, language habitually wrests its subject-matter in some measure from its real context and transfers it to a represented and secondary world, the world of logic and reflection. Concretions in existence are subsumed, when named, under concretions in discourse. Grammar lays violent hands upon experience, and everything becomes a prey to wit and fancy, a material for fiction and eloquence. Man's intellectual progress has a poetic phase, in which he imagines the world; and then a scientific phase, in which he sifts and tests what he has imagined.

SOUND AND OBJECT, IN THEIR SENSUOUS PRESENCE, MAY HAVE AFFINITY

In what measure do inflection and syntax represent anything in the subject-matter of discourse? In what measure are they an independent play of expression, a quasi-musical, quasi-mathematical veil interposed between reflection and existence? One who knows only languages of a single family can give but a biassed answer to this question. There are doubtless many approaches to correct symbolism in language, which grammar may have followed up at different times in strangely different ways. That the medium in every art has a character of its own, a character limiting its representative value, may perhaps be safely asserted, and this intrinsic character in the medium antedates and permeates all representation. Phonetic possibilities and phonetic habits belong, in language, to this indispensable vehicle; what the throat and lips can emit easily and distinguishably, and what sequences can appeal to the ear and be retained, depend alike on physiological conditions; and no matter how convenient or inconvenient these conditions may be for signification, they will always make themselves felt and may sometimes remain predominant. In poetry they are still conspicuous. Euphony, metre, and rhyme colour the images they transmit and add a charm wholly extrinsic and imputed. In this immersion of the message in the medium and in its intrinsic movement the magic of poetry lies; and the miracle grows as there is more and more native analogy between the movement of the medium and that of the subject-matter.

Both language and ideas involve processes in the brain. The two processes may be wholly disparate if we regard their objects only and forget their seat, as Athena is in no way linked to an elephant's tusk; yet in perception all processes are contiguous and exercise a single organism, in which they may find themselves in sympathetic or antipathetic vibration. On this circumstance hangs that subtle congruity between subject and vehicle which is otherwise such a mystery in expression. If to think of Athena and to look on ivory are congruous physiological processes, if they sustain or heighten each other, then to represent Athena in ivory will be a happy expedient, in which the very nature of the medium will already be helping us forward. Scent and form go better together, for instance, in the violet or the rose than in the hyacinth or the poppy: and being better compacted for human perception they seem more expressive and can be linked more unequivocally with other sources of feeling. So a given vocal sound may have more or less analogy to the thing it is used to signify; this analogy may be obvious, as in onomatopœia, or subtle, as when short, sharp sounds go with decision, or involved rhythms and vague reverberations with a floating dream. What seems exquisite to one poet may accordingly seem vapid to another, when the texture of experience in the two minds differs, so that a given composition rustles through one man's fancy as a wind might through a wood, but finds no sympathetic response in the other organism, nerved as it may be, perhaps, to precision in thought and action.

SYNTAX POSITIVELY REPRESENTATIVE

The structure of language, when it passes beyond the phonetic level, begins at once to lean upon existences and to imitate the structure of things. We distinguish the parts of speech, for instance, in subservience to distinctions which we make in ideas.

The feeling or quality represented by an adjective, the relation indicated by a verb, the substance or concretion of qualities designated by a noun, are diversities growing up in experience, by no means attributable to the mere play of sound. The parts of speech are therefore representative. Their inflection is representative too, since tenses mark important practical differences in the distribution of events described, and cases express the respective rôles played by objects in the operation. "I struck him and he will strike me," renders in linguistic symbols a marked change in the situation; the variation in phrase is not rhetorical. Language here, though borrowed no doubt from ancestral poetry, has left all revery far behind, and has been submerged in the Life of Reason.

YET IT VITIATES WHAT IT REPRESENTS

The medium, however, constantly reasserts itself. An example may be found in gender, which, clearly representative in a measure, cuts loose in language from all genuine representation and becomes a feature in abstract linguistic design, a formal characteristic in expression. Contrasted sentiments permeate an animal's dealings with his own sex and with the other; nouns and adjectives represent this contrast by taking on masculine and feminine forms. The distinction is indeed so important that wholly different words —man and woman, bull and cow—stand for the best-known animals of different sex; while adjectives, where declension is extinct, as in English, often take on a connotation of gender and are applied to one sex only—as we say a beautiful woman, but hardly a beautiful man.

But gender in language extends much farther than sex, and even if by some subtle analogy all the masculine and feminine nouns in a language could be attached to something suggesting sex in the objects they designate, yet it can hardly be maintained that the elaborate concordance incident upon that distinction is representative of any felt quality in the things. So remote an analogy to sex could not assert itself pervasively. Thus Horace says:

> Quis multa gracilis te puer in rosa
> perfusis liquidis urget odoribus
> grato, Pyrrha, sub antro?

Here we may perceive why the rose was instinctively made feminine, and we may grant that the bower, though the reason escape us, was somehow properly masculine; but no one would urge that a *profusion* of roses was also intrinsically feminine, or that the *pleasantness* of a bower was ever specifically masculine to sense. The epithets *multa* and *grato* take their gender from the nouns, even though the quality they designate fails to do so. Their gender is therefore non-representative and purely formal; it marks an intra-linguistic accommodation. The medium has developed a syntactical structure apart from any intrinsic significance thereby accruing to its elements. Artificial concordance in gender does not express gender: it merely emphasises the grammatical links in the phrases and makes greater variety possible in the arrangement of words.

DIFFICULTY IN SUBDUING A LIVING MEDIUM

This example may prepare us to understand a general principle: that language, while essentially significant viewed in its function, is indefinitely wasteful, being mechanical and tentative in its origin. It overloads itself, and being primarily music, and a labyrinth of sounds, it develops an articulation and method of its own, which only in the end, and with much inexactness, reverts to its function of expression. How great the possibilities of effect are in developing a pure medium we can best appreciate in music; but in language a similar development goes on while it is being applied to representing things. The organ is spontaneous, the function adventitious and superimposed. Rhetoric and utility keep language going, as centrifugal and centripetal forces keep a planet in its course. Euphony, verbal analogy, grammatical fancy, poetic confusion, continually drive language afield, in its own tangential

direction; while the business of life, in which language is employed, and the natural lapse of rhetorical fashions, as continually
draw it back towards convenience and exactitude.

LANGUAGE FORESHORTENS EXPERIENCE

Between music and bare symbolism language has its florid expansion. Until music is subordinated, speech has little sense; it can
hardly tell a story or indicate an object unequivocally. Yet if music
were left behind altogether, language would pass into a sort of
algebra or vocal shorthand, without literary quality; it would become wholly indicative and record facts without colouring them
ideally. This medium and its intrinsic development, though they
make the bane of reproduction, make the essence of art; they give
representation a new and specific value such as the object, before
representation, could not have possessed. Consciousness itself is
such a medium in respect to diffuse existence, which it foreshortens
and elevates into synthetic ideas. Reason, too, by bringing the
movement of events and inclinations to a head in single acts of
reflection, thus attaining to laws and purposes, introduces into life
the influence of a representative medium, without which life could
never pass from a process into an art. Language acquires scope in
the same way, by its kindly infidelities; its metaphors and syntax
lend experience perspective. Language vitiates the experience it
expresses, but thereby makes the burden of one moment relevant
to that of another. The two experiences, identified roughly with
the same concretion in discourse, are pronounced similar or comparable in character. Thus a proverb, by its verbal pungency and
rhythm, becomes more memorable than the event it first described
would ever have been if not translated into an epigram and rendered, so to speak, applicable to new cases; for by that translation
the event has become an idea.

To turn events into ideas is the function of literature. Music,
which in a certain sense is a mass of pure forms, must leave its
"ideas" imbedded in their own medium—they are musical ideas—
and cannot impose them on any foreign material, such as human
affairs. Science, on the contrary, seeks to disclose the bleak anatomy
of existence, stripping off as much as possible the veil of prejudice
and words. Literature takes a middle course and tries to subdue

313

music, which for its purposes would be futile and too abstract, into conformity with general experience, making music thereby significant.

IT IS A PERPETUAL MYTHOLOGY

Literary art in the end rejects all unmeaning flourishes, all complications that have no counterpart in things or no use in expressing their relations; at the same time it aspires to digest that reality to which it confines itself, making it over into ideal substance and material for the mind. It looks at things with an incorrigibly dramatic eye, turning them into permanent unities (which they never are) and almost into persons, grouping them by their imaginative or moral affinities and retaining in them chiefly what is incidental to their being, namely, the part they may chance to play in man's adventures.

Such literary art demands a subject-matter other than the literary impulse itself. The literary man is an interpreter and hardly succeeds, as the musician may, without experience and mastery of human affairs. His art is half genius and half fidelity. He needs inspiration; he must wait for automatic musical tendencies to ferment in his mind, proving it to be fertile in devices, comparisons, and bold assimilations. Yet inspiration alone will lead him astray, for his art is relative to something other than its own formal impulse; it comes to clarify the real world, not to encumber it; and it needs to render its native agility practical and to attach its volume of feeling to what is momentous in human life. Literature has its piety, its conscience; it cannot long forget, without forfeiting all dignity, that it serves a burdened and perplexed creature, a human animal struggling to persuade the universal Sphinx to propose a more intelligible riddle. Irresponsible and trivial in its abstract impulse, man's simian chatter becomes noble as it becomes symbolic; its representative function lends it a serious beauty, its utility endows it with moral worth.

IT MAY BE APT OR INAPT, WITH EQUAL RICHNESS

These relations, in determining the function of language, determine the ideal which its structure should approach. Any sort of grammar and rhetoric, the most absurd and inapplicable as well as the most descriptive, can be spontaneous; fit organisms are not less natural than those that are unfit. Felicitous genius is so called because it meets experience half-way. A genius which flies in the opposite direction, though not less fertile internally, is externally inept and is called madness. Ineptitude is something which language needs to shake off. Better surrender altogether some verbal categories and start again, in that respect, with a clean slate, than persist in any line of development that alienates thought from reality. The language of birds is excellent in its way, and those ancient sages who are reported to have understood it very likely had merely perceived that it was not meant to be intelligible; for it is not to understand nature to reduce her childishly to a human scale. Man, who is merged in universal nature at the roots of his being, is not without profound irrational intuitions by which he can half divine her secret processes; and his heart, in its own singing and fluttering, might not wholly misinterpret the birds. But human discourse is not worth having if it is mere piping, and helps not at all in mastering things; for man is intelligent, which is another way of saying that he aspires to envisage in thought what he is dealing with in action. Discourse that absolved itself from that observant duty would not be cognitive; and in failing to be cognitive it would fail to redeem the practical forces it ignored from their brute externality, and to make them tributary to the Life of Reason. Thus its own dignity and continued existence depend on its learning to express momentous facts, facts important for action and happiness; and there is nothing which so quickly discredits itself as empty rhetoric and dialectic, or poetry that wanders in dim and private worlds.

ABSOLUTE LANGUAGE A POSSIBLE BUT FOOLISH ART

If pure music, even with its immense sensuous appeal, is so easily tedious, what a universal yawn must meet the verbiage which develops nothing but its own iridescence. Absolute versification and absolute dialectic may have their place in society; they give play to an organ that has its rights like any other, and that, after serving for a while in the economy of life, may well claim a holiday in which to disport itself irresponsibly among the fowls of the air and the lilies of the field. But the exercise is trivial; and if its high priests go through their mummeries with a certain unction, and pretend to be wafted by them into a higher world, the phenomenon is neither new nor remarkable. Language is a wonderful and pliant medium, and why should it not lend itself to imposture? A systematic abuse of words, as of other things, is never without some inner harmony or propriety that makes it prosper; only the man who looks beyond and sees the practical results awakes to the villainy of it. In the end, however, those who play with words lose their labour, and pregnant as they feel themselves to be with new and wonderful universes, they cannot humanise the one in which they live and rather banish themselves from it by their persistent egotism and irrelevance.

POETRY AND
PROSE

FORCE OF PRIMARY EXPRESSIONS

THERE IS both truth and illusion in the saying that primitive poets are sublime. Genesis and the Iliad (works doubtless backed by a long tradition) are indeed sublime. Primitive men, having perhaps developed language before the other arts, used it with singular directness to describe the chief episodes of life, which was all that life as yet contained. They had frank passions and saw things from single points of view. A breath from that early world seems to enlarge our natures, and to restore to language, which we have sophisticated, all its magnificence and truth. But there is more, for (as we have seen) language is spontaneous; it constitutes an act before it registers an observation. It gives vent to emotion before it is adjusted to things external and reduced, as it were, to its own echo rebounding from a refractory world. The lion's roar, the bellowing of bulls, even the sea's cadence has a great sublimity. Though hardly in itself poetry, an animal cry, when still audible in human language, renders it also the unanswerable, the ultimate voice of nature. Nothing can so pierce the soul as the uttermost sigh of the body. There is no utterance so thrilling as that of absolute impulse, if absolute impulse has learned to speak at all. An intense, inhospitable mind, filled with a single idea, in which all animal, social, and moral interests are fused together, speaks a language of incomparable force. Thus the Hebrew prophets, in their savage concentration, poured into one torrent all that their souls possessed or could dream of. What other men are wont to pursue in politics, business, religion, or art, they looked for from one wave of national repentance and consecration. Their age, swept by this ideal passion, possessed at the same time a fresh and homely vocabulary; and the result was an eloquence so elemental and combative, so imaginative and so bitterly practical, that the world has never heard its like. Such single-mindedness, with such heroic simplicity in words and images, is hardly possible in a late civilisation. Cultivated poets are not unconsciously sublime.

ITS EXCLUSIVENESS AND NARROWNESS

The sublimity of early utterances should not be hailed, however, with unmixed admiration. It is a sublimity born of defect or at least of disproportion. The will asserts itself magnificently; images, like thunder-clouds, seem to cover half the firmament at once. But such a will is sadly inexperienced; it has hardly tasted or even conceived any possible or high satisfactions. Its lurid firmament is poor in stars. To throw the whole mind upon something is not so great a fear when the mind has nothing else to throw itself upon. Every animal when goaded becomes intense; and it is perhaps merely the apathy in which mortals are wont to live that keeps them from being habitually sublime in their sentiments. The sympathy that makes a sheep hasten after its fellows, in vague alarm or in vague affection; the fierce premonitions that drive a bull to the heifer; the patience with which a hen sits on her eggs; the loyalty which a dog shows to his master—what thoughts may not all these instincts involve, which it needs only a medium of communication to translate into poetry?

Man, though with less wholeness of soul, enacts the same dramas. He hears voices on all occasions; he incorporates what little he observes of nature into his verbal dreams; and as each new impulse bubbles to the surface he feels himself on the verge of some inexpressible heaven or hell. He needs but to abandon himself to that seething chaos which perpetually underlies conventional sanity—a chaos in which memory and prophecy, vision and impersonation, sound and sense, are inextricably jumbled together—to find himself at once in a magic world, irrecoverable, largely unmeaning, terribly intricate, but, as he will conceive, deep, inward, and absolutely real. He will have reverted, in other words, to crude experience, to primordial illusion. The movement of his animal or vegetative mind will be far from delightful; it will be unintelligent and unintelligible; nothing in particular will be represented therein; but it will be a movement in the soul and for the soul, as exciting and compulsive as the soul's volume can make it. In this muddy torrent words also may be carried down; and if these words are by chance strung together into a cadence, and are afterwards written down, they may remain for a memento of that turbid moment. Such words we may at first hesitate to call poetry, since very likely they are nonsense; but this nonsense will have some quality —some rhyme or rhythm—that makes it memorable (else it would not have survived); and moreover the words will probably show, in their connotation and order, some sympathy with the dream that cast them up. For the man himself, in whom such a dream may be partly recurrent, they may consequently have a considerable power of suggestion, and they may even have it for others, whenever the rhythm and incantation avail to plunge them also into a similar trance.

RUDIMENTARY POETRY AN INCANTATION OR CHARM

Memorable nonsense, or sound with a certain hypnotic power, is the really primitive and radical form of poetry. Nor is such poetry yet extinct: children still love and compose it, and every genuine poet, on one side of his genius, reverts to it from explicit speech. As all language has acquired its meaning, and did not have it in the beginning, so the man who launches a new locution, the poet who creates a symbol, must do so without knowing what significance it may eventually acquire, and conscious at best only of the emotional background from which it emerged. Pure poetry is pure experiment; and it is not strange that nine-tenths of it should be pure failure. For it matters little what unutterable things may have originally gone together with a phrase in the dreamer's mind; if they were not uttered and the phrase cannot call them back, this verbal relic is none the richer for the high company it may once have kept. Expressiveness is a most accidental matter. What a line suggests at one reading, it may never suggest again even to the same person. For this reason, among others, poets are partial to their own compositions; they truly discover there depths of meaning which exist for nobody else. Those readers who appropriate a poet and make him their own fall into a similar illusion; they attribute to him what they themselves supply, and whatever he reels out, lost in his own personal revery, seems to them, like *sortes biblicæ*, written to fit their own case.

INSPIRATION IRRESPONSIBLE

Justice has never been done to Plato's remarkable consistency and boldness in declaring that poets are inspired by a divine madness and yet, when they transgress rational bounds, are to be banished from an ideal republic, though not without some marks of Platonic regard. Instead of fillets, a modern age might assign them a coterie of flattering dames, and instead of banishment, starvation; but the result would be the same in the end. A poet is inspired because what occurs in his brain is a true experiment in creation. His apprehension plays with words and their meanings as nature, in any spontaneous variation, plays with her own structure. A mechanical force shifts the kaleidoscope; a new direction is given to growth or a new gist to signification. This inspiration, moreover, is mad, being wholly ignorant of its own issue; and though it has a confused fund of experience and verbal habit on which to draw, it draws on this fund blindly and quite at random, consciously possessed by nothing but a certain stress and pregnancy and the pains, as it were, of parturition. Finally the new birth has to be inspected critically by the public censor before it is allowed to live; most probably it is too feeble and defective to prosper in the common air, or is a monster that violates some primary rule of civic existence, tormenting itself to disturb others.

PLATO'S DISCRIMINATING VIEW

Plato seems to have exaggerated the havoc which these poetic dragons can work in the world. They are in fact more often absurd than venomous, and no special legislation is needed to abolish them. They soon die quietly of universal neglect. The poetry that ordinarily circulates among a people is poetry of a secondary and conventional sort that propagates established ideas in trite metaphors. Popular poets are the parish priests of the Muse, retailing her ancient divinations to a long since converted public. Plato's quarrel was not so much with poetic art as with ancient myth and emotional laxity: he was preaching a crusade against the established church. For naturalistic deities he wished to substitute moral symbols; for the joys of sense, austerity and abstraction. To proscribe Homer was a marked way of protesting against the frivolous reigning ideals. The case is much as if we should now proscribe the book of Genesis, on account of its mythical cosmogony, or in order to proclaim the philosophic truth that the good, being an adequate expression to be attained by creation, could not possibly have preceded it or been its source. We might admit at the same time that Genesis contains excellent images and that its poetic force is remarkable; so that if serious misunderstanding could be avoided the censor might be glad to leave it in everybody's hands. Plato in some such way recognised that Homer was poetical and referred his works, mischievous as they might prove incidentally, to divine inspiration. Poetic madness, like madness in prophecy or love, bursts the body of things to escape from it into some ideal; and even the Homeric world, though no model for a rational state, was a cheerful heroic vision, congenial to many early impulses and dreams of the mind.

Homer, indeed, was no primitive poet; he was a consummate master, the heir to generations of discipline in both life and art. This appears in his perfect prosody, in his limpid style, in his sense for proportion, his abstentions, and the frank pathos of his portraits and principles, in which there is nothing gross, subjective, or arbitrary. The inspirations that came to him never carried him into crudeness or absurdity. Every modern poet, though the world he describes may be more refined in spots and more elaborate, is less advanced in his art; for art is made rudimentary not by its date but by its irrationality. Yet even if Homer had been primitive he might well have been inspired, in the same way as a Bacchic frenzy or a mystic trance; the most blundering explosions may be justified antecedently by the plastic force that is vented in them. They may be expressive, in the physical sense of this ambiguous word; for, far as they may be from conveying an idea, they may betray a tendency and prove that something is stirring in the soul.

EXPLOSIVE AND PREGNANT EXPRESSION

Expressiveness is often sterile; but it is sometimes fertile and capable of reproducing in representation the experience from which it sprang. As a tree in the autumn sheds leaves and seeds together, so a ripening experience comes indifferently to various manifestations, some barren and without further function, others fit to carry the parent experience over into another mind, and give it a new embodiment there. Expressiveness in the former case is dead, like that of a fossil; in the latter it is living and efficacious, recreating its original. The first is idle self-manifestation, the second rational art.

NATURAL HISTORY OF INSPIRATION

Self-manifestation, so soon as it is noted and accepted as such, seems to present the same marvel as any ideal success. Such self-manifestation is incessant, many-sided, unavoidable; yet it seems a miracle when its conditions are looked back upon from the vantage ground of their result. By reading spirit out of a work we turn it into a feat of inspiration. Thus even the crudest and least coherent utterances, when we suspect some soul to be groping in them, and striving to address us, become oracular; a divine afflatus breathes behind their gibberish and they seem to manifest some deep intent. The miracle of creation or inspiration consists in nothing but this, that an external effect should embody an inner intention. The miracle, of course, is apparent only, and due to an inverted and captious point of view. In truth the tendency that executed the work was what first made its conception possible; but this conception, finding the work responsive in some measure to its inner demand, attributes that response to its own magic preroga-tive. Hence the least stir and rumble of formative processes, when it generates a soul, makes itself somehow that soul's interpreter; and dim as the spirit and its expression may both remain, they are none the less in profound concord, a concord which wears a mirac-ulous providential character when it is appreciated without being understood.

EXPRESSIONS TO BE UNDERSTOOD MUST BE RECREATED, AND SO CHANGED

Primitive poetry is the basis of all discourse. If we open any ancient book we come at once upon an elaborate language, and on divers conventional concepts, of whose origin and history we hear nothing. We must read on, until by dint of guessing and by confronting instances we grow to understand those symbols. The writer was himself heir to a linguistic tradition which he made his own by the same process of adoption and tentative use by which we, in turn, interpret his phrases: he understood what he heard in terms of his own experience, and attributed to his predecessors (no matter what their incommunicable feelings may have been) such ideas as their words generated in his own thinking. In this way expressions continually change their sense; they can communicate a thought only by diffusing a stimulus, and in passing from mouth to mouth they will wholly reverse their connotation, unless some external object or some recurring human situation gives them a constant standard, by which private aberrations may be checked. Thus in the first phrase of Genesis, "In the beginning God created the heavens and the earth," the words have a stable meaning only in so far as they are indicative and bring us back to a stable object. What "heavens" and "earth" stand for can be conveyed by gestures, by merely pointing up and down; but beyond that sensuous connotation their meaning has entirely changed since they were here written; and no two minds, even to-day, will respond to these familiar words with exactly the same images. "Beginning" and "created" have a superficial clearness, though their implications cannot be defined without precipitating the most intricate metaphysics, which would end in nothing but a proof that both terms were ambiguous and unthinkable. As to the word "God," all mutual understanding is impossible. It is a floating literary symbol, with a value which, if we define it scientifically, becomes quite algebraic. As no experienced object corresponds to it, it is without fixed indicative force, and admits any sense which its context in any mind may happen to give it. In the first sentence of Genesis its meaning, we may safely say, is "a masculine being by whom heaven and earth were created." To fill out this implication other instances of the word would have to be gathered, in each of which, of course, the word would appear with a new and perhaps incompatible meaning.

EXPRESSIONS MAY BE RECAST PERVERSELY, HUMOUROUSLY, OR SUBLIMELY

Whenever a word appears in a radically new context it has a radically new sense: the expression in which it so figures is a poetic figment, a fresh literary creation. Such invention is sometimes perverse, sometimes humourous, sometimes sublime; that is, it may either buffet old associations without enlarging them, or give them a plausible but impossible twist, or enlarge them to cover, with unexpected propriety, a much wider or more momentous experience. The force of experience in any moment—if we abstract from represented values—is emotional; so that for sublime poetry what is required is to tap some reservoir of feeling. If a phrase opens the flood-gates of emotion, it has made itself most deeply significant. Its discursive range and clearness may not be remarkable; its emotional power will quite suffice. For this reason again primitive poetry may be sublime: in its inchoate phrases there is affinity to raw passion and their very blindness may serve to bring that passion back. Poetry has body; it represents the volume of experience as well as its form, and to express volume a primitive poet will rely rather on rhythm, sound, and condensed suggestion than on discursive fulness or scope.

THE NATURE OF PROSE

The descent from poetry to prose is in one sense a progress. When use has worn down a poetic phrase to its external import, and rendered it an indifferent symbol for a particular thing, that phrase has become prosaic; it has also become, by the same process, transparent and purely instrumental. In poetry feeling is transferred by contagion; in prose it is communicated by bending the attention upon determinate objects; the one stimulates and the other informs. Under the influence of poetry various minds radiate from a somewhat similar core of sensation, from the same vital mood, into the most diverse and incommunicable images. Interlocutors speaking prose, on the contrary, pelt and besiege one another with a peripheral attack; they come into contact at sundry superficial points and thence push their agreement inwards, until perhaps a practical coincidence is arrived at in their thought. Agreement is produced by controlling each mind externally, through a series of checks and little appeals to possible sensation; whereas in poetry the agreement, where it exists, is vague and massive; there is an initial fusion of minds under hypnotic musical influences, from which each listener, as he awakes, passes into his own thoughts and interpretations. In prose the vehicle for communication is a conventional sign, standing in the last analysis for some demonstrable object or controllable feeling. By marshalling specific details a certain indirect suasion is exercised on the mind, as nature herself, by continual checks and denials, gradually tames the human will. The elements of prose are always practical, if we run back and reconstruct their primitive essence, for at bottom every experience is an original and not a copy, a nucleus for ideation rather than an object to which ideas may refer. It is when these stimulations are shaken together and become a system of mutual checks that they begin to take on ideally a rhythm borrowed from the order in which they actually recurred. Then a prophetic or representative movement arises in thought. Before this comes about, experience remains a constantly renovated dream, as poetry to the end conspires to keep it. For poetry, while truly poetical, never loses sight of its initial feelings and underlying appeals; it is incorrigibly transcendental, and takes every present passion and every private dream in turn for the core of the universe. By creating new signs, or by recasting and crossing those which have become conventional, it keeps communication massive and instinctive, immersed in music, and inexhaustible by clear thought.

IT IS MORE ADVANCED AND RESPONSIBLE THAN POETRY

Lying is a privilege of poets because they have not yet reached the level on which truth and error are discernible. Veracity and significance are not ideals for a primitive mind; we learn to value them as we learn to live, when we discover that the spirit cannot be wholly free and solipsistic. To have to distinguish fact from fancy is so great a violence to the inner man that not only poets, but theologians and philosophers, still protest against such a distinction. They urge (what is perfectly true for a rudimentary creature) that facts are mere conceptions and conceptions full-fledged facts; but this interesting embryonic lore they apply, in their intellectual weakness, to retracting or undermining those human categories which, though alone fruitful or applicable in life, are not congenial to their half-formed imagination. Retreating deeper into the inner chaos, they bring to bear the whole momentum of an irresponsible dialectic to frustrate the growth of representative ideas. In this they are genuine, if somewhat belated, poets, experimenting anew with solved problems, and fancying how creation might have moved upon other lines. The great merit that prose shares with science is that it is responsible. Its conscience is a new and wiser imagination, by which creative thought is rendered cumulative and progressive; for a man does not build less boldly or solidly if he takes the precaution of building in baked brick. Prose is in itself meagre and bodiless, merely indicating the riches of the world. Its transparency helps us to look through it to the issue, and the signals it gives fill the mind with an honest assurance and a prophetic art far nobler than any ecstasy.

MATURITY BRINGS LOVE OF PRACTICAL TRUTH

As men of action have a better intelligence than poets, if only their action is on a broad enough stage, so the prosaic rendering of experience has the greater value, if only the experience rendered covers enough human interests. Youth and aspiration indulge in poetry; a mature and masterful mind will often despise it, and prefer to express itself laconically in prose. It is clearly proper that prosaic habits should supervene in this way on the poetical; for youth, being as yet little fed by experience, can find volume and depth only in the soul; the half-seen, the supra-mundane, the inexpressible, seem to it alone beautiful and worthy of homage. Time modifies this sentiment in two directions. It breeds lassitude and indifference towards impracticable ideals, originally no less worthy than the practicable. Ideals which cannot be realised, and are not fed at least by partial realisations, soon grow dormant. Life-blood passes to other veins; the urgent and palpitating interests of life appear in other quarters. While things impossible thus lose their serious charm, things actual reveal their natural order and variety; these not only can entertain the mind abstractly, but they can offer a thousand material rewards in observation and action. In their presence, a private dream begins to look rather cheap and hysterical. Not that existence has any dignity or prerogative in the presence of will, but that will itself, being elastic, grows definite and firm when it is fed by success; and its formed and expressible ideals then put to shame the others, which have remained vague for want of practical expression. Mature interests centre on soluble problems and tasks capable of execution; it is at such points that the ideal can be really served. The individual's dream straightens and reassures itself by merging with the dream of humanity. To dwell, as irrational poets do, on some private experience, on some emotion without representative or ulterior value, then seems a waste of time. Fiction becomes less interesting than affairs, and poetry turns into a sort of incompetent whimper, a childish foreshortening of the outspread world.

PURE PROSE WOULD TEND TO EFFACE ITSELF

On the other hand, prose has a great defect, which is abstractness. It drops the volume of experience in finding bodiless algebraic symbols by which to express it. The verbal form, instead of transmitting an image, seems to constitute it, in so far as there is an image suggested at all; and the ulterior situation is described only in the sense that a change is induced in the hearer which prepares him to meet that situation. Prose seems to be a use of language in the service of material life. It would tend, in that case, to undermine its own basis; for in proportion as signals for action are quick and efficacious they diminish their sensuous stimulus and fade from consciousness. Were language such a set of signals it would be something merely instrumental, which if made perfect ought to be automatic and unconscious. It would be a buzzing in the ears, not a music native to the mind. Such a theory of language would treat it as a necessary evil and would look forward hopefully to the extinction of literature, in which it would recognise nothing ideal. There is of course no reason to deprecate the use of vocables, or of any other material agency, to expedite affairs; but an art of speech, if it is to add any ultimate charm to life, has to supervene upon a mere code of signals. Prose, could it be purely representative, would be ideally superfluous. A literary prose accordingly owns a double allegiance, and its life is amphibious. It must convey intelligence, but intelligence clothed in a language that lends the message an intrinsic value, and makes it delightful to apprehend apart from its importance in ultimate theory or practice. Prose is in that measure a fine art. It might be called poetry that had become pervasively representative, and was altogether faithful to its rational function.

FORM ALONE, OR SUBSTANCE ALONE, MAY BE POETICAL

We may therefore with good reason distinguish prosaic form from prosaic substance. A novel, a satire, a book of speculative philosophy, may have a most prosaic exterior; every phrase may convey its idea economically; but the substance may nevertheless be poetical, since these ideas may be irrelevant to all ulterior events, and may express nothing but the imaginative energy that called them forth. On the other hand, a poetic vehicle in which there is much ornamental play of language and rhythm may clothe a dry ideal skeleton. So those tremendous positivists, the Hebrew prophets, had the most prosaic notions about the goods and evils of life. So Lucretius praised, I will not say the atoms merely, but even fecundity and wisdom. The motives, to take another example, which Racine attributed to his personages, were prosaically conceived; a physiologist could not be more exact in his calculations, for even love may be made the mainspring in a clockwork of emotions. Yet that Racine was a born poet appears in the music, nobility, and tenderness of his medium; he clothed his intelligible characters in magical and tragic robes; the aroma of sentiment rises like a sort of pungent incense between them and us, and no dramatist has ever had so sure a mastery over transports and tears.

POETRY HAS ITS PLACE IN THE MEDIUM

In the medium a poet is at home; in the world he tries to render, he is a child and a stranger. Poetic notions are false notions; in so far as their function is representative they are vitiated by containing elements not present in things. Truth is a jewel which should not be painted over; but it may be set to advantage and shown in a good light. The poetic way of idealising reality is dull, bungling, and impure; a better acquaintance with things renders such flatteries ridiculous. That very effort of thought by which opaque masses of experience were first detached from the flux and given a certain individuality, seeks to continue to clarify them until they become as transparent as possible. To resist this clarification, to love the chance incrustations that encumber human ideas, is a piece of timid folly, and poetry in this respect is nothing but childish confusion. Poetic apprehension is a makeshift, in so far as its cognitive worth is concerned; it is exactly, in this respect, what myth is to science. Approaching its subject-matter from a distance, with incongruous categories, it translates it into some vague and misleading symbol rich in emotions which the object as it is could never arouse and is sure presently to contradict. What lends these hybrid ideas their temporary eloquence and charm is their congruity with the mind that breeds them and with its early habits. Falsification, or rather clouded vision, gives to poetry a more human accent and a readier welcome than to truth. In other words, it is the medium that asserts itself; the apperceptive powers indulge their private humours, and neglect the office to which they were assigned once for all by their cognitive essence.

IT IS THE BEST MEDIUM POSSIBLE

That the medium should so assert itself, however, is no anomaly, the cognitive function being an ulterior one to which ideas are by no means obliged to conform. Apperception is itself an activity or art, and like all others terminates in a product which is a good in itself, apart from its utilities. If we abstract, then, from the representative function which may perhaps accrue to speech, and regard it merely as an operation absorbing energy and occasioning delight, we see that poetic language is language at its best. Its essential success consists in fusing ideas in charming sounds or in metaphors that shine by their own brilliance. Poetry is an eloquence justified by its spontaneity, as eloquence is a poetry justified by its application. The first draws the whole soul into the situation, and the second puts the whole situation before the soul.

329

MIGHT IT NOT CONVEY WHAT IT IS BEST TO KNOW?

Is there not, we may ask, some ideal form of discourse in which apperceptive life could be engaged with all its volume and transmuting power, and in which at the same time no misrepresentation should be involved? Transmutation is not erroneous when it is intentional; misrepresentation does not please for being false, but only because truth would be more congenial if it resembled such a fiction. Why should not discourse, then, have nothing but truth in its import and nothing but beauty in its form? With regard to euphony and grammatical structure there is evidently nothing impossible in such an ideal; for these radical beauties of language are independent of the subject-matter. They form the body of poetry; but the ideal and emotional atmosphere which is its soul depends on things external to language, which no perfection in the medium could modify. It might seem as if the brilliant substitutions, the magic suggestions essential to poetry, would necessarily vanish in the full light of day. The light of day is itself beautiful; but would not the loss be terrible if no other light were ever suffered to shine?

A RATIONAL POETRY WOULD EXCLUDE MUCH NOW THOUGHT POETICAL

The Life of Reason involves sacrifice. What forces yearn for the ideal, being many and incompatible, have to yield and partly deny themselves in order to attain any ideal at all. There is something sad in all possible attainment so long as the rational virtue (which wills such attainment) is not pervasive; and even then there is limitation to put up with, and the memory of many a defeat. Rational poetry is possible and would be infinitely more beautiful than the other; but the charm of unreason, if unreason seem charming, it certainly could not preserve. In what human fancy demands, as at present constituted, there are irrational elements. The given world seems insufficient; impossible things have to be imagined, both to extend its limits and to fill in and vivify its texture. Homer has a mythology without which experience would have seemed to him undecipherable; Dante has his allegories and his mock science; Shakespeare has his romanticism; Goethe his symbolic characters and artificial machinery. All this lumber seems to have been somehow necessary to their genius; they could not reach expression in more honest terms. If such indirect expression could be discarded, it would not be missed; but while the mind, for want of a better vocabulary, is reduced to using these symbols, it pours into them a part of its own life and makes them beautiful. Their loss is a real blow, while the incapacity that called for them endures; and the soul seems to be crippled by losing its crutches.

ALL APPERCEPTION MODIFIES ITS OBJECT

There are certain adaptations and abbreviations of reality which thought can never outgrow. Thought is representative; it enriches each soul and each moment with premonitions of surrounding existences. If discourse is to be significant it must transfer to its territory and reduce to its scale whatever objects it deals with: in other words, thought has a point of view and cannot see the world except in perspective. This point of view is not, for reason, locally or naturally determined; sense alone is limited in that material fashion, being seated in the body and looking thence centrifugally upon things in so far as they come into dynamic relations with that body. Intelligence, on the contrary, sallies from that physical stronghold and consists precisely in shifting and universalising the point of view, neutralising all local, temporal, or personal conditions. Yet intelligence, notwithstanding, has its own centre and point of origin, not explicitly in space or in a natural body, but in some specific interest or moral aim. It translates animal life into moral endeavour, and what figured in the first as a local existence figures in the second as a specific good. Reason accordingly has its essential bias, and looks at things as they affect the particular form of life which reason expresses; and though all reality should be ultimately swept by the eye of reason, the whole would still be surveyed by a particular method, from a particular starting-point, for a particular end; nor would it take much shrewdness to perceive that this nucleus for discourse and estimation, this ideal life, corresponds in the moral world to that animal body which gave sensuous experience its seat and centre; so that rationality is nothing but the ideal function or aspect of natural life. Reason is universal in its outlook and in its sympathies: it is the faculty of changing places ideally and representing alien points of view; but this very self-transcendence manifests a certain special method in life, an equilibrium which a far-sighted being is able to establish between itself and its comprehended conditions. Reason remains to the end essentially human and, in its momentary actuality, necessarily personal.

REASON HAS ITS OWN BIAS AND METHOD

We have here an essential condition of discourse which renders it at bottom poetical. Selection and applicability govern all thinking, and govern it in the interests of the soul. Reason is itself a specific medium; so that prose can never attain that perfect transparency and mere utility which we were attributing to it. We should not wish to know "things in themselves," even if we were able. What it concerns us to know about them is merely the service or injury they are able to do us, and in what fashion they can affect our lives. To know this would be, in so far, truly to know them; but it would be to know them through our own faculties and through their supposed effects; it would be to know them by their appearance. A singular proof of the frivolous way in which philosophers often proceed, when they think they are particularly profound, is seen in this puzzle, on which they solemnly ask us to fix our thoughts: How is it possible to know reality, if all we can attain in experience is but appearance? The meaning of knowledge, which is an intellectual and living thing, is here forgotten, and the notion of sensation, or bodily possession, is substituted for it; so what we are really asked to consider is how, had we no understanding, we should be able to understand what we endure. It is by conceiving what we endure to be the appearance of something beyond us, that we reach knowledge that something exists beyond us, and that it plays in respect to us a determinate rôle. There could be no knowledge of reality if what conveyed that knowledge were not felt to be appearance; nor can a medium of knowledge better than appearance be by any possibility conceived. To have such appearances is what makes realities knowable. Knowledge transcends sensation by relating it to other sensation, and thereby rising to a supersensuous plane, the plane of principles and causes by which sensibles are identified in character and distributed in existence. These principles and causes are what we call the intelligible or the real world; and the sensations, when they have been so interpreted and underpinned, are what we call experience.

RATIONAL POETRY WOULD ENVELOP EXACT KNOWLEDGE IN ULTIMATE EMOTIONS

If a poet could clarify the myths he begins with, so as to reach ultimate scientific notions of nature and life, he would still be dealing with vivid feeling and with its imaginative expression. The prosaic landscape before him would still be a work of art, painted on the human brain by human reason. If he found that landscape uninteresting, it would be because he was not really interested in life; if he found it dull and unpoetical, he would be manifesting his small capacity and childish whims. Tragic, fatal, intractable, he might well feel that the truth was; but these qualities have never been absent from that half-mythical world through which poets, for want of a rational education, have hitherto wandered. A rational poet's vision would have the same moral functions which myth was asked to fulfil, and fulfilled so treacherously; it would employ the same ideal faculties which myth expressed in a confused and hasty fashion. More detail would have been added, and more variety in interpretation. To deal with so great an object, and retain his mastery over it, a poet would doubtless need a robust genius. If he possessed it, and in transmuting all existence falsified nothing, giving that picture of everything which human experience in the end would have drawn, he would achieve an ideal result. In prompting mankind to imagine, he would be helping them to live. His poetry, without ceasing to be a fiction in its method and ideality, would be an ultimate truth in its practical scope. It would present in graphic images the total efficacy of real things. Such a poetry would be more deeply rooted in human experience than is any casual fancy, and therefore more appealing to the heart. Such a poetry would represent more thoroughly than any formula the concrete burden of experience; it would become the most trustworthy of companions. The images it had worked out would confront human passion more intelligibly than does the world as at present conceived, with its mechanism half ignored and its ideality half invented; they would represent vividly the uses of nature, and thereby make all natural situations seem so many incentives to art.

AN ILLUSTRATION

Rational poetry is not wholly unknown. When Homer mentions an object, how does he render it poetical? First, doubtless, by the euphony of its name or the sensuous glow of some epithet coupled with it. Sometimes, however, even this ornamental epithet is not merely sensuous; it is very likely a patronymic, the name of some region or some mythical ancestor. In other words, it is a signal for widening our view and for conceiving the object, not only vividly and with pause, but in an adequate historic setting. Macbeth tells us that his dagger was "unmannerly breeched in gore." Achilles would not have amused himself with such a metaphor, even if breeches had existed in his day, but would rather have told us whose blood, on other occasions, had stained the same blade, and perhaps what father or mother had grieved for the slaughtered hero, or what brave children remained to continue his race. Shakespeare's phrase is ingenious and fanciful; it dazzles for a moment, but in the end it seems violent and crude. What Homer would have said, on the contrary, being simple and true, might have grown, as we dwelt upon it, always more noble, pathetic, and poetical. Shakespeare too, beneath his occasional absurdities of plot and diction, ennobles his stage with actual history, with life painted to the quick, with genuine human characters, politics, and wisdom; and surely these are not the elements that do least credit to his genius. In every poet, indeed, there is some fidelity to nature, mixed with that irrelevant false fancy with which poetry is sometimes identified; and the degree in which a poet's imagination dominates reality is, in the end, the exact measure of his importance and dignity.

VOLUME CAN BE FOUND IN SCOPE BETTER THAN IN SUGGESTION

Before prosaic objects are descried, the volume and richness needful for poetry lie in a blurred and undigested chaos; but after the common world has emerged and has called on prose to describe it, the same volume and richness may be recovered; and a new and clarified poetry may arise through synthesis. Scope is a better thing than suggestion, and more truly poetical. It has expressed what suggestion pointed to and felt in the bulk: it possesses what was yearned for. A real thing, when all its pertinent natural associates are discerned, touches wonder, pathos, and beauty on every side; the rational poet is one who, without feigning anything unreal, perceives these momentous ties, and presents his subject loaded with its whole fate, missing no source of worth which is in it, no ideal influence which it may have. Homer remains, perhaps, the greatest master in this art. The world he glorified by showing in how many ways it could serve reason and beauty was but a simple world, and an equal genius in these days might be distracted by the Babel about him, and be driven, as poets now are, into incidental dreams. Yet the ideal of mastery and idealisation remains the same, if any one could only attain it: mastery, to see things as they are and dare to describe them ingenuously; idealisation, to select from this reality what is pertinent to ultimate interests and can speak eloquently to the soul.

LITERARY FORM

THE MOST remarkable and characteristic problem of æsthetics is that of beauty of form. Where there is a sensuous delight, like that of colour, and the impression of the object is in its elements agreeable, we have to look no farther for an explanation of the charm we feel. Where there is expression, and an object indifferent to the senses is associated with other ideas which are interesting, the problem, although complex and varied, is in principle comparatively plain. But there is an intermediate effect which is more mysterious, and more specifically an effect of beauty. It is found where sensible elements, by themselves indifferent, are so united as to please in combination. There is something unexpected in this phenomenon, so much so that those who cannot conceive its explanation often reassure themselves by denying its existence. To reduce beauty of form, however, to beauty of elements would not be easy, because the creation and variation of effect, by changing the relation of the simplest lines, offers too easy an experiment in refutation. And it would, moreover, follow to the comfort of the vulgar that all marble houses are equally beautiful.

To attribute beauty of form to expression is more plausible. If I take the meaningless short lines in the figure and arrange them in the given ways, intended to represent the human face, there appear at once notably different æsthetic values. Two of the forms are differently grotesque and one approximately beautiful. Now these effects are due to the expression of the lines; not only because they make one think of fair or ugly faces, but because, it may be said, these faces would in reality be fair or ugly according to their expression, according to the vital and moral associations of the different types.

Nevertheless, beauty of form cannot be reduced to expression

336

without denying the existence of immediate æsthetic values altogether, and reducing them all to suggestions of moral good. For if the object expressed by the form, and from which the form derives its value, had itself beauty of form, we should not advance; we must come somewhere to the point where the expression is of something else than beauty; and this something else would of course be some practical or moral good. Moralists are fond of such an interpretation, and it is a very interesting one. It puts beauty in the same relation to morals in which morals stand to pleasure and pain; both would be intuitions, qualitatively new, but with the same materials; they would be new perspectives of the same object.

But this theory is actually inadmissible. Innumerable æsthetic effects, indeed all specific and unmixed ones, are direct transmutations of pleasures and pains; they express nothing extrinsic to themselves, much less moral excellences. The detached lines of our figure signify nothing, but they are not absolutely uninteresting; the straight line is the simplest and not the least beautiful of forms. To say that it owes its interest to the thought of the economy of travelling over the shortest road, or of other practical advantages, would betray a feeble hold on psychological reality. The impression of a straight line differs in a certain almost emotional way from that of a curve, as those of various curves do from one another. The quality of the sensation is different, like that of various colours or sounds. To attribute the character of these forms to association would be like explaining sea-sickness as the fear of shipwreck. There is a distinct quality and value, often a singular beauty, in these simple lines that is intrinsic in the perception of their form.

It would be pedantic, perhaps, anywhere but in a treatise on æsthetics, to deny to this quality the name of expression; we might commonly say that the circle has one expression and the oval another. But what does the circle express except circularity, or the oval except the nature of the ellipse? Such expression *expresses* nothing; it is really *im*pression. There may be analogy between it and other impressions; we may admit that odours, colours, and sounds correspond, and may mutually suggest one another; but this analogy is a superadded charm felt by very sensitive natures, and does not constitute the original value of the sensations. The common emotional tinge is rather what enables them to suggest one another, and what makes them comparable. Their expression, such as it is, is therefore due to the accident that both feelings have a kindred quality; and this quality has its effectiveness for sense independently of the perception of its recurrence in a different sphere. We shall accordingly take care to reserve the term "expression" for the suggestion of some other and assignable object, from which the expressive thing borrows an interest; and we shall speak of the intrinsic quality of forms as their emotional tinge or specific value. . . .

ORIGIN OF TYPES

A most important thing . . . in the perception of form is the formation of types in our mind, with reference to which examples are to be judged. I say the formation of them, for we can hardly consider the theory that they are eternal as a possible one in psychology. The Platonic doctrine on that point is a striking illustration of an equivocation we mentioned in the beginning; namely, that the import of an experience is regarded as a manifestation of its cause—the product of a faculty substituted for the description of its function. Eternal types are the instrument of æsthetic life, not its foundation. Take the æsthetic attitude, and you have for the moment an eternal idea; an idea, I mean, that you treat as an absolute standard, just as when you take the perceptive attitude you have an external object which you treat as an absolute existence. But the æsthetic, like the perceptive faculty, can be made an object of study in turn, and its theory can be sought; and then the eternal idea, like the external object, is seen to be a product of human nature, a symbol of experience, and an instrument of thought.

The question whether there are not, in external nature or in the mind of God, objects and eternal types, is indeed not settled, it is not even touched by this inquiry; but it is indirectly shown

338

to be futile, because such transcendent realities, if they exist, can have nothing to do with our ideas of them. The Platonic idea of a tree may exist; how should I deny it? How should I deny that I might some day find myself outside the sky gazing at it, and feeling that I, with my mental vision, am beholding the plenitude of arboreal beauty, perceived in this world only as a vague essence haunting the multiplicity of finite trees? But what can that have to do with my actual sense of what a tree should be? Shall we take the Platonic myth literally, and say the idea is a memory of the tree I have already seen in heaven? How else establish any relation between that eternal object and the type in my mind? But why, in that case, this infinite variability of ideal trees? Was the Tree Beautiful an oak, or a cedar, an English or an American elm? My actual types are finite and mutually exclusive; that heavenly type must be one and infinite. The problem is hopeless.

Very simple, on the other hand, is the explanation of the existence of that type as a residuum of experience. Our idea of an individual thing is a compound and residuum of our several experiences of it; and in the same manner our idea of a class is a compound and residuum of our ideas of the particulars that compose it. Particular impressions have, by virtue of their intrinsic similarity or of the identity of their relations, a tendency to be merged and identified, so that many individual perceptions leave but a single blurred memory that stands for them all, because it combines their several associations. Similarly, when various objects have many common characteristics, the mind is incapable of keeping them apart. It cannot hold clearly so great a multitude of distinctions and relations as would be involved in naming and conceiving separately each grain of sand, or drop of water, each fly or horse or man that we have ever seen. The mass of our experience has therefore to be classified, if it is to be available at all. Instead of a distinct image to represent each of our original impressions, we have a general resultant—a composite photograph—of those impressions.

This resultant image is the idea of the class. It often has very few, if any, of the sensible properties of the particulars that underlie it, often an artificial symbol—the sound of a word—is the only element, present to all the instances, which the generic image clearly contains. For, of course, the reason why a name can represent a class of objects is that the name is the most conspicuous element of identity in the various experiences of objects in that class. We have seen many horses, but if we are not lovers of the animal, nor particularly keen observers, very likely we retain no clear image of all that mass of impressions except the reverberation of the sound "horse," which really or mentally has accompanied all those impressions. This sound, therefore, is the content of our general idea, and to it cling all the associations which constitute our sense of what the word means. But a person with a memory predominantly visual would probably add to this remembered sound a more or less detailed image of the animal; some particular horse in some particular attitude might possibly be recalled, but more probably some imaginative construction, some dream image, would accompany the sound. An image which reproduced no particular horse exactly, but which was a spontaneous fiction of the fancy, would serve, by virtue of its felt relations, the same purpose as the sound itself. Such a spontaneous image would be, of course, variable. In fact, no image can, strictly speaking, ever recur. But these percepts, as they are called, springing up in the mind like flowers from the buried seeds of past experience, would inherit all the powers of suggestion which are required by any instrument of classification.

These powers of suggestion have probably a cerebral basis. The new percept—the generic idea—repeats to a great extent, both in nature and localisation, the excitement constituting the various original impressions; as the percept reproduces more or less of these it will be a more or less full and impartial representative of them. Not all the suggestions of a word or image are equally ripe. A generic idea or type usually presents to us a very inadequate and biassed view of the field it means to cover. As we reflect and seek to correct this inadequacy, the percept changes on our hands. The very consciousness that other individuals and other qualities fall under our concept, changes this concept, as a psychological presence, and alters its distinctness and extent. When I remember, to use a classical example, that the triangle is not isosceles, nor scalene, nor rectangular, but each and all of those, I reduce my percept to the word and its definition, with perhaps a sense of the general motion of the hand and eye by which we trace a three-cornered figure.

Since the production of a general idea is thus a matter of subjective bias, we cannot expect that a type should be the exact average of the examples from which it is drawn. In a rough way, it is the average; a fact that in itself is the strongest of arguments against the independence or priority of the general idea. The beautiful horse, the beautiful speech, the beautiful face, is always a medium between the extremes which our experience has offered. It is enough that a given characteristic should be generally present in our experience, for it to become an indispensable element of the ideal. There is nothing in itself beautiful or necessary in the shape of the human ear, or in the presence of nails on the fingers and toes; but the ideal of man, which the preposterous conceit of our judgment makes us set up as divine and eternal, requires these precise details; without them the human form would be repulsively ugly.

It often happens that the accidents of experience make us in this way introduce into the ideal, elements which, if they could be excluded without disgusting us, would make possible satisfactions greater than those we can now enjoy. Thus the taste formed by one school of art may condemn the greater beauties created by another. In morals we have the same phenomenon. A barbarous ideal of life requires tasks and dangers incompatible with happiness; a rude and oppressed conscience is incapable of regarding as good a state which excludes its own acrid satisfactions. So, too, a fanatical imagination cannot regard God as just unless he is represented as infinitely cruel. The purpose of education is, of course, to free us from these prejudices, and to develop our ideals in the direction of the greatest possible good. Evidently the ideal has been formed by the habit of perception; it is, in a rough way, that average form which we expect and most readily apperceive. The propriety and necessity of it is entirely relative to our experience and faculty of apperception. The shock of surprise, the incongruity with the formed percept, is the essence and measure of ugliness.

THE AVERAGE MODIFIED IN THE DIRECTION OF PLEASURE

Nevertheless we do not form æsthetic ideals any more than other general types, entirely without bias. We have already observed that a percept seldom gives an impartial compound of the objects of which it is the generic image. This partiality is due to a variety of

341

circumstances. One is the unequal accuracy of our observation. If some interest directs our attention to a particular quality of objects, that quality will be prominent in our percept; it may even be the only content clearly given in our general idea; and any object, however similar in other respects to those of the given class, will at once be distinguished as belonging to a different species if it lacks that characteristic on which our attention is particularly fixed. Our percepts are thus habitually biassed in the direction of practical interest, if practical interest does not indeed entirely govern their formation. In the same manner, our æsthetic ideals are biassed in the direction of æsthetic interest. Not all parts of an object are equally congruous with our perceptive faculty; not all elements are noted with the same pleasure. Those, therefore, which are agreeable are chiefly dwelt upon by the lover of beauty, and his percept will give an average of things with a great emphasis laid on that part of them which is beautiful. The ideal will thus deviate from the average in the direction of the observer's pleasure.

For this reason the world is so much more beautiful to a poet or an artist than to an ordinary man. Each object, as his æsthetic sense is developed, is perhaps less beautiful than to the uncritical eye; his taste becomes difficult, and only the very best gives him unalloyed satisfaction. But while each work of nature and art is thus apparently blighted by his greater demands and keener susceptibility, the world itself, and the various natures it contains, are to him unspeakably beautiful. The more blemishes he can see in men, the more excellence he sees in man, and the more bitterly he laments the fate of each particular soul, the more reverence and love he has for the soul in its ideal essence. Criticism and idealisation involve each other. The habit of looking for beauty in everything makes us notice the shortcomings of things; our sense, hungry for complete satisfaction, misses the perfection it demands. But this demand for perfection becomes at the same time the nucleus of our observation; from every side a quick affinity draws what is beautiful together and stores it in the mind, giving body there to the blind yearnings of our nature. Many imperfect things crystallise into a single perfection. The mind is thus peopled by general ideas in which beauty is the chief quality; and these ideas are at the same time the types of things. The type is still a natural resultant of particular impressions; but the formation of it has been guided by a deep subjective bias in favour of what has delighted the eye.

This theory can be easily tested by asking whether, in the case where the ideal differs from the average form of objects, this variation is not due to the intrinsic pleasantness or impressiveness of the quality exaggerated. For instance, in the human form, the ideal differs immensely from the average. In many respects the extreme or something near it is the most beautiful. Xenophon describes the women of Armenia as καλαὶ καὶ μεγάλαι, and we should still speak of one as fair and tall and of another as fair but little. Size is therefore, even where least requisite, a thing in which the ideal exceeds the average. And the reason—apart from associations of strength—is that unusual size makes things conspicuous. The first prerequisite of effect is impression, and size helps that; therefore in the æsthetic ideal the average will be modified by being enlarged, because that is a change in the direction of our pleasure, and size will be an element of beauty.[1]

Similarly the eyes, in themselves beautiful, will be enlarged also; and generally whatever makes by its sensuous quality, by its abstract form, or by its expression, a particular appeal to our attention and contribution to our delight, will count for more in the ideal type than its frequency would warrant. The generic image has been constructed under the influence of a selective attention, bent upon æsthetic worth.

To praise any object for approaching the ideal of its kind is therefore only a roundabout way of specifying its intrinsic merit and expressing its direct effect on our sensibility. If in referring to the ideal we were not thus analysing the real, the ideal would be an irrelevant and unmeaning thing. We know what the ideal is because we observe what pleases us in the reality. If we allow the general notion to tyrannise at all over the particular impression and to blind us to new and unclassified beauties which the latter may contain, we are simply substituting words for feelings, and making a verbal classification pass for an æsthetic judgment. Then

---

[1]The contention of Burke that the beautiful is small is due to an arbitrary definition. By beautiful he means pretty and charming; agreeable as opposed to impressive. He only exaggerates the then usual opposition of the beautiful to the sublime.

the sense of beauty is gone to seed. Ideals have their uses, but their authority is wholly representative. They stand for specific satisfactions, or else they stand for nothing at all.

In fact, the whole machinery of our intelligence, our general ideas and laws, fixed and external objects, principles, persons and gods, are so many symbolic, algebraic expressions. They stand for experience; experience which we are incapable of retaining and surveying in its multitudinous immediacy. We should flounder hopelessly, like the animals, did we not keep ourselves afloat and direct our course by these intellectual devices. Theory helps us to bear our ignorance of fact.

The same thing happens, in a way, in other fields. Our armies are devices necessitated by our weakness; our property an encumbrance required by our need. If our situation were not precarious, these great engines of death and life would not be invented. And our intelligence is such another weapon against fate. We need not lament the fact, since, after all, to build these various structures is, up to a certain point, the natural function of human nature. The trouble is not that the products are always subjective, but that they are sometimes unfit and torment the spirit which they exercise. The pathetic part of our situation appears only when we so attach ourselves to those necessary but imperfect fictions, as to reject the facts from which they spring and of which they seek to be prophetic. We are then guilty of that substitution of means for ends, which is called idolatry in religion, absurdity in logic, and folly in morals. In æsthetics the thing has no name, but is nevertheless very common; for it is found whenever we speak of what ought to please, rather than of what actually pleases. . . .

FORM IN WORDS

The main effect of language consists in its meaning, in the ideas which it expresses. But no expression is possible without a presentation, and this presentation must have a form. This form of the instrument of expression is itself an element of effect, although in practical life we may overlook it in our haste to attend to the meaning it conveys. It is, moreover, a condition of the kind of expression possible, and often determines the manner in which the object suggested shall be apperceived. No word has the exact value of any other in the same or in another language.[2] But the intrinsic effect of language does not stop there. The single word is but a stage in the series of formations which constitute language, and which preserve for men the fruit of their experience, distilled and concentrated into a symbol.

This formation begins with the elementary sounds themselves, which have to be discriminated and combined to make recognisable symbols. The evolution of these symbols goes on spontaneously, suggested by our tendency to utter all manner of sounds, and preserved by the ease with which the ear discriminates these sounds when made. Speech would be an absolute and unrelated art, like music, were it not controlled by utility. The sounds have indeed no resemblance to the objects they symbolise; but before the system of sounds can represent the system of objects, there has to be a correspondence in the groupings of both. The structure of language, unlike that of music, thus becomes a mirror of the structure of the world as presented to the intelligence.

Grammar, philosophically studied, is akin to the deepest metaphysics, because in revealing the constitution of speech, it reveals the constitution of thought, and the hierarchy of those categories by which we conceive the world. It is by virtue of this parallel development that language has its function of expressing experience with exactness, and the poet—to whom language is an instrument of art—has to employ it also with a constant reference to meaning and veracity; that is, he must be a master of experience before he can become a true master of words. Nevertheless, language is primarily a sort of music, and the beautiful effects which it produces are due to its own structure, giving, as it crystallises in a new fashion, an unforeseen form to experience.

Poets may be divided into two classes: the musicians and the psychologists. The first are masters of significant language as harmony; they know what notes to sound together and in succession; they can produce, by the marshalling of sounds and images, by

[2]Not only are words untranslatable when the exact object has no name in another language, as "home" or "mon ami," but even when the object is the same, the attitude toward it, incorporated in one word, cannot be rendered by another. Thus, to my sense, "bread" is as inadequate a translation of the human intensity of the Spanish "pan" as "Dios" is of the awful mystery of the English "God." This latter word does not designate an object at all, but a sentiment, a psychosis, not to say a whole chapter of religious history. English is remarkable for the intensity and variety of the colour of its words. No language, I believe, has so many words specifically poetic.

345

the fugue of passion and the snap of wit, a thousand brilliant effects out of old materials. The Ciceronian orator, the epigrammatic, lyric, and elegiac poets, give examples of this art. The psychologists, on the other hand, gain their effect not by the intrinsic mastery of language, but by the closer adaptation of it to things. The dramatic poets naturally furnish an illustration.

But however transparent we may wish to make our language, however little we may call for its intrinsic effects, and direct our attention exclusively to its expressiveness, we cannot avoid the limitations of our particular medium. The character of the tongue a man speaks, and the degree of his skill in speaking it, must always count enormously in the æsthetic value of his compositions; no skill in observation, no depth of thought or feeling, but is spoiled by a bad style and enhanced by a good one. The diversities of tongues and their irreducible æsthetic values, begin with the very sound of the letters, with the mode of the utterance, and the characteristic inflections of the voice; notice, for instance, the effect of the French of these lines of Alfred de Musset,

> Jamais deux yeux plus doux n'ont du ciel le plus pur
> Sondé la profondeur et réfléchi l'azur.

and compare with its flute-like and treble quality the breadth, depth, and volume of the German in this inimitable stanza of Goethe's:

> Ueber allen Gipfeln
> Ist Ruh,
> In allen Wipfeln
> Spürest du
> Kaum einen Hauch;
> Die Vögelein schweigen im Walde.
> Warte nur, balde
> Ruhest du auch.

Even if the same tune could be played on both these vocal instruments, the difference in their *timbre* would make the value of the melody entirely distinct in each case.

SYNTACTICAL FORM

The known impossibility of adequate translation appears here at the basis of language. The other diversities are superadded upon this diversity of sound. The syntax is the next source of effect. What could be better than Homer, or what worse than almost any translation of him? And this holds even of languages so closely allied as the Indo-European, which, after all, have certain correspondences of syntax and inflection. If there could be a language with other parts of speech than ours,—a language without nouns, for instance,—how would that grasp of experience, that picture of the world, which all our literature contains, be reproduced in it? Whatever beauties that language might be susceptible of, none of the effects produced on us, I will not say by poets, but even by nature itself, could be expressed in it.

Nor is such a language inconceivable. Instead of summarising all our experiences of a thing by one word, its name, we should have to recall by appropriate adjectives the various sensations we had received from it; the objects we think of would be disintegrated, or, rather, would never have been unified. For "sun" they would say "high, yellow, dazzling, round, slowly moving," and the enumeration of these qualities (as we call them), without any suggestion of a unity at their source, might give a more vivid and profound, if more cumbrous, representation of the facts. But how could the machinery of such an imagination be capable of repeating the effects of ours, when the objects to us most obvious and real would be to those minds utterly indescribable?

The same diversity appears in the languages we ordinarily know, only in a lesser degree. The presence or absence of case-endings in nouns and adjectives, their difference of gender, the richness of inflections in the verbs, the frequency of particles and conjunctions,—all these characteristics make one language differ from another entirely in genius and capacity of expression. Greek is probably the best of all languages in melody, richness, elasticity, and simplicity; so much so, that in spite of its complex inflections, when once a vocabulary is acquired, it is more easy and natural for a modern than his ancestral Latin itself. Latin is the stiffer tongue; it is by nature at once laconic and grandiloquent, and the exceptional condensation and transposition of which it is capable make its effects entirely foreign to a modern, scarcely inflected, tongue. Take, for instance, these lines of Horace:

> me tabula sacer
> votiva paries indicat uvida
> suspendisse potenti
> vestimenta maris deo,

or these of Lucretius:

> Jamque caput quassans grandis suspirat arator
> Crebrius incassum magnum cecidisse laborem.

What conglomerate plebeian speech of our time could utter the stately grandeur of these Lucretian words, every one of which is noble, and wears the toga?

As a substitute for the inimitable interpenetration of the words in the Horatian strophe, we might have the external links of rhyme; and it seems, in fact, to be a justification of rhyme, that besides contributing something to melody and to the distribution of parts, it gives an artificial relationship to the phrases between which it obtains, which, but for it, would run away from one another in a rapid and irrevocable flux. In such a form as the sonnet, for instance, we have, by dint of assonance, a real unity forced upon the thought; for a sonnet in which the thought is not distributed appropriately to the structure of the verse, has no excuse for being a sonnet. By virtue of this inter-relation of parts, the sonnet, the *non plus ultra* of rhyme, is the most classic of modern poetical forms: much more classic in spirit than blank verse, which lacks almost entirely the power of synthesising the phrase, and making the unexpected seem the inevitable.

This beauty given to the ancients by the syntax of their language, the moderns can only attain by the combination of their rhymes. It is a bad substitute perhaps, but better than the total absence of form, favoured by the atomic character of our words, and the flat juxtaposition of our clauses. The art which was capable of making a gem of every prose sentence,—the art which, carried, perhaps, to a pitch at which it became too conscious, made the phrases of Tacitus a series of cameos,—that art is inapplicable to our looser medium; we cannot give clay the finish and nicety of marble. Our poetry and speech in general, therefore, start out upon a lower level; the same effort will not, with this instrument, attain the same beauty. If equal beauty is ever attained, it comes from the wealth of suggestion, or the refinement of sentiment. The art of words remains hopelessly inferior. And what best proves this, is that when, as in our time, a reawakening of the love of beauty has prompted a refinement of our poetical language, we pass so soon into extravagance, obscurity, and affectation. Our modern languages are not susceptible of great formal beauty.

LITERARY FORM. THE PLOT

The forms of composition in verse and prose which are practised in each language are further organisations of words, and have formal values. The most exacting of these forms and that which has been carried to the greatest perfection is the drama; but it belongs to rhetoric and poetics to investigate the nature of these effects, and we have here sufficiently indicated the principle which underlies them. The plot, which Aristotle makes, and very justly, the most important element in the effect of a drama, is the formal element of the drama as such: the ethos and sentiments are the expression, and the versification, music, and stage settings are the materials. It is in harmony with the romantic tendency of modern times that modern dramatists—Shakespeare as well as Molière, Calderon, and the rest—excel in ethos rather than in plot; for it is the evident characteristic of modern genius to study and enjoy expression,—the suggestion of the not-given,—rather than form, the harmony of the given.

Ethos is interesting mainly for the personal observations which it summarises and reveals, or for the appeal to one's own actual or imaginative experience; it is portrait-painting, and enshrines something we love independently of the charm which at this moment and in this place it exercises over us. It appeals to our affections; it does not form them. But the plot is the synthesis of actions, and is a reproduction of those experiences from which our notion of men and things is originally derived; for character can never be observed in the world except as manifested in action.

Indeed, it would be more fundamentally accurate to say that a character is a symbol and mental abbreviation for a peculiar set of acts, than to say that acts are a manifestation of character. For the acts are the data, and the character the inferred principle, and a principle, in spite of its name, is never more than a description *a posteriori*, and a summary of what is subsumed under it. The plot, moreover, is what gives individuality to the play, and exercises invention; it is, as Aristotle again says, the most difficult portion of dramatic art, and that for which practice and training are most indispensable. And this plot, giving by its nature a certain picture of human experience, involves and suggests the ethos of its actors.

What the great characterisers, like Shakespeare, do, is simply to elaborate and develop (perhaps far beyond the necessities of the plot) the suggestion of human individuality which that plot contains. It is as if, having drawn from daily observation some knowledge of the tempers of our friends, we represented them saying and doing all manner of ultra-characteristic things, and in an occasional soliloquy laying bare, even more clearly than by any possible action, that character which their observed behaviour had led us to impute to them. This is an ingenious and fascinating invention, and delights us with the clear discovery of a hidden personality; but the serious and equable development of a plot has a more stable worth in its greater similarity to life, which allows us to see other men's minds through the medium of events, and not events through the medium of other men's minds.

CHARACTER AS AN ÆSTHETIC FORM

We have just come upon one of the unities most coveted in our literature, and most valued by us when attained,—the portrait, the individuality, the character. The construction of a plot we call invention, but that of a character we dignify with the name of creation. It may therefore not be amiss, in finishing our discussion of form, to devote a few pages to the psychology of character-drawing. How does the unity we call a character arise, how is it described, and what is the basis of its effect?

We may set it down at once as evident that we have here a case of the type: the similarities of various persons are amalgamated, their differences cancelled, and in the resulting percept those traits emphasised which have particularly pleased or interested us. This, in the abstract, may serve for a description of the origin of an idea of character quite as well as of an idea of physical form. But the different nature of the material—the fact that a character is not a presentation to sense, but a rationalistic synthesis of successive acts and feelings, not combinable into any image—makes such a description much more unsatisfying in this case than in that of material forms. We cannot understand exactly how these summations and cancellings take place when we are not dealing with a visible object. And we may even feel that there is a wholeness and inwardness about the development of certain ideal characters, that makes such a treatment of them fundamentally false and artificial. The subjective element, the spontaneous expression of our own passion and will, here counts for so much, that the creation of an ideal character becomes a new and peculiar problem.

There is, however, a way of conceiving and delineating character which still bears a close resemblance to the process by which the imagination produces the type of any physical species. We may gather, for instance, about the nucleus of a word, designating some human condition or occupation, a number of detached observations. We may keep a note-book in our memory, or even in our pocket, with studious observations of the language, manners, dress, gesture, and history of the people we meet, classifying our statistics under such heads as innkeepers, soldiers, housemaids, governesses, adventuresses, Germans, Frenchmen, Italians, Americans, actors, priests, and professors. And then, when occasion offers, to describe, or to put into a book or a play, any one of these types, all we have to do is to look over our notes, to select according to the needs of the moment, and if we are skilful in reproduction, to obtain by that means a life-like image of the sort of person we wish to represent.

This process, which novelists and playwrights may go through deliberately, we all carry on involuntarily. At every moment experience is leaving in our minds some trait, some expression, some image, which will remain there attached to the name of a person, a class, or a nationality. Our likes and dislikes, our summary judgments on whole categories of men, are nothing but the distinct survival of some such impression. These traits have vivacity. If the picture they draw is one-sided and inadequate, the sensation they recall may be vivid, and suggestive of many other aspects of the thing. Thus the epithets in Homer, although they are often far from describing the essence of the object—γλαυκῶπις Ἀθήνη, εὐκνήμιδες Ἀχαιοι—seem to recall a sensation, and to give vitality to the narrative. By bringing you, through one sense, into the presence of the object, they give you that same hint of further discovery, that same expectation of experience, which we have at the sight of whatever we call real.

The graphic power of this method of observation and aggregation of characteristic traits is thus seen to be great. But it is not by this method that the most famous or most living characters have been conceived. This method gives the average, or at most the salient, points of the type, but the great characters of poetry—a Hamlet, a Don Quixote, an Achilles—are no averages, they are not even a collection of salient traits common to certain classes of men. They seem to be persons; that is, their actions and words seem to spring from the inward nature of an individual soul. Goethe is reported to have said that he conceived the character of his Gretchen entirely without observation of originals. And, indeed, he would probably not have found any. His creation rather is the original to which we may occasionally think we see some likeness in real maidens. It is the fiction here that is the standard of naturalness. And on this, as on so many occasions, we may repeat the saying that poetry is truer than history. Perhaps no actual maid ever spoke and acted so naturally as this imaginary one.

If we think there is any paradox in these assertions, we should reflect that the standard of naturalness, individuality, and truth is in us. A real person seems to us to have character and consistency when his behaviour is such as to impress a definite and simple image upon our mind. In themselves, if we could count all their undiscovered springs of action, all men have character and consistency alike: all are equally fit to be types. But their characters are not equally intelligible to us, their behaviour is not equally deducible, and their motives not equally appreciable. Those who appeal most to us, either in themselves or by the emphasis they borrow from their similarity to other individuals, are those we remember and regard as the centres around which variations oscillate. These men are natural: all others are more or less eccentric.

IDEAL CHARACTER

The standard of naturalness being thus subjective, and determined by the laws of our imagination, we can understand why a spontaneous creation of the mind can be more striking and living than any reality, or any abstraction from realities. The artist can invent a form which, by its adaptation to the imagination, lodges there, and becomes a point of reference for all observations, and a standard of naturalness and beauty. A type may be introduced to the mind suddenly, by the chance presentation of a form that by its intrinsic impressiveness and imaginative coherence, acquires that pre-eminence which custom, or the mutual reinforcement of converging experiences, ordinarily gives to empirical percepts.

This method of originating types is what we ordinarily describe as artistic creation. The name indicates the suddenness, originality, and individuality of the conception thus attained. What we call idealisation is often a case of it. In idealisation proper, however, what happens is the elimination of individual eccentricities; the result is abstract, and consequently meagre. This meagreness is often felt to be a greater disadvantage than the accidental and picturesque imperfection of real individuals, and the artist therefore turns to the brute fact, and studies and reproduces that with indiscriminate attention, rather than lose strength and individuality in the presentation of an insipid type. He seems forced to a choice between an abstract beauty and an unlovely example.

But the great and masterful presentations of the ideal are somehow neither the one nor the other. They present ideal beauty with just that definiteness with which nature herself sometimes presents it. When we come in a crowd upon an incomparably beautiful face, we know it immediately as an embodiment of the ideal; while it contains the type,—for if it did not we should find it monstrous and grotesque,—it clothes that type in a peculiar splendour of form, colour, and expression. It has an individuality. And just so the imaginary figures of poetry and plastic art may have an individuality given them by the happy affinities of their elements in the imagination. They are not idealisations, they are spontaneous variations, which can arise in the mind quite as easily as in the world. They spring up in

The wreathèd trellis of a working brain;
. . . With all the gardener fancy e'er could feign
Who, breeding flowers, will never breed the same.

Imagination, in a word, generates as well as abstracts; it observes, combines, and cancels; but it also dreams. Spontaneous syntheses arise in it which are not mathematical averages of the images it receives from sense; they are effects of diffused excitements left in the brain by sensations. These excitements vary constantly in their various renewals, and occasionally take such a form that the soul is surprised by the inward vision of an unexampled beauty. If this inward vision is clear and steady, we have an æsthetic inspiration, a vocation to create; and if we can also command the technique of an appropriate art, we shall hasten to embody that inspiration, and realise an ideal. This ideal will be gradually recognised as supremely beautiful for the same reason that the object, had it been presented in the real world, would have been recognised as supremely beautiful; because while embodying a known type of form,—being, that is, a proper man, animal, or vegetable,—it possessed in an extraordinary degree those direct charms which most subjugate our attention.

Imaginary forms then differ in dignity and beauty not according to their closeness to fact or type in nature, but according to the ease with which the normal imagination reproduces the synthesis they contain. To add wings to a man has always been a natural fancy; because man can easily imagine himself to fly, and the idea is delightful to him. The winged man is therefore a form generally recognised as beautiful; although it can happen, as it did to Michael Angelo, that our appreciation of the actual form of the human body should be too keen and overmastering to allow us to relish even so charming and imaginative an extravagance. The centaur is another beautiful monster. The imagination can easily follow the synthesis of the dream in which horse and man melted into one, and first gave the glorious suggestion of their united vitality.

The same condition determines the worth of imaginary personalities. From the gods to the characters of comedy, all are, in proportion to their beauty, natural and exhilarating expressions of possible human activity. We sometimes remould visible forms into imaginary creatures; but our originality in this respect is meagre compared with the profusion of images of action which arise in us, both asleep and awake; we constantly dream of new situations, extravagant adventures, and exaggerated passions. Even our soberer thoughts are very much given to following the possible fortunes of some enterprise, and foretasting the satisfactions of love and ambition. The mind is therefore particularly sensitive to pictures of action and character; we are easily induced to follow the fortunes of any hero, and share his sentiments.

Our will, as Descartes said in a different context, is infinite, while our intelligence is finite; we follow experience pretty closely in our ideas of things, and even the furniture of fairyland bears a sad resemblance to that of earth; but there is no limit to the elasticity of our passion; and we love to fancy ourselves kings and beggars, saints and villains, young and old, happy and unhappy. There seems to be a boundless capacity of development in each of us, which the circumstances of life determine to a narrow channel; and we like to revenge ourselves in our reveries for this imputed limitation, by classifying ourselves with all that we are not, but might so easily have been. We are full of sympathy for every manifestation of life, however unusual; and even the conception of infinite knowledge and happiness—than which nothing could be more removed from our condition or more unrealisable to our fancy—remains eternally interesting to us.

The poet, therefore, who wishes to delineate a character need not keep a note-book. There is a quicker road to the heart—if he has the gift to find it. Probably his readers will not themselves have kept note-books, and his elaborate observations will only be effective when he describes something which they also happen to have noticed. The typical characters describable by the empirical method are therefore few: the miser, the lover, the old nurse, the ingénue, and the other types of traditional comedy. Any greater specification would appeal only to a small audience for a short time, because the characteristics depicted would no longer exist to be recognised. But whatever experience a poet's hearers may have had, they are men. They will have certain imaginative capacities to conceive and admire those forms of character and action which, although never actually found, are felt by each man to express what he himself might and would have been, had circumstances been more favourable.

The poet has only to study himself, and the art of expressing his own ideals, to find that he has expressed those of other people. He has but to enact in himself the part of each of his personages, and if he possesses that pliability and that definiteness of imagination which together make genius, he may express for his fellows those inward tendencies which in them have remained painfully dumb. He will be hailed as master of the human soul. He may know nothing of men, he may have almost no experience; but his creations will pass for models of naturalness, and for types of humanity. Their names will be in every one's mouth, and the lives of many generations will be enriched by the vision, one might almost say by the friendship, of these imaginary beings. They have individuality without having reality, because individuality is a thing acquired in the mind by the congeries of its impressions. They have power, also, because that depends on the appropriateness of a stimulus to touch the springs of reaction in the soul. And they of course have beauty, because in them is embodied the greatest of our imaginative delights,—that of giving body to our latent capacities, and of wandering, without the strain and contradiction of actual existence, into all forms of possible being.

THE RELIGIOUS IMAGINATION

The greatest of these creations have not been the work of any one man. They have been the slow product of the pious and poetic imagination. Starting from some personification of nature or some memory of a great man, the popular and priestly tradition has refined and developed the ideal; it has made it an expression of men's aspiration and a counterpart of their need. The devotion of each tribe, shrine, and psalmist has added some attribute to the god or some parable to his legend; and thus, around the kernel of some original divine function, the imagination of a people has gathered every possible expression of it, creating a complete and beautiful personality, with its history, its character, and its gifts. No poet has ever equalled the perfection or significance of these religious creations. The greatest characters of fiction are uninteresting and unreal compared with the conceptions of the gods; so much so that men have believed that their gods have objective reality.

The forms men see in dreams might have been a reason for believing in vague and disquieting ghosts; but the belief in individual and well-defined divinities, with which the visions of the dreams might be identified, is obviously due to the intrinsic coherence and impressiveness of the conception of those deities. The visions would never have suggested the legend and attributes of the god; but when the figure of the god was once imaginatively conceived, and his name and aspect fixed in the imagination, it would be easy to recognise him in any hallucination, or to interpret any event as due to his power. These manifestations, which constitute the evidence of his actual existence, can be regarded as manifestations of him, rather than of a vague, unknown power, only when the imagination already possesses a vivid picture of him, and of his appropriate functions. This picture is the work of a spontaneous fancy.

No doubt, when the belief is once specified, and the special and intelligible god is distinguished in the night and horror of the all-pervading natural power, the belief in his reality helps to concentrate our attention on his nature, and thus to develop and enrich our idea. The belief in the reality of an ideal personality brings about its further idealisation. Had it ever occurred to any Greek seer to attribute events to the influence of Achilles, or to offer sacrifices to him in the heat of the enthusiasm kindled by the thought of his beauty and virtue, the legend of Achilles, now become a god, would have grown and deepened; it would have been moralised like the legend of Hercules, or naturalised like that of Persephone, and what is now but a poetic character of extraordinary force and sublimity would have become the adored patron of generation after generation, and a manifestation of the divine man.

Achilles would then have been as significant and unforgettable a figure as Apollo or his sister, as Zeus, Athena, and the other greater gods. If ever, while that phase of religion lasted, his character had been obscured and his features dimmed, he would have been recreated by every new votary: poets would never have tired of singing his praises, or sculptors of rendering his form. When, after the

357

hero had been the centre and subject of so much imaginative labour, the belief in his reality lapsed, to be transferred to some other conception of cosmic power, he would have remained an ideal of poetry and art, and a formative influence of all cultivated minds, This he is still, like all the great creations of avowed fiction, but he would have been immensely more so, had belief in his reality kept the creative imagination continuously intent upon his nature.

The reader can hardly fail to see that all this applies with equal force to the Christian conception of the sacred personalities. Christ, the Virgin Mary, and the saints may have been exactly what our imagination pictures them to be; that is entirely possible; nor can I see that it is impossible that the conceptions of other religions might themselves have actual counterparts somewhere in the universe. That is a question of faith and empirical evidence with which we are not here concerned. But however descriptive of truth our conceptions may be, they have evidently grown up in our minds by an inward process of development. The materials of history and tradition have been melted and recast by the devout imagination into those figures in the presence of which our piety lives.

That is the reason why the reconstructed logical gods of the metaphysicians are always an offense and a mockery to the religious consciousness. There is here, too, a bare possibility that some one of these absolutes may be a representation of the truth; but the method by which this representation is acquired is violent and artificial; while the traditional conception of God is the spontaneous embodiment of passionate contemplation and long experience.

As the God of religion differs from that of metaphysics, so does the Christ of tradition differ from that of our critical historians. Even if we took the literal narrative of the Gospels and accepted it as all we could know of Christ, without allowing ourselves any imaginative interpretation of the central figure, we should get an ideal of him, I will not say very different from that of St. Francis or St. Theresa, but even from that of the English prayer-book. The Christ men have loved and adored is an ideal of their own hearts, the construction of an ever-present personality, living and intimately understood, out of the fragments of story and doctrine connected with a name. This subjective image has inspired all the prayers, all the conversions, all the penances, charities, and sacrifices, as well as half the art of the Christian world.

The Virgin Mary, whose legend is so meagre, but whose power over the Catholic imagination is so great, is an even clearer illustration of this inward building up of an ideal form. Everything is here spontaneous sympathetic expansion of two given events: the incarnation and the crucifixion. The figure of the Virgin, found in these mighty scenes, is gradually clarified and developed, until we come to the thought on the one hand of her freedom from original sin, and on the other to that of her universal maternity. We thus attain the conception of one of the noblest of conceivable rôles and of one of the most beautiful of characters. It is a pity that a foolish iconoclasm should so long have deprived the Protestant mind of the contemplation of this ideal.

Perhaps it is a sign of the average imaginative dulness or fatigue of certain races and epochs that they so readily abandon these supreme creations. For, if we are hopeful, why should we not believe that the best we can fancy is also the truest; and if we are distrustful in general of our prophetic gifts, why should we cling only to the most mean and formless of our illusions? From the beginning to the end of our perspective and imaginative activity, we are synthesising the material of experience into unities the independent reality of which is beyond proof, nay, beyond the possibility of a shadow of evidence. And yet the life of intelligence, like the joy of contemplation, lies entirely in the formation and inter-relation of these unities. This activity yields us all the objects with which we can deal, and endows them with the finer and more intimate part of their beauty. The most perfect of these forms, judged by its affinity to our powers and its stability in the presence of our experience, is the one with which we should be content; no other kind of veracity could add to its value.

The greatest feats of synthesis which the human mind has yet accomplished will, indeed, be probably surpassed and all ideals yet formed be superseded, because they were not based upon enough experience, or did not fit that experience with adequate precision. It is also possible that changes in the character of the facts, or in the powers of intelligence, should necessitate a continual reconstruction of our world. But unless human nature suffers an inconceivable change, the chief intellectual and æsthetic value of our ideas will always come from the creative action of the imagination.

EXPRESSION IN
LITERATURE

EXPRESSION DEFINED

W<small>E HAVE</small> found in the beauty of material and form the objectification of certain pleasures connected with the process of direct perception, with the formation, in the one case of a sensation, or quality, in the other of a synthesis of sensations or qualities. But the human consciousness is not a perfectly clear mirror, with distinct boundaries and clear-cut images, determinate in number and exhaustively perceived. Our ideas half emerge for a moment from the dim continuum of vital feeling and diffused sense, and are hardly fixed before they are changed and transformed, by the shifting of attention and the perception of new relations, into ideas of really different objects. This fluidity of the mind would make reflection impossible, did we not fix in words and other symbols certain abstract contents; we thus become capable of recognising in one perception the repetition of another, and of recognising in certain recurrences of impressions a persistent object. This discrimination and classification of the contents of consciousness is the work of perception and understanding, and the pleasures that accompany these activities make the beauty of the sensible world.

But our hold upon our thoughts extends even further. We not only construct visible unities and recognisable types, but remain aware of their affinities to what is not at the time perceived; that is, we find in them a certain tendency and quality, not original to them, a meaning and a tone, which upon investigation we shall see to have been the proper characteristics of other objects and feelings, associated with them once in our experience. The hushed reverberations of these associated feelings continue in the brain, and by modifying our present reaction, colour the image upon

361

which our attention is fixed. The quality thus acquired by objects through association is what we call their expression. Whereas in form or material there is one object with its emotional effect, in expression there are two, and the emotional effect belongs to the character of the second or suggested one. Expression may thus make beautiful by suggestion things in themselves indifferent, or it may come to heighten the beauty which they already possess.

Expression is not always distinguishable in consciousness from the value of material or form, because we do not always have a distinguishable memory of the related idea which the expressiveness implies. When we have such a memory, as at the sight of some once frequented garden, we clearly and spontaneously attribute our emotion to the memory and not to the present fact which it beautifies. The revival of a pleasure and its embodiment in a present object which in itself might have been indifferent, is here patent and acknowledged.

The distinctness of the analysis may indeed be so great as to prevent the synthesis; we may so entirely pass to the suggested object, that our pleasure will be embodied in the memory of that, while the suggestive sensation will be overlooked, and the expressiveness of the present object will fail to make it beautiful. Thus the mementos of a lost friend do not become beautiful by virtue of the sentimental associations which may make them precious. The value is confined to the images of the memory; they are too clear to let any of that value escape and diffuse itself over the rest of our consciousness, and beautify the objects which we actually behold. We say explicitly: I value this trifle for its associations. And so long as this division continues, the worth of the thing is not for us æsthetic.

But a little dimming of our memory will often make it so. Let the images of the past fade, let them remain simply as a halo and suggestion of happiness hanging about a scene; then this scene, however empty and uninteresting in itself, will have a deep and intimate charm; we shall be pleased by its very vulgarity. We shall not confess so readily that we value the place for its associations; we shall rather say: I am fond of this landscape; it has for me an ineffable attraction. The treasures of the memory have been melted and dissolved, and are now gilding the object that supplants them; they are giving this object expression.

Expression then differs from material or formal value only as habit differs from instinct—in its origin. Physiologically, they are both pleasurable radiations of a given stimulus; mentally, they are both values incorporated in an object. But an observer, looking at the mind historically, sees in the one case the survival of an experience, in the other the reaction of an innate disposition. This experience, moreover, is generally rememberable, and then the extrinsic source of the charm which expression gives becomes evident even to the consciousness in which it arises. A word, for instance, is often beautiful simply by virtue of its meaning and associations; but sometimes this expressive beauty is added to a musical quality in the word itself. In all expression we may thus distinguish two terms: the first is the object actually presented, the word, the image, the expressive thing; the second is the object suggested, the further thought, emotion, or image evoked, the thing expressed.

These lie together in the mind, and their union constitutes expression. If the value lies wholly in the first term, we have no beauty of expression. The decorative inscriptions in Saracenic monuments can have no beauty of expression for one who does not read Arabic; their charm is wholly one of material and form. Or if they have any expression, it is by virtue of such thoughts as they might suggest, as, for instance, of the piety and oriental sententiousness of the builders and of the aloofness from us of all their world. And even these suggestions, being a wandering of our fancy rather than a study of the object, would fail to arouse a pleasure which would be incorporated in the present image. The scroll would remain without expression, although its presence might have suggested to us interesting visions of other things. The two terms would be too independent, and the intrinsic values of each would remain distinct from that of the other. There would be no visible expressiveness, although there might have been discursive suggestions.

Indeed, if expression were constituted by the external relation of object with object, everything would be expressive equally, indeterminately, and universally. The flower in the crannied wall would express the same thing as the bust of Cæsar or the *Critique of Pure Reason*. What constitutes the individual expressiveness of these things is the circle of thoughts allied to each in a given mind;

my words, for instance, express the thoughts which they actually arouse in the reader; they may express more to one man than to another, and to me they may have expressed more or less than to you. My thoughts remain unexpressed, if my words do not arouse them in you, and very likely your greater wisdom will find in what I say the manifestation of a thousand principles of which I never dreamed. Expression depends upon the union of two terms, one of which must be furnished by the imagination; and a mind cannot furnish what it does not possess. The expressiveness of everything accordingly increases with the intelligence of the observer.

But for expression to be an element of beauty, it must, of course, fulfil another condition. I may see the relations of an object, I may understand it perfectly, and may nevertheless regard it with entire indifference. If the pleasure fails, the very substance and protoplasm of beauty is wanting. Nor, as we have seen, is even the pleasure enough; for I may receive a letter full of the most joyous news, but neither the paper, nor the writing, nor the style, need seem beautiful to me. Not until I confound the impressions, and suffuse the symbols themselves with the emotions they arouse, and find joy and sweetness in the very words I hear, will the expressiveness constitute a beauty; as when they sing, *Gloria in excelsis Deo*.

The value of the second term must be incorporated in the first; for the beauty of expression is as inherent in the object as that of material or form, only it accrues to that object not from the bare act of perception, but from the association with it of further processes, due to the existence of former impressions. We may conveniently use the word "expressiveness" to mean all the capacity of suggestion possessed by a thing, and the word "expression" for the æsthetic modification which that expressiveness may cause in it. Expressiveness is thus the power given by experience to any image to call up others in the mind; and this expressiveness becomes an æsthetic value, that is, becomes expression, when the value involved in the associations thus awakened are incorporated in the present object. . . .

ÆSTHETIC VALUE IN THE SECOND TERM

That the noble associations of any object should embellish that object is very comprehensible. Homer furnishes us with a good illustration of the constant employment of this effect. The first term, one need hardly say, leaves with him little to be desired. The verse is beautiful. Sounds, images, and composition conspire to stimulate and delight. This immediate beauty is sometimes used to clothe things terrible and sad; there is no dearth of the tragic in Homer. But the tendency of his poetry is nevertheless to fill the outskirts of our consciousness with the trooping images of things no less fair and noble than the verse itself. The heroes are virtuous. There is none of importance who is not admirable in his way. The palaces, the arms, the horses, the sacrifices, are always excellent. The women are always stately and beautiful. The ancestry and the history of every one are honourable and good. The whole Homeric world is clean, clear, beautiful, and providential, and no small part of the perennial charm of the poet is that he thus immerses us in an atmosphere of beauty; a beauty not concentrated and reserved for some extraordinary sentiment, action, or person, but permeating the whole and colouring the common world of soldiers and sailors, war and craft, with a marvellous freshness and inward glow. There is nothing in the associations of life in this world or in another to contradict or disturb our delight. All is beautiful, and beautiful through and through.

Something of this quality meets us in all simple and idyllic compositions. There is, for instance, a popular demand that stories and comedies should "end well." The hero and heroine must be young and handsome; unless they die,—which is another matter,—they must not in the end be poor. The landscape in the play must be beautiful; the dresses pretty; the plot without serious mishap. A pervasive presentation of pleasure must give warmth and ideality to the whole. In the proprieties of social life we find the same principle; we study to make our surroundings, manner, and conversation suggest nothing but what is pleasing. We hide the ugly and disagreeable portion of our lives, and do not allow the least hint of it to come to light upon festive and public occasions. Whenever, in a word, a thoroughly pleasing effect is found, it is found by the expression, as well as presentation, of what is in itself pleasing—and when this effect is to be produced artificially, we attain it by the suppression of all expression that is not suggestive of something good.

If our consciousness were exclusively æsthetic, this kind of expression would be the only one allowed in art or prized in nature. We should avoid as a shock or an insipidity, the suggestion of anything not intrinsically beautiful. As there would be no values not æsthetic, our pleasure could never be heightened by any other kind of interest. But as contemplation is actually a luxury in our lives, and things interest us chiefly on passionate and practical grounds, the accumulation of values too exclusively æsthetic produces in our minds an effect of closeness and artificiality. So selective a diet cloys, and our palate, accustomed to much daily vinegar and salt, is surfeited by such unmixed sweet.

Instead we prefer to see through the medium of art—through the beautiful first term of our expression—the miscellaneous world which is so well known to us—perhaps so dear, and at any rate so inevitable, an object. We are more thankful for this presentation of the unlovely truth in a lovely form, than for the like presentation of an abstract beauty; what is lost in the purity of the pleasure is gained in the stimulation of our attention, and in the relief of viewing with æsthetic detachment the same things that in practical life hold tyrannous dominion over our souls. The beauty that is associated only with other beauty is therefore a sort of æsthetic dainty; it leads the fancy through a fairyland of lovely forms, where we must forget the common objects of our interest. The charm of such an idealisation is undeniable; but the other important elements of our memory and will cannot long be banished. Thoughts of labour, ambition, lust, anger, confusion, sorrow, and death must needs mix with our contemplation and lend their various expressions to the objects with which in experience they are so closely allied. Hence the incorporation in the beautiful of values of other sorts, and the comparative rareness in nature or art of expressions the second term of which has only æsthetic value. . . .

NEGATIVE VALUES IN THE SECOND TERM

All subjects, even the most repellent, when the circumstances of life thrust them before us, can thus be observed with curiosity and treated with art. The calling forth of these æsthetic functions softens the violence of our sympathetic reaction. If death, for instance, did not exist and did not thrust itself upon our thoughts with painful importunity, art would never have been called upon to soften and dignify it, by presenting it in beautiful forms and surrounding it with consoling associations. Art does not seek out the pathetic, the tragic, and the absurd; it is life that has imposed them upon our attention, and enlisted art in their service, to make the contemplation of them, since it is inevitable, at least as tolerable as possible.

The agreeableness of the presentation is thus mixed with the horror of the thing; the result is that while we are saddened by the truth we are delighted by the vehicle that conveys it to us. The mixture of these emotions constitutes the peculiar flavour and poignancy of pathos. But because unlovely objects and feelings are often so familiar as to be indifferent or so momentous as to be alone in the mind, we are led into the confusion of supposing that beauty depends upon them for its æsthetic value; whereas the truth is that only by the addition of positive beauties can these evil experiences be made agreeable to contemplation.

There is, in reality, no such paradox in the tragic, comic, and sublime, as has been sometimes supposed. We are not pleased by virtue of the suggested evils, but in spite of them; and if ever the charm of the beautiful presentation sinks so low, or the vividness of the represented evil rises so high, that the balance is in favour of pain, at that very moment the whole object becomes horrible, passes out of the domain of art, and can be justified only by its scientific or moral uses. As an æsthetic value it is destroyed; it ceases to be a benefit; and the author of it, if he were not made harmless by the neglect that must soon overtake him, would have to be punished as a malefactor who adds to the burden of mortal life. For the sad, the ridiculous, the grotesque, and the terrible, unless they become æsthetic goods, remain moral evils.

We have, therefore, to study the various æsthetic, intellectual, and moral compensations by which the mind can be brought to contemplate with pleasure a thing which, if experienced alone, would be the cause of pain. There is, to be sure, a way of avoiding this inquiry. We might assert that since all moderate excitement is pleasant, there is nothing strange in the fact that the representation of evil should please; for the experience is evil by virtue of the pain it gives; but it gives pain only when felt with great intensity. Observed from afar, it is a pleasing impression; it is vivid enough to interest, but not acute enough to wound. This simple explanation is possible in all those cases where æsthetic effect is gained by the inhibition of sympathy.

The term "evil" is often a conventional epithet; a conflagration may be called an evil, because it usually involves loss and suffering; but if, without caring for a loss and suffering we do not share, we are delighted by the blaze, and still say that what pleases us is an evil, we are using this word as a conventional appellation, not as the mark of a felt value. We are not pleased by an evil; we are pleased by a vivid and exciting sensation, which is a good, but which has for objective cause an event which may indeed be an evil to others, but about the consequences of which we are not thinking at all. There is, in this sense, nothing in all nature, perhaps, which is not an evil; nothing which is not unfavourable to some interest, and does not involve some infinitesimal or ultimate suffering in the universe of life.

But when we are ignorant or thoughtless, this suffering is to us as if it did not exist. The pleasures of drinking and walking are not tragic to us, because we may be poisoning some bacillus or crushing some worm. To an omniscient intelligence such acts may be tragic by virtue of the insight into their relations to conflicting impulses; but unless these impulses are present to the same mind, there is no consciousness of tragedy. The child that, without understanding of the calamity, should watch a shipwreck from the shore, would have a simple emotion of pleasure as from a jumping jack; what passes for tragic interest is often nothing but this. If he understood the event, but was entirely without sympathy, he would have the æsthetic emotion of the careless tyrant, to whom the notion of suffering is no hindrance to the enjoyment of the lyre. If the temper of his tyranny were purposely cruel, he might add to that æsthetic delight the luxury of *Schadenfreude;* but the pathos and horror of the sight could only appeal to a man who realised and shared the sufferings he beheld.

A great deal of brutal tragedy has been endured in the world because the rudeness of the representation, or of the public, or of both, did not allow a really sympathetic reaction to arise. We all smile when Punch beats Judy in the puppet show. The treatment and not the subject is what makes a tragedy. A parody of *Hamlet* or of *King Lear* would not be a tragedy; and these tragedies themselves are not wholly such, but by the strain of wit and nonsense they contain are, as it were, occasional parodies on themselves. By treating a tragic subject bombastically or satirically we can turn it into an amusement for the public; they will not feel the griefs which we have been careful to harden them against by arousing in them contrary emotions. A work, nominally a work of art, may also appeal to non-æsthetic feelings by its political bias, brutality, or obscenity. But if an effect of true pathos is sought, the sympathy of the observer must be aroused; we must awaken in him the emotion we describe. The intensity of the impression must not be so slight that its painful quality is not felt; for it is this very sense of pain, mingling with the æsthetic excitement of the spectacle, that gives it a tragic or pathetic colouring.

We cannot therefore rest in the assertion that the slighter degree of excitement is pleasant, when a greater degree of the same would be disagreeable; for that principle does not express the essence of the matter, which is that we must be aware of the evil, and conscious of it as such, absorbed more or less in the experience of the sufferer, and consequently suffering ourselves, before we can experience the essence of tragic emotion. This emotion must therefore be complex; it must contain an element of pain overbalanced by an element of pleasure; in our delight there must be a distinguishable touch of shrinking and sorrow; for it is this conflict and rending of our will, this fascination by what is intrinsically terrible or sad, that gives these turbid feelings their depth and pungency.

INFLUENCE OF THE FIRST TERM IN THE PLEASING EXPRESSION OF EVIL

A striking proof of the compound nature of tragic effects can be given by a simple experiment. Remove from any drama—say from *Othello*—the charm of the medium of presentation; reduce the tragedy to a mere account of the facts and of the words spoken, such as our newspapers almost daily contain; and the tragic dignity and beauty is entirely lost. Nothing remains but a disheartening item of human folly, which may still excite curiosity, but which will rather defile than purify the mind that considers it. A French poet has said:

> *Il n'est de vulgaire chagrin*
> *Que celui d'une âme vulgaire.*

The counterpart of this maxim is equally true. There is no noble sorrow except in a noble mind, because what is noble is the reaction upon the sorrow, the attitude of the man in its presence, the language in which he clothes it, the associations with which he surrounds it, and the fine affections and impulses which shine through it. Only by suffusing some sinister experience with this moral light, as a poet may do who carries that light within him, can we raise misfortune into tragedy and make it better for us to remember our lives than to forget them.

There are times, although rare, when men are noble in the very moment of passion: when that passion is not unqualified, but already mastered by reflection and levelled with truth. Then the experience is itself the tragedy, and no poet is needed to make it beautiful in representation, since the sufferer has been an artist himself, and has moulded what he has endured. But usually these two stages have to be successive: first we suffer, afterwards we sing. An interval is necessary to make feeling presentable, and subjugate it to that form in which alone it is beautiful.

This form appeals to us in itself, and without its aid no subject-matter could become an æsthetic object. The more terrible the experience described, the more powerful must the art be which is to transform it. For this reason prose and literalness are more tolerable in comedy than in tragedy; any violent passion, any overwhelming pain, if it is not to make us think of a demonstration in pathology, and bring back the smell of ether, must be rendered in the most exalted style. Metre, rhyme, melody, the widest flights of allusion, the highest reaches of fancy, are there in place. For these enable the mind swept by the deepest cosmic harmonies, to endure and absorb the shrill notes which would be intolerable in a poorer setting.

The sensuous harmony of words, and still more the effects of rhythm, are indispensable at this height of emotion. Evolutionists have said that violent emotion naturally expresses itself in rhythm. That is hardly an empirical observation, nor can the expressiveness of rhythms be made definite enough to bear specific association with complex feelings. But the suspension and rush of sound and movement have in themselves a strong effect; we cannot undergo them without profound excitement; and this, like martial music, nerves us to courage and, by a sort of intoxication, bears us along amid scenes which might otherwise be sickening. The vile effect of literal and disjointed renderings of suffering, whether in writing or acting, proves how necessary is the musical quality to tragedy—a fact Aristotle long ago set forth. The afflatus of rhythm, even if it be the pomp of the Alexandrine, sublimates the passion, and clarifies its mutterings into poetry. This breadth and rationality are necessary to art, which is not skill merely, but skill in the service of beauty.

MIXTURE OF OTHER EXPRESSIONS, INCLUDING THAT OF TRUTH

To the value of these sensuous and formal elements must be added the continual suggestion of beautiful and happy things, which no tragedy is sombre enough to exclude. Even if we do not go so far as to intersperse comic scenes and phrases into a pathetic subject,—a rude device, since the comic passages themselves need that purifying which they are meant to effect,—we must at least relieve our theme with pleasing associations. For this reason we have palaces for our scene, rank, beauty, and virtue in our heroes, nobility in their passions and in their fate, and altogether a sort of glorification of life without which tragedy would lose both in depth of pathos—since things so precious are destroyed—and in subtlety of charm, since things so precious are manifested.

Indeed, one of the chief charms that tragedies have is the suggestion of what they might have been if they had not been tragedies. The happiness which glimmers through them, the hopes, loves, and ambitions of which it is made, these things fascinate us, and win our sympathy; so that we are all the more willing to suffer with our heroes, even if we are at the same time all the more sensitive to their suffering. Too wicked a character or too unrelieved a situation revolts us for this reason. We do not find enough expression of good to make us endure the expression of the evil.

A curious exception to this rule, which, however, admirably illustrates the fundamental principle of it, is where by the diversity of evils represented the mind is relieved from painful absorption

in any of them. There is a scene in *King Lear,* where the horror
of the storm is made to brood over at least four miseries, that of
the king, of the fool, of Edgar in his real person, and of Edgar in
his assumed character. The vividness of each of these portrayals,
with its different note of pathos, keeps the mind detached and free,
forces it to compare and reflect, and thereby to universalise the
spectacle. Yet even here, the beautiful effect is not secured without
some touches of good. How much is not gained by the dumb fidelity of the fool, and by the sublime humanity of Lear, when he
says, "Art cold? There is a part of me is sorry for thee yet."

Yet all these compensations would probably be unavailing but
for another which the saddest things often have,—the compensation of being true. Our practical and intellectual nature is deeply
interested in truth. What describes fact appeals to us for that
reason; it has an inalienable interest. However unpleasant truth
may prove, we long to know it, partly perhaps because experience
has shown us the prudence of this kind of intellectual courage, and
chiefly because the consciousness of ignorance and the dread of the
unknown are more tormenting than any possible discovery. A
primitive instinct makes us turn the eyes full upon any object that
appears in the dim borderland of our field of vision—and this all
the more quickly, the more terrible that object threatens to be.

This physical thirst for seeing has its intellectual extension. We
covet truth, and to attain it, amid all accidents, is a supreme satisfaction. Now this satisfaction the representation of evil can also
afford. Whether we hear the account of some personal accident, or
listen to the symbolic representation of the inherent tragedy of
life, we crave the same knowledge; the desire for truth makes us
welcome eagerly whatever comes in its name. To be sure, the relief
of such instruction does not of itself constitute an æsthetic pleasure: the other conditions of beauty remain to be fulfilled. But the
satisfaction of so imperious an intellectual instinct insures our
willing attention to the tragic object, and strengthens the hold
which any beauties it may possess will take upon us. An intellectual
value stands ready to be transmuted into an æsthetic one, if once
its discursiveness is lost, and it is left hanging about the object as
a vague sense of dignity and meaning.

To this must be added the specific pleasure of recognition, one
of the keenest we have, and the sentimental one of nursing our

own griefs and dignifying them by assimilation to a less inglorious representation of them. Here we have truth on a small scale; conformity in the fiction to incidents of our personal experience. Such correspondences are the basis of much popular appreciation of trivial and undigested works that appeal to some momentary phase of life or feeling, and disappear with it. They have the value of personal stimulants only; they never achieve beauty. Like the souvenirs of last season's gayeties, or the diary of an early love, they are often hideous in themselves in proportion as they are redolent with personal associations. But however hopelessly mere history or confession may fail to constitute a work of art, a work of art that has an historical warrant, either literal or symbolical, gains the support of that vivid interest we have in facts. And many tragedies and farces, that to a mind without experience of this sublunary world might seem monstrous and disgusting fictions, may come to be forgiven and even perhaps preferred over all else, when they are found to be a sketch from life.

Truth is thus the excuse which ugliness has for being. Many people, in whom the pursuit of knowledge and the indulgence in sentiment have left no room for the cultivation of the æsthetic sense, look in art rather for this expression of fact or of passion than for the revelation of beauty. They accordingly produce and admire works without intrinsic value. They employ the procedure of the fine arts without an eye to what can give pleasure in the effect. They invoke rather the *a priori* interest which men are expected to have in the subject-matter, or in the theories and moral implied in the presentation of it. Instead of using the allurements of art to inspire wisdom, they require an appreciation of wisdom to make us endure their lack of art.

Of course, the instruments of the arts are public property and any one is free to turn them to new uses. It would be an interesting development of civilisation if they should now be employed only as methods of recording scientific ideas and personal confessions. But the experiment has not succeeded and can hardly succeed. There are other simpler, clearer, and more satisfying ways of expounding truth. A man who is really a student of history or philosophy will never rest with the vague and partial oracles of poetry, not to speak of the inarticulate suggestions of the plastic arts. He will at once make for the principles which art cannot express,

even if it can embody them, and when those principles are attained, the works of art, if they had no other value than that of
suggesting them, will lapse from his mind. Forms will give place
to formulas as hieroglyphics have given place to the letters of the
alphabet.

If, on the other hand, the primary interest is really in beauty,
and only the confusion of a moral revolution has obscured for a
while the vision of the ideal, then as the mind regains its mastery
over the world, and digests its new experience, the imagination
will again be liberated, and create its forms by its inward affinities,
leaving all the weary burden, archæological, psychological, and
ethical, to those whose business is not to delight. But the sudden
inundation of science and sentiment which has made the mind
of the nineteenth century so confused, by overloading us with
materials and breaking up our habits of apperception and our
ideals, has led to an exclusive sense of the value of expressiveness,
until this has been almost identified with beauty. This exaggeration can best prove how the expression of truth may enter into the
play of æsthetic forces, and give a value to representations which,
but for it, would be repulsive.

THE LIBERATION OF SELF

Hitherto we have been considering those elements of a pathetic
presentation which may mitigate our sympathetic emotion, and
make it on the whole agreeable. These consist in the intrinsic
beauties of the medium of presentation, and in the concomitant
manifestation of various goods, notably of truth. The mixture of
these values is perhaps all we have in mildly pathetic works, in the
presence of which we are tolerably aware of a sort of balance and
compensation of emotions. The sorrow and the beauty, the hope-
lessness and the consolation, mingle and merge into a kind of joy
which has its poignancy, indeed, but which is far too passive and
penitential to contain the louder and sublimer of our tragic moods.
In these there is a wholeness, a strength, and a rapture, which still
demand an explanation.

Where this explanation is to be found may be guessed from the
following circumstance. The pathetic is a quality of the object, at
once lovable and sad, which we accept and allow to flow in upon

the soul; but the heroic is an attitude of the will, by which the voices of the outer world are silenced, and a moral energy, flowing from within, is made to triumph over them. If we fail, therefore, to discover, by analysis of the object, anything which could make it sublime, we must not be surprised at our failure. We must remember that the object is always but a portion of our consciousness: that portion which has enough coherence and articulation to be recognised as permanent and projected into the outer world. But consciousness remains one, in spite of this diversification of its content, and the object is not really independent, but is in constant relation to the rest of the mind, in the midst of which it swims like a bubble on a dark surface of water.

The æsthetic effect of objects is always due to the total emotional value of the consciousness in which they exist. We merely attribute this value to the object by a projection which is the ground of the apparent objectivity of beauty. Sometimes this value may be inherent in the process by which the object itself is perceived; then we have sensuous and formal beauty; sometimes the value may be due to the incipient formation of other ideas, which the perception of this object evokes; then we have beauty of expression. But among the ideas with which every object has relation there is one vaguest, most comprehensive, and most powerful one, namely, the idea of self. The impulses, memories, principles, and energies which we designate by that word baffle enumeration; indeed, they constantly fade and change into one another; and whether the self is anything, everything, or nothing depends on the aspect of it which we momentarily fix, and especially on the definite object with which we contrast it.

Now, it is the essential privilege of beauty so to synthesise and bring to a focus the various impulses of the self, so to suspend them to a single image, that a great peace falls upon that perturbed kingdom. In the experience of these momentary harmonies we have the basis of the enjoyment of beauty, and of all its mystical meanings. But there are always two methods of securing harmony: one is to unify all the given elements, and another is to reject and expunge all the elements that refuse to be unified. Unity by inclusion gives us the beautiful; unity by exclusion, opposition, and isolation gives us the sublime. Both are pleasures: but the pleasure of the one is warm, passive, pervasive; that of the other, cold, imperious, and keen. The one identifies us with the world, the other raises us above it.

There can be no difficulty in understanding how the expression of evil in the object may be the occasion of this heroic reaction of the soul. In the first place, the evil may be felt; but at the same time the sense that, great as it may be in itself, it cannot touch us, may stimulate extraordinarily the consciousness of our own wholeness. This is the sublimity which Lucretius calls "sweet" in the famous lines in which he so justly analyses it. We are not pleased because another suffers an evil, but because, seeing it is an evil, we see at the same time our own immunity from it. We might soften the picture a little, and perhaps make the principle even clearer by so doing. The shipwreck observed from the shore does not leave us wholly unmoved; we suffer, also, and if possible, would help. So, too, the spectacle of the erring world must sadden the philosopher even in the Acropolis of his wisdom; he would, if it might be, descend from his meditation and teach. But those movements of sympathy are quickly inhibited by despair of success; impossibility of action is a great condition of the sublime. If we could count the stars, we should not weep before them. While we think we can change the drama of history, and of our own lives, we are not awed by our destiny. But when the evil is irreparable, when our life is lived, a strong spirit has the sublime resource of standing at bay and of surveying almost from the other world the vicissitudes of this.

The more intimate to himself the tragedy he is able to look back upon with calmness, the more sublime that calmness is, and the more divine the ecstasy in which he achieves it. For the more of the accidental vesture of life we are able to strip ourselves of, the more naked and simple is the surviving spirit; the more complete its superiority and unity, and, consequently, the more unqualified its joy. There remains little in us, then, but that intellectual essence, which several great philosophers have called eternal and identified with the Divinity.

A single illustration may help to fix these principles in the mind. When Othello has discovered his fatal error, and is resolved to take his own life, he stops his groaning, and addresses the ambassadors of Venice thus:

376

Speak of me as I am: nothing extenuate,
Nor set down aught in malice: then, must you speak
Of one that loved, not wisely, but too well;
Of one not easily jealous, but, being wrought,
Perplexed in the extreme; of one whose hand,
Like the base Indian, threw a pearl away
Richer than all his tribe; of one whose subdued eyes,
Albeit unusèd to the melting mood,
Drop tears as fast as the Arabian trees
Their medicinal gum. Set you down this:
And say, besides, that in Aleppo once
When a malignant and a turbaned Turk
Beat a Venetian, and traduced the state,
I took by the throat the circumcisèd dog,
And smote him, thus.

There is a kind of criticism that would see in all these allusions, figures of speech, and wandering reflections, an unnatural rendering of suicide. The man, we might be told, should have muttered a few broken phrases, and killed himself without this pomp of declamation, like the jealous husbands in the daily papers. But the conventions of the tragic stage are more favourable to psychological truth than the conventions of real life. If we may trust the imagination (and in imagination lies, as we have seen, the test of propriety), this is what Othello would have felt. If he had not expressed it, his dumbness would have been due to external hindrances, not to the failure in his mind of just such complex and rhetorical thoughts as the poet has put into his mouth. The height of passion is naturally complex and rhetorical. Love makes us poets, and the approach of death should make us philosophers. When a man knows that his life is over, he can look back upon it from a universal standpoint. He has nothing more to live for, but if the energy of his mind remains unimpaired, he will still wish to live, and, being cut off from his personal ambitions, he will impute to himself a kind of vicarious immortality by identifying himself with what is eternal. He speaks of himself as he is, or rather as he was. He sums himself up, and points to his achievement. This I have been, says he, this I have done.

This comprehensive and impartial view, this synthesis and objectification of experience, constitutes the liberation of the soul
and the essence of sublimity. That the hero attains it at the end
consoles us, as it consoles him, for his hideous misfortunes. Our
pity and terror are indeed purged; we go away knowing that, however tangled the net may be in which we feel ourselves caught,
there is liberation beyond, and an ultimate peace.

THE SUBLIME INDEPENDENT OF THE EXPRESSION OF EVIL

So natural is the relation between the vivid conception of great
evils, and that self-assertion of the soul which gives the emotion
of the sublime, that the sublime is often thought to depend upon
the terror which these conceived evils inspire. To be sure, that
terror would have to be inhibited and subdued, otherwise we
should have a passion too acute to be incorporated in any object;
the sublime would not appear as an æsthetic quality in things, but
remain merely an emotional state in the subject. But this subdued
and objectified terror is what is commonly regarded as the essence
of the sublime, and so great an authority as Aristotle would seem
to countenance some such definition. The usual cause of the sublime is here confused, however, with the sublime itself. The
suggestion of terror makes us withdraw into ourselves: there
with the supervening consciousness of safety or indifference comes
a rebound, and we have that emotion of detachment and liberation
in which the sublime really consists.

Thoughts and actions are properly sublime, and visible things
only by analogy and suggestion when they induce a certain moral
emotion; whereas beauty belongs properly to sensible things, and
can be predicated of moral facts only by a figure of rhetoric. What
we objectify in beauty is a sensation. What we objectify in the
sublime is an act. This act is necessarily pleasant, for if it were not
the sublime would be a bad quality and one we should rather
never encounter in the world. The glorious joy of self-assertion in
the face of an uncontrollable world is indeed so deep and entire,
that it furnishes just that transcendent element of worth for which
we were looking when we tried to understand how the expression
of pain could sometimes please. It can please, not in itself, but
because it is balanced and annulled by positive pleasures, espe-

cially by this final and victorious one of detachment. If the expression of evil seems necessary to the sublime, it is so only as a condition of this moral reaction.

We are commonly too much engrossed in objects and too little centred in ourselves and our inalienable will, to see the sublimity of a pleasing prospect. We are then enticed and flattered, and won over to a commerce with these external goods, and the consummation of our happiness would lie in the perfect comprehension and enjoyment of their nature. This is the office of art and of love; and its partial fulfilment is seen in every perception of beauty. But when we are checked in this sympathetic endeavour after unity and comprehension; when we come upon a great evil or an irreconcilable power, we are driven to seek our happiness by the shorter and heroic road; then we recognise the hopeless foreignness of what lies before us, and stiffen ourselves against it. We thus for the first time reach the sense of our possible separation from our world, and of our abstract stability; and with this comes the sublime.

But although experience of evil is the commonest approach to this attitude of mind, and we commonly become philosophers only after despairing of instinctive happiness, yet there is nothing impossible in the attainment of detachment by other channels. The immense is sublime as well as the terrible; and mere infinity of the object, like its hostile nature, can have the effect of making the mind recoil upon itself. Infinity, like hostility, removes us from things, and makes us conscious of our independence. The simultaneous view of many things, innumerable attractions felt together, produce equilibrium and indifference, as effectually as the exclusion of all. If we may call the liberation of the self by the consciousness of evil in the world, the Stoic sublime, we may assert that there is also an Epicurean sublime, which consists in liberation by equipoise. Any wide survey is sublime in that fashion. Each detail may be beautiful. We may even be ready with a passionate response to its appeal. We may think we covet every sort of pleasure, and lean to every kind of vigorous, impulsive life. But let an infinite panorama be suddenly unfolded; the will is instantly paralysed, and the heart choked. It is impossible to desire everything at once, and when all is offered and approved, it is impossible to choose everything. In this suspense, the mind soars into a kind of heaven, benevolent but unmoved.

379

This is the attitude of all minds to which breadth of interest or length of years has brought balance and dignity. The sacerdotal quality of old age comes from this same sympathy in disinterestedness. Old men full of hurry and passion appear as fools, because we understand that their experience has not left enough mark upon their brain to qualify with the memory of other goods any object that may be now presented. We cannot venerate any one in whom appreciation is not divorced from desire. And this elevation and detachment of the heart need not follow upon any great disappointment; it is finest and sweetest where it is the gradual fruit of many affections now merged and mellowed into a natural piety. Indeed, we are able to frame our idea of the Deity on no other model.

When the pantheists try to conceive all the parts of nature as forming a single being, which shall contain them all and yet have absolute unity, they find themselves soon denying the existence of the world they are trying to deify; for nature, reduced to the unity it would assume in an omniscient mind, is no longer nature, but something simple and impossible, the exact opposite of the real world. Such an opposition would constitute the liberation of the divine mind from nature, and its existence as a self-conscious individual. The effort after comprehensiveness of view reduces things to unity, but this unity stands out in opposition to the manifold phenomena which it transcends, and rejects as unreal.

Now this destruction of nature, which the metaphysicians since Parmenides have so often repeated (nature nevertheless surviving still), is but a theoretical counterpart and hypostasis of what happens in every man's conscience when the comprehensiveness of his experience lifts him into thought, into abstraction. The sense of the sublime is essentially mystical: it is the transcending of distinct perception in favour of a feeling of unity and volume. So in the moral sphere, we have the mutual cancelling of the passions in the breast that includes them all, and their final subsidence beneath the glance that comprehends them. This is the Epicurean approach to detachment and perfection; it leads by systematic acceptance of instinct to the same goal which the stoic and the ascetic reach by systematic rejection of instinct. It is thus possible to be moved to that self-enfranchisement which constitutes the sublime, even when the object contains no expression of evil.

This conclusion supports that part of our definition of beauty which declares that the values beauty contains are all positive; a definition which we should have had to change if we had found that the sublime depended upon the suggestion of evil for its effect. But the sublime is not the ugly, as some descriptions of it might lead us to suppose; it is the supremely, the intoxicatingly beautiful. It is the pleasure of contemplation reaching such an intensity that it begins to lose its objectivity, and to declare itself, what it always fundamentally was, an inward passion of the soul. For while in the beautiful we find the perfection of life by sinking into the object, in the sublime we find a purer and more inalienable perfection by defying the object altogether. The surprised enlargement of the vision, the sudden escape from our ordinary interests and the identification of ourselves with something permanent and superhuman, something much more abstract and inalienable than our changing personality, all this carries us away from the blurred objects before us, and raises us into a sort of ecstasy.

In the trite examples of the sublime, where we speak of the vast mass, strength, and durability of objects, or of their sinister aspect, as if we were moved by them on account of our own danger, we seem to miss the point. For the suggestion of our own danger would produce a touch of fear; it would be a practical passion, or if it could by chance be objectified enough to become æsthetic, it would merely make the object hateful and repulsive, like a mangled corpse. The object is sublime when we forget our danger, when we escape from ourselves altogether, and live as it were in the object itself, energising in imitation of its movement, and saying, "Be thou me, impetuous one!" This passage into the object, to live its life, is indeed a characteristic of all perfect contemplation. But when in thus translating ourselves we rise and play a higher personage, feeling the exhilaration of a life freer and wilder than our own, then the experience is one of sublimity. The emotion comes not from the situation we observe, but from the powers we conceive; we fail to sympathise with the struggling sailors because we sympathise too much with the wind and waves. And this mystical cruelty can extend even to ourselves; we can so feel the fascination of the cosmic forces that engulf us as to take a fierce joy in the thought of our own destruction. We can identify ourselves with the abstractest essence of reality, and, raised to that height, despise the human accidents of our own nature. Lord, we say, though thou slay me, yet will I trust in thee. The sense of suffering disappears in the sense of life and the imagination overwhelms the understanding.

THE COMIC

Something analogous takes place in the other spheres where an æsthetic value seems to arise out of suggestions of evil, in the comic, namely, and the grotesque. But here the translation of our sympathies is partial, and we are carried away from ourselves only to become smaller. The larger humanity, which cannot be absorbed, remains ready to contradict the absurdity of our fiction. The excellence of comedy lies in the invitation to wander along some by-path of the fancy, among scenes not essentially impossible, but not to be actually enacted by us on account of the fixed circumstances of our lives. If the picture is agreeable, we allow ourselves to dream it true. We forget its relations; we forbid the eye to wander beyond the frame of the stage, or the conventions of the fiction. We indulge an illusion which deepens our sense of the essential pleasantness of things.

So far, there is nothing in comedy that is not delightful, except, perhaps, the moment when it is over. But fiction, like all error or abstraction, is necessarily unstable; and the awakening is not always reserved for the disheartening moment at the end. Everywhere, when we are dealing with pretension or mistake, we come upon sudden and vivid contradictions; changes of view, transformations of apperception which are extremely stimulating to the imagination. We have spoken of one of these: when the sudden dissolution of our common habits of thought lifts us into a mystical contemplation, filled with the sense of the sublime; when the transformation is back to common sense and reality, and away from some fiction, we have a very different emotion. We feel cheated, relieved, abashed, or amused, in proportion as our sympathy attaches more to the point of view surrendered or to that attained.

The disintegration of mental forms and their redintegration is the life of the imagination. It is a spiritual process of birth and death, nutrition and generation. The strongest emotions accompany these changes, and vary infinitely with their variations. All the qualities of discourse, wit, eloquence, cogency, absurdity, are feelings incidental to this process, and involved in the juxtapositions, tensions, and resolutions of our ideas. Doubtless the last explanation of these things would be cerebral; but we are as yet confined to verbal descriptions and classifications of them, which are always more or less arbitrary.

The most conspicuous headings under which comic effects are gathered are perhaps incongruity and degradation. But clearly it cannot be the logical essence of incongruity or degradation that constitutes the comic; for then contradiction and deterioration would always amuse. Amusement is a much more directly physical thing. We may be amused without any idea at all, as when we are tickled, or laugh in sympathy with others by a contagious imitation of their gestures. We may be amused by the mere repetition of a thing at first not amusing. There must therefore be some nervous excitement on which the feeling of amusement directly depends, although this excitement may most often coincide with a sudden transition to an incongruous or meaner image. Nor can we suppose that particular ideational excitement to be entirely dissimilar to all others; wit is often hardly distinguishable from brilliancy, as humour from pathos. We must, therefore, be satisfied with saying vaguely that the process of ideation involves various feelings of movement and relation,—feelings capable of infinite gradation and complexity, and ranging from sublimity to tedium and from pathos to uncontrollable merriment.

Certain crude and obvious cases of the comic seem to consist of little more than a shock of surprise: a pun is a sort of jack-in-the-box, popping from nowhere into our plodding thoughts. The liveliness of the interruption, and its futility, often please; *dulce est desipere in loco;* and yet those who must endure the society of inveterate jokers know how intolerable this sort of scintillation can become. There is something inherently vulgar about it; perhaps because our train of thought cannot be very entertaining in itself when we are so glad to break in upon it with irrelevant nullities. The same undertone of disgust mingles with other amusing surprises, as when a dignified personage slips and falls, or some disguise is thrown off, or those things are mentioned and described which convention ignores. The novelty and the freedom please, yet the shock often outlasts the pleasure, and we have cause to wish we had been stimulated by something which did not involve this degradation. So, also, the impossibility in plausibility which tickles the fancy in Irish bulls, and in wild exaggerations, leaves an uncomfortable impression, a certain after-taste of foolishness.

The reason will be apparent if we stop to analyse the situation. We have a prosaic background of common sense and every-day reality; upon this background an unexpected idea suddenly impinges. But the thing is a futility. The comic accident falsifies the nature before us, starts a wrong analogy in the mind, a suggestion that cannot be carried out. In a word, we are in the presence of an absurdity; and man, being a rational animal, can like absurdity no better than he can like hunger or cold. A pinch of either may not be so bad, and he will endure it merrily enough if you repay him with abundance of warm victuals; so, too, he will play with all kinds of nonsense for the sake of laughter and good fellowship and the tickling of his fancy with a sort of caricature of thought. But the qualm remains, and the pleasure is never perfect. The same exhilaration might have come without the falsification, just as repose follows more swiftly after pleasant than after painful exertions.

Fun is a good thing, but only when it spoils nothing better. The best place for absurdity is in the midst of what is already absurd— then we have the play of fancy without the sense of ineptitude. Things amuse us in the mouth of a fool that would not amuse us in that of a gentleman; a fact which shows how little incongruity and degradation have to do with our pleasure in the comic. In fact, there is a kind of congruity and method even in fooling. The incongruous and the degraded displease us even there, as by their nature they must at all times. The shock which they bring may sometimes be the occasion of a subsequent pleasure, by attracting our attention, or by stimulating passions, such as scorn, or cruelty, or self-satisfaction (for there is a good deal of malice in our love of fun); but the incongruity and degradation, as such, always remain unpleasant. The pleasure comes from the inward rationality and movement of the fiction, not from its inconsistency with anything else. There are a great many topsy-turvy worlds possible to our fancy, into which we like to drop at times. We enjoy the stimulation and the shaking up of our wits. It is like getting into a new posture, or hearing a new song.

Nonsense is good only because common sense is so limited. For reason, after all, is one convention picked out of a thousand. We love expansion, not disorder, and when we attain freedom without incongruity we have a much greater and a much purer delight. The excellence of wit can dispense with absurdity. For on the same prosaic background of common sense, a novelty might have appeared that was not absurd, that stimulated the attention quite as much as the ridiculous, without so baffling the intelligence. This purer and more thoroughly delightful amusement comes from what we call wit.

WIT

Wit also depends upon transformation and substitution of ideas. It has been said to consist in quick association by similarity. The substitution must here be valid, however, and the similarity real, though unforeseen. Unexpected justness makes wit, as sudden incongruity makes pleasant foolishness. It is characteristic of wit to penetrate into hidden depths of things, to pick out there some telling circumstance or relation, by noting which the whole object appears in a new and clearer light. Wit often seems malicious because analysis in discovering common traits and universal principles assimilates things at the poles of being; it can apply to cookery the formulas of theology, and find in the human heart a case of the fulcrum and lever. We commonly keep the departments of experience distinct; we think that different principles hold in each and that the dignity of spirit is inconsistent with the explanation of it by physical analogy, and the meanness of matter unworthy of being an illustration of moral truths. Love must not be classed under physical cravings, nor faith under hypnotisation. When, therefore, an original mind overleaps these boundaries, and recasts its categories, mixing up our old classifications, we feel that the values of things are also confused. But these depended upon a deeper relation, upon their response to human needs and aspirations. All that can be changed by the exercise of intelligence is our sense of the unity and homogeneity of the world. We may come to hold an object of thought in less isolated respect, and another in less hasty derision; but the pleasures we derive from all, or our total happiness and wonder, will hardly be diminished. For this reason the malicious or destructive character of intelligence must not be regarded as fundamental. Wit belittles one thing and dignifies another; and its comparisons are as often flattering as ironical.

The same process of mind that we observed in wit gives rise to those effects we call charming, brilliant, or inspired. When Shakespeare says,

> *Come and kiss me,* sweet and twenty,
> *Youth's a stuff will not endure,*

the fancy of the phrase consists in a happy substitution, a merry way of saying something both true and tender. And where could we find a more exquisite charm? So, to take a weightier example, when St. Augustine is made to say that pagan virtues were *splendid vices,* we have—at least if we catch the full meaning—a pungent assimilation of contrary things, by force of a powerful principle; a triumph of theory, the boldness of which can only be matched by its consistency. In fact, a phrase could not be more brilliant, or better condense one theology and two civilisations. The Latin mind is particularly capable of this sort of excellence. Tacitus alone could furnish a hundred examples. It goes with the power of satirical and bitter eloquence, a sort of scornful rudeness of intelligence, that makes for the core of a passion or of a character, and affixes to it a more or less scandalous label. For in our analytical zeal it is often possible to condense and abstract too much. Reality is more fluid and elusive than reason, and has, as it were, more dimensions than are known even to the latest geometry. Hence the understanding, when not suffused with some glow of sympathetic emotion or some touch of mysticism, gives but a dry, crude image of the world. The quality of wit inspires more admiration than confidence. It is a merit we should miss little in any one we love.

The same principle, however, can have more sentimental embodiments. When our substitutions are brought on by the excitement of generous emotion, we call wit inspiration. There is the same finding of new analogies, and likening of disparate things; there is the same transformation of our apperception. But the brilliancy is here not only penetrating, but also exalting. For instance:

> *Peace, peace, he is not dead, he doth not sleep,*
> *He hath awakened from the dream of life:*
> *'Tis we that wrapped in stormy visions keep*
> *With phantoms an unprofitable strife.*

There is here paradox, and paradox justified by reflection. The poet analyses, and analyses without reserve. The dream, the storm, the phantoms, and the unprofitableness could easily make a satirical picture. But the mood is transmuted; the mind takes an upward flight, with a sense of liberation from the convention it dissolves, and of freer motion in the vagueness beyond. The disintegration of our ideal here leads to mysticism, and because of this effort towards transcendence, the brilliancy becomes sublime.

HUMOUR

A different mood can give a different direction to the same processes. The sympathy by which we reproduce the feeling of another, is always very much opposed to the æsthetic attitude to which the whole world is merely a stimulus to our sensibility. In the tragic, we have seen how the sympathetic feeling, by which suffering is appreciated and shared, has to be overlaid by many incidental æsthetic pleasures, if the resulting effect is to be on the whole good. We have also seen how the only way in which the ridiculous can be kept within the sphere of the æsthetically good is abstracting it from its relations, and treating it as an independent and curious stimulus; we should stop laughing and begin to be annoyed if we tried to make sense out of our absurdity. The less sympathy we have with men the more exquisite is our enjoyment of their folly: satirical delight is closely akin to cruelty. Defect and mishap stimulate our fancy, as blood and tortures excite in us the passions of the beast of prey. The more this inhuman attitude yields to sympathy and reason, the less are folly and error capable of amusing us. It would therefore seem impossible that we should be pleased by the foibles or absurdities of those we love. And in fact we never enjoy seeing our own persons in a satirical light, or any one else for whom we really feel affection. Even in farces, the hero and heroine are seldom made ridiculous, because that would jar upon the sympathy with which we are expected to regard them.

Nevertheless, the essence of what we call humour is that amusing weaknesses should be combined with an amicable humanity. Whether it be in the way of ingenuity, or oddity, or drollery, the humourous person must have an absurd side, or be placed in an absurd situation. Yet this comic aspect, at which we ought to wince, seems to endear the character all the more. This is a parallel case to that of tragedy, where the depth of the woe we sympathise with seems to add to our satisfaction. And the explanation of the paradox is the same. We do not enjoy the expression of evil, but only the pleasant excitements that come with it; namely, the physical stimulus and the expression of good. In tragedy, the misfortunes help to give the impression of truth, and to bring out the noble qualities of the hero, but are in themselves depressing, so much so that over-sensitive people cannot enjoy the beauty of the representation. So also in humour, the painful suggestions are felt as such, and need to be overbalanced by agreeable elements. These come from both directions, from the æsthetic and the sympathetic reaction. On the one hand there is the sensuous and merely perceptive stimulation, the novelty, the movement, the vivacity of the spectacle. On the other hand, there is the luxury of imaginative sympathy, the mental assimilation of another congenial experience, the expansion into another life.

The juxtaposition of these two pleasures produces just that tension and complication in which the humourous consists. We are satirical, and we are friendly at the same time. The consciousness of the friendship gives a regretful and tender touch to the satire, and the sting of the satire makes the friendship a trifle humble and sad. Don Quixote is mad; he is old, useless, and ridiculous, but he is the soul of honour, and in all his laughable adventures we follow him like the ghost of our better selves. We enjoy his discomfitures too much to wish he had been a perfect Amadis; and we have besides a shrewd suspicion that he is the only kind of Amadis there can ever be in this world. At the same time it does us good to see the courage of his idealism, the ingenuity of his wit, and the simplicity of his goodness. But how shall we reconcile our sympathy with his dream and our perception of its absurdity? The situation is contradictory. We are drawn to some different point of view, from which the comedy may no longer seem so amusing. As humour becomes deep and really different from satire, it changes into pathos, and passes out of the sphere of the comic altogether. The mischances that were to amuse us as scoffers now grieve us as men, and the value of the representation depends on the touches of beauty and seriousness with which it is adorned.

THE GROTESQUE

Something analogous to humour can appear in plastic forms, when we call it the grotesque. This is an interesting effect produced by such a transformation of an ideal type as exaggerates one of its elements or combines it with other types. The real excellence of this, like that of all fiction, consists in re-creation; in the formation of a thing which nature has not, but might conceivably have offered. We call these inventions comic and grotesque when we are considering their divergence from the natural rather than their inward possibility. But the latter constitutes their real charm; and the more we study and develop them, the better we understand it. The incongruity with the conventional type then disappears, and what was impossible and ridiculous at first takes its place among recognised ideals. The centaur and the satyr are no longer grotesque; the type is accepted. And the grotesqueness of an individual has essentially the same nature. If we like the inward harmony, the characteristic balance of his features, we are able to disengage this individual from the class into which we were trying to force him; we can forget the expectation which he was going to disappoint. The ugliness then disappears, and only the reassertion of the old habit and demand can make us regard him as in any way extravagant.

What appears as grotesque may be intrinsically inferior or superior to the normal. That is a question of its abstract material and form. But until the new object impresses its form on our imagination, so that we can grasp its unity and proportion, it appears to us as a jumble and distortion of other forms. If this confusion is absolute, the object is simply null; it does not exist æsthetically, except by virtue of materials. But if the confusion is not absolute, and we have an inkling of the unity and character in the midst of the strangeness of the form, then we have the grotesque. It is the half-formed, the perplexed, and the suggestively monstrous.

The analogy to the comic is very close, as we can readily conceive that it should be. In the comic we have this same juxtaposition of a new and an old idea, and if the new is not futile and really inconceivable, it may in time establish itself in the mind, and cease to be ludicrous. Good wit is novel truth, as the good grotesque is novel beauty. But there are natural conditions of organisation, and we must not mistake every mutilation for the creation of a new form. The tendency of nature to establish well-marked species of animals shows what various combinations are most stable in the face of physical forces, and there is a fitness also for survival in the mind, which is determined by the relation of any form to our fixed method of perception. New things are therefore generally bad because, as has been well said, they are incapable of becoming old. A thousand originalities are produced by defect of faculty, for one that is produced by genius. For in the pursuit of beauty, as in that of truth, an infinite number of paths lead to failure, and only one to success.

THE POSSIBILITY OF FINITE PERFECTION

If these observations have any accuracy, they confirm this important truth,—that no æsthetic value is really founded on the experience or the suggestion of evil. This conclusion will doubtless seem the more interesting if we think of its possible extension to the field of ethics and of the implied vindication of the ideal of moral perfection as something essentially definable and attainable. But without insisting on an analogy to ethics, which might be misleading, we may hasten to state the principle which emerges from our analysis of expression. Expressiveness may be found in any one thing that suggests another, or draws from association with that other any of its emotional colouring. There may, therefore, of course, be an expressiveness of evil; but this expressiveness will not have any æsthetic value. The description or suggestion of suffering may have a worth as science or discipline, but can never in itself enhance any beauty. Tragedy and comedy please in spite of this expressiveness and not by virtue of it; and except for the pleasures they give, they have no place among the fine arts. Nor have they, in such a case, any place in human life at all; unless they are instruments of some practical purpose and serve to preach a moral, or achieve a bad notoriety. For ugly things can attract attention, although they cannot keep it; and the scandal of a new horror may secure a certain vulgar admiration which follows whatever is momentarily conspicuous, and which is attained even by crime. Such admiration, however, has nothing æsthetic about it, and is only made possible by the bluntness of our sense of beauty.

The effect of the pathetic and comic is therefore never pure; since the expression of some evil is mixed up with those elements by which the whole appeals to us. These elements we have seen to be the truth of the presentation, which involves the pleasures of recognition and comprehension, the beauty of the medium, and the concomitant expression of things intrinsically good. To these sources all the æsthetic value of comic and tragic is due; and the sympathetic emotion which arises from the spectacle of evil must never be allowed to overpower these pleasures of contemplation, else the entire object becomes distasteful and loses its excuse for being. Too exclusive a relish for the comic and pathetic is accordingly a sign of bad taste and of comparative insensibility to beauty.

This situation has generally been appreciated in the practice of the arts, where effect is perpetually studied; but the greatest care has not always succeeded in avoiding the dangers of the pathetic, and history is full of failures due to bombast, caricature, and unmitigated horror. In all these the effort to be expressive has transgressed the conditions of pleasing effect. For the creative and imitative impulse is indiscriminate. It does not consider the eventual beauty of the effect, but only the blind instinct of self-expression. Hence an untrained and not naturally sensitive mind cannot distinguish or produce anything good. This critical incapacity has always been a cause of failure and a just ground for ridicule; but it remained for some thinkers of our time—a time of little art and much undisciplined production—to erect this abuse into a principle and declare that the essence of beauty is to express the artist and not to delight the world. But the conditions of effect, and the possibility of pleasing, are the only criterion of what is capable and worthy of expression. Art exists and has value by its adaptation to these universal conditions of beauty.

Nothing but the good of life enters into the texture of the beautiful. What charms us in the comic, what stirs us in the sublime and touches us in the pathetic, is a glimpse of some good; imperfection has value only as an incipient perfection. Could the labours and sufferings of life be reduced, and a better harmony between man and nature be established, nothing would be lost to the arts; for the pure and ultimate value of the comic is discovery, of the pathetic, love, of the sublime, exaltation; and these would still subsist. Indeed, they would all be increased; and it has ever been, accordingly, in the happiest and most prosperous moments of humanity, when the mind and the world were knit into a brief embrace, that natural beauty has been best perceived, and art has won its triumphs. But it sometimes happens, in moments less propitious, that the soul is subdued to what it works in, and loses its power of idealisation and hope. By a pathetic and superstitious self-depreciation, we then punish ourselves for the imperfection of nature. Awed by the magnitude of a reality that we can no longer conceive as free from evil, we try to assert that its evil also is a good; and we poison the very essence of the good to make its extension universal. We confuse the causal connexion of those things in nature which we call good or evil by an adventitious denomination with the logical opposition between good and evil themselves; because one generation makes room for another, we say death is necessary to life; and because the causes of sorrow and joy are so mingled in this world, we cannot conceive how, in a better world, they might be disentangled.

This incapacity of the imagination to reconstruct the conditions of life and build the frame of things nearer to the heart's desire is dangerous to a steady loyalty to what is noble and fine. We surrender ourselves to a kind of miscellaneous appreciation, without standard or goal; and calling every vexatious apparition by the name of beauty, we become incapable of discriminating its excellence or feeling its value. We need to clarify our ideals, and enliven our vision of perfection. No atheism is so terrible as the absence of an ultimate ideal, nor could any failure of power be more contrary to human nature than the failure of moral imagination, or more incompatible with healthy life. For we have faculties, and habits, and impulses. These are the basis of our demands. And these demands, although variable, constitute an ever-present intrinsic standard of value by which we feel and judge. The ideal is immanent in them; for the ideal means that environment in which our faculties would find their freest employment, and their most congenial world. Perfection would be nothing but life under those conditions. Accordingly our consciousness of the ideal becomes distinct in proportion as we advance in virtue and in proportion to the vigour and definiteness with which our faculties work. When the vital harmony is complete, when the *act* is *pure*, faith in perfection passes into vision. That man is unhappy indeed, who in all his life has had no glimpse of perfection, who in the ecstasy of love, or in the delight of contemplation, has never been able to say: It is attained. Such moments of inspiration are the source of the arts, which have no higher function than to renew them.

A work of art is indeed a monument to such a moment, the memorial to such a vision; and its charm varies with its power of recalling us from the distractions of common life to the joy of a more natural and perfect activity. . . .

LITERARY PSYCHOLOGY

Scientific psychology is a part of physics, or the study of nature; it is the record of how animals act. Literary psychology is the art of imagining how they feel and think. Yet this art and that science are practised together, because one characteristic habit of man, namely speech, yields the chief terms in which he can express his thoughts and feelings. Still it is not the words, any more than the action and attitude which accompany them, that are his *understanding* of the words, or his *sense* of his attitude and action. These can evidently be apprehended only dramatically, by imitative sympathy; so that literary psychology, however far scientific psychology may push it back, always remains in possession of the moral field.

When nature was still regarded as a single animal, this confusion extended to science as a whole, and tinctured the observation of nature with some suggestion of how a being that so acts must be minded, and what thoughts and sentiments must animate it. Such myths cannot be true; not because nature or its parts may not be animate in fact, but because there is no vital analogy between the cosmos and the human organism; so that if nature is animate as a whole, or in her minute or gigantic cycles, animation there is sure not to resemble human discourse, which is all we can attribute to her. Myth and natural theology are accordingly fabulous essentially and irremediably. If literary psychology is to interpret the universe at large, it can be only very cautiously, after I have explored nature scientifically as far as I can, and am able to specify the degree of analogy and the process of concretion that connect my particular life with the universal flux.

Myth is now extinct (which is a pity) and theology discredited; but the same confusion subsists in the quarters where it is not fashionable to doubt. History, for instance, is partly a science, since it contains archæological and antiquarian lore and a study of documents; but it is also, in most historians, an essay in dramatic art, since it pretends to rehearse the ideas and feelings of dead men. These would not be recoverable even if the historian limited himself to quoting their recorded words, as he would if he was conscientious; because even these words are hard to interpret afterwards, so as to recover the living sentiment they expressed. At least authentic phrases, like authentic relics, have an odour of antiquity about them which helps us to feel transported out of ourselves, even if we are transported in fact only into a more romantic and visionary stratum of our own being. Classic historians, however, are not content with quoting recorded words: they compose speeches for their characters, under the avowed inspiration of Clio; or less honestly, in modern times, they explain how their heroes felt, or what influences were at work in the spirit of the age, or what dialectic drove public opinion from one sentiment to another. All this is shameless fiction; and the value of it, when it has a value, lies exclusively in the eloquence, wisdom, or incidental information found in the historian. Such history can with advantage be written in verse, or put upon the stage; its virtue is not at all to be true, but to be well invented.

Philosophy fell into the same snare when in modern times it ceased to be the art of thinking and tried to become that impossible thing, the science of thought. Thought can be found only by being enacted. I may therefore guide my thoughts according to some prudent rule, and appeal as often as I like to experience for a new starting-point or a controlling perception in my thinking; but I cannot by any possibility make experience or mental discourse at large the object of investigation: it is invisible, it is past, it is nowhere. I can only surmise what it might have been, and rehearse it imaginatively in my own fancy. It is an object of literary psychology. The whole of British and German philosophy is only literature. In its deepest reaches it simply appeals to what a man says to himself when he surveys his adventures, re-pictures his perspectives, analyses his curious ideas, guesses at their origin, and imagines the varied experience which he would like to possess, cumulative and dramatically unified. The universe is a novel of which the ego is the hero; and the sweep of the fiction (when the ego is learned and omnivorous) does not contradict its poetic essence. The composition is perhaps pedantic, or jejune, or overloaded; but on the other hand it is sometimes most honest and appealing, like the autobiography of a saint; and taken as the confessions of a romantic scepticism trying to shake itself loose from the harness of convention and of words, it may have a great dramatic interest and profundity. But not one term, not one conclusion in it has the least scientific value, and it is only when this philosophy is good literature that it is good for anything.

The literary character of such accounts of experience would perhaps have been more frankly avowed if the interest guiding them had been truly psychological, like that of pure dramatic poetry or fiction. What kept philosophers at this task—often quite unsuited to their powers—was anxiety about the validity of knowledge in physics or in theology. They thought that by imagining how their ideas might have grown up they could confirm themselves in their faith or in their scepticism. Practising literary psychology with this motive, they did not practise it freely or sympathetically; they missed, in particular, the decided dominance of the passions over the fancy, and the nebulous and volatile nature of fancy itself. For this reason the poets and novelists are often better psychologists than the philosophers. But the most pertinent effect of this appeal of science to a romantic psychology was the *hypostasis of an imagined experience,* as if experience could go on in a void without any material organs or occasions, and as if its entire course could be known by miracle, as the experiences of the characters in a novel are known to the author.

Criticism of knowledge is thus based on the amazing assumption that a man can have an experience which is past, or which was never his own. Although criticism can have no first principle, I have endeavoured in this book to show how, if genuinely and impartially sceptical, it may retreat to the actual datum and find there some obvious essence, necessarily without any given place, date, or inherence in any mind. But from such a datum it would not be easy to pass to belief in anything; and if the leap were finally taken, it would be confessedly at the instance of animal faith, and in the direction of vulgar and materialistic convictions. Modern critics of knowledge have had more romantic prepossessions. Often they were not really critics, saying *It seems,* but rebels saying *I find,*

I know, or empiricists saying *Everybody finds, Everybody knows.*
Their alleged criticism of science is pure literary psychology, gossip, and story-telling. They are miraculously informed that there
are many minds, and that these all have a conventional experience.
What this experience contains, they think is easily stated. You have
but to ask a friend, or make an experiment, or imagine how you
would feel in another man's place. So confident is this social convention, that the natural world in which these experiences are reported to occur, and the assumed existence of which renders them
imaginable, may be theoretically resolved into a picture contained
in them. Thus the ground is removed which sustained all this
literary psychology and suggested the existence of minds and their
known experience at all; yet the groundless belief in these minds,
and in copious knowledge of their fortunes, is retained as obvious;
and this novelesque universe is called the region of facts, or of
immediate experience, or of radical empiricism. Literary psychology thus becomes a metaphysics for novelists. It supplies one of the
many thinkable systems of the universe, though a fantastic one;
and I shall return to it, under the name of psychologism, when
considering the realm of matter. Here I am concerned only with
the evidence that such masses of experience exist or are open to
my inspection.

No inspection is competent to discover anything but an essence;
what social intuition touches is therefore always a dramatic illusion of life in others or in myself, never the actual experience that
may have unfolded itself elsewhere as a matter of fact. Yet this
dramatic illusion, like any given essence, may be a true symbol for
the material events upon which the psyche is then directed; in this
case, the life of other people, or my own past life, as scientific
psychology might describe it. A good literary psychologist, who can
read people's minds intuitively, is likely to anticipate their conduct
correctly. His psychological imagination is not a link in this practical sagacity but a symptom of it, a poetic by-product of fineness
in instinct and in perception. Slight indications in the attitude or
temper of the persons observed, much more than their words, will
suggest to the sympathetic instinct of the observer what those persons are in the habit of doing, or are inclined to do; and the stock
idea assigned to them, or the stock passion attributed to them, will
be but a sign in the observer's discourse for that true observation.

I watch a pair of lovers; and it requires no preternatural insight for me to see whether the love is genuine, whether it is mutual, whether it is waxing or waning, irritable or confident, sensual or friendly. I may make it the nucleus of a little novel in my own mind; and it will be a question of my private fancy and literary gift whether I can evolve language and turns of sentiment capable of expressing all the latent dispositions which the behaviour of those lovers, unconscious of my observation, suggested to me. Have I read their minds? Have I divined their fate? It is not probable; and yet it is infinitely probable that minds and fates were really evolving there, not generically far removed from those which I have imagined.

The only facts observable by the psychologist are physical facts, and the only events that can test the accuracy of his theories are material events; he is therefore in those respects simply a scientific psychologist, even if his studies are casual and desultory. Whence, then, his literary atmosphere? For there is not only the medium of words which intervenes in any science, but the ulterior sympathetic echo of feelings truly felt and thoughts truly rehearsed and intended. I reply that whereas scientific psychology is addressed to the bodies and the material events composing the animate world, literary psychology restores the essences intervening in the perception of those material events, and re-echoes the intuitions aroused in those bodies. This visionary stratum is the true immediate as well as the imagined ultimate. Even in the simplest perceptions on which scientific psychology, or any natural science, can be based, there is an essence present which only poetry can describe or sympathy conceive. Schoolroom experiments in optics, for instance, are initially a play of intuitions, and exciting in that capacity; I see, and am confident and pleased that others see with me, this colour of an after-image, this straight stick bent at the surface of the water, the spokes of this wheel vanishing as it turns. For science, these given essences are only stepping-stones to the conditions under which they arise, and their proper æsthetic nature, which is trivial in itself, is forgotten in the curious knowledge I may acquire concerning light and perspective and refraction and the structure of the eye. Yet in that vast, vibrating, merciless realm of matter I am, as it were, a stranger on his travels. The adventure is exhilarating, and may be profitable, but it is endless and, in a sense, disappointing; it takes me far from home. I may seem to myself to have gained the whole world and lost my own soul. Of course I am still at liberty to revert in a lyrical moment to the immediate, to the intuitions of my childish senses; yet for an intelligent being such a reversion is a sort of *gran rifiuto* in the life of mind, a collapse into lotus-eating and dreaming. It is here that the Muses come to the rescue, with their dramatic and epic poetry, their constructive music, and their literary psychology. Knowledge of nature and experience of life are presupposed; but as at first, in the beginnings of science, intuition was but a sign for material facts to be discovered, so now all material facts are but a pedestal for images of other intuitions. The poet feels the rush of emotion on the other side of the deployed events; he wraps them in an atmosphere of immediacy, luminous or thunderous; and his spirit, that piped so thin a treble in its solitude, begins to sing in chorus. Literary psychology pierces to the light, to the shimmer of passion and fancy, behind the body of nature, like Dante issuing from the bowels of the earth at the antipodes, and again seeing the stars.

Such a poetic interpretation of natural things has a double dignity not found in sensuous intuitions antecedent to any knowledge of the world. It has the dignity of virtual truth, because there are really intuitions in men and animals, varying with their fortunes, often much grander and sweeter than any that could come to me. The literary psychologist is like some antiquary rummaging in an old curiosity shop, who should find the score of some ancient composition, in its rude notation, and should sit down at a wheezy clavichord and spell out the melody, wondering at the depth of soul in that archaic art, so long buried, and now so feebly revealed. This curious music, he will say to himself, was mighty and glorious in its day; this moonlight was once noon. There is no illusion in this belief in life long past or far distant; on the contrary, the sentimentalist errs by defect of imagination, not by excess of it, and his pale water-colours do no justice to the rugged facts. The other merit that dignifies intuitions mediated by knowledge of things, is that they release capabilities in one's own soul which one's personal fortunes may have left undeveloped. This makes the mainspring of fiction, and its popular charm. The illusion of projecting one's own thoughts into remote or imaginary characters is only half an illusion: these thoughts were never there, but they were always here, or knocking at the gate; and there is an indirect victory in reaching and positing elsewhere, in an explicit form, the life which accident denied me, and thereby enjoying it *sub rosa* in spite of fate. And there are many experiences which are only tolerable in this dream-like form, when their consequences are negligible and their vehemence is relieved by the distance at which they appear, and by the show they make. Thus both the truth and the illusion of literary psychology are blessings: the truth by revealing the minds of others, and the illusion by expanding one's own mind.

These imaginative blessings, however, are sometimes despised, and philosophers, when they suspect that they have no evidence for their psychological facts, or become aware of their literary flavour, sometimes turn away from this conventional miscellany of experience, and ask what is the substantial texture of experience beneath. Suppose I strain my introspection in the hope of discovering it; the picture (for such a method can never yield anything but pictures) may be transformed in two ways, to which two schools of recent literary psychology are respectively wedded. One transformation turns experience, intensely gaped at, into a mere strain, a mere sense of duration or tension; the other transformation unravels experience into an endless labyrinth of dreams. In the one case, experience loses its articulation to the extent of becoming a dumb feeling; and it is hard to see how, if one dumb undifferentiated feeling is the only reality, the illusion of many events and the intuition of many pictures could be grafted upon it. In the other case experience increases its articulation to the extent of becoming a chaos; and the sensitive psychology that dips into these subterranean dreams needs, and easily invents, guiding principles by which to classify them. Especially it reverts to sexual and other animal instincts, thus grafting literary psychology (which in this field is called psycho-analysis) again on natural substance and the life of animals, as scientific psychology may report it.

This natural setting restores literary psychology to its normal status; it is no longer a chimerical metaphysics, but an imaginative version, like a historical novel, of the animation that nature, in some particular regions, may actually have possessed. The fineness and complexity of mental discourse within us may well be greater than we can easily remember or describe; and there is piety as well as ingenuity in rescuing some part of it from oblivion. But here, as elsewhere, myth is at work. We make a romance of our incoherence, and compose new unities in the effort to disentangle those we are accustomed to, and find their elements. Discourse is not a chemical compound; its past formations are not embedded in its present one. It is a life with much iteration in it, much recapitulation, as well as much hopeless loss and forgetfulness. As the loom shifts, or gets out of order, the woof is recomposed or destroyed. It is a living, a perpetual creation; and the very fatality that forces me, in conceiving my own past or future, or the animation of nature at large, to imagine that object afresh, with my present vital resources and on the scale and in the style of my present discourse —this very fatality, I say, reveals to me the nature of discourse everywhere, that it is poetry. But it is poetry about facts, or means to be; and I need not fear to be too eloquent in expressing my forgotten sentiments, or the unknown sentiments of others. Very likely those sentiments, when living, were more eloquent than I am now.

MYTHOLOGY

Primitive thought has the form of poetry and the function of prose. Being thought, it distinguishes objects from the experience that reveals them and it aspires to know things as they are; but being poetical, it attributes to those objects all the qualities which the experience of them contains, and builds them out imaginatively in all directions, without distinguishing what is constant and efficacious in them. This primitive habit of thought survives in mythology, which is an observation of things encumbered with all they can suggest to a dramatic fancy. It is neither conscious poetry nor valid science, but the common root and raw material of both. Free poetry is a thing which early man is too poor to indulge in; his wide-open eyes are too intently watching this ominous and treacherous world. For pure science he has not enough experience, no adequate power to analyse, remember, and abstract; his soul is too hurried and confused, too thick with phantoms, to follow abstemiously the practical threads through the labyrinth. His view of things is immensely overloaded; what he gives out for description is more than half soliloquy; but his expression of experience is for that very reason adequate and quite sincere. Belief, which we have come to associate with religion, belongs really to science; myths are not believed in, they are conceived and understood. To demand belief for an idea is already to contrast interpretation with knowledge; it is to assert that that idea has scientific truth. Mythology cannot flourish in that dialectical air; it belongs to a deeper and more ingenuous level of thought, when men pored on the world with intense indiscriminate interest, accepting and recording the mind's vegetation no less than that observable in things, and mixing the two developments together in one wayward drama.

IT REQUIRES GENIUS

A good mythology cannot be produced without much culture and intelligence. Stupidity is not poetical. Nor is mythology essentially a half-way house between animal vagueness in the soul and scientific knowledge. It is conceivable that some race, not so dreamful as ours, should never have been tempted to use psychic and passionate categories in reading nature, but from the first should have kept its observations sensuous and pure, elaborating them only on their own plane, mathematically and dialectically. Such a race, however, could hardly have had lyric or dramatic genius, and even in natural science, which requires imagination, they might never have accomplished anything. The Hebrews, denying themselves a rich mythology, remained without science and plastic art; the Chinese, who seem to have attained legality and domestic arts and a tutored sentiment without passing through such imaginative tempests as have harassed us, remain at the same time without a serious science or philosophy. The Greeks, on the contrary, precisely the people with the richest and most irresponsible myths, first conceived the cosmos scientifically, and first wrote rational history and philosophy. So true it is that vitality in any mental function is favourable to vitality in the whole mind. Illusions incident to mythology are not dangerous in the end, because illusion finds in experience a natural though painful cure. Extravagant error is unstable, unless it be harmless and confined to a limbo remote from all applications; if it touches experience it is stimulating and brief, while the equipoise of dulness may easily render dulness eternal. A developed mythology shows that man has taken a deep and active interest both in the world and in himself, and has tried to link the two, and interpret the one by the other. Myth is therefore a natural prologue to philosophy, since the love of ideas is the root of both. Both are made up of things admirable to consider.

IT ONLY HALF DECEIVES

Nor is the illusion involved in fabulous thinking always so complete and opaque as convention would represent it. In taking fable for fact, good sense and practice seldom keep pace with dogma.

There is always a race of pedants whose function it is to materialise everything ideal, but the great world, half shrewdly, half doggedly, manages to escape their contagion. Language may be entirely permeated with myth, since the affinities of language have much to do with men gliding into such thoughts; yet the difference between language itself and what it expresses is not so easily obliterated. In spite of verbal traditions, people seldom take a myth in the same sense in which they would take an empirical truth. All the doctrines that have flourished in the world about immortality have hardly affected men's natural sentiment in the face of death, a sentiment which those doctrines, if taken seriously, ought wholly to reverse. Men almost universally have acknowledged a Providence, but that fact has had no force to destroy natural aversions and fears in the presence of events; and yet, if Providence had ever been really trusted, those preferences would all have lapsed, being seen to be blind, rebellious, and blasphemous. Prayer, among sane people, has never superseded practical efforts to secure the desired end; a proof that the sphere of expression was never really confused with that of reality. Indeed, such a confusion, if it had passed from theory to practice, would have changed mythology into madness. With rare exceptions this declension has not occurred and myths have been taken with a grain of salt which not only made them digestible, but heightened their savour.

It is always by its applicability to things known, not by its revelation of things unknown and irrelevant, that a myth at its birth appeals to mankind. When it has lost its symbolic value and sunk to the level of merely false information, only an inert and stupid tradition can keep it above water. Parables justify themselves but dogmas call for an apologist. The genial offspring of prophets and poets then has to be kept alive artificially by professional doctors. A thing born of fancy, moulded to express universal experience and its veritable issues, has to be hedged about by misrepresentation, sophistry, and party spirit. The very apologies and unintelligent proofs offered in its defence in a way confess its unreality, since they all strain to paint in more plausible colours what is felt to be in itself extravagant and incredible.

ITS INTERPRETATIVE ESSENCE

Yet if the myth was originally accepted it could not be for this falsity plainly written on its face; it was accepted because it was understood, because it was seen to express reality in an eloquent metaphor. Its function was to show up some phase of experience in its totality and moral issue, as in a map we reduce everything geographically in order to overlook it better in its true relations. Had those symbols for a moment descended to the plane of reality they would have lost their meaning and dignity; they would tell us merely that they themselves existed bodily, which would be false, while about the real configuration of life they would no longer tell us anything. Such an error, if carried through to the end, would nullify all experience and arrest all life. Men would be reacting on expressions and meeting with nothing to express. They would all be like word-eating philosophers or children learning the catechism.

The true function of mythical ideas is to present and interpret events in terms relative to spirit. Things have uses in respect to the will which are direct and obvious, while the inner machinery of these same things is intricate and obscure. We therefore conceive things roughly and superficially by their eventual practical functions and assign to them, in our game, some counterpart of the interest they affect in us. This counterpart, to our thinking, constitutes their inward character and soul. So conceived, soul and character are purely mythical, being arrived at by dramatising events according to our own fancy and interest. Such ideas may be adequate in their way if they cover all the uses we may eventually find in the objects they transcribe for us dramatically. But the most adequate mythology is mythology still; it does not, like science, set things before us in the very terms they will wear when they are gradually revealed to experience. Myth is expression, it is not prophecy. For this reason myth is something on which the mind rests; it is an ideal interpretation in which the phenomena are digested and transmuted into human energy, into imaginative tissue.

CONTRAST WITH SCIENCE

Scientific formulas, on the contrary, cry aloud for retranslation into perceptual terms, they are like tight-ropes, on which a man may walk but on which he cannot stand still. These unstable symbols lead, however, to real facts and define their experimental relations; while the mind reposing contentedly in a myth needs to have all observation and experience behind it, for it will not be driven to gather more. The perfect and stable myth would rest on a complete survey and steady focussing of all interests really affecting the one from whose point of view the myth was framed. Then each physical or political unit would be endowed with a character really corresponding to all its influence on the thinker. This symbol would render the diffuse natural existences which it represented in an eloquent figure; and since this figure would not mislead practically it might be called true. But truth, in a myth, means a sterling quality and standard excellence, not a literal or logical truth. It will not, save by a singular accident, represent their proper internal being, as a forthright unselfish intellect would wish to know it. It will translate into the language of a private passion the smiles and frowns which that passion meets with in the world.

IMPORTANCE OF THE MORAL FACTOR

There are accordingly two factors in mythology, a moral consciousness and a corresponding poetic conception of things. Both factors are variable, and variations in the first, if more hidden, are no less important than variations in the second. Had fable started with a clear perception of human values, it would have gained immensely in significance, because its pictures, however wrong the external notions they built upon, would have shown what, in the world so conceived, would have been the ideals and prizes of life. Thus Dante's bad cosmography and worse history do not detract from the spiritual penetration of his thought, though they detract from its direct applicability. Had nature and destiny been what Dante imagined, his conception of the values involved would have been perfect, for the moral philosophy he brought into play was Aristotelian and rational. So his poem contains a false instance or imaginary rehearsal of true wisdom. It describes the Life of Reason in a fantastic world. We need only change man's situation to that in which he actually finds himself, and let the soul, fathomed and chastened as Dante left it, ask questions and draw answers from this steadier dream.

ITS SUBMERGENCE

Myth travels among the people, and in their hands its poetic factor tends to predominate. It is easier to carry on the dialectic or drama proper to a fable than to confront it again with the facts and give them a fresh and more genial interpretation. The poet makes the fable; the sophist carries it on. Therefore historians and theologians discuss chiefly the various forms which mythical beings have received, and the internal logical or moral implications of those hypostases. They would do better to attend instead to the moral factor. However interesting a fable may be in itself, its religious value lies wholly in its revealing some function which nature has in human life. Not the beauty of the god makes him adorable, but his dispensing benefits and graces. Side by side with Apollo (a god having moral functions and consequently inspiring a fervent cult and tending himself to assume a moral character) there may be a Helios or a Phaëthon, poetic figures expressing just as well the sun's physical operation, and no less capable, if the theologian took hold of them, of suggesting psychological problems. The moral factor, however, was not found in these minor deities. Only a verbal and sensuous poetry had been employed in defining them; the needs and hopes of mankind had been ignored. Apollo, on the contrary, in personifying the sun, had embodied also the sun's relations to human welfare. The vitality, the healing, the enlightenment, the lyric joy flowing into man's heart from that highest source of his physical being are all beautifully represented in the god's figure and fable. The religion of Apollo is therefore a true religion, as religions may be true: the mythology which created the god rested on a deep, observant sense for moral values, and drew a vivid, if partial, picture of the ideal, attaching it significantly to its natural ground.

The first function of mythology is to justify magic. The weak hope on which superstition hangs, the gambler's instinct which divines in phenomena a magic solicitude for human fortunes, can scarcely be articulated without seeking to cover and justify itself by some fable.

MYTH JUSTIFIES MAGIC

A magic function is most readily conceived and defined by attributing to the object intentions hostile or favourable to men, together with human habits of passion and discourse. For lack of resources and observations, reason is seldom able to discredit magic altogether. Reasonable men are forced, therefore, in order to find some satisfaction, to make magic as intelligible as possible by assimilating it to such laws of human action as may be already mastered and familiar. Magic is thus reduced to a sort of system, regulated by principles of its own and naturalised, as it were, in the commonwealth of science.

MYTHS MIGHT BE METAPHYSICAL

Such an avowed and defended magic usually takes one of two forms. When the miracle is interpreted dramatically, by analogy to human life, we have mythology; when it is interpreted rationalistically, by analogy to current logic or natural science, we have metaphysics or theosophy. The metaphysical sort of superstition has never taken deep root in the western world. Pythagorean mysteries and hypnotisations, although periodically fashionable, have soon shrivelled in our too salubrious and biting air. Even such charming exotics as Plato's myths have not been able to flourish without changing their nature and passing into ordinary dramatic mythology—into a magic system in which all the forces, once terms in moral experience, became personal angels and demons. Similarly with the Christian sacraments: these magic rites, had they been established in India among a people theosophically minded, might have furnished cues to high transcendental mysteries. Baptism might have been interpreted as a symbol for the purged and abolished will, and Communion as a symbol for the escape from personality. But European races, though credulous enough, are naturally positivistic, so that, when they were called upon to elucidate their ceremonial mysteries, what they lit upon was no metaphysical symbolism but a material and historical drama. Communion became a sentimental interview between the devout soul and the person of Christ; baptism became the legal execution of a mythical contract once entered into between the first and second persons of the Trinity. Thus, instead of a metaphysical interpretation, the extant magic received its needful justification through myths.

THEY APPEAR READY MADE, LIKE PARTS OF THE SOCIAL FABRIC

When mythology first appears in western literature it already possesses a highly articulate form. The gods are distinct personalities, with attributes and histories which it is hard to divine the source of and which suggest no obvious rational interpretation. The historian is therefore in the same position as a child who inherits a great religion. The gods and their doings are *prima facie* facts in his world like any other facts, objective beings that convention puts him in the presence of and with which he begins by having social relations. He envisages them with respect and obedience, or with careless defiance, long before he thinks of questioning or proving their existence. The attitude he assumes towards them makes them in the first instance factors in his moral world. Much subsequent scepticism and rationalising philosophy will not avail to efface the vestiges of that early communion with familiar gods. It is hard to reduce to objects of science what are essentially factors in moral intercourse. All thoughts on religion remain accordingly coloured with passion, and are felt to be, above all, a test of loyalty and an index to virtue. The more derivative, unfathomable, and opaque is the prevalent idea of the gods, the harder it is for a rational feeling to establish itself in their regard. Sometimes the most complete historical enlightenment will not suffice to dispel the shadow which their moral externality casts over the mind. In vain do we discard their fable and the thin proofs of their existence when, in spite of ourselves, we still live in their presence.

THEY PERPLEX THE CONSCIENCE

This pathetic phenomenon is characteristic of religious minds that have outgrown their traditional faith without being able to restate the natural grounds and moral values of that somehow precious system in which they no longer believe. The dead gods, in such cases, leave ghosts behind them, because the moral forces which the gods once expressed, and which, of course, remain, remain inarticulate; and therefore, in their dumbness, these moral forces persistently suggest their only known but now discredited symbols. To regain moral freedom—without which knowledge cannot be put to its rational use in the government of life—we must rediscover the origin of the gods, reduce them analytically to their natural and moral constituents, and then proceed to rearrange those materials, without any quantitative loss, in forms appropriate to a maturer reflection.

Of the innumerable and rather monotonous mythologies that have flourished in the world, only the Græco-Roman and the Christian need concern us here, since they are by far the best known to us and the best defined in themselves, as well as the only two likely to have any continued influence on the western mind. Both these systems presuppose a long prior development. The gods of Greece and of Israel have a full-blown character when we first meet them in literature. In both cases, however, we are fortunate in being able to trace somewhat further back the history of mythology, and do not depend merely on philosophic analysis to reach the elements which we seek.

INCIPIENT MYTH IN THE VEDAS

In the Vedic hymns there survives the record of a religion remarkably like the Greek in spirit, but less dramatic and articulate in form. The gods of the Vedas are unmistakably natural elements. Vulcan is there nothing but fire, Jupiter nothing but the sky. This patriarchal people, fresh from the highlands, had not yet been infected with the manias and diseases of the jungle. It lived simply, rationally, piously, loving all natural joys and delighted with all the instruments of a rude but pure civilisation. It saluted without servility the forces of nature which ministered to its needs. It burst into song in the presence of the magnificent panorama spread out before it—day-sky and night-sky, dawn and gloaming, clouds, thunder and rain, rivers, cattle and horses, grain, fruit, fire, and wine. Nor were the social sanctities neglected. Commemoration was made of the stages of mortal life, of the bonds of love and kinship, of peace, of battle, and of mourning for the dead. By a very intelligible figure and analogy the winds became shepherds, the clouds flocks, the day a conqueror, the dawn a maid, the night a wise sibyl and mysterious consort of heaven. These personifications were tentative and vague, and the consequent mythology was a system of rhetoric rather than of theology. The various gods had interchangeable attributes, and, by a voluntary confusion, quite in the manner of later Hindu poetry, each became on occasion any or all of the others.

Here the Indian pantheistic vertigo begins to appear. Many dark superstitions, no doubt, bubbled up in the torrent of that plastic reverie; for this people, clean and natural as on the whole it appears, cannot have been without a long and ignoble ancestry. The Greeks themselves, heirs to kindred general traditions, retained some childish and obscene practices in their worship. But such hobgoblins naturally vanish under a clear and beneficent sun and are scattered by healthy mountain breezes. A cheerful people knows how to take them lightly, play with them, laugh at them, and turn them again into figures of speech. Among the early speakers of Sanskrit, even more than among the Greeks, the national religion seems to have been nothing but a poetic naturalism.

Such a mythology, however, is exceedingly plastic and unstable. If the poet is observant and renews his impressions, his myths will become more and more accurate descriptions of the facts, and his hypotheses about phenomena will tend to be expressed more and more in terms of the phenomena themselves; that is, will tend to become scientific. If, on the contrary and as usually happens, the inner suggestions and fertility of his fables absorb his interest, and he neglects to consult his external perceptions any further, or even forgets that any such perceptions originally inspired the myth, he will tend to become a dramatic poet, guided henceforth in his fictions only by his knowledge and love of human life.

NATURAL SUGGESTIONS SOON EXHAUSTED

When we transport ourselves in fancy to patriarchal epochs and Arcadian scenes, we can well feel the inevitable tendency of the mind to mythologise and give its myths a more and more dramatic character. The phenomena of nature, unintelligible rationally but

411

immensely impressive, must somehow be described and digested. But while they compel attention they do not, after a while, enlarge experience. Husbandmen's lore is profound, practical, poetic, superstitious, but it is singularly stagnant. The cycle of natural changes goes its perpetual round and the ploughman's mind, caught in that narrow vortex, plods and plods after the seasons. Apart from an occasional flood, drought, or pestilence, nothing breaks his laborious torpor. The most cursory inspection of field and sky yields him information enough for his needs. Practical knowledge with him is all instinct and tradition. His mythology can for that very reason ride on nature with a looser rein.

THEY WILL BE CARRIED OUT IN ABSTRACT FANCY

If at the same time, however, his circumstances are auspicious and he feels practically secure, he will have much leisure to ripen inwardly and to think. He will hasten to unfold in meditation the abstract potentialities of his mind. His social and ideal passions, his aptitude for art and fancy, will arouse within him a far keener and more varied experience than his outer life can supply. Yet all his fortunes continue to be determined by external circumstances and to have for their theatre this given and uncontrollable world. Some conception of nature and the gods—that is, in his case, some mythology—must therefore remain before him always and stand in his mind for the real forces controlling experience.

His moral powers and interests have meantime notably developed. His sense for social relations has grown clear and full in proportion as his observation of nature has sunk into dull routine. Consequently, the myths by which reality is represented lose, so to speak, their birthright and first nationality. They pass under the empire of abstract cogitation and spontaneous fancy. They become naturalised in the mind. The poet cuts loose from nature and works out instead whatever hints of human character or romantic story the myth already supplies. Analogies drawn from moral and passionate experience replace the further portraiture of outer facts. Human tastes, habits, and dreams enter the fable, expanding it into some little drama, or some mystic anagram of mortal life. While in the beginning the sacred poet had transcribed nothing but joyous perceptions and familiar industrial or martial actions, he now introduces intrigue, ingenious adventures, and heroic passions.

THEY MAY BECOME MORAL IDEALS

When we turn from the theology of the Vedas to that of Homer we see this revolution already accomplished. The new significance of mythology has obscured the old, and what was a symbol for material facts has become a drama, an apologue, and an ideal. Thus one function of mythology has been nothing less than to carry religion over from superstition into wisdom, from an excuse and apology for magic into an ideal representation of moral goods. In his impotence and sore need a man appeals to magic; this appeal he justifies by imagining a purpose and a god behind the natural agency. But after his accounts with the phenomena are settled by his own labour and patience, he continues to be fascinated by the invisible spirit he has evoked. He cherishes this image; it becomes his companion, his plastic and unaccountable witness and refuge in all the exigencies of life. Dwelling in the mind continually, the deity becomes acclimated there; the worship it receives endows it with whatever powers and ideal faculties are most feared or honoured by its votary. Now the thunder and the pestilence which were once its essence come to be regarded as its disguises and its foils. Faith comes to consist in disregarding what it was once religion to regard, namely, the ways of fortune and the conditions of earthly happiness. Thus the imagination sets up its ideals over against the world that occasioned them, and mythology, instead of cheating men with false and magic aids to action, moralises them by presenting an ideal standard for action and a perfect object for contemplation.

THE SUN-GOD MORALISED

If we consider again, for instance, Apollo's various attributes and the endless myths connected with his name, we shall find him changing his essence and forgetting to be the material sun in order to become the light of a cultivated spirit. At first he is the sky's child, and has the moon for twin sister. His mother is an impersonation of darkness and mystery. He travels yearly from the hyperborean regions towards the south, and daily he traverses the firmament in a chariot. He sleeps in a sea-nymph's bosom or rises from the dawn's couch. In all this we see clearly a scarcely figurative description of the material sun and its motions. A quasi-scientific fancy spins these fables almost inevitably to fill the vacuum not yet occupied by astronomy. Such myths are indeed compacted out of wonders, not indeed to add wonder to them (for the original and greatest marvel persists always in the sky), but to entertain us with pleasant consideration of them and with their assimilation to our own fine feats. This assimilation is unavoidable in a poet ignorant of physics, whom human life must supply with all his vocabulary and similes. Fortunately in this need of introducing romance into phenomena lies the leaven that is to leaven the lump, the subtle influence that is to moralise religion. For presently Apollo becomes a slayer of monsters (a function no god can perform until he has ceased to be a monster himself), he becomes the lovely and valorous champion of humanity, the giver of prophecy, of music, of lyric song, even the patron of medicine and gymnastics.

THE LEAVEN OF RELIGION IS MORAL IDEALISM

What a humane and rational transformation! The spirit of Socrates was older than the man and had long been at work in the Greeks. Interest had been transferred from nature to art, from the sources to the fruits of life. We in these days are accustomed as a matter of course to associate religion with ideal interests. Our piety, unlike our barbarous pantheistic theology, has long lost sight of its rudimentary material object, and habituated us to the worship of human sanctity and human love. We have need all the more to remember how slowly and reluctantly religion has suffered spiritualisation, how imperfectly as yet its superstitious origin has been outgrown. We have need to retrace with the greatest attention the steps by which a moral value has been insinuated into what would otherwise be nothing but a medley of magic rites and poetic physics. It is this submerged idealism which alone, in an age that should have finally learned how to operate in nature and how to conceive her processes, could still win for religion a philosopher's attention or a legislator's mercy.